SOMETHING ABOUT THE AUTHOR®

Something about
the Author *was named
an*"**Outstanding
Reference Source,**"
*the highest honor given
by the American
Library Association
Reference and Adult
Services Division.*

ISSN 0276-816X

SOMETHING ABOUT THE AUTHOR®

**Facts and Pictures about Authors
and Illustrators of Books for Young People**

volume 240

GALE
CENGAGE Learning®

Detroit • New York • San Francisco • New Haven, Conn • Waterville, Maine • London

GALE
CENGAGE Learning®

Something about the Author, Volume 240

Project Editor: Lisa Kumar

Permissions: Robyn Young

Imaging and Multimedia: John Watkins, Robyn Young

Composition and Electronic Capture: Amy Darga

Manufacturing: Rhonda Dover

Product Manager: Mary Onorato

For product information and technology assistance, contact us at
Gale Customer Support, 1-800-877-4253.
For permission to use material from this text or product,
submit all requests online at **www.cengage.com/permissions.**
Further permissions questions can be emailed to
permissionrequest@cengage.com

Since this page cannot legibly accommodate all copyright notices, the acknowledgments constitute an extension of the copyright notice.

While every effort has been made to ensure the reliability of the information presented in this publication, Gale, a part of Cengage Learning, does not guarantee the accuracy of the data contained herein. Gale accepts no payment for listing; and inclusion in the publication of any organization, agency, institution, publication, service, or individual does not imply endorsement of the editors or publisher. Errors brought to the attention of the publisher and verified to the satisfaction of the publisher will be corrected in future editions.

EDITORIAL DATA PRIVACY POLICY: Does this publication contain information about you as an individual? If so, for more information about our editorial data privacy policies, please see our Privacy Statement at www.gale.cengage.com.

Gale, Cengage Learning
27500 Drake Rd.
Farmington Hills, MI, 48331-3535

LIBRARY OF CONGRESS CATALOG CARD NUMBER 62-52046

ISBN-13: 978-1-4144-8096-1
ISBN-10: 1-4144-8096-2

ISSN 0276-816X

This title is also available as an e-book.
ISBN-13: 978-1-4144-8242-2
ISBN-10: 1-4144-8242-6
Contact your Gale, Cengage Learning sales representative for ordering information.

Printed in Mexico
1 2 3 4 5 6 7 16 15 14 13 12

Contents

Authors in Forthcoming Volumes

Below are some of the authors and illustrators that will be featured in upcoming volumes of *SATA*. These include new entries on the swiftly rising stars of the field, as well as completely revised and updated entries (indicated with *) on some of the most notable and best-loved creators of books for children.

Elizabeth Berkley ▮ An actress best known for her role on television's *Saved by the Bell* and *CSI: Miami,* Berkley has also channeled her celebrity into a second career as a workshop-leader and author. Inspired by her presentations for teenage girls, her book *Ask Elizabeth* shares advice about looks, love, and many other aspects of teen life, winning trust through her use of a first-person, diary format.

*Orson Scott Card ▮ Although best known for his "Ender" science-fiction series, Card has also produced fantasy, history, thrillers, stage plays, and faith-based nonfiction. His works of fantasy include the quest novel *Wyrms* as well as the mythic *Enchantment,* while the supernatural enters the mix in *Lost Boys, Treasure Box,* and *Pathfinder.* In 2008 Card was awarded the ALA's Margaret A. Edwards Award for Lifetime Achievement in Young-Adult literature.

Margie Gelbwasser ▮ Born in Russia and raised in the United States, Gelbwasser tapped her Russian-Jewish immigrant heritage in her first novel, *Inconvenient.* She continues to examine adolescent lives in *Pieces of Us,* a novel that finds the teen talent for reinvention distorted by dark secrets.

Ben Hodson ▮ An award-winning artist, Hodson has been inspired in his career by his love of nature and his many travel adventures throughout the world. In addition to creating art for Laura Crawford's *In Arctic Waters* and Joanna Boutilier's *Pigs Aren't Dirty, Bears Aren't Slow,* the Canadian illustrator also shares his quirky humor in the colorful art he contributes to beginning readers, chapter books, and picture books such as *Richard Was a Picker* by Carolyn Beck.

Matthew J. Kirby ▮ In addition to his work as a teacher, Kirby writes for middle graders and is best known for his novels *The Clockwork Three* and *Icefall.* Mixing fantasy, history, and steampunk elements, *The Clockwork Three* attracted comparisons to Brian Selznick's *The Invention of Hugo Cabret,* while *Icefall* draws readers into a northern world wherein three siblings must survive the treachery of their kingly father's hidden enemies.

*Anita Lobel ▮ Celebrated as both an artist and author, Lobel's picture books, fantasies, and concept books pair a theatrical approach and a keen sense of design. Her illustrations have brought to life stories by Meindert de Jong, Doris Orgel, Clement Clarke Moore, Penelope Lively, and Charlotte Zolotow in detailed paintings featuring richly patterned landscapes, opulent costumes and tapestries, and colorful flowers. As a writer, Lobel characteristically taps folk and fairy-tale traditions, salting them with humor as well as more serious themes. She chronicles her life as a Polish immigrant in her award-winning memoir *No Pretty Pictures: A Child of War.*

*Yuyi Morales ▮ Born in Mexico, Morales is an award-winning illustrator and author whose original self-illustrated picture books include *Just in Case: A Trickster Tale and Spanish Alphabet Book* and *Little Night.* Noted for her bright, stylized, child-friendly art, she is a two-time winner of the Pura Belpré Illustrator Award, which honors Latino authors and illustrators whose work shares the best elements of Hispanic culture in a way that will inspire children.

*Cynthia Rylant ▮ Award-winning author/illustrator Rylant frequently sets her stories in the Appalachian region where she was raised. Her many works range from novels and beginning readers to short stories, verse, autobiography, and nonfiction. Among her books for younger children are the beloved "Henry and Mudge," "Mr. Putter and Tabby," and "Poppleton" stories, while her picture book include *Ludie's Life, Snow,* and *Long Night Moon.*

*Kate Thompson ▮ Thompson draws on the lore and locales of her adopted Ireland in her award-winning futuristic novels *The New Policeman, The Last of the High Kings,* and *The White Horse Trick.* Her other novels for young adults include *Creature of the Night* as well as the "Switchers" and "Missing Link" books, all of which mix fantasy elements with a story grounded in science. Younger readers are Thompson's focus in *Highway Robbery* and *Most Wanted,* the latter of which finds a young boy guided by a powerful horse into an adventure in ancient Rome.

Kiersten White ▮ White's first novel, *Paranormalcy,* hit bestseller status and has been followed by the equally popular sequels *Supernaturally* and *Endlessly.* Tapping the urban fantasy trend, her high-action stories follow a teenager charged with keeping faeries, shape-shifters, and other creatures below the human radar while also navigating romance and following her preordained destiny.

Introduction

Something about the Author (*SATA*) is an ongoing reference series that examines the lives and works of authors and illustrators of books for children. *SATA* includes not only well-known writers and artists but also less prominent individuals whose works are just coming to be recognized. This series is often the only readily available information source on emerging authors and illustrators. You'll find *SATA* informative and entertaining, whether you are a student, a librarian, an English teacher, a parent, or simply an adult who enjoys children's literature.

What's Inside *SATA*

SATA provides detailed information about authors and illustrators who span the full time range of children's literature, from early figures like John Newbery and L. Frank Baum to contemporary figures like Judy Blume and Richard Peck. Authors in the series represent primarily English-speaking countries, particularly the United States, Canada, and the United Kingdom. Also included, however, are authors from around the world whose works are available in English translation. The writings represented in *SATA* include those created intentionally for children and young adults as well as those written for a general audience and known to interest younger readers. These writings cover the entire spectrum of children's literature, including picture books, humor, folk and fairy tales, animal stories, mystery and adventure, science fiction and fantasy, historical fiction, poetry and nonsense verse, drama, biography, and nonfiction. Obituaries are also included in many volumes of *SATA* and are intended not only as death notices but also as concise overviews of people's lives and work. Additionally, each edition features newly revised and updated entries for a selection of *SATA* listees who remain of interest to today's readers and who have been active enough to require extensive revisions of their earlier biographies.

Autobiography Feature

Beginning with Volume 103, many volumes of *SATA* feature one or more specially commissioned autobiographical essays. These unique essays, averaging about ten thousand words in length and illustrated with an abundance of personal photos, present an entertaining and informative first-person perspective on the lives and careers of prominent authors and illustrators profiled in *SATA*.

Two Convenient Indexes

In response to suggestions from librarians, *SATA* indexes no longer appear in every volume but are included in alternate (odd-numbered) volumes of the series, beginning with Volume 57.

SATA continues to include two indexes that cumulate with each alternate volume: the Illustrations Index, arranged by the name of the illustrator, gives the number of the volume and page where the illustrator's work appears in the current volume as well as all preceding volumes in the series; the Author Index gives the number of the volume in which a person's biographical sketch, autobiographical essay, or obituary appears in the current volume as well as all preceding volumes in the series.

These indexes also include references to authors and illustrators who appear in *Gale's Yesterday's Authors of Books for Children, Children's Literature Review,* and *Something about the Author Autobiography Series.*

Easy-to-Use Entry Format

Whether you're already familiar with the *SATA* series or just getting acquainted, you will want to be aware of the kind of information that an entry provides. In every *SATA* entry the editors attempt to give as complete a picture of the person's life and work as possible. A typical entry in *SATA* includes the following clearly labeled information sections:

PERSONAL: date and place of birth and death, parents' names and occupations, name of spouse, date of marriage, names of children, educational institutions attended, degrees received, religious and political affiliations, hobbies and other interests.

ADDRESSES: complete home, office, electronic mail, and agent addresses, whenever available.

CAREER: name of employer, position, and dates for each career post; art exhibitions; military service; memberships and offices held in professional and civic organizations.

MEMBER: professional, civic, and other association memberships and any official posts held.

AWARDS, HONORS: literary and professional awards received.

WRITINGS: title-by-title chronological bibliography of books written and/or illustrated, listed by genre when known; lists of other notable publications, such as plays, screenplays, and periodical contributions.

ADAPTATIONS: a list of films, television programs, plays, CD-ROMs, recordings, and other media presentations that have been adapted from the author's work.

WORK IN PROGRESS: description of projects in progress.

SIDELIGHTS: a biographical portrait of the author or illustrator's development, either directly from the biographee—and often written specifically for the *SATA* entry—or gathered from diaries, letters, interviews, or other published sources.

BIOGRAPHICAL AND CRITICAL SOURCES: cites sources quoted in "Sidelights" along with references for further reading.

EXTENSIVE ILLUSTRATIONS: photographs, movie stills, book illustrations, and other interesting visual materials supplement the text.

How a *SATA* Entry Is Compiled

SATA editors examine a wide variety of published sources to gather information for an entry. Biographical and bibliographic sources are consulted, as are book reviews, feature articles, published interviews, and material sometimes obtained from the biographee's family, publishers, agent, or other associates. Whenever possible, the author or illustrator is sent a copy of the entry to check for accuracy and completeness.

Entries that have not been verified by the biographees or their representatives are marked with an asterisk (*).

Contact the Editor

We encourage our readers to examine the entire *SATA* series. Please write and tell us if we can make *SATA* even more helpful to you. Give your comments and suggestions to the editor:

Editor
Something about the Author
Gale, Cengage Learning
27500 Drake Rd.
Farmington Hills MI 48331-3535

Toll-free: 800-877-GALE
Fax: 248-699-8070

Something about the Author Product Advisory Board

The editors of *Something about the Author* are dedicated to maintaining a high standard of excellence by publishing comprehensive, accurate, and highly readable entries on a wide array of writers for children and young adults. In addition to the quality of the content, the editors take pride in the graphic design of the series, which is intended to be orderly yet inviting, allowing readers to utilize the pages of *SATA* easily and with efficiency. Despite the longevity of the *SATA* print series, and the success of its format, we are mindful that the vitality of a literary reference product is dependent on its ability to serve its users over time. As literature, and attitudes about literature, constantly evolve, so do the reference needs of students, teachers, scholars, journalists, researchers, and book club members. To be certain that we continue to keep pace with the expectations of our customers, the editors of *SATA* listen carefully to their comments regarding the value, utility, and quality of the series. Librarians, who have firsthand knowledge of the needs of library users, are a valuable resource for us. The *Something about the Author* Product Advisory Board, made up of school, public, and academic librarians, is a forum to promote focused feedback about *SATA* on a regular basis. The nine-member advisory board includes the following individuals, whom the editors wish to thank for sharing their expertise:

Eva M. Davis
Director,
Canton Public Library,
Canton, Michigan

Joan B. Eisenberg
Lower School Librarian,
Milton Academy,
Milton, Massachusetts

Francisca Goldsmith
Teen Services Librarian,
Berkeley Public Library,
Berkeley, California

Susan Dove Lempke
Children's Services Supervisor,
Niles Public Library District,
Niles, Illinois

Robyn Lupa
Head of Children's Services,
Jefferson County Public Library,
Lakewood, Colorado

Victor L. Schill
Assistant Branch Librarian/Children's Librarian,
Harris County Public Library/Fairbanks Branch,
Houston, Texas

Caryn Sipos
Community Librarian,
Three Creeks Community Library,
Vancouver, Washington

Steven Weiner
Director,
Maynard Public Library,
Maynard, Massachusetts

SOMETHING ABOUT THE AUTHOR

ADOFF, Arnold 1935-

Personal

Born July 16, 1935, in New York, NY; son of Aaron Jacob (a pharmacist) and Rebecca Adoff; married Virginia Hamilton (a writer), March 19, 1960 (died, 2002); children: Leigh Hamilton (daughter), Jaime Levi (son). *Education:* City College of New York (now City College of the City University of New York), B.A. (history and literature), 1956; graduate studies at Columbia University, 1956-58; attended New School for Social Research, 1965-67. *Religion:* "Freethinking pragmatist." *Hobbies and other interests:* History, music.

Addresses

Home—Yellow Springs, OH. *Office*—Arnold Adoff Agency, P.O. Box 293, Yellow Springs, OH 45387.

Career

Poet, writer of fiction and nonfiction, and anthologist. Teacher in New York City public schools, 1957-69; Arnold Adoff Agency, Yellow Springs, OH, literary agent, beginning 1977. Instructor in federal projects at New York University, Connecticut College, and other institutions; visiting professor, Queens College, 1986-87. Lecturer at colleges throughout the United States; consultant in children's literature, poetry, and creative writing. Member of planning commission, Yellow Springs. *Military service:* Served with New York National Guard.

Arnold Adoff (Photograph by Kacy Cook. Reproduced by permission.)

Awards, Honors

Children's Books of the Year citation, Child Study Association of America, 1968, for *I Am the Darker Brother,* 1969, for *City in All Directions,* and 1986, for *Sports Pages;* Notable Children's Trade Book citation, National Council for the Social Studies/Children's Book Council (NCSS-CBC), 1974, and Children's Choice citation, International Reading Association/CBC, 1985, both for *My Black Me;* Art Books for Children Award for *MA nDA LA,* 1975; Books for the Teen Age citation, New York Public Library, 1980, 1981, 1982, all for *It Is the Poem Singing into Your Eyes;* Jane Addams Children's Book Award special recognition, 1983, for *All the Colors of the Race;* Parents' Choice Award (picture-book category), 1988, for *Flamboyan;* National Council of Teachers of English Award in Excellence in Poetry for Children, 1988; Notable Book citation, American Library Association, 1995, for *Slow Dance Heartbreak Blues; Riverbank Review* Children's Book of Distinction selection, 1997, for *Love Letters.*

Writings

FOR CHILDREN

Malcolm X (nonfiction), illustrated by John Wilson, Crowell, 1970, revised edition, HarperCollins (New York, NY), 2000.

MA nDA LA, illustrated by Emily Arnold McCully, Harper (New York, NY), 1971.

Black Is Brown Is Tan, illustrated by Emily Arnold McCully, Harper (New York, NY), 1973, published with new illustrations by McCully, HarperCollins (New York, NY), 2002.

Make a Circle Keep Us In: Poems for a Good Day, illustrated by Ronald Himler, Delacorte (New York, NY), 1975.

Big Sister Tells Me That I'm Black, illustrated by Lorenzo Lynch, Holt (New York, NY), 1976.

Tornado!, illustrated by Ronald Himler, Delacorte (New York, NY), 1977.

Under the Early Morning Trees, illustrated by Ronald Himler, Dutton (New York, NY), 1978.

Where Wild Willie, illustrated by Emily Arnold McCully, Harper (New York, NY), 1978.

Eats, illustrated by Susan Russo, Lothrop (New York, NY), 1979.

I Am the Running Girl, illustrated by Ronald Himler, Harper (New York, NY), 1979.

Friend Dog, illustrated by Troy Howell, Lippincott (Philadelphia, PA), 1980.

OUTside/INside Poems, illustrated by John Steptoe, Lothrop (New York, NY), 1981.

Today We Are Brother and Sister, illustrated by Glo Coalson, Lothrop (New York, NY), 1981.

Birds, illustrated by Troy Howell, Lippincott (Philadelphia, PA), 1982.

All the Colors of the Race, illustrated by John Steptoe, Lothrop (New York, NY), 1982.

The Cabbages Are Chasing the Rabbits, illustrated by Janet Stevens, Harcourt (New York, NY), 1985.

Sports Pages, illustrated by Steven Kuzma, Lippincott (Philadelphia, PA), 1986.

Greens, illustrated by Betsy Lewin, Morrow (New York, NY), 1988.

Flamboyan, illustrated by Karen Barbour, Harcourt (New York, NY), 1988.

Chocolate Dreams, illustrated by Turi MacCombie, Lothrop (New York, NY), 1988.

Hard to Be Six, illustrated by Cheryl Hanna, Lothrop (New York, NY), 1990.

In for Winter, out for Spring, illustrated by Jerry Pinkney, Harcourt (New York, NY), 1991.

The Return of Rex and Ethel, illustrated by Catherine Deeter, Harcourt (New York, NY), 1993.

Street Music: City Poems, illustrated by Karen Barbour, HarperCollins (New York, NY), 1995.

Slow Dance Heart Break Blues, illustrated by William Cotton, Lothrop (New York, NY), 1995.

Touch the Poem, illustrated by Bill Creevy, Scholastic, Inc. (New York, NY), 1996.

Love Letters, illustrated by Lisa Desimini, Scholastic, Inc. (New York, NY), 1997.

The Basket Counts, illustrated by Mike Weaver, Simon & Schuster Books for Young Readers (New York, NY), 2000.

Daring Dog and Captain Cat, illustrated by Joe Cepeda, Simon & Schuster Books for Young Readers (New York, NY), 2001.

Roots and Blues: A Celebration, illustrated by R. Gregory Christie, Clarion Books (New York, NY), 2011.

EDITOR

I Am the Darker Brother: An Anthology of Modern Poems by Negro Americans, illustrated by Benny Andrews, Macmillan (New York, NY), 1968, revised with a new afterword by Adoff, 1997.

Black on Black: Commentaries by Negro Americans, Macmillan (New York, NY), 1968.

City in All Directions: An Anthology of Modern Poems, illustrated by Donald Carrick, Macmillan (New York, NY), 1969.

Black Out Loud: An Anthology of Modern Poems by Black Americans, illustrated by Alvin Hollingsworth, Macmillan (New York, NY), 1970.

Brothers and Sisters: Modern Stories by Black Americans, Macmillan (New York, NY), 1970.

It Is the Poem Singing in Your Eyes: An Anthology of New Young Poets, Harper (New York, NY), 1971.

The Poetry of Black America: An Anthology of the Twentieth Century, introduction by Gwendolyn Brooks, Harper (New York, NY), 1973.

My Black Me: A Beginning Book of Black Poetry, Dutton (New York, NY), 1974.

Celebrations: A New Anthology of Black American Poetry, Follett, 1977.

(With Kacy Cook) *Virginia Hamilton: Speeches, Essays, and Conversations,* Blue Sky Press (New York, NY), 2010.

Contributor of articles and reviews to periodicals.

Adoff's research library was bequeathed to Bolinga Black Cultural Center, Wright State University, as part of Virginia Hamilton and Arnold Adoff Resource Center, 2010.

Sidelights

Poet, biographer, anthologist, and educator Arnold Adoff is recognized as one of the early champions of multiculturalism in literature for children and young adults. Adoff reflects the African-American experience in many of his works, most notably in the anthologies *I Am the Darker Brother: An Anthology of Modern Poems by Negro Americans* and *City in All Directions: An Anthology of Modern Poems* as well as in his illustrated biography *Malcolm X* and picture books such as the award-winning *Black Is Brown Is Tan.*

As a poet, Adoff characteristically utilizes free verse, vivid images, and unusual structures and sounds to express a variety of moods and tones. His poetry is noted for its invention and innovation as well as for its idiosyncratic use of capitalization and punctuation as a way to visually represent the meaning of words. As an anthologist, Adoff is acknowledged for creating carefully selected poetry and prose collections that feature African-American writers and focus on themes of survival, transcendence, and hope. In his collections for young adults, he includes works by Langston Hughes, Lucille Clifton, Paul Laurence Dunbar, Gwendolyn Brooks, Arna Bontemps, and Nikki Giovanni as well as a number of talented but lesser-known poets.

Adoff was born in New York City and grew up in a mixed working-class neighborhood in the South Bronx. His father, who operated a pharmacy, immigrated to the United States from a town near the Polish/Russian border. "In our home, as in so many others, the emphasis was on being American with a keen sense of Jewish," Adoff once told *SATA.* The Adoff family was well read, and numerous magazines and newspapers could be found around the house—the exception being comics, which Adoff's grandmother strictly forbade as too low brow. Lively discussions on issues of the day were frequently exchanged. "Discussions were volatile, emotional as well as intellectual," Adoff told *SATA.* "In order to hold status within the family, you had to speak loudly . . . on such burning topics as economics, socialism, the Soviet Union, and how to be assimilated into the larger society without losing one's Jewishness."

Around the age of ten, Adoff attended a neighborhood Zionist school, where, as he told *SATA,* he "studied the Old Testament and . . . Zionism as well as other aspects of Jewish history and culture," supplementing his studies with books that included *Little Women* and *The Five Little Peppers and How They Grew.* As a teenager, he read such authors as Shakespeare, Balzac, Dos Passos, Steinbeck, and De Maupassant; in addition, he was exposed to the writings of Havelock Ellis and the work of psychologists such as Menninger, Steckel, and Horney. Adoff's favorite poets are the ones "who can sing and can control their word-songs with all-important craft," he once noted: among his most important influences were Dylan Thomas, e.e. cummings, Rilke, Marianne Moore, Gwendolyn Brooks, and Robert Hayden. At age sixteen, Adoff began writing poetry; he also be-

Adoff's award-winning Black Is Brown Is Tan *has been reissued with new illustrations by original artist Emily Arnold McCully.* (Illustration copyright © 2002 by Emily Arnold McCully. Reproduced by permission of Amistad, an imprint of HarperCollins Children's, a division of HarperCollins Publishers.)

gan sneaking into New York City jazz clubs to hear jazz legends such as Dizzy Gillespie, Charlie Parker, and Sarah Vaughan. Jazz demonstrated to Adoff, as he remarked to *SATA,* that "what was called 'American culture' most often did not include black or Latino culture. . . . By the time I graduated high school, jazz was the only music I listened to. It pushed out the boundaries of my world."

Adoff enrolled at the Columbia University School of Pharmacy, but withdrew to major in history and literature at City College. He wrote for the college newspaper and literary magazine and was politically active, participating in protests for civil liberties. During college, he was introduced to James Joyce and Gertrude Stein, writers who experimented with language and wordplay. He was also greatly influenced by jazz artist Charles Mingus, who lectured before the jazz club of which Adoff was president and became the young poet's friend. Later, while Adoff was substitute teaching and living in Greenwich Village, he became Mingus's manager and maintained "running chronicles of the Village club scene." It was through Mingus that Adoff would meet his future wife, African-American novelist and children's writer Virginia Hamilton; the couple was married in 1960.

While at graduate school at Columbia University, Adoff began teaching seventh-grade social studies at a *yeshiva* in the Brownsville section of Brooklyn. This job, he once told *SATA,* "gave me confidence knowing I could stay alive outside grad school." Although he finished the required coursework for a Ph.D. in American history, he left before completing his dissertation, pulled by his desire to write. He moved to Greenwich Village and alternated substitute teaching in New York City public schools with writing and going to jazz clubs in the Village. The Village scene included "a vibrant community of painters, writers, musicians who would meet in the coffeehouses and talk art. . . . Man Ray was an important influence, as was Picasso, the Russian Constructivists, and other painters and sculptors influenced by technology and things industrial." Shortly after Adoff and Virginia Hamilton were married, they moved to Spain and France to work on writing projects. During their stay in Europe, the civil rights movement was intensifying in the United States and they decided to return. "Virginia [was] black, our children brown—we felt somehow it would be wrong to stay," Adoff recalled to *SATA.* "Besides, it all seemed very exciting and we didn't want to be removed from the action. So we returned to New York, where we threw ourselves into our work and as much political work as we could handle."

Adoff began teaching students in Harlem and on Manhattan's Upper West Side. In addition, he told *SATA,* "I resumed collecting black literature, which I had begun in the late 1950s and early 1960s. . . . I would dig up

Adoff and award-winning artist John Steptoe team up in **All the Colors of the Race,** *featuring poems about a girl growing up in a biracial family.* (Illustration copyright © 1982 by John Steptoe. Reproduced by permission of the Estate of John Steptoe. All rights reserved.)

old magazines like *Dial* and look for specifically black periodicals. . . . I'd haunt bookshops all over town." He also became aware of the lack of materials available to ethnically diverse children that reflected their reality. "As a teacher I had students who wanted life in those dusty classrooms," he would write in the preface to his anthology *The Poetry of Black America: An Anthology of Twentieth-Century America.* They wanted pictures of themselves inside themselves. . . . I was the dealer. The pusher of poems and stories. Plays and paintings. Jazz and blues. And my students began to push on me. To deal their sounds and write their poems. And I was made to become serious about myself. To get my head together and attempt to go beyond the classrooms and students and schools. To go beyond the racist textbooks and anthologies that were on the shelves and in the bookstores."

Adoff began to assemble some of the poems that he had been collecting and sharing with his students, and he included 600 of these in his first anthology, *I Am the Darker Brother,* published in 1968. In compiling a more-recent work, *It Is the Poem Singing into Your Eyes,* Adoff solicited work from young poets across the country and received over 6,000 submissions. Among the young poets included in this collection was August Wilson, who would later become a Pulitzer prize-winning playwright.

In an interview with Lee Bennett Hopkins in *More Books by More People,* Adoff explained that his objective in producing black literature anthologies is to portray a truer cultural picture of literary America. "I want my anthologies of Black American writing to make black kids strong in their knowledge of themselves and their great literary heritage—give them facts and people and power. I also want . . . to give knowledge to white kids around the country, so that mutual respect and understanding will come from mutual learning. . . . Children have to understand that the oversimplifications they get in classrooms, along with the token non-white artists represented, are not the true American literature," and "using an anthology is the first step to discovery. The anthology then leads to individual works of the writers."

In 1971, Adoff published *MA nDA LA,* a story poem for children that uses only words containing the sound "ah." Brought to life in watercolor illustrations by Emily Arnold McCully, the book relates the cycle of family life in a small African village. As Adoff explained of *MA nDA LA* in *SATA,* "I use the image of invisible rubber bands pulling the reader's eye from the last letter of the last word in the first line down to the first letter of the first word in the last line. . . . The music of language greatly affects meaning. . . . Ideally, each poem should be read three times: for meaning; for rhythm; for technical tricks. My poems demand active participation."

Throughout the 1970s and 1980s, Adoff published several volumes of poetry for young people that display his characteristic use of free verse, vivid sensory images,

Adoff's musical celebration, **Roots and Blues,** *comes to life in colorful paintings by R. Gregory Christie.* (Illustration copyright © 2011 by R. Gregory Christie. Reproduced by permission of Clarion Books, an imprint of Houghton Mifflin Harcourt Publishing Company. All rights reserved.)

striking word pictures, and lively rhythms while offering sensitive portrayals of family life and interior emotions. Modeled after his own family, *Black Is Brown Is Tan* became one of the first children's books to depict interracial families, while in *All The Colors of the Race* Adoff explores the feelings of a girl with a black mother and a white father in "contemplative, jubilant, and questioning . . . verses [that] stress the young person's humanity in terms of gifts received from her forebears," according to Ruth M. Stein in *Language Arts.* Another work for children, *OUTside/INside Poems* recreates a day in the life of a small boy and expresses his range of feelings. In *SATA* Adoff once described this work as "a great vehicle for teaching young readers to write poetry. Also, this is the one that really has the greatest element of reality/fantasy."

In *Where Wild Willie,* which Stein described as "Adoff's paean to independence" in her *Language Arts* review, the poet describes a child who temporarily leaves her family to go on her own adventure of learning. The poem recounts the girl's journey and is interspersed with the encouraging words of her parents. Zena Sutherland wrote in *Bulletin of the Center for Children's Books* that *Where Wild Willie* "describes with lilting fluency Willie's rambles and then the voices from home speak for themselves, an antiphonal arrangement in which the two draw closer until Willie comes home."

Adoff considers his middle-grade poetry collection *Sports Pages* to be "a breakthrough [because I] worked in a longer form of a combination of poetic prose and poetry and dealt with some autobiographical material using individual voice in the midst of organized activity." Another collection designed to appeal to young athletes, *The Basket Counts* pairs twenty-eight poems by Adoff with paintings by Mike Weaver. As a reviewer acknowledged in the *Bulletin of the Center for Children's Books, Sports Pages* "is one of his best collections," while a critic in *Kirkus Reviews* predicted that the work will "easily lure the adolescent" due to Adoff's "sensitivity and acuity." In *Booklist* Gillian Engberg noted of *The Basket Counts* that the poet's focus is the game "played on driveways, on neighborhood course, through a bedroom-door hoop," and his "words bounce back and forth in staccato dribbling."

With *Flamboyan* Adoff uses poetic prose to paint a picture-book fantasy about a Puerto Rican girl who longs to fly with the birds that circle above her yard. Illustrated by Karen Barbour, the book contains an unusual typographic device: a red leaf that appears in the text to provide directions for reading aloud. Called "a magical story of a girl's yearning to be outside her own life" by a reviewer in *Publishers Weekly, Flamboyan* will "appeal to all who long to go beyond the ordinary," the critic added, and in *School Library Journal* Ruth K. MacDonald praised the book's "dazzling combination of . . . text and illustration."

Chocolate Dreams is also inspired by Adoff's life, in this case his—and his children's—favorite subject: food. Described by Betsy Hearne in *Bulletin of the Center for Children's Books* as a "rich confection of wordplay, rhythms, and unexpected twists of rhyme and meaning from a poet in his element," *Chocolate Dreams* reveals Adoff's ability to combine "invention and control, depth and delight."

A collection of jazzy poems in free verse, Adoff's *Street Music: City Poems* celebrates the vibrancy of city life, while in *Slow Dance Heart Break Blues* he captures the thoughts and experiences that are common among early teens. According to a critic in *Kirkus Reviews, Slow Dance Heart Break Blues* "is laden with empathy," and in *School Library Journal* Sharon Korbeck concluded of the same work that the poet challenges readers to question what poetry is and to reexamine "who and where they are in light of today's fast-moving issues and society." Writing in *Horn Book*, Robert D. Hale stated that the "on-target" collection shows that "Adoff knows what teenagers are thinking and feeling."

Music is the inspiration for Adoff's *Roots and Blues: A Celebration*, which is illustrated by talented artist R. Gregory Christie. Here the author mixes poetry and

Adoff offers young readers a collection of twenty poems written in the form of valentine notes, Love Letters, *illustrated by Lisa Desimini.* (Illustration copyright © 1997 by Lisa Desmini. Reproduced by permission of Scholastic, Inc.)

lyrical prose in sharing his love of an uniquely American musical form that is rooted in the slave culture of the rural South. Praised by a *Kirkus Reviews* writer as "a moving meditation on the roots of American blues," the book's sixty poems resonate with the strong religious faith and resilience of the men and woman who wove the music out of their multicultural experience. Christie's "haunting, acrylic images" also added to the book's power, prompting Marilyn Taniguchi to described *Roots and Blues* as a "splendid addition to American history" studies in her *School Library Journal* review.

Love Letters is one of two collaborations with artist Lisa Desimini, Here Adoff presents primary graders with twenty valentines written as anonymous notes. Described by *School Library Journal* contributor Jane Marino as "funny, joyful, and creative," *Touch the Poem* inspires readers to reconnect with their five senses as they pass through a single day. Reviewing *Love Letters,* Dulcy Brainard wrote in *Publishers Weekly* that "much of the pleasure" comes from the author's and illustrator's "abilities to evoke not only . . . everyday feelings but the more complicated sense of privacy and mystery they summon." The "striking mixed-media collages" in *Touch the Poem* "make consistently pertinent use of off-center techniques," observed a *Publishers Weekly* critic, and serve as "an effective contrast to Adoff's low-key approach."

While most of Adoff's books for children contain a selection of verses, he shares both his love of animals and his talent for storytelling in *The Return of Rex and Ethel* and *Daring Dog and Captain Cat*. In the first book, two best friends and neighbors have shared their childhood with their two dogs, Rex and Ethel. As the girls grow up, the pets grow old and finally pass away, both on the same day, leaving their human friends inspired to honor them by caring for other pets in need. From contemplative, the author's tone turns rambunctious in *Daring Dog and Captain Cat,* as Joe Cepeda's art energizes a free-verse story about two pets who have exciting adventures after their human housemates go to sleep each night. With their characteristic use of capitalization, "Adoff's shaped lines crank up the verbal intensity," wrote a *Kirkus Reviews* writer in an appraisal of *Daring Dog and Captain Cat*. For *School Library Journal* critic Nina Lindsay, the poet's "free verse dashes and leaps across the page and tongue" in a way that will entertain story-hour audiences. With its "vibrantly colored" illustrations, the book treats children to "a delightful domestic swashbuckler," concluded *Booklist* contributor Annie Ayres.

"I began writing for kids because I wanted to effect a change in American society . . . ," Adoff once told *SATA*. "By the time we reach adulthood, we are closed and set in our attitudes. The chances of a poet reaching us are very slim. But I can open a child's imagination, develop his appetite for poetry, and most importantly, show him that poetry is a natural part of everyday life.

We all need someone to point out that the emperor is wearing no clothes. That is the poet's job." In an interview with Jeffrey S. Copeland in *Speaking of Poets,* Adoff added another perspective: "I'm still attempting to influence kids one way or another, whether it is the way they view the color of skin or reality and fantasy. I hope always to be considered perhaps controversial, perhaps dangerous, to the status quo. . . . It is a struggle to create something you hope is art. I work long and hard at my craft. I like to feel I have good instincts when it comes to language. All in all, I am very proud of what I've done."

Biographical and Critical Sources

BOOKS

Hopkins, Lee Bennett, *More Books by More People: Interviews with Sixty-five Authors of Books for Children,* Citation Press, 1974.
Speaking of Poets: Interviews with Poets Who Write for Children and Young Adults, National Council of Teachers of English, 1993.

PERIODICALS

American Libraries, April, 2010, interview with Adoff, p. 22.
Booklist, January 1, 1997, Ilene Cooper, review of *Love Letters,* p. 863; February 15, 1997, Hazel Rochman, review of *I Am the Darker Brother: An Anthology of Modern Poems by African Americans,* p. 1013; February 1, 2000, Gillian Engberg, review of *The Basket Counts,* p. 1017; February 15, 2000, Hazel Rochman, review of *Malcolm X,* p. 1103; March 15, 2000, Ilene Cooper, review of *Touch the Poem,* p. 1378; October 1, 2001, Annie Ayres, review of *Daring Dog and Captain Cat,* p. 322; April 15, 2002, Hazel Rochman, review of *Black Is Brown Is Tan,* p. 1405; March 1, 2010, Hazel Rochman, review of *Virginia Hamilton: Speeches, Essays, and Conversations,* p. 58.
Bulletin of the Center for Children's Books, March, 1979, Zena Sutherland, review of *Where Wild Willie,* p. 109; June, 1986, review of *Sports Pages,* p, 181; November, 1989, Betsy Hearne, review of *Chocolate Dreams,* p. 49; March, 1997, Elizabeth Bush, review of *Love Letters,* p. 239.
Horn Book, November-December, 1995, Robert D. Hale, review of *Slow Dance Heart Break Blues,* p. 770.
Kirkus Reviews, May 1, 1986, review of *Sports Pages,* p. 721; July 1, 1995, review of *Slow Dance Heart Break Blues,* p. 942; August 15, 2001, review of *Daring Dog and Captain Cat*; December 15, 2010, review of *Roots and Blues.*
Language Arts, September, 1979, Ruth M. Stein, review of *Where Wild Willie,* pp. 690-691; April, 1983, Ruth M. Stein, review of *All the Colors of the Race,* pp. 483-484.
Publishers Weekly, August 26, 1988, review of *Flamboyan,* p. 88; December 2, 1997, Dulcy Brainard, review of *Love Letters;* January 10, 2000, review of *The Basket Counts,* p. 68; April 17, 2000, review of *Touch the Poem,* p. 80; May 15, 2000, review of *The Return of Rex and Ethel,* p. 118; September 24, 2001, review of *Daring Dog and Captain Cat,* p. 93; March 25, 2002, review of *We're Back!,* p. 66; November 29, 2010, review of *Roots and Blues,* p. 48.
New York Times Book Review, April 25, 1982, Ardis Kimzey, "Verse First, Poetry Next," p. 37.
School Library Journal, October, 1988, Ruth K. MacDonald, review of *Flamboyan,* p. 114; September, 1995, Sharon Korbeck, review of *Slow Dance Heart Break Blues,* p. 221; June, 2000, Margaret Bush, review of *The Return of Rex and Ethel,* p. 200, and Jane Marino, review of *Touch the Poem,* p. 128; September, 2001, Nina Lindsay, review of *Daring Dog and Captain Cat,* p. 182; July, 2002, Dorothy N. Bowen, review of *Black Is Brown Is Tan,* p. 76; March, 2010, Margaret A. Chang, review of *Virginia Hamilton,* p. 188; February, 2011, Marilyn Taniguchi, review of *Roots and Blues,* p. 122.
Top of the News, January, 1972, interview with Adoff, pp. 153-155.
Voice of Youth Advocates, August, 2010, Courtney Huse Wika, review of *Virginia Hamilton,* p. 276.

ONLINE

Arnold Adoff Home Page, http://www.arnoldadoff.com (March 7, 2012).
Cynsations Web log, http://cynthialeitichsmith.blogspot.com (March 31, 2010), "Guest Post: Arnold Adoff and Kacy Cook on Virginia Hamilton."*

*   *   *

AMINI-HOLMES, Liz

Personal

Born in San Francisco, CA; married Mark Holmes (an artist and writer); children: twin sons. *Education:* Academy of Art College, B.F.A. (illustration); also attended Stanford University and University of California, Berkeley.

Addresses

Home—Woodside, CA. *E-mail*—liz@lunavilla.com.

Career

Illustrator, art director, and educator. Taught at Academy of Art University, San Francisco, CA; conducts adult and children's art workshops. *Exhibitions:* Work exhibited at galleries in San Francisco Bay area and in New York, NY.

Member

Society of Children's Book Writers and Illustrators, Graphic Artists Guild, San Francisco Society of Illustrators.

Awards, Honors

Outstanding International Books Honor listee, U.S. Board on Books for Young People (USBBY), Best Books for Kids and Teens selection, Canadian Children's Book Centre, Sheila A. Egoff Children's Literature Prize finalist, and Information Book Award nomination, Children's Literature Roundtables of Canada, all 2011, all for *Fatty Legs* by Margaret Pokiak-Fenton and Christy Jordan-Fenton; Outstanding International Books Award, USBBY, 2012, for *A Stranger at Home* by Pokiak-Fenton and Jordan-Fenton.

Illustrator

Christy Jordan-Fenton and Margaret Pokiak-Fenton, *Fatty Legs: A True Story,* Annick Press (Toronto, Ontario, Canada), 2010.

Christy Jordan-Fenton and Margaret Pokiak-Fenton, *A Stranger at Home: A True Story* (sequel to *Fatty Legs: A True Story*), Annick Press (Toronto, Ontario, Canada), 2011.

Contributor to periodicals and poetry books.

Sidelights

A respected illustrator who works primarily in acrylics, Liz Amini-Holmes has provided the artwork for *Fatty Legs: A True Story* and its sequel, *A Stranger at Home: A True Story.* Written by Christy Jordan-Fenton and her mother-in-law, Margaret Pokiak-Fenton, the books present an autobiographical account of a young girl's traumatic experiences at a residential school in the Canadian arctic. Set in the 1940s, *Fatty Legs* introduces eight-year-old Olemaun, an Inuit girl who convinces her father to let her attend a church-run school so she can learn to read. An abusive nun known as the "Raven" takes an instant dislike to the strong-willed youngster, renaming her Margaret and forcing her to perform exhausting manual labor. When the Raven demands that Margaret wear unflattering red stockings, making her the brunt of her classmates' jokes, the girl finally stands up for herself and protests the harsh treatment. "Dark, expressive original paintings are dotted throughout the story and complement the serious tone of the narrative," observed *School Library Journal* critic Jody Kopple in her review of *Fatty Legs*. A writer in *Kirkus Reviews* also praised "Amini-Holmes' slightly surreal paintings, which capture the alien flavor of these schools for their students."

A Stranger at Home continues Margaret's story, focusing on the girl's difficult readjustment to village life. After two years at the residential school, Margaret returns to Tuktoyaktuk, but the homecoming is not a pleasant one: her mother and siblings do not recognize her at first, and she struggles to speak in her native tongue. With her father's help, Margaret eventually reconnects with her old way of life, going on a hunt and even driving her own dog sled. According to Cynthia O'Brien in *Quill & Quire*, "Amini-Holmes's illustra-

Margaret Pokiak-Fenton teams up with daughter-in-law Christy Jordan-Fenton to share her childhood experiences in Fatty Legs, *a middle-grade novel featuring artwork by Liz Amini-Holmes.* (Artwork copyright © 2010 by Liz Amini-Holmes. Reproduced with permission of Annick Press Ltd.)

tions are beautifully rendered, capturing the landscape in rich, saturated colours. In combination with Margaret's story, they help create a textured, compelling book."

Biographical and Critical Sources

PERIODICALS

Canadian Review of Materials, November 12, 2010, Shelbey Krahn, review of *Fatty Legs: A True Story;* February 17, 2012, Shelbey Krahn, review of *a Stranger at Home: A True Story.*

Kirkus Reviews, November 15, 2010, review of *Fatty Legs;* October 15, 2011, review of *A Stranger at Home.*

Quill & Quire, November, 2010, Jean Mills, review of *Fatty Legs;* November, 2011, Cynthia O'Brien, review of *A Stranger at Home.*

School Library Journal, December, 2010, Jody Kopple, review of *Fatty Legs,* p. 139; December, 2011, Jody Kopple, review of *A Stranger at Home,* p. 140.

ONLINE

Annick Press Web site, http://www.annickpress.com/ (March 1, 2012), "Liz Amini-Holmes."

Children's Illustrators Web site, http://www.childrens illustrators.com/ (March 1, 2012), "Liz Amini-Holmes."

Graphic Artists Guild Web site, http://norcal.gag.org/ members/ (March 1, 2012), "Liz Amini-Holmes."

Liz Amini-Holmes Home Page, http://www.lunavilla.com (March 1, 2012).

Liz Amini-Holmes Web log, http://lunavilla.blogspot.com (March 1, 2012).*

* * *

ASTOR, Kristi
See COOK, Kristi

* * *

ATWATER-RHODES, Amelia 1984-

Personal

Born April 16, 1984, in Silver Spring, MD; daughter of William Rhodes (a public-policy consultant in econometrics) and Susan Atwater-Rhodes (a school vice principal); married; July 4, 2010; partner's name Mandi. *Education:* University of Massachusetts, B.A.; Northeastern University, M.A. *Hobbies and other interests:* Cross-stitch, playing piano, gardening, cooking, carpentry, debate, learning new things.

Addresses

Home—Framingham, MA.

Career

Novelist and educator. Teaches English and special education.

Awards, Honors

"Twenty Teens Who Will Change the World" listee, *Teen People* magazine; Quick Picks for Reluctant Young Readers citation, American Library Association (ALA), 2001, for *In the Forests of the Night;* Quick Picks for Reluctant Young Readers citation, ALA, 2001, and Young-Adults Choice selection, International Reading Association (IRA), 2002, both for *Demon in My View;* Quick Picks for Reluctant Young Readers citation, 2002, and IRA Young-Adult Choice selection, 2003, both for *Shattered Mirror;* Quick Picks for Reluctant Young Readers citation, 2003, for *Midnight Predator;* IRA Young-Adults Choice selection, 2003, for *Wolfcry;* honors from numerous state reading associations.

Writings

Persistence of Memory, Delacorte (New York, NY), 2008.
Token of Darkness, Delacorte (New York, NY), 2010.

"DEN OF SHADOWS" NOVEL SERIES

In the Forests of the Night, Delacorte (New York, NY), 1999.
Demon in My View, Delacorte (New York, NY), 2000.
Shattered Mirror, Delacorte (New York, NY), 2001.
Midnight Predator, Delacorte (New York, NY), 2002.
The Den of Shadows Quartet (omnibus), Delacorte (New York, NY), 2009.
All Just Glass, Delacorte (New York, NY), 2011.

"KIESHA'RA" NOVEL SERIES

Hawksong, Delacorte (New York, NY), 2003.
Snakecharm, Delacorte (New York, NY), 2004.
Falcondance, Delacorte (New York, NY), 2005.
Wolfcry, Delacorte (New York, NY), 2006.
Wyvernhail, Delacorte (New York, NY), 2007.
The Shapeshifters: Kiesha'ra of the Den of Shadows (omnibus), Delacorte (New York, NY), 2010.

Adaptations

The "Kiesha'ra" series has been adapted for audiobook by Recorded Books.

Sidelights

At an age when most girls are contemplating their first date, Amelia Atwater-Rhodes was already a successful novelist with a young-adult bestseller under her belt. she had an early dose of fame when *In the Forests of the Night,* her first published book, garnered critical acclaim and sold over 50,000 copies only months after publication. In the years since, Atwater-Rhodes has continued to develop as a writer, producing both the "Den of Shadows" series (or "Nyeusigrube", as the author refers to her fictional vampire world), and her "Kiesha'ra" fantasy series as well as several stand-alone novels.

Not surprisingly, considering the author's celebrity, Atwater-Rhodes' books continue to be popular with teen readers. "Writing has always been, to me, a way of interacting with the world on a different level," the author stated in an essay on the Random House Web site. "I write when I'm angry; I write when I'm happy; I write when I'm depressed. Writing is for me a way of communicating not only with others but with myself. The keyboard is my medium for painting the world around me. What I'm thinking, what I see, what I hear, what I do, and who I meet; I write it all."

Atwater-Rhodes was born in Silver Spring, Maryland, in 1984, but subsequently moved to Concord, Massachusetts, where she attended high school. While both parents—her mother is a high-school vice principal and her father is a public-policy consultant—acknowledged being fans of the books of horror fiction-writer Anne Rice, Atwater-Rhodes particularly credits her mother with whetting her appetite for the genre. As she told

USA Today writer Katy Kelly, "She pretty much raised me on Stephen King and Dracula and aliens. She'd say, 'Just keep in mind: it's fiction. You're not supposed to take an ax to your neighbor. You're not to bite your friend.'"

The urge to create seized Atwater-Rhodes early, and she was at work on a science-fiction novel by the second grade. "I have always loved to create stories," she noted on her home page, *Den of Shadows.* "My imagination has always been my driving characteristic." By age nine, she had discovered Christopher Pike's *The Last Vampire,* a book that, as she once explained, "served as an inspiration by pointing out that vampires do not have to fit into stereotypes." She began writing in earnest following fifth grade, working after school, in the middle of the night, or whenever inspiration struck. Sometimes she would write sixty pages at a sitting, and while composing *In the Forests of the Night* she balanced a tiger Beanie Baby on her head and took inspiration from singer Alanis Morisette's *Jagged Little Pill* album. After reading the novel, a former teacher signed on as her agent and sent the novel to Delacorte Press. While celebrating her fourteenth birthday, Atwater-Rhodes received a phone call telling her that the publisher had accepted *In the Forests of the Night* for publication.

Taking place in the present day and set in its author's New England hometown, *In the Forests of the Night* is the story of a 300-year-old vampire named Risika, who was "turned" while a teenager living in colonial Concord. Risika's human persona, Rachel Weatere, was born in 1684; now, after centuries living as the Undead Risika, she has adjusted to her status and, as Holly Koelling noted in *Booklist,* "has grown distant from the mortal world. Humans are prey, needed solely for nourishment." Risika sleeps by day and goes hunting in New York City by night, seeking fresh blood. One night, returning home, she discovers a black rose on her pillow just as she had centuries before, on the eve of her own transition from human to vampire. The rose is a sign, a challenge from her archenemy, a powerful vampire named Aubrey, who long ago helped Risika arrange her transformation and who she believes murdered her human brother. Risika goes into action, deciding to confront her old enemy.

Reviews of *In the Forests of the Night* were generally favorable, albeit with some reservations. A reviewer for *Publishers Weekly* described Atwater-Rhodes as "skillful at building atmosphere, insightful in creating characters and imaginative in varying and expanding upon vampire lore," while also noting a strain of "easy, adolescent cynicism." In *Booklist,* Koelling dubbed the novel's storyline "derivative" and "meandering," but went on to comment that its "use of language is surprisingly mature and polished for a thirteen-year-old writer." As Koelling correctly predicted, "Both the book's subject and the age of the author will ensure its popularity, especially with middle-schoolers, and it may

encourage other young writers to pursue the craft." Kendra Nan Skellen, reviewing the novel for *School Library Journal,* wrote that *In the Forests of the Night* "is well written and very descriptive, and has in-depth character development . . . . This first novel by an author with great ability and promise is sure to be popular." *New Yorker* contributor Melanie Thernstrom summed up the overall critical response by writing that Atwater Rhodes "has an uncanny understanding of the kind of narrative that makes for a successful potboiler: she's skilled at creating characters the reader easily and instantly bonds with, and she's resourceful when it comes to putting them in jeopardy."

Atwater-Rhodes served up another slice of horror in her second novel, *Demon in My View.* Like *In the Forests of the Night, Demon in My View* chronicles a portion of her elaborately crafted genealogy of vampires and related supernatural beings created by the author. The novel focuses on Jessica Ashley Allodola, a high school student who briefly appeared in *In the Forests of the*

Cover of Amelia Atwater-Rhodes' young-adult novel Demon in My View, *featuring cover art by Cliff Nielsen.* (Illustration © by Shannon Associates. All rights reserved. Reproduced by permission.)

Night. Writing under the pen name Ash Night, Jessica has just published her first novel, a vampire tale titled *Tiger, Tiger.* At school she is an outsider, something of a misfit, but writing takes her into a dreamlike state in which she can describe the world of vampires and witches in vivid detail. Jessica marvels at the way her fertile imagination works; what she does not realize is that these visions are, in fact, real. As a reviewer for *Publishers Weekly* noted of the novel's plot, the vampires "aren't too happy that she's spilled their secrets and wittingly alerted vampire-hunting witches to the location of their undead village, New Mayhem." To gain vengeance, Aubrey—the nemesis of *In the Forests of the Night*—appears at Jessica's high school disguised as a new student named Alex. Attracted to Jessica's aura, he is torn between a desire for revenge and the wish to turn her into a vampire like himself. Meanwhile, the plot thickens with the arrival of new student Caryn, who is actually a witch of the Smoke Line who has arrived to protect Jessica from the vampires. "The clash between the witches and the vampires and the truth of Jessica's birth take the plot down many twisting and suspenseful paths," wrote Jane Halsall in a review of *Demon in My View* for *School Library Journal.*

Atwater-Rhodes's vampire and witch saga continues in the novels *Shattered Mirror* and *Midnight Predator.* *Shattered Mirror* tells the story of Sara Vida, a high-school student and witch who must grapple with her upbringing and values when she befriends brother and sister vampires Christopher and Nissa. When Sara learns that Christopher's twin brother is Nikolas, a notoriously evil vampire who murdered one of Sara's own ancestors, the tension and suspense build. *Midnight Predator* finds relentless vampire hunter Turquoise Draka joining fellow tracker Ravyn on the trail of notorious undead Jeshickah, even though the creature's trail leads into the vampire realm known as the Midnight Empire.

While a *Publishers Weekly* contributor found that "some of [Atwater-Rhodes's] writing . . . is over the top," in *Shattered Mirror* the young author "chooses an interesting theme . . . and she builds some creative elements around it." Similarly, *School Library Journal* contributor Elaine Baran Black commented that with *Shattered Mirror,* "Atwater-Rhodes does another fine job of building a suspenseful mood and sustaining it throughout." Black further remarked that, "though the ending isn't necessarily a big surprise, readers will be racing to reach it as they devour this compelling tale." Praising *Midnight Predator* for its "thoughtful" conclusion, Molley S. Kinney noted in *School Library Journal* that Atwater-Rhodes' "plot and characters are . . . skillfully intertwined," and "the harshness and violence" of her story are balanced by "the soulful searching" of the tale's central protagonists.

In 2003 Atwater-Rhodes introduced her "Kiesha'ra" series with *Hawksong.* A shapeshifter who can move from human to hawk form, Danica Shardae is heir to the throne of her kingdom. Hoping to end the war between

Cover of Atwater-Rhodes' young-adult novel **All Just Glass,** *featuring cover art by Miranda Adria.* (Jacket cover copyright © 2011 by Delacorte Press. Reproduced by Delacorte Press, an imprint of Random House Children's Books, a division of Random House, Inc.)

her kind and the serpiente, she agrees to wed Zane Cobriana. Professing an equal commitment to a peace between their two shapeshifter races, Zane nonetheless presents a real threat to his bride while in his alternate cobra form, a fact that forces Danica to keep removed from him in private. As some attempt to end their alliance, Danica and Zane try to forge a bond of trust in a novel that *School Library Journal* contributor Saleena L. Davidson dubbed an "engaging fantasy" that is both "a love story and . . . an intriguing look at a world that is teeming with tension and danger and beauty." While a *Kirkus Reviews* writer bemoaned Atwater-Rhodes' use of a "stock romance plot," the critic added that *Hawksong* is "enjoyable for that genre," and in *Publishers Weekly* a critic praised the author for "creat[ing] . . . impressively complex cultures for both the avian and serpiente people."

Atwater-Rhodes continues her "Kiesha'ra" saga with *Snakecharm, Falcondance,* and *Wolfcry,* all which continue to detail the fragile alliance between avian and serpiente shapeshifters. In *Snakecharm* Danica and Zane hope that their heir will strengthen the bond between their peoples, until Syfka, a member of the falcon clan, arrives and begins to stir up discontent in the Wyvern court. *Falcondance* finds falcon Nicias Silvermead isolated from his kind and living amid the avians and serpientes as a guard to Danica and Zane's daughter, Oliza Shardae Cobriana, in the Wyvern court. Haunted by visions of his home in Anhmik, Nicias finally returns to his homeland, hoping to find the powerful falcon that can help him harness his growing magic powers. Back in the Wyvern court, Princess Oliza comes of age and hopes for a peaceful future, until her kidnapping by a wolf band forces her to realize that peace in her kingdom is a fragile thing. According to Lisa Prolman in *School Library Journal, Snakecharm* contains a "compelling" story in which "there is enough suspense to keep readers interested," while the tale unfolding in *Falcondance* is "detailed and intertwined with [falcon] myth and legend," according to Janis Flint-Ferguson in her *Kliatt* review.

The series goes forward with *Wolfcry.* It is time for Oliza to marry, though she fears that her choice will bring discord to the kingdom—were she to choose a snake for a mate, the birds would find fault, and vice versa. She begins to see in this dilemma the roots of prejudice and also how easily her kingdom could be undone. Reviewing *Wolfcry* in *Kliatt,* Flint-Ferguson wrote that the author "is a master at integrating the needed details from past volumes without losing momentum in the narrative she is telling." *School Library Journal* contributor June H. Keuhn also had praise for the novel, describing *Wolfcry* as "a tale of the spirit and love" that the rulers have for their subjects.

The "Kiesha'ra" series comes to completion in *Wyvernhail,* as the focus turns Oliza's cousin Hai, the daughter of a falcon and cobra, and as such, a potential heir to the throne. However, the Wyvern Court now is ruled by the serpent Salem Cobriana and the avian Sive Hardae. Hai sees trouble for the kingdom with this unworkable co-regency and finds herself in the midst of court turmoil, trying to decide whether or not she should intercede to become regent and save the realm. Flint-Ferguson, in her review of *Wyvernhail,* wrote that "fans of the series will not be disappointed" in this finale. *School Library Journal* contributor Amy J. Chow similarly thought that "the conclusion, filled with betrayal, tenderness, and peace for diverse peoples, will satisfy, despite ending a little too neatly."

Atwater-Rhodes's first stand-alone novel, *Persistence of Memory,* concerns a schizophrenic girl's struggle to control her violent, vampiric alter-ego. The work centers on Erin Misrahe, a teenager who, after years of institutionalization, is finally allowed to attend public school. Soon, however, Erin experiences bizarre episodes in which she trades places with Shevaun, an inhabitant of Nyeusigrube, who threatens to kill Erin to sever their otherworldly connection. Amy Alessio, critiquing the book for *Teenreads.com,* commended *Persistence of Memory* for its thoughtful themes. She opined that "Atwater-Rhodes takes what readers love

about fantasy . . . and challenges boundaries in creative ways to bring fresh ideas." Flint-Ferguson also commended this novel, calling it a "cleverly crafted story of a collision between the fantasy world and the known world." Likewise, *School Library Journal* contributor Mara Alpert asserted that "the world that Atwater-Rhodes has created is believable and intriguing."

Token of Darkness is the author's second stand-alone novel, although it is also connected to her larger Nyeusigrube universe). The novel opens with teenager Cooper Blake waking in the hospital following a traffic accident. The trauma he suffered has made him aware of another dimension containing the spirit of a young woman named Samantha. Cooper is drawn to the dilemma of Samantha who, though she has no memory of her former self, wants to end her current existence. Cooper takes it as his mission to bring her peace, and he is aided in his efforts by telepathic fellow student Brent, cheerleader and sorceress Delilah, and Ryan le Coire, a friend with knowledge of magic. A *Publishers Weekly* reviewer termed *Token of Darkness* a "fast-paced supernatural thriller," and *Voice of Youth Advocates*

Cover of Atwater-Rhodes' novel* Token of Darkness, *featuring artwork by Amanda Abram. (Jacket cover copyright © by Delacorte Press. Reproduced by permission of Delacorte Press, an imprint of Random House Children's Books, a division of Random House, Inc.)

contributor Cheryl Clark observed that Atwater-Rhodes' inclusion of "unexpected twists make it a page-turner." Likewise, *School Library Journal* contributor Anthony C. Doyle deemed *Token of Darkness* a "chilling tale with enough plot twists to keep readers guessing."

In an interview with Kellie Vaughan for *Teen People,* fourteen-year-old Atwater-Rhodes asserted that, "as a teen, I bring a different perspective to writing. I can offer immediate emotions, experiences and insight that adult writers often have to reach back and find in order to write about them." Nearly a decade, she observed in a *Bildungsroman* online interview: "My writing in general has grown in just about every way since I first started to publish. The world is more complex in my head—both the fictional one, which has grown with each story, and the real one, which I have lived in and studied through high school and college classes." "Beyond that," she added, "my sense of a story and what goes into it has matured. I have more awareness of my audience as I write, which is both good and bad. I can deal with more of the plot at a time, planning more than I used to."

Biographical and Critical Sources

PERIODICALS

Booklist, June 1, 1999, Holly Koelling, review of *In the Forests of the Night,* p. 1812; September 1, 2001, John Peters, review of *Shattered Mirror,* p. 96; August, 2002, Debbie Carton, review of *Midnight Predator,* p. 1948; December 1, 2008, Krista Hutley, review of *Persistence of Memory,* p. 43.
Detroit Free Press, July 16, 2000, Ellen Creager, "Fifteen Year Old Is on a Roll with Her Second Novel," p. E5.
Kirkus Reviews, June 15, 2003, review of *Hawksong,* p. 855; September 1, 2004, review of *Snakecharm,* p. 859; November 15, 2008, review of *Persistence of Memory;* January 15, 2010, review of *Token of Darkness.*
Kliatt, September, 2005, Janis Flint-Ferguson, review of *Falcondance,* p. 5; September, 2006, Janis Flint-Ferguson, review of *Wolfcry,* p. 6; September, 2007, Janis Flint-Ferguson, review of *Wyvernhail,* p. 6; November, 2008, Janis Flint-Ferguson, review of *Persistence of Memory,* p. 6.

Los Angeles Times, July 30, 2000, Susan Carpenter, "Teen Author's Novel Approach," p. E2.
New Yorker, October 18-25, 1999, Melanie Thernstrom, "The Craft," pp. 136, 138, 140-142.
People, August 9, 1999, William Plummer and Tom Duffy, "Author Rising," pp. 103-104.
Publishers Weekly, May 24, 1999, review of *In the Forests of the Night,* p. 80; April 24, 2000, review of *Demon in My View,* p. 92; September 24, 2001, review of *Shattered Mirror,* p. 94; June 30, 2003, review of *Hawksong,* p. 80; February 1, 2010, review of *Token of Darkness,* p. 51.
School Library Journal, July, 1999, Kendra Nan Skellen, review of *In the Forests of the Night,* p. 92; May, 2000, Jane Halsall, review of *Demon in My View,* p. 166; September, 2001, Elaine Baran Black, review of *Shattered Mirror,* p. 223; May, 2002, Molley S. Kinney, review of *Midnight Predator,* p. 146; August, 2003, Saleena L. Davidson, review of *Hawksong,* p. 154; October, 2004, Lisa Prolman, review of *Snakecharm,* p. 154; September, 2005, Sharon Rawlins, review of *Falcondance,* p. 198; October, 2006, June H. Keuhn, review of *Wolfcry,* p. 147; December, 2007, Amy J. Chow, review of *Wyvernhail,* p. 118; February, 2009, Mara Alpert, review of *Persistence of Memory,* p. 96; January, 2010, Anthony C. Doyle, review of *Token of Darkness,* p. 95; March, 2011, Donna Rosenblum, review of *All Just Glass,* p. 154.
Teen People, February, 1999, Kellie Vaughan, interview with Atwater-Rhodes.
USA Today, May 6, 1999, Katy Kelly, "A Writer Grave beyond Her Years," p. D1.
Voice of Youth Advocates, August, 2010, Cheryl Clark, review of *Token of Darkness,* p. 206.

ONLINE

Bildungsroman Web log, http://slayground.livejournal.com/ (July 22, 2008), interview with Atwater-Rhodes.
Den of Shadows Web site, http://www.nyeusigrube.com (March 1, 2012).
Powells.com, http://www.powells.com/ (August 5, 2009), "Kids' Q&A: Amelia Atwater-Rhodes."
Random House Web site, http://www.randomhouse.com/ (March 1, 2012), "Amelia Atwater-Rhodes."
Teenreads.com, http://www.teenreads.com/ (October 23, 2001), Serena Burns, interview with Atwater-Rhodes; (August 5, 2009) Amy Alessio, review of *Persistence of Memory;* (March 11, 2011) Melanie Smith, review of *Token of Darkness.**

B-C

BARBER, Ronde 1975-

Personal
Name pronounced RON-day; born Jamael Oronde Barber, April 7, 1975, in Roanoke, VA; son of James "J.B." and Geraldine (a financial director) Barber; married; wife's name Claudia; children: Yammile Rose, Justyce Rosina. *Education:* University of Virginia, B.A. (marketing), 1997.

Addresses
Home—Tampa, FL. *Office*—c/o Tampa Bay Buccaneers, One Buccaneer Pl., Tampa, FL 33607.

Career
Professional football player and broadcaster. Played college football at University of Virginia; Tampa Bay Buccaneers, Tampa, FL, cornerback, 1997—. *Sunday Sports Extra,* WFLA, co-host, 2000, 2002-03; *The Ronde Barber Show* (radio program), Tampa, host; *The Barber Shop,* Sirius Satellite Radio, co-host, 2005-06.

Member
Fellowship of Christian Athletes.

Awards, Honors
Society of Professional Journalists Award, for *Sunday Sports Extra;* named National Football League (NFL) Alumni Defensive Back of the Year, 2001; named to NFL All-Pro team, Associated Press, 2001, 2004, 2005; selected to NFL Pro Bowl, 2001, 2004, 2005, 2006, 2008; inducted into Virginia High School Hall of Fame, 2006; Christopher Award, 2006, for *Game Day;* named to NFL 2000's All Decade-Team.

Writings

(With brother, Tiki Barber, and Robert Burleigh) *By My Brother's Side,* illustrated by Barry Root, Simon & Schuster Books for Young Readers (New York, NY), 2004.

Ronde Barber (Photograph by Bill Kostroun. AP Images.)

(With Tiki Barber and Robert Burleigh) *Game Day,* illustrated by Barry Root, Simon & Schuster Books for Young Readers (New York, NY), 2005.

(With Tiki Barber and Robert Burleigh) *Teammates,* illustrated by Barry Root, Simon & Schuster Books for Young Readers (New York, NY), 2006.

(With Tiki Barber and Paul Mantell) *Kickoff!,* Simon & Schuster Books for Young Readers (New York, NY), 2007.

(With Tiki Barber and Paul Mantell) *Go Long!,* Simon & Schuster Books for Young Readers (New York, NY), 2008.

(With Tiki Barber and Paul Mantell) *Wild Card,* Simon & Schuster Books for Young Readers (New York, NY), 2009.

(With Tiki Barber and Paul Mantell) *Red Zone,* Simon & Schuster Books for Young Readers (New York, NY), 2010.

(With Tiki Barber and Paul Mantell) *Goal Line,* Simon & Schuster Books for Young Readers (New York, NY), 2011.

Sidelights

Ronde Barber, an All-Pro cornerback with the National Football League's Tampa Bay Buccaneers, joins his identical twin brother Tiki Barber as coauthors of *Teammates, Go Long!,* and several other well-received sports books for children. The multi-talented brothers, whose off-field activities include radio and television broadcasting, have made literacy a cornerstone of their volunteer efforts. "We work essentially as spokesmen and conduits to get the message of literacy to the public," Ronde Barber told Suzanne Rust in the *Black Issues Book Review.* "Most people in the public eye are role models by default."

Born April 7, 1975 (Ronde is older by seven minutes), the Barbers excelled at both sports and academics at Cave Spring High School in Roanoke, Virginia. They decided to play football and room together at the University of Virginia, where they earned All-Atlantic Coast Conference honors their senior year and graduated from the McIntire School of Commerce. Ronde Barber, who was drafted in the third round by the Buccaneers, earned a Super Bowl ring in 2003 and has been selected to the National Football League Pro Bowl five times. The brothers were encouraged to enter the publishing field by editor Paula Wiseman, whose son avidly followed their careers. "It just so happens that the idea fell right into line with the initiatives and ideals that are important to my brother and me," Ronde Barber recalled to *Publishers Weekly* interviewer Shannon Maughan.

In their debut work, *By My Brother's Side,* the Barbers recount a defining moment from their childhood that taught them about love and perseverance. The virtually inseparable twins must spend their first summer apart after Tiki suffers a severe leg injury in a bicycle accident. With Ronde's support and encouragement, Tiki makes a full recovery, joining his brother in time for their team's Pee Wee football league opener in the fall. According to a *Publishers Weekly* reviewer, the Barbers "give a warm focus to the family foundation they believe is instrumental to their successes and their lives." *By My Brother's Side* "will inspire those peewee football players out there who are recuperating from their own breaks," observed a critic in *Kirkus Reviews.*

Game Day focuses on the Barbers' exploits with the Cave Spring Vikings, their Pee Wee league team. Tiki, the squad's star halfback, gets most of the credit for his team's success. This leaves Ronde feeling a bit underappreciated, because his devastating blocks clear the way for his brother's touchdown runs. The boys' coach has noticed Ronde's contributions, however, and he devises a trick play that allows Ronde to showcase his talents. "What works best here is the feel-good mood,"

remarked *Booklist* contributor Ilene Cooper, and a *Publishers Weekly* reviewer similarly noted that the narrative "is equal parts sunny reminiscence and inspirational game-day pep talk; the text sails along like a skillfully thrown spiral." Mary Hazelton, writing in *School Library Journal,* described *Game Day* as "an engaging memoir that touches on themes of cooperation and individual differences."

In *Teammates* the brothers develop a novel solution to a vexing problem. After Tiki fumbles the ball during a critical possession, his coach notes the importance of developing good habits during practice. In response, the Barbers start a secret early-morning practice club, "leading to an ending that is believable as well as happy," wrote *Booklist* contributor Carolyn Phelan. "Tiki and Ronde have a warm, supportive relationship, rare in tales featuring siblings," remarked Rachel G. Payne in *School Library Journal.*

With *Kickoff!* the Barbers create a chapter book for older readers that was inspired by their experiences in junior high school Written in collaboration with Paul Mantell, the story focuses on the challenges the brothers face as they navigate the hallways of a much-larger school, where they are enrolled in separate classes for the first time. The twins also find it tough going on the

Ronde and Tiki Barber share an inspiring story in Teammates, *a picture book featuring energy-filled artwork by Barry Root.* (Illustration copyright © 2006 by Barry Root. Reprinted by permission of Simon & Schuster Books for Young Readers, an imprint of Simon & Schuster Publishing Division.)

football field practicing with their new team, the Hidden Valley Eagles. Smaller and less experienced than many of their teammates, Tiki and Ronde are buried on the bench as the season begins. They rise to the occasion, however, when they are finally offered field time during a pivotal game against a longstanding rival. "Even as the game races to an expected outcome," a *Publishers Weekly* critic noted, "the swift action" in *Kickoff!* "delivers genuine tension." According to Cheryl Ashton, reviewing *Kickoff!* for *School Library Journal*, "football enthusiasts will . . . recognize how the value of team sports is portrayed throughout the book."

In another chapter book, *Go Long!*, the Barbers enter eighth grade prepared to help their team defend the district championship. Unfortunately, their popular and respected coach announces that he has been offered a job at Cave Spring High School, and Mr. Wheeler, a science teacher at Hidden Valley, is tapped to lead the junior-high squad. When the unexpected coaching change divides the team's loyalties, Tiki and Ronde must assume leadership roles to pull the squad together. Although *School Library Journal* contributor Laura Lutz wrote that *Go Long!* contains some complex football terminology, she predicted that the Barbers' story will appeal to its intended audience of "avid football fans."

Wild Card addresses the notion of the student-athlete. As the Eagles gear up for the playoffs, they learn that their star kicker has been placed on academic probation and cannot play again until he raises his grades. Realizing that their friend needs help, Tiki and Ronde devise a clever solution to the problem. The brothers' sports-themed chapter books continue with *Red Zone*, which finds the Hidden Valley Eagles among the teams favored to win the state championship until an outbreak of chicken pox hits the school. When the Barbers fall ill their teammates rally around them. Audiences "looking for play-by-play football action will find plenty here," Carolyn Phelan maintained in her approving review of *Red Zone* for *Booklist*.

Biographical and Critical Sources

BOOKS

Contemporary Black Biography, Volume 41, Gale (Detroit, MI), 2004.

PERIODICALS

Black Issues Book Review, September-October, 2004, Suzanne Rust, "He Ain't Heavy," p. 60.
Booklist, September 1, 2004, Todd Morning, review of *By My Brother's Side*, p. 114; September 1, 2005, Ilene Cooper, review of *Game Day*, p. 119; September 1, 2006, Carolyn Phelan, review of *Teammates*, p. 116; September 1, 2007, Carolyn Phelan, review of *Kick-

off!*, p. 136; September 15, 2009, Carolyn Phelan, review of *Wild Card*, p. 60; September 1, 2010, Carolyn Phelan, review of *Red Zone*, p. 120.
Bulletin of the Center for Children's Books, January, 2006, Elizabeth Bush, review of *Game Day*, p. 218.
Ebony, December, 2005, review of *Game Day*, p. 30.
Kirkus Reviews, September 15, 2004, review of *By My Brother's Side*, p. 909; September 15, 2005, review of *Game Day*, p. 1020; July 1, 2010, review of *Red Zone*.
New York Times, August 12, 1997, Bill Pennington, "The Barber Brothers Stay in Touch as Rookie Rivals with the Giants and Bucs"; November 29, 1997, Bill Pennington, "It's Barber vs. Barber When Giants Play Bucs."
Publishers Weekly, August 30, 2004, Shannon Maughan, "Double Duty," p. 54, and review of *By My Brother's Side*, p. 55; October 3, 2005, review of *Game Day*, p. 70; October 15, 2007, review of *Kickoff!*, p. 61.
St. Petersburg Times, August 7, 2011, Gary Shelton, "Barber Keeps Defying Age," p. C1.
Sarasota Herald Tribune, October 29, 2006, Tom Balog, "Barbers' Final Meeting?," p. C3.
School Library Journal, November, 2004, Ann M. Holcomb, review of *By My Brother's Side*, p. 122; January, 2006, Mary Hazelton, review of *Game Day*, p. 116; November, 2006, Rachel G. Payne, review of *Teammates*, p. 117; December, 2007, Cheryl Ashton, review of *Kickoff!*, p. 148; October, 2008, Laura Lutz, review of *Go Long!*, p. 138.
Sports Illustrated, July 23, 2001, John Ed Bradley, "Play Mates," p. 52.

ONLINE

National Football League Web site, http://www.nfl.com/ (March 1, 2012), "Ronde Barber."
Tampa Bay Buccaneers Web site, http://www.buccaneers.com (March 1, 2012), "Ronde Barber."
University of Virginia Magazine Online, http://www.uvamagazine.org/ (spring, 2006), Ben Cramer, "The Power of Two."*

* * *

BEITIA, Sara 1977-

Personal

Surname pronounced "BAY-tee-uh"; born 1977; married Paul Marshall. *Education:* College of Idaho, B.A. (philosophy and creative writing), 2003.

Addresses

Home—Southeast ID. *Agent*—Kate Schafer Testerman, KT Literary, Highlands Ranch, CO 80129; contact@ktliterary.com. *E-mail*—sabeitia@gmail.com.

Career

Writer. Worked variously as a field worker, legal secretary, and bookkeeper. *Boise Weekly*, Boise, ID, former staff writer and arts editor.

Awards, Honors

Popular Paperbacks for Young Adults designation, American Library Association, 2011, for *The Last Good Place.*

Writings

The Last Good Place of Lily Odilon, Flux (Woodbury, MN), 2010.

Sidelights

A teenager's frantic search for his missing girlfriend is at the heart of *The Last Good Place of Lily Odilon,* the debut novel of Sara Beitia. The work centers on Albert Morales, a high-school student. Albert finds himself the prime suspect in the disappearance of girlfriend Lily Odilon after she left his company one night and vanished. Interestingly, Lily had been suffering from memory lapses since breaking into her stepfather's den-

Cover of Sara Beitia's coming-of-age novel The Last Good Place of Lily Odilon, *which focuses on a teen's search for a missing friend.* (Jacket cover photographs © Yellow Studios/iStockphoto.com (tree); Vladimir Piskunov/ iStockphoto.com (woman). Reproduced by Flux, an imprint of Llewellyn Worldwide, Ltd.)

tal office and overdosing on laughing gas some eighteen months earlier. With help from Lily's sister, Olivia, Albert attempts to locate his girlfriend, his only clue the cryptic note she left behind describing her whereabouts.

In *The Last Good Place of Lily Odilon* Beitia employs an unusual narrative structure: the story's action unfolds in three distinct time threads. One describes Lily and Albert's budding romance; another explores the hours just after Lily's disappearance; and a third chronicles Albert and Olivia's efforts to track Lily. The author told *Cynsations* online interviewer Cynthia Leitich Smith that this complex structure "serves the plot by piecing out certain information at certain times, to balance suspense with coherence and propel the story to the end."

According to *Booklist* critic Connie Fletcher, *The Last Good Place of Lily Odilon* "boasts a strong narrative drive, deft scene setting, and isn't bad at delivering catch-your-breath suspense," and a *Kirkus Reviews* writer asserted that Beitia's "noir thriller hooks readers with realistic dialogue, fully fleshed characters and plenty of twists." A contributor in *Publishers Weekly* applauded the novel's taut ending, noting that it "caps off a journey well worth taking."

Beitia enjoys writing for a young-adult audience because adolescents have reached "an interesting and hopeful and highly emotional period of life," as she told Amy Atkins for the *Boise Weekly* online. "The whole world is in front of them," she added; "they're right on the cusp of being good, bad and indifferent. I found that really compelling."

Biographical and Critical Sources

PERIODICALS

Booklist, November 15, 2010, Connie Fletcher, review of *The Last Good Place of Lily Odilon,* p. 43.

Kirkus Reviews, September 15, 2010, review of *The Last Good Place of Lily Odilon.*

Publishers Weekly, October 11, 2010, review of *The Last Good Place of Lily Odilon,* p. 46.

School Library Journal, February, 2011, Colleen S. Banick, review of *The Last Good Place of Lily Odilon,* p. 101.

Voice of Youth Advocates, December, 2010, C.J. Bott, review of *The Last Good Place of Lily Odilon,* p. 444.

ONLINE

Boise Weekly Online, http://www.boiseweekly.com/ (October 6, 2010), Amy Atkins, interview with Beitia and review of *The Last Good Place of Lily Odilon.*

Cynsations Web log, http://cynthialeitichsmith.blogspot. com/ (October 11, 2010), Cynthia Leitich Smith, interview with Beitia.

Sara Beitia Home Page, http://www.sarabeitia.com (March 1, 2012).

Sara Beitia Web log, http://owlishness.blogspot.com (March 1, 2012).

* * *

BLACKABY, Susan 1953-

Personal

Born 1953, in CA; married; children: one daughter. *Education:* University of California, Santa Cruz, B.A. (Western civilization), 1975.

Addresses

Home—Portland, OR.

Career

Educational author. Addison-Wesley Publishing Co., Menlo Park, CA, former editor.

Awards, Honors

New York Public Library Top 100 Book selection, 2010, for *Nest, Nook, and Cranny.*

Writings

JUVENILE NONFICTION

A Bird for You: Caring for Your Bird, illustrated by Charlene DeLage, Picture Window Books (Minneapolis, MN), 2003.

A Cat for You: Caring for Your Cat, illustrated by Charlene DeLage, Picture Window Books (Minneapolis, MN), 2003.

A Dog for You: Caring for Your Dog, illustrated by Charlene DeLage, Picture Window Books (Minneapolis, MN), 2003.

A Guinea Pig for You: Caring for Your Guinea Pig, illustrated by Charlene DeLage, Picture Window Books (Minneapolis, MN), 2003.

A Rabbit for You: Caring for Your Rabbit, illustrated by Charlene DeLage, Picture Window Books (Minneapolis, MN), 2003.

Buds and Blossoms: A Book about Flowers, illustrated by Charlene DeLage, Picture Window Books (Minneapolis, MN), 2003.

Catching Sunlight: A Book about Leaves, illustrated by Charlene DeLage, Picture Window Books (Minneapolis, MN), 2003.

Fish for You: Caring for Your Fish, illustrated by Charlene DeLage, Picture Window Books (Minneapolis, MN), 2003.

Green and Growing: A Book about Plants, illustrated by Charlene DeLage, Picture Window Books (Minneapolis, MN), 2003.

Plant Packages: A Book about Seeds, illustrated by Charlene DeLage, Picture Window Books (Minneapolis, MN), 2003.

Plant Plumbing: A Book about Roots and Stems, illustrated by Charlene DeLage, Picture Window Books (Minneapolis, MN), 2003.

The World's Largest Plants: A Book about Trees, illustrated by Charlene DeLage, Picture Window Books (Minneapolis, MN), 2003.

Drop, Drip, an Underwater Trip, School Specialty Pub. (Columbus, OH), 2007.

It Stinks to Be Extinct!, School Specialty Pub. (Columbus, OH), 2007.

Salty, Sandy, Soggy Homes, School Specialty Pub. (Columbus, OH), 2007.

Sea Cows Don't Moo!, School Specialty Pub. (Columbus, OH), 2007.

Splishy, Splashy Mammals, School Specialty Pub. (Columbus, OH), 2007.

Cleopatra: Egypt's Last and Greatest Queen, Sterling (New York, NY), 2009.

Water Wise, illustrated by Susan DeSantis, Picture Window Books (Minneapolis, MN), 2009.

Contributor to periodicals, including *Explorer.*

FICTION FOR YOUNG CHILDREN

Rembrandt's Hat, illustrated by Mary Newell DePalma, Houghton Mifflin Company (Boston, MA), 2002.

Classroom Cookout, illustrated by Amy Bailey Muehlenhardt, Picture Window Books (Minneapolis, MN), 2004.

A Fire Drill with Mr. Dill, illustrated by Amy Bailey Muehlenhardt, Picture Window Books (Minneapolis, MN), 2005.

A Place for Mike, illustrated by Mernie Gallagher-Cole, Picture Window Books (Minneapolis, MN), 2005.

A Pup Shows Up, illustrated by Amy Bailey Muehlenhardt, Picture Window Books (Minneapolis, MN), 2005.

A Year of Fun, illustrated by Natalie Magnuson, Picture Window Books (Minneapolis, MN), 2005.

Ann Plants a Garden, illustrated by Roberta Collier-Morales, Picture Window Books (Minneapolis, MN), 2005.

Bess and Tess, illustrated by Ronnie Rooney, Picture Window Books (Minneapolis, MN), 2005.

Dan Gets Set, illustrated by Ryan Haugen, Picture Window Books (Minneapolis, MN), 2005.

Fishing Trip, illustrated by Ryan Haugen, Picture Window Books (Minneapolis, MN), 2005.

Hatching Chicks, illustrated by Amy Bailey Muehlenhardt, Picture Window Books (Minneapolis, MN), 2005.

Jen Plays, illustrated by Mernie Gallagher-Cole, Picture Window Books (Minneapolis, MN), 2005.

Mary's Art, illustrated by Ryan Haugen, Picture Window Books (Minneapolis, MN), 2005.

Meg Takes a Walk, illustrated by Sharon Holme, Picture Window Books (Minneapolis, MN), 2005.

Moving Day, illustrated by Ryan Haugen, Picture Window Books (Minneapolis, MN), 2005.

Pat Picks Up, illustrated by Ryan Haugen, Picture Window Books (Minneapolis, MN), 2005.

Sunny Bumps the Drum, illustrated by Amy Bailey Muehlenhardt, Picture Window Books (Minneapolis, MN), 2005.

The Best Soccer Player, illustrated by Ryan Haugen, Picture Window Books (Minneapolis, MN), 2005.

The Word of the Day, illustrated by Amy Bailey Muehlenhardt, Picture Window Books (Minneapolis, MN), 2005.

Wes Gets a Pet, illustrated by Mernie Gallagher-Cole, Picture Window Books (Minneapolis, MN), 2005.

Winter Fun for Kat, illustrated by Roberta Collier-Morales, Picture Window Books (Minneapolis, MN), 2005.

A Trip to the Zoo, illustrated by Amy Bailey Muehlenhardt, Picture Window Books (Minneapolis, MN), 2006.

Coco on the Go, illustrated by Amy Bailey Muehlenhardt, Picture Window Books (Minneapolis, MN), 2006.

Riley Flies a Kite, illustrated by Matthew Skeens, Picture Window Books (Minneapolis, MN), 2006.

Shopping for Lunch, illustrated by James Demski, Jr, Picture Window Books (Minneapolis, MN), 2006.

Syd's Room, illustrated by Frances Moore, Picture Window Books (Minneapolis, MN), 2006.

The Missing Tooth, illustrated by Ryan Haugen, Picture Window Books (Minneapolis, MN), 2006.

Allie's Bike, illustrated by Shawna J.C. Tenney, Picture Window Books (Minneapolis, MN), 2007.

Greg Gets a Hint, illustrated by Zachary Trover, Picture Window Books (Minneapolis, MN), 2007.

Jake Skates, illustrated by Troy Olin, Picture Window Books (Minneapolis, MN), 2007.

New to Drew, illustrated by Hye Won Yi, Picture Window Books (Minneapolis, MN), 2007.

One up for Brad, illustrated by Len Epstein, Picture Window Books (Minneapolis, MN), 2007.

Tricky Twins, illustrated by Len Epstein, Picture Window Books (Minneapolis, MN), 2007.

Who's in Your Class?, School Specialty Pub. (Columbus, OH), 2007.

Groceries for Grandpa, illustrated by Jisun Lee, Picture Window Books (Minneapolis, MN), 2008.

Lost on Owl Lane, illustrated by Amy Bailey Muehlenhardt, Picture Window Books (Minneapolis, MN), 2008.

The Blue Stone Plot, illustrated by Len Epstein, Picture Window Books (Minneapolis, MN), 2008.

The Carnival Committee, illustrated by Ryan Haugen, Picture Window Books (Minneapolis, MN), 2008.

The Secret Warning, illustrated by Len Epstein, Picture Window Books (Minneapolis, MN), 2008.

The Shepherd and the Racehorse, illustrated by Len Epstein, Picture Window Books (Minneapolis, MN), 2008.

The Torchbearer, illustrated by Len Epstein, Picture Window Books (Minneapolis, MN), 2008.

Todd's Fire Drill, illustrated by Justin Greathouse, Picture Window Books (Minneapolis, MN), 2008.

Jenna and the Three R's, illustrated by Sharon Lane Holm, Picture Window Books (Minneapolis, MN), 2009.

Brownie Groundhog and the February Fox, illustrated by Carmen Segovia, Sterling (New York, NY), 2010.

Nest, Nook, and Cranny: Poems, illustrated by Jamie Hogan, Charlesbridge (Watertown, MA), 2010.

Author's work has been translated into Spanish.

"READ-IT! READERS FAIRY TALES" SERIES

(Adapter) Hans Christian Andersen, *The Emperor's New Clothes,* illustrated by Charlene DeLage, Picture Window Books (Minneapolis, MN), 2004.

(Adapter) Hans Christian Andersen, *The Little Mermaid,* illustrated by Charlene DeLage, Picture Window Books (Minneapolis, MN), 2004.

(Adapter) Hans Christian Andersen, *The Princess and the Pea,* illustrated by Charlene DeLage, Picture Window Books (Minneapolis, MN), 2004.

(Adapter) Hans Christian Andersen, *The Steadfast Tin Soldier,* illustrated by Charlene DeLage, Picture Window Books (Minneapolis, MN), 2004.

(Adapter) Hans Christian Andersen, *The Ugly Duckling: A Retelling,* illustrated by Charlene DeLage, Picture Window Books (Minneapolis, MN), 2004.

(Adapter) Hans Christian Andersen, *Thumbelina,* illustrated by Charlene DeLage, Picture Window Books (Minneapolis, MN), 2004.

Sidelights

In her many books for young children, Susan Blackaby encourages budding readers while also expanding their knowledge of the world around them. A former editor for an educational publisher, the Oregon-based Blackaby

Susan Blackaby's nature-themed picture book **Nest, Nook, and Cranny** *features Jamie Hogan's detailed art.* (Illustration copyright © 2010 by Jamie Hogan. Reproduced by permission of Charlesbridge Publishing, Inc., Watertown, MA. All rights reserved.)

published her first trade picture book, *Rembrandt's Hat,* in 2002. In the years since, she has contributed to the easy-reading "Picture Window" series with *Catching Sunlight: A Book about Leaves* and *Plant Packages: A Book about Seeds,* as well as producing fairy-tale retellings, entertaining beginning readers, and standalone picture books that include *Brownie Groundhog and the February Fox* and *Nest, Nook, and Cranny: Poems.*

In *Rembrandt's Hat* Blackaby tells the story of a blue-eyed stuffed bear named Rembrandt and the fretful day when the wind swept away his favorite hat. Knowing that he must now replace the beloved head covering, Rembrandt is first aided by three animal friends—a bluebird, a rabbit, and a cat—each of whom volunteers unsuccessfully to function as a hat. The determined bear then goes shopping and tries on a wide variety of hats, caps, chapeaus, berets, and bonnets before finding a suitable successor. In *Publishers Weekly,* a contributor praised *Rembrandt's Hat* as a "satisfyingly spontaneous and quirky tale" that also serves as "a finely tuned collaboration between" author and illustrator. Praising the "distinctive" mixed-media artwork created for the story by Mary Newell DePalma, with its "cool colors and . . . French flavor," a *Kirkus Reviews* writer concluded that "Blackaby hits a high note" in her picture-book debut. In a review for *School Library Journal,* Robin L. Gibson cited the author's ability to craft a "clearly written" text, adding that her story's "short sentences" create a "good pacing for reading aloud."

Illustrated by Jamie Hoga, *Nest, Nook, and Cranny* features a selection of poems representing a range of rhyme forms. These verses introduce young children to the varied animals, birds, and bugs that inhabit five main ecosystems: woodlands, grasslands, deserts, wetlands, and the shoreline. Blackaby's poems also offer factual information that highlights the varied things animals eat as well as how they make their homes, raise their young, and evade predators. Illustrating these poems are charcoal sketches by Jamie Hogan that also give a naturalist-like feel to the book. Serving as a beginners guide to both poetic forms and habitats, *Nest, Nook, and Cranny* was recommended by *Booklist* contributor Hazel Rochman as a "lively" work that could be used in both "science and creative-writing classes," and Susan Scheps recommended it in *School Library Journal* as "a special book that . . . nature lovers will treasure." Discussing Blackaby's approach on the *School Library Journal* Web log, Elizabeth Bird concluded that, "with her words as an aid, kids won't just learn the facts about a place. They'll get the feel, the sounds, and the veritable smells as well. Here's to poetry with a purpose."

A childhood friend—a biology professor who also studies hibernating mammals—inspired Blackaby to write *Brownie Groundhog and the February Fox,* a picture book that focuses on Groundhog Day. In an unusual twist on picture-book writing, Blackaby created her story to fit a series of illustrations already created by artist Carmen Segovia. In the tale, Brownie the groundhog wakes up from her long sleep right on schedule, but a peek outside her cozy burrow on February 2nd reveals that winter is not yet over. A fox with an empty tummy spots Brownie and begins to plan a meal of groundhog stew, but the clever woodchuck ultimately traps the fox and then befriends him by sharing a cup of cocoa and some cinnamon toast. Praising *Brownie Groundhog and the February Fox* in *Kirkus Reviews,* a contributor commended Blackaby's ability to "economically develop . . . likeable characters and deliver . . . plenty of chuckles and wordplay" in her story. Citing Segovia's ink-and-wash images, which "evoke the two-color classics of the mid-20th century," a *Publishers Weekly* writer noted that the "comforting pace" of Blackaby's Groundhog Day story makes it "a promising bedtime selection," while *School Library Journal* critic C.J. Connor deemed *Brownie Groundhog and the February Fox* both "endearing" and "delightful."

Biographical and Critical Sources

PERIODICALS

Booklist, April 15, 2002, Kay Weisman, review of *Rembrandt's Hat,* p. 1405; February, 2010, Hazel Rochman, review of *Nest, Nook, and Cranny: Poems,* p. 40.
Kirkus Reviews, February 1, 2002, review of *Rembrandt's Hat,* p. 176; November 15, 2010, review of *Brownie Groundhog and the February Fox.*
Publishers Weekly, January 14, 2002, review of *Rembrandt's Hat,* p. 59; November 8, 2010, review of *Brownie Groundhog and the February Fox,* p. 57.
School Library Journal, July, 2002, Robin L. Gibson, review of *Rembrandt's Hat,* p. 83; January, 2004, Anne Knickerbocker, review of *The Little Mermaid,* p. 88; May, 2004, Karen Land, review of *The Ugly Duckling: A Retelling,* p. 128; March, 2005, Phyllis M. Simon, review of *Classroom Cookout,* p. 166; September, 2005, Blair Christolon, review of *Bess and Tess,* p. 166; August, 2009, Lana Miles, review of *Cleopatra: Egypt's Last and Greatest Queen,* p. 118; March, 2010, Susan Scheps, review of *Nest, Nook, and Cranny,* p. 173; February, 2011, C.J. Connor, review of *Brownie Groundhog and the February Fox,* p. 75.

ONLINE

Today@Colorado State Online, http://www.today.colostate.edu/ (February 24, 2011), Emily Wimsen, "Author Dedicates Book to Biology Professor, Childhood Chum."
School Library Journal Web log, http://blog.schoollibraryjournal.com/afuse8production/ (December 4, 2010), Elizabeth Bird, review of *Nest, Nook, and Cranny.**

* * *

BODEEN, S.A.
See STUVE-BODEEN, Stephanie

BONDOUX, Anne-Laure 1971-

Personal

Born April 23, 1971, in Bois-Colombes, France; children: two. *Education:* Attended University of Paris—Nanterre.

Addresses

Home—Paris, France.

Career

Writer and editor. Bayard Presse, Paris, France, magazine editor, 1996-2000; freelance writer, 2000—. Has also worked in the theater.

Awards, Honors

Fondation de France award; Prix Sorcières and Prix littéraire des collégiens du Bessin-Bocage, both 2004, both for *Les larmes de l'assassin*; Prix Coup de Coeur Jeunesse, 2006, for *Le destin de Linus Hoppe*; Prix Livrentête, 2006, for *Pépites;* Mildred L. Batchelder Award, 2007, for *The Killer's Tears,* translated by Y. Maudet; Mildred L. Batchelder Award, 2011, for *A Time of Miracles,* translated by Maudet.

Writings

YOUNG-ADULT NOVELS

Le destin de Linus Hoppe, Bayard (Paris, France), 2001, translated by Catherine Temerson as *The Destiny of Linus Hoppe,* Delacorte (New York, NY), 2005.
La seconde vie de Linus Hoppe, Bayard (Paris, France), 2002, translated by Catherine Temerson as *The Second Life of Linus Hoppe,* Delacorte (New York, NY), 2005.
Les larmes de l'assassin, Bayard (Paris, France), 2003, translated by Y. Maudet as *The Killer's Tears,* Delacorte (New York, NY), 2006.
La princetta et le capitaine, Hachette (Paris, France), 2004, translated by Anthea Bell as *The Princetta,* Bloomsbury (New York, NY), 2006, published as *The Princess and the Captain,* Bloomsbury (London, England), 2006.
La vie comme elle vient, École des Loisirs (Paris, France), 2004, translated by Anthea Bell as *Life as It Comes,* Delacorte (New York, NY), 2007.
La Tribu, Bayard (Paris, France), 2004, translated by Y. Maudet as *Vasco, Leader of the Tribe,* Delacorte Press (New York, NY), 2007.
Pépites, Bayard (Paris, France), 2005.
Temps des miracles, Bayard (Paris, France), 2009, translated by Y. Maudet as *A Time of Miracles,* Delacorte Press (New York, NY), 2010.
Coutre moitré de moi-même, Bayard (Paris, France), 2011.

Author's work has been translated into several languages, including German and Spanish.

"PEOPLE OF THE RATS" NOVEL TRILOGY

La grande menace (title means "The Great Threat"), Bayard (Paris, France), 2001.
Au coeur de la tourmente (title means "In the Heart of the Storm"), Bayard (Paris, France), 2002.
La tribu des forêts (title means "The Tribe of the Forests"), Bayard (Paris, France), 2002.

CHAPTER BOOKS

Noémie superstar!, Syros (Paris, France), 1999.
Qu'est-ce que tu vas faire de toi?, Nathan (Paris, France), 2000.
Voilà comment je suis devenu un héros!, Livre de Poche (Paris, France), 2002.
Le prince Nino à la maternouille, illustrated by Roser Capdevila, Bayard (Paris, France), 2003.
Les bottes de grand-chemin, illustrated by Émile Bravo, Bayard (Paris, France), 2004.
Mon amie d'Amérique, illustrated by Nicolas Wintz, Bayard (Paris, France), 2005.
Le croquemitaine, illustrated by Serge Bloch, Bayard (Paris, France), 2005.

Cover of Anne-Laure Bondoux's young-adult novel The Destiny of Linus Hoppe, *featuring cover art by John Ritter.* (Jacket cover copyright © 2006 by Yearling. Reproduced by permission of Yearling, an imprint of Random House Children's Books, a division of Random House, Inc.)

Lancelot du lac, illustrated by Joëlle Jolivet, Tourbillon (France), 2011.

Sidelights

Based in France, Anne-Laure Bondoux is the author of several highly regarded novels for young adults, among them *The Destiny of Linus Hoppe, Life as It Comes,* and *A Time of Miracles.* Raised near Paris, Bondoux attended the University of Paris—Nanterre, where she established a series of writing workshops for students with special needs, earning a national award from the Fondation de France for her efforts. She spent some time in the theater before joining the staff of Paris-based publisher Bayard Presse in 1996. At Bayard she edited *J'aime Lire,* an educational magazine for children, and helped launch another periodical for children titled *Maximum.* Bondoux published her first book, *Noémie superstar!,* in 1999, and a year later she became a full-time writer.

In her futuristic science-fiction novel, *The Destiny of Linus Hoppe*—published in its original French as *Le destin de Linus Hoppe*—Bondoux follows the exploits of a teenager who lives a comfortable life with his family in Realm One, a safe, clean section of Paris that is reserved for the city's elite. Upon reaching age fourteen, all Parisians are tested by the Great Processor to determine how they will spend the remainder of their lives; those who achieve the highest scores are assigned to Realm One while others must work in the factories of squalid Realm Two or face the terrifying prospect of "reeducation" in Realm Three. Through the Internet, Linus makes contact with Yosh, a boy from Realm Two who, like Linus, is approaching his fourteenth birthday. With the help of some friends, the boys "hatch a plan to scramble their test results and choose their own destinies, an unheard-of idea," observed a critic in *Kirkus Reviews.* Praising *The Destiny of Linus Hoppe,* Holly Koelling wrote in *Booklist* that "Bondoux's action-oriented story is an intriguing attempt at [presenting] a utopian/dystopian future from the teen perspective."

Bondoux continues Linus's story in *The Second Life of Linus Hoppe* (originally published as *La seconde vie de Linus Hoppe*). Having successfully undermined the system, the teen now faces a life of exhausting manual labor in Realm Two. Then he meets Mr. Zanz, a member of the underground resistance movement that opposes the rigid caste system. Using identification cards stolen from dead citizens, Linus is able to move between realms and ultimately helps to expose a government plot involving corruption at the testing bureau. Although some critics maintained that Bondoux's sequel does not live up to the promise of *The Destiny of Linus Hoppe,* *Booklist* contributor Jennifer Hubert stated that the author's "premise . . . is intriguing enough to please fans of the first book."

Bondoux received the prestigious Prix Sorcières for *Les larmes de l'assassin,* a novel translated into English as *The Killer's Tears.* Described as "a haunting exploration of guilt and innocence, and of the redemptive power of a loving relationship," by *Kliatt* reviewer Claire Rosser, the work opens as Angel Allegria, a drifter with a sinister past, arrives at the home of young Paolo Poloverdo, who lives with his parents on a small, desolate farm on the southern tip of Chile. In need of a place to hide, Angel brutally murders Paolo's parents and settles into his victims' home, sparing their son's life. When another wanderer, Luis Secunda, also happens upon the farm, he is invited to stay and over time he teaches Paolo to read and write. His presence also affects Angel, who has grown so attached to Paolo that he acts the role of the boy's father. Eventually the trio heads for town to purchase livestock; once they arrive, Angel is identified as a wanted criminal and imprisoned, triggering a series of disastrous events.

"In commanding, starkly poetic language that lends an almost magical beauty to the harsh landscape and events," *Horn Book* contributor Christine M. Hepperman observed, Bondoux demonstrates how the "two outcasts become emotionally dependent on each other" in *The Killer's Tears.* Noting the focus on "Angel's awakening conscience," B. Allison Gray added in her *School Library Journal* review that, "through his relationship with the boy, he begins to see the importance

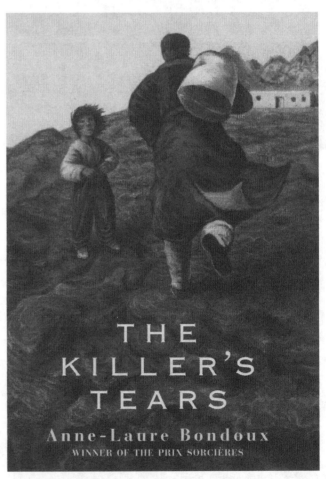

Cover of Bondoux's prize-winning novel The Killer's Tears, ***featuring artwork by Fabian Negrin.*** (Jacket cover copyright © 2010 by Delacorte Press. Reproduced by permission of Delacorte Press, an imprint of Random House Children's Books, a division of Random House, Inc.)

of life and love." "Bondoux's prose is as parched as the land, her symbols and images knife-sharp: the spirits of dead children, a broken pitcher, a handful of dirt," noted a contributor in *Kirkus Reviews* in praise of the novel, while a *Publishers Weekly* reviewer maintained that the author's "affecting fable-like style and absorbing narrative sustain this unusual story to its redemptive conclusion." Gillian Engberg, writing in *Booklist,* praised Bondoux's willingness to explore important themes, remarking of *The Killer's Tears* that, "with unsparing, emotional truth, she describes a world in which the morality of the heart doesn't always match the morality of civilized society."

Bondoux introduces readers to a world of make believe in *La princetta et le capitaine,* a story translated into English as *The Princetta.* In the novel, Malva, the princess of Galnicia, bristles at the thought of her upcoming marriage to the prince of Andemark. On the eve of her wedding Malva escapes from the palace and boards a ship that will carry her to freedom. A fierce storm shipwrecks the princess, however, and brave Orpheus McBott sets out to rescue her. "Things get swirlingly complicated, with sea beasts, mysterious lands and new allies," noted a *Kirkus Reviews* critic in appraising *The Princetta.* Citing the book's "rich descriptive language," Lynn Rutan commented in *Booklist* that Bondoux's "swashbuckling fantasy . . . is chock-full of action."

Another adventure tale, *Vasco, Leader of the Tribe* (first published as *La Tribu*) concerns the reluctant leader of a band of rodents that has been targeted for extermination. After his rat clan is nearly decimated by a powerful new toxin designed by humans, young Vasco gathers the survivors and leads them from their threatened home. Seeking a safe haven, Vasco and his new tribe board a freighter, enduring a perilous ocean crossing before the ship lands and they venture into a lush rain forest. There the group encounters even greater dangers, including battles with rival tribes of rats, all which test the sensitive and intelligent Vasco's burgeoning leadership skills. "Animal lovers who crave edge-of-your-seat action and the triumph of reason over violence will love this page-turner," Nicki Clausen-Grace predicted in *School Library Journal.* John Peters, writing in *Booklist,* commended Bondoux's anthropomorphic cast of characters in *Vasco, Leader of the Tribe,* adding that she "endows her furry fugitives with a smooth blend of rodentine and human characteristics."

Bondoux's *La vie comme elle vient,* published in the United States as *Life as It Comes,* focuses on the often-difficult relationship between two dissimilar Parisian sisters. After their parents are killed in an automobile accident, twenty-year-old Patty becomes the legal guardian of her serious and studious fifteen-year-old sister, Mado. When Patty confesses that she is several months pregnant, Mado—the more responsible of the pair—fears that the authorities may now place her in foster care. She convinces Patty to travel with her to their family home in southern France, where her sister gives birth to a baby boy. When Patty fails to bond with

her child, however, she returns to Paris, leaving Mado to care for the infant. "How all this evolves makes for a riveting story of grief, sibling conflict, and acknowledgement of personal responsibility and change," Claire Rosser observed in her *Kliatt* review of *Life as It Comes.* Joyce Adams Burner applauded Bondoux's fully realized portrait of the book's narrator, writing in *School Library Journal* that "Mado is a believable if overburdened teen, juggling the anxieties of schoolwork with domestic responsibilities and an unpredictable guardian."

In *A Time of Miracles* (originally published as *Temps des miracles*), Bondoux "tells another unusual, wrenching story of a vulnerable child," in the words of *Booklist* contributor Gillian Engberg. After the collapse of the U.S.S.R., seven-year-old Koumail flees the Russian Republic of Georgia with his guardian, Gloria, who has cared for him since a train wreck killed his mother. During their journey to France, where Koumail was born, the pair endures all manner of hardship and is forced to seek shelter in refugee camps and gypsy settlements. After years of traveling through the war-torn region, Gloria and Koumail reach France, only to

Cover of **A Time of Miracles,** *Bondoux's novel about an orphan growing up in the U.S.S.R. at a time of political unrest.* (Jacket cover copyright © 2010 by Delacorte Press. Reproduced by permission of Delacorte Press, an imprint of Random House Children's Books, a division of Random House, Inc.)

be separated, suddenly and agonizingly. *A Time of Miracles* "is written in beautiful, quiet prose and offers a touch of hope, along with tragedy," Sharon Senser McKellar reported in *School Library Journal,* and Christine M. Heppermann noted in *Horn Book* that Bondoux takes readers on a "journey in prose that is both exquisitely poetic and unsparing."

Biographical and Critical Sources

PERIODICALS

Booklist, April 15, 2005, Holly Koelling, review of *The Destiny of Linus Hoppe,* p. 1463; November 1, 2005, Jennifer Hubert, review of *The Second Life of Linus Hoppe,* p. 37; January 1, 2006, Gillian Engberg, review of *The Killer's Tears,* p. 92; September 1, 2006, Lynn Rutan, review of *The Princetta,* p. 109; March 1, 2007, Frances Bradburn, review of *Life as It Comes,* p. 73; December 1, 2007, John Peters, review of *Leader of the Tribe,* p. 44; December 15, 2010, Gillian Engberg, review of *A Time of Miracles,* p. 50.
Bookseller, February 17, 2006, review of *The Princetta,* p. 36.
Horn Book, March-April, 2006, Christine M. Hepperman, review of *The Killer's Tears,* p. 179; January-February, 2011, Christine M. Hepperman, review of *A Time of Miracles,* p. 89.
Kirkus Reviews, April 15, 2005, review of *The Destiny of Linus Hoppe,* p. 469; October 1, 2005, review of *The Second Life of Linus Hoppe,* p. 1076; February 1, 2006, review of *The Killer's Tears,* p. 128; July 1, 2006, review of *The Princetta,* p. 674; January 15, 2007, review of *Life as It Comes,* p. 70; October 1, 2007, review of *Leader of the Tribe*; October 15, 2010, review of *A Time of Miracles.*
Kliatt, January, 2006, Claire Rosser, review of *The Killer's Tears,* p. 4; January, 2007, Claire Rosser, review of *Life as It Comes,* p. 8.
Publishers Weekly, January 16, 2006, review of *The Killer's Tears,* p. 65; January 29, 2007, review of *Life as It Comes,* p. 73; November 8, 2010, review of *A Time of Miracles,* p. 63.
School Library Journal, July, 2005, Jessi Platt, review of *The Destiny of Linus Hoppe,* p. 96; January, 2006, Kelly Vikstrom, review of *The Second Life of Linus Hoppe,* p. 128; February, 2006, B. Allison Gray, review of *The Killer's Tears,* p. 128; March, 2007, Joyce Adams Burner, review of *Life as It Comes,* p. 206; March, 2008, Nicki Clausen-Grace, review of *Leader of the Tribe,* p. 194; January, 2011, Sharon Senser McKellar, review of *A Time of Miracles,* p. 100.

PERIODICALS

Anne-Laure Bondoux Home Page, http://www.bondoux.net (March 1, 2012).*

*   *   *

BOSWORTH, Lauren
See BOSWORTH, Lo

BOSWORTH, Lo 1986-
(Lauren Bosworth)

Personal
Born September 29, 1986, in CA. *Education:* Attended University of California, Santa Barbara, 2004-05; University of California, Los Angeles, B.A. (art history), 2008.

Addresses
Home—Los Angeles, CA.

Career
Television celebrity and producer and author. Appeared on television reality series, including *Laguna Beach: The Real Orange County,* 2004-05; *The Hills,* 2008-10; Octagon Entertainment, Los Angeles, CA, television producer.

Member
Kappa Kappa Gamma.

Cover of Lo Bosworth's entertaining **The Lo-down,** *a chronicle of her experiences on a television reality show.* (Jacket cover art © 2011 by Eleonora Ivanova/iStockphoto.com.)

Writings

The Lo-Down, Simon & Schuster (New York, NY), 2011.

Sidelights

Lo Bosworth became a celebrity through her performance on television's *Laguna Beach: The Real Orange County,* a mock-reality series broadcast on MTV that followed a group of affluent Southern California teens during their final year of high school and into the summer following graduation. After taking a few years off to complete her college education, Bosworth returned to television, this time as a costar of the reality program *The Hills,* which focuses on the fashion career of Lauren Conrad, a friend of Bosworth's as well as a fellow *Laguna Beach* alum. Her involvement in these television productions inspired Bosworth to move into the television industry, where she now works for Octagon Entertainment. As a celebrity, her advice on dating and other relationship advice has also been sought, and Bosworth comes to the aid of the modern teen in her self-help book *The Lo-Down.*

Divided into five parts, *The Lo-Down* ranges in focus from dating mishaps and the romantic personality types to avoid to self-esteem boosters and techniques for dating on a budget. In prose that a *Publishers Weekly* contributor characterized as "conversational and accessible," Bosworth weaves stories from her own and her friends' dating experience as well as self-graded quizzes and exercises designed to help readers increase their dating I.Q. Noting that the publication of *The Lo-Down* was timed to coordinate with her advice Web site of the same name, Elaine Gass Hirsch added in *Voice of Youth Advocates* that the author's sincerity shines through in her "worthwhile" and upbeat message and her "end goal of helping" teens to "build . . . strong relationships." "Bosworth . . . is building a brand for herself: the sensible-yet-sexy older cousin," quipped a *Kirkus Reviews* writer, the critic adding that the advice dispensed in the celebrity's book is sensible, responsible, and dispensed in "a breezy, knowing tone." Comparing Bosworth to her celebrity co-stars, Elaine Baran Black asserted in her *School Library Journal* review of *The Lo-Down:* "She's the kind of friend who listens to the dating woes of others and honestly wants to help."

Biographical and Critical Sources

PERIODICALS

Kirkus Reviews, December 1, 2010, review of *The Lo-Down.*
Publishers Weekly, November 22, 2010, review of *The Lo-Down,* p. 59.
School Library Journal, February, 2011, Elaine Baran Black, review of *The Lo-Down,* p. 124.
Voice of Youth Advocates, February, 2011, Elaine Gass Hirsch, review of *The Lo-Down,* p. 581.

ONLINE

Lo Bosworth Home Page, http://thelodown.com (March 1, 2012).*

* * *

BROWN, Judy
See CHAYIL, Eishes

* * *

BRYANT, Laura J.

Personal

Born in FL. *Education:* Maryland Institute College of Art, degree.

Addresses

Home and office—Asheville, NC. *E-mail*—info@ LauraBryant.com.

Career

Illustrator and designer. Worked previously in the display industry; children's book illustrator, 1997—.

Awards, Honors

International Reading Association/Children's Book Council Children's Choice Award, 2005, for *Smudge Bunny* by Bernie Segal; National Parenting Publications Honors Award, 2005, for *If You Were My Baby* by Fran Hodgkins, and 2011, for *Jo MacDonald Saw a Pond* by Mary Quattlebaum; Bank Street College of Education Best Children's Book of the Year designation, 2002, for *Where Fish Go in Winter, and Other Great Mysteries* by Amy Goldman Koss, 2003, for *A Fairy in a Dairy* by Lucy Nolan, and 2011, for *If You Were My Baby* by Hodgkins; Top Ten Picks for Early Readers, American Library Association, 2002, for *Where Fish Go in Winter, and Other Great Mysteries* by Koss.

Illustrator

Dan Piparo, *Listen for the Rattle,* McGraw-Hill (New York, NY), 1999.
Caroline Walsh, *What's the Trick?,* Perfection Learning (Logan, IA), 1999.
Nancy Tolson, reteller, *Tales of Africa: Retold Timeless Classics,* Perfection Learning (Logan, IA), 1999.
Lisa Tawn Bergren, *God Gave Us You,* WaterBrook Press (Colorado Springs, CO), 2000.
Eleanor Hudson, *The Special Valentine,* Little Simon (New York, NY), 2000.
Eleanor Hudson, *A Valentine Bouquet,* Little Simon (New York, NY), 2000.
Akimi Gibson, *Lewis Latimer: An Inventive Mind,* McGraw-Hill (New York, NY), 2000.

Laura J. Bryant (Reproduced by permission.)

David Haynes, *Gumma Wars,* Perfection Learning (Logan, IA), 2001.

Teresa Turner, *Every Flower Is Beautiful,* Steck-Vaughn (Orlando, FL), 2001.

Lisa Tawn Bergren, *God Gave Us Two,* WaterBrook Press (Colorado Springs, CO), 2001.

David Haynes, *Business as Usual,* Perfection Learning (Logan, IA), 2001.

Paula J. Reece, reteller, *Tales of William Shakespeare: The Comedies,* Perfection Learning (Logan, IA), 2001.

Susan Nastasic, *The Galaxy Diner,* Perfection Learning (Logan, IA), 2001.

Amy Goldman Koss, *Where Fish Go in Winter, and Other Great Mysteries,* Dial (New York, NY), 2002.

Melissa Blackwell Burke, *One Farm,* Steck-Vaughn (Orlando, FL), 2002.

Candice F. Ransom, *Goldilocks and the Three Bears,* McGraw-Hill (New York, NY), 2002.

David Haynes, *Who's Responsible?,* Perfection Learning (Logan, IA), 2002.

Steve Metzger, *Five Little Penguins Slipping on the Ice,* Scholastic (New York, NY), 2003.

David Haynes, *The Kevin Show,* Perfection Learning (Logan, IA), 2003.

Lucy Nolan, *A Fairy in a Dairy,* Marshall Cavendish (New York, NY), 2003.

Patricia J. Murphy, *I Need You,* Children's Press (New York, NY), 2003.

Mary Ann McCabe Riehle, *M Is for Mountain State: A West Virginia Alphabet,* Sleeping Bear Press (Chelsea, MI), 2004.

Bernie Siegel, *Smudge Bunny,* Starseed Press (Tiburon, CA), 2004.

Steve Metzger, *Five Little Bats Flying in the Night,* Scholastic (New York, NY), 2004.

Steve Metzger, *Five Little Sharks Swimming in the Sea,* Scholastic (New York, NY), 2004.

Joanne Barkan, *Goodnight, Summer Lights,* Reader's Digest (New York, NY), 2005.

Fran Hodgkins, *If You Were My Baby: A Wildlife Lullaby,* Dawn Publications (Nevada City, CA), 2005.

Sean Callahan, *The Bear Hug,* Albert Whitman (Morton Grove, IL), 2006.

Steve Metzger, *Five Little Bunnies Hopping on a Hill,* Scholastic (New York, NY), 2006.

Candice F. Ransom, *Tractor Day,* Walker & Company (New York, NY), 2007.

Lisa Tawn Bergren, *How Big Is God?,* HarperCollins (New York, NY), 2008.

Lisa Tawn Bergren, *God Gave Us Heaven,* WaterBrook Press (Colorado Springs, CO), 2008.

Bill Martin, Jr., and Michael Sampson, *Kitty Cat, Kitty Cat, Are You Waking Up?,* Marshall Cavendish (New York, NY), 2008.

Lisa McCourt, *Yummiest Love,* Orchard Books (New York, NY), 2009.

Lisa Tawn Bergren, *God Gave Us Love,* WaterBrook Press (Colorado Springs, CO), 2009.

Lisa Tawn Bergren, *God Found Us You,* HarperCollins (New York, NY), 2009.

Julie Stiegemeyer, *Seven Little Bunnies,* Marshall Cavendish (Tarrytown, NY), 2010.

Jean Monrad Thomas, *How Many Kisses Good Night?,* Random House (New York, NY), 2010.

Ann Tompert, *Little Fox Goes to the End of the World,* Marshall Cavendish (Tarrytown, NY), 2010.

Melita Morales, *Jam and Honey,* Tricycle Press (Berkeley, CA), 2011.

Bill Martin, Jr., and Michael Sampson, *Kitty Cat, Kitty Cat, Are You Going to Sleep?,* Marshall Cavendish (New York, NY), 2011.

Mary Quattlebaum, *Jo MacDonald Saw a Pond,* Dawn Publications (Nevada City, CA), 2011.

Anne Graham Lotz, *Heaven: God's Promise for Me,* Zonderkidz (Grand Rapids, MI), 2011.

Lisa Tawn Bergren, *God Gave Us the World,* WaterBrook Press (Colorado Springs, CO), 2011.

Lisa Tawn Bergren, *God Gave Us So Much,* WaterBrook Press (Colorado Springs, CO), 2011.

Mary Quattlebaum, *Jo MacDonald Had a Garden,* Dawn Publications (Nevada City, CA), 2011.

Adaptations

Five Little Penguins Slipping on the Ice was adapted for audiocassette, read by Steven Blane, Scholastic, 2002. *Five Little Bunnies Hopping on a Hill* was adapted for audiocassette and CD, read by Kirsten Krohn, Scholastic, 2006.

Sidelights

A respected artist, Laura J. Bryant features elements from the natural environment into her watercolor illustrations for children's books, many of which feature animal characters. Among the picture books featuring Bryant's art are *The Bear Hug* by Sean Callaghan, Ann Tompert's *Little Fox Goes to the End of the World,* and *Jam and Honey* by Melita Morales. Stylistically, Bryant's illustrations are often cited for their delicate quality and air of whimsy. As a *Kirkus Reviews* critic commented in appraising her contributions to Fran Hodgkins' *If You Were My Baby: A Wildlife Lullaby,* the story comes to life in images that "are beautifully detailed and yet softly muted at the same time."

In discussing Bryant's illustrations, reviewers often comment on her ability to create humorous, detailed, and engaging images with instant child appeal. For example, a *Publishers Weekly* reviewer wrote that her artwork for Lucy Nolan's *A Fairy in a Dairy* brings to life the story's rural, small-town setting via "detailed, meticulously tinted watercolors" in which "every picture bubbles with a spunky, homespun energy." A *Kirkus Reviews* noted of *Where Fish Go in Winter, and Other Great Mysteries* that the book's illustrations "add to the humorous flair of the poetry, with buggy-eyed fish, cuddly cats, and a mysterious man in the moon." Leslie Barban, in a *School Library Journal* review of the same book, cited the playfulness of Bryant's pictures, commenting that "the funny, spirited illustrations, well executed in watercolors, will make children chuckle."

Bryant's "lighthearted pictures" were cited by a *Publishers Weekly* critic as a highlight of Callahan's *The Bear Hug,* which focuses on the tender relationship be-

Candace Ransom's rural-themed story in **Tractor Day** *comes to life in Bryant's colorful art.* (Illustration copyright © 2007 by Laura J. Bryant. Reproduced by permission of Walker Publishing, an imprint of Bloomsbury Publishing, Inc.)

tween a young cub and its grandfather. *Yummiest Love,* a tale by Lisa McCourt that celebrates parental affection, also features a pair of ursine protagonists. Here, according to *School Library Journal* reviewer Amy Lilien-Harper, "Bryant's cuddly personified bears . . . are appealingly sweet, and are a good match for the text."

A mother's concern for her youngster is at the heart of *Little Fox Goes to the End of the World,* a picture book by Ann Tompert. In the work, a young fox describes an imaginative and somewhat dangerous adventure she plans to take, prompted in part by her mother's gentle questions. According to Blair Christolon in *School Library Journal,* "Bryant's dramatic watercolor artwork frequently fills the spreads." A bedtime tale for young readers, Julie Stiegemeyer's *Seven Little Bunnies* follows a group of energetic rabbits that prefers playing to sleeping. "Bryant's winsome watercolors showcase the busy activities," Linda Ludke remarked in her *School Library Journal* appraisal of the picture book.

In *Tractor Day,* a story by Candice F. Ransom, a family attends to a multitude of chores on their busy farm. According to *School Library Journal* reviewer Carolyn Janssen, Bryant's "watercolor illustrations reflect the lilting rhythm of the narrative." *Jam and Honey,* another nature-themed tale, finds a young girl picking berries from an urban park while a bee dances around the flowers, searching for nectar. Here "Bryant's softly col-

Melita Morales creates the story that Bryant brings to life via lovable characters in **Jam and Honey.** (Illustration copyright © 2011 by Laura J. Bryant. Reproduced by permission of Tricycle Press, an imprint of Random House Children's Books, a division of Random House, Inc.)

ored watercolor-and-pencil illustrations nicely juxtapose the two perspectives," noted a *Kirkus Reviews* writer. "Done from a variety of vantage points," Lilien-Harper similarly remarked, "the artwork draws listeners through the plot" of Morales's tale.

Bryant has enjoyed a successful collaboration with Lisa Tawn Bergren on a number of faith-centered works, beginning with *God Gave Us You*, which has turned into a best-selling series selling over one million copies. Other collaborations include *How Big Is God?* and *God Found Us You*. In the former, a young boy and his mother ponder the existence of a higher power, and *School Library Journal* critic Lisa Egly Lehmuller noted that the story's "subdued watercolor illustrations of rosy-nosed, slightly disheveled characters suit Bergren's quiet musings." *God Found Us You* centers on a conversation between a mother fox and her adopted son. Here "Bryant's appealing images, mostly gentle pastels, are sweet but not saccharine," Abby Nolan stated in *Booklist*.

Among her many illustration projects, Bryant has teamed up with coauthors Bill Martin, Jr., and Michael Sampson on two humorous tales about a spunky young feline. Told in rhyming verse, *Kitty Cat, Kitty Cat, Are You Waking Up?* concerns a mother cat's efforts to get her dawdling kitten off to school. "Bryant's illustrations, rendered in watercolor and colored pencil, are playful, light, and absolutely adorable," Kara Schaff Dean commented in her *School Library Journal* review of the book. In the companion volume, *Kitty Cat, Kitty Cat, Are You Going to Sleep?*, the youngster finds a variety of ways to delay the inevitable bedtime, much to the consternation of her mother. "Bryant depicts Kitty Cat and Mother's nightly rituals with soothing watercolor and colored pencil spreads," a *Publishers Weekly* contributor maintained.

Biographical and Critical Sources

PERIODICALS

Booklist, November 1, 2003, Connie Fletcher, review of *A Fairy in a Dairy,* p. 505; January 1, 2007, Randall Enos, review of *Tractor Day,* p. 116; July 1, 2008, Connie Fletcher, review of *Kitty Cat, Kitty Cat, Are You Waking Up?,* p. 72; May 1, 2009, Abby Nolan, review of *God Found Us You,* p. 85; February 15, 2010, Hazel Rochman, review of *Seven Little Bunnies,* p. 82; December 1, 2010, Diane Foote, review of *Little Fox Goes to the End of the World,* p. 65; February 15, 2011, Hazel Rochman, review of *Jam and Honey,* p. 77; March 15, 2011, Carolyn Phelan, review of *Kitty Cat, Kitty Cat, Are You Going to Sleep?,* p. 62.

Kirkus Reviews, August 1, 2002, review of *Where Fish Go in Winter, and Other Great Mysteries,* p. 1134; September 15, 2003, review of *A Fairy in a Dairy,* p. 1179; August 15, 2005, review of *If You Were My Baby: A Wildlife Lullaby,* p. 915; February 15, 2006, review of *The Bear Hug,* p. 179; August 15, 2008, review of *Kitty Cat, Kitty Cat, Are You Waking Up?*; November 15, 2008, review of *Yummiest Love*; May 15, 2009, review of *God Found Us You*; November 15, 2010, review of *Jam and Honey*; February 15, 2011, review of *Kitty Cat, Kitty Cat, Are You Going to Sleep?*; August 1, 2011, review of *Heaven: God's Promise for Me.*

Publishers Weekly, December 15, 2003, review of *A Fairy in a Dairy,* p. 72; March 6, 2006, review of *The Bear Hug,* p. 72; January 28, 2008, review of *How Big Is God?,* p. 71; December 8, 2008, review of *Yummiest Love,* p. 57; January 24, 2011, review of *Kitty Cat, Kitty Cat, Are You Going to Sleep?,* p. 150.

School Library Journal, November, 2003, Leslie Barban, review of *A Fairy in a Dairy,* p. 110; March, 2006, Angela J. Reynolds, review of *The Bear Hug,* p. 185; March, 2007, Carolyn Janssen, review of *Tractor Day,* p. 184; April, 2008, Lisa Egly Lehmuller, review of *How Big Is God?,* p. 103; September, 2008, Kara Schaff Dean, review of *Kitty Cat, Kitty Cat, Are You Waking Up?,* p. 155; January, 2009, Amy Lilien-Harper, review of *Yummiest Love,* p. 80; April, 2009, Linda L. Walkins, review of *God Found Us You,* p. 100; April, 2010, Linda Ludke, review of *Seven Little Bunnies,* p. 140; October, 2010, Blair Christolon, review of *Little Fox Goes to the End of the World,* p. 95; March, 2011, Amy Lilien-Harper, review of *Jam and Honey,* p. 130; May, 2011, Carolyn Janssen, review of *Kitty Cat, Kitty Cat, Are You Going to Sleep?,* p. 83.

ONLINE

Dawn Publications Web site, http://www.dawnpub.com/ (March 1, 2012), "Laura J. Bryant."

Lisa McCourt's engaging bedtime story **Yummiest Love** *gains a new layer of whimsey through Bryant's illustrations.* (Illustration copyright © 2009 by Laura J. Bryant. Reproduced by permission of Scholastic, Inc.)

Laura J. Bryant Home Page, http://www.laurabryant.com (March 1, 2012).

*   *   *

CHAVARRI, Elisa

Personal

Born in Lima, Peru; immigrated to United States; married; husband's name Matt. *Education:* Savannah College of Art and Design, B.A. (classical animation; with honors).

Addresses

Home—Alpena, MI. *E-mail*—elisachavarri@gmail.com.

Career

Illustrator and animator. *Exhibitions:* Work exhibited at Art in the Loft, Alpena, MI; Red Gallery, Savannah, GA; Gallery 1600, Atlanta, GA; Gallery 231, Marquette, MI; Biddle Gallery, Wyandotte, MI; j3fm Gallery, Hannover, Germany; Bodhi Gallery, London, England; Canteen Gallery, Ottawa, Ontario, Canada; and in Argentina.

Illustrator

Anne Margaret Lewis, *Santa Goes Green,* Mackinac Island Press (Traverse City, MI), 2008.

Chavarri's illustrations exhibit her talent for mixing color and design. (Courtesy of Elisa Chavarri.)

Esmé Raji Codell, *Fairly Fairy Tales,* Aladdin (New York, NY), 2011.

Anne Margaret Lewis, *Fly Blanky Fly,* HarperCollins (New York, NY), 2012.

Contributor to periodicals, including *American Girl, Guide, Humpty Dumpty, Jack & Jill, Michigan History, Michigan History for Kids, Shine Brightly, Sparkle, Turtle,* and *USA Weekend.*

Sidelights

Born in Peru and now based in the midwestern United States, Elisa Chavarri shares her cheerful and colorful illustrations with young children in the pages of popular children's magazines as well as in books. An animator as well as illustrator, Chavarri has created story boards and designed characters for films and she has exhibited her artwork at galleries both close to home and internationally. "I like to create things that are beautiful, have an element of fun, and hopefully, bring a smile to others," Chavarri noted on her home page. "My works are a mixture of my experiences, what I find inspiring, and what I would like to see. They are constantly evolving."

The picture books that feature Chavarri's artwork include *Santa Goes Green,* a holiday story by Anne Mar-

Elisa Chavarri (Reproduced by permission.)

Chavarri's illustration projects include creating the artwork for Esmé Raji Codell's Fairly Fairy Tales. (Illustration copyright © 2011 by Elisa Chavarri. Reproduced by permission of Aladdin, an imprint of Simon & Schuster Children's Publishing Division.)

garet Lewis, a as well as Lewis's whimsical *Fly Blanky Fly*. Another illustration project, Esmé Raji Codell's humorous *Fairly Fairy Tales*, finds a busy mom putting a modern-day spin on tried-and-true bedtime tales such as "The Three Little Pigs," "Cinderella," and "Red Riding Hood" in her hurry to get her young son off to bed. Reviewing *Fairly Fairy Tales*, a *Publishers Weekly* critic wrote that "Chavarri renders the traditional fairy tale elements in tidy, pretty spot illustrations," and Karen Cruze wrote in *Booklist* that her artwork is "packed with details delighted readers will pore over." "Busy illustrations, humorously fractured tales and a [text] . . . that encourages audience participation ensure that this will see repeat readings," predicted a *Kirkus Reviews* writer in reviewing *Fairly Fairy Tales*.

Biographical and Critical Sources

PERIODICALS

Booklist, February 1, 2011, Karen Cruze, review of *Fairly Fairy Tales*, p. 81.
Bulletin of the Center for Children's Books, February, 2011, Hope Morrison, review of *Fairly Fairy Tales*, p. 273.
Kirkus Reviews, December 1, 2010, review of *Fairly Fairy Tales*.
Publishers Weekly, review of *Fairly Fairy Tales*, p. 55.
School Library Journal, February, 2011, C.J. Connor, review of *Fairly Fairy Tales*, p. 76.

ONLINE

Elisa Chavarri Home Page, http://www.elisachavarri.com (March 1, 2012).
Elisa Chavarri Web log, http://echavarri.xanga.com (March 1, 2012).

*   *   *

CHAYIL, Eishes
[A pseudonym]
(Judy Brown)

Personal

Born Judy Brown; pen name pronounced "AY-shis CHEYE-el". *Education:* Bachelor's degree; M.F.A. (creative writing). *Religion:* Jewish.

Addresses

Home—Brooklyn, NY.

Career

Writer. Journalist for international Orthodox Jewish newspapers.

Awards, Honors

William C. Morris Young-Adult Debut Award finalist, and Sydney Taylor Book Award Teen Honor selection, American Association of Jewish Libraries, both 2011, both for *Hush.*

Writings

Hush (novel), Walker & Company (New York, NY), 2010.

Sidelights

Published under the pseudonym Eishes Chayil, Judy Brown's controversial debut novel *Hush* explores the aftermath of a horrific incident of child sexual abuse. The fictional work is based on an event from the author's life: as a youngster growing up in Brooklyn, New York, Brown witnessed the sexual molestation of one of her friends. She remained silent about the abuse for decades because in her insular Chassidic community families are discouraged from reporting cases of rape and sexual abuse to the police. At the age of twenty-three, however, Brown disclosed the incident to a therapist, and after meeting with other victims she felt compelled to publicly tell her story, fictionalizing it in the novel *Hush.* "It's been an extremely painful process for me, as the entire issue of abuse remains an open wound in the Orthodox community," the author remarked to *Tablet* contributor Marjorie Ingall. "Things are slowly opening up but will take a long time."

The Chassidic community's reluctance to address the topic of abuse prompted Brown, a journalist, to publishe *Hush* under a pen name to avoid fearing a backlash from members of the community and the book's release sparked several threats to her publisher. Refusing to be intimidated, however, Brown subsequently revealed her true identity in "Orthodox Jewish Child Abuse: Shattering a Traumatic Silence," an essay published online through the *Huffington Post.* "For too long we have tiptoed around our flaws with fear and caution, pushing them into the shadows in hopes they will disappear," she wrote. "For too long, victims have been made to be the villains, and abuse was called *loshon harah,* evil talk. For too long, we have refused to honestly discuss the horrific possibilities, and in doing so allowed our children to fall victim to them. And for too long, I have allowed my own fear to make me part of a wall of silence—guilty for what I had seen, guilty for what I had written."

In *Hush* Brown tells the story of Gittel Klein. Seventeen-year-old Gittel is preparing for her upcoming marriage, one arranged by a matchmaker in her Chassidic community. Although she is on the cusp of adulthood, Gittel is still haunted by the memories of her best friend from childhood, Devory. Years earlier, during a slee-pover at Devory's house, Gittel witnessed Devory's sibling, Shmuli, force his younger sister to commit a sexual act. When Gittel tells her mother about the episode, she advises her daughter to keep quiet, and members of the community lie to the police after Devory commits suicide. Once Gittel gives birth to her own child, however, she realizes that she can no longer remain silent.

Brown's "thoughtful, disturbing, and insightful novel provides an insider's view of an insular society," Carolyn Lehman remarked in her review of *Hush* for *School Library Journal,* and *Booklist* contributor Ilene Cooper described the work as "powerful stuff and a glimpse into places not often seen." A number of critics praised the author's sensitive and balanced picture of Borough Park, home to one of the largest Orthodox Jewish populations in the United States. "The portrait of Gittel's closed community is simultaneously affectionate and critical," Ingall wrote, and *School Library Journal Web log* contributor Elizabeth Burns observed that "*Hush* is not a condemnation of a community. This is a condem-

Cover of Hush, *a book first published under Judy Brown's pen name* Eishes Chayil. (Jacket cover photograph © Photodisc/Getty Images. Reproduced by permission of Walker Publishing, an imprint of Bloomsbury Publishing, Inc.)

nation of how a community reacts to something tragic and horrible." "For the reader who is willing to stick with this complex novel, it will strike a deep emotional chord," Jennifer McConnel predicted in her appraisal of Brown's novel for *Voice of Youth Advocates.*

Biographical and Critical Sources

PERIODICALS

Booklist, October 15, 2010, Ilene Cooper, review of *Hush,* p. 59.

Bulletin of the Center for Children's Books, October, 2010, Elizabeth Bush, review of *Hush,* p. 73.

Kirkus Reviews, August 1, 2010, review of *Hush.*

School Library Journal, September, 2010, Carolyn Lehman, review of *Hush,* p. 148.

Tablet, November 8, 2010, Marjorie Ingall, "Out of the Silence," review of *Hush*

Voice of Youth Advocates, December, 2010, Jennifer McConnel, review of *Hush,* p. 448.

ONLINE

Huffington Post Web site, http://www.huffingtonpost.com/ (August 1, 2011), Eishes Chayil, "Orthodox Jewish Child Abuse: Shattering a Traumatic Silence."

Kirkus Reviews Web log, http://www.kirkusreviews.com/ blog/ (December 2, 2010), Jenny Brown, review of *Hush.*

School Library Journal Web log, http://blog.schoollibrary journal.com/teacozy/ (November 19, 2010), Elizabeth Burns, review of *Hush.**

*   *   *

CHOLDENKO, Gennifer 1957-

Personal

Born October 20, 1957, in Santa Monica, CA; daughter of Jimmy (a business executive) and Ann (a physical therapist) Johnson; married Jacob Brown; children: Ian Brown, Kai Brown. *Education:* Brandeis University, B.A. (English and American literature; cum laude); Rhode Island School of Design, B.F.A. (illustration).

Addresses

Home—San Francisco Bay area, CA. *E-mail*—choldenko@earthlink.net.

Career

Writer. Worked in various jobs, including horseback riding instructor for seeing-and hearing-impaired children. Presenter at schools.

Awards, Honors

New York Library Top 100 Book designation, and National Parenting Center Seal of Approval, both 1997, both for *Moonstruck;* California Book Award Silver

Gennifer Choldenko (Photograph by Pat Stroud. Courtesy of Gennifer Choldenko.)

Medal for Young Adults, and International Reading Association/Children's Book Council (CBC) Children's Choice selection, both 2001, both for *Notes from a Liar and Her Dog;* Newbery Honor Book designation, Carnegie Medal shortlist, American Library Association Notable Book designation, New York Public Library Books for the Teen Age inclusion, CBC/National Council for Social Studies Notable Social Studies Trade Book designation, Special Needs Award (UK), Beatty Award, California Library Association, Judy Lopez Honor Award, Northern California Book Award, and Parents' Choice Silver Medal, all 2005, and California Young Readers Medal, Garden State Teen Book Award, and Keystone State Reading Association Young-Adult Book Award, all 2007, all for *Al Capone Does My Shirts;* Indie Choice Honor selection, 2010, for *Al Capone Shines My Shoes.*

Writings

PICTURE BOOKS

Moonstruck: The True Story of the Cow Who Jumped over the Moon, illustrated by Paul Yalowitz, Hyperion (New York, NY), 1997.

How to Make Friends with a Giant, illustrated by Amy Walrod, Putnam (New York, NY), 2006.

Louder, Lili, illustrated by S.D. Schindler, Putnam (New York, NY), 2007.

A Giant Crush, illustrated by Melissa Sweet, G.P. Putnam's Sons (New York, NY), 2011.

MIDDLE-GRADE NOVELS

Notes from a Liar and Her Dog, Putnam (New York, NY), 2001.

Al Capone Does My Shirts, Putnam's (New York, NY), 2004.

If a Tree Falls at Lunch Period, Harcourt (Orlando, FL), 2007.

Al Capone Shines My Shoes, Dial Books for Young Readers (New York, NY), 2009.

No Passengers beyond This Point, Dial Books for Young Readers (New York, NY), 2011.

Al Capone Does My Homework, Dial Books for Young Readers (New York, NY), 2013.

Contributor to anthologies, including *Guys Read: Thrillers,* edited by Jon Scieszka, HarperCollins (New York, NY), 2011.

Choldenko's books have been translated into nine languages, including Chinese, French, German, Japanese, Korean, and Spanish.

Adaptations

Notes from a Liar and Her Dog was adapted for audiocassette, Listening Library, 2001. *Al Capone Does My Shirts* was adapted for audiocassette, Recorded Books, 2004, and Listening Library, 2009. *Al Capone Shines My Shoes* was adapted for audiocassette by Listening Library, 2009. *If a Tree Falls at Lunch Period* was adapted for audiocassette, Recorded Books, 2007. *No Passengers beyond This Point* was adapted for audiocassette, Listening Library, 2011.

Sidelights

Selling her first book manuscript to a publisher at age thirty-three, Gennifer Choldenko has gone on to become an award-winning author of both picture books for young children and novels for middle-grade readers. In her fast-paced novels, Choldenko focuses on serious topics that range from chronic lying to autism, but she makes them seem fresh through her light, witty touch. Featuring both her characteristic humor and her offbeat perspective, her novel *Al Capone Does My Shirts* earned the prestigious 2005 Newbery Honor Book designation, one of several honors accorded the book. Crediting her father, an unpublished but passionate writer, for inspiring her own efforts as an author, Choldenko added on her home page: "It took me a long time to . . . be willing to take the risks necessary to pursue a career as a writer."

Choldenko was born in Santa Monica, California, in the late 1950s, the youngest in a family that included four boisterous children. As a child, her first love was horses,

and her second was writing and making up stories. Choldenko's interests turned to poetry in high school, but while completing her studies at Brandeis University she returned to prose and graduated *cum laude* with a dual major in American literature and English because the school did not yet offer a major in creative writing. Later, she earned an illustration degree from the prestigious Rhode Island School of Design, where she produced her first picture-book text, *Moonstruck: The True Story of the Cow Who Jumped over the Moon.*

Featuring illustrations by Paul Yalowitz, *Moonstruck* sheds new light on the nursery-rhyme line "And the cow jumped over the moon," which has perplexed generations of listeners, both young and old. In Choldenko's version, the rhyme's narrator—a horse—explains that the black-and-white bovine in question accomplished the high-flying task after training with a group of agile horses that regularly made the leap into the night sky to skim the top of the moon and return to Earth. Calling the picture book "a giggle from beginning to end," a *Publishers Weekly* contributor noted that

Cover of Choldenko's middle-grade novel **Notes from a Liar and Her Dog,** *featuring artwork by Mark Ulriksen.* (Illustration © 2001 by Mark Ulriksen. Reproduced by permission of Puffin Books, a division of Penguin Young Readers Group, a member of Penguin Group (USA) Inc., 375 Hudson Street, New York, NY 10014. All rights reserved.)

the author "clearly had fun setting tradition on its ear, and her glee is evident throughout." In her review of Choldenko's debut for *Booklist,* Ilene Cooper dubbed *Moonstruck* "fractured and funny" and called it "a fun read-aloud—and a tribute to hard work."

Notes from a Liar and Her Dog, Choldenko's first novel for middle-grade readers, introduces preteen narrator Antonia "Ant" MacPherson, a middle sibling who finds herself constantly on the outs with her two perfect sisters: "Your Highness Elizabeth" and "Katherine the Great." Because her relationship with her parents is equally strained, Ant's only confidants are a Chihuahua named Pistachio and her best friend Harrison, an artist who is obsessed with poultry. As a way to mask her unhappiness, the sixth grader embroiders her life with elaborate falsehoods until a perceptive teacher helps her come to terms with her own role in her difficult family relationship. Noting that Choldenko "vividly captures the feelings of a middle child torn between wanting to be noticed and wanting to be invisible," a *Publishers Weekly* contributor called *Notes from a Liar and Her Dog* a "funny and touching novel." Reviewing the book for *School Library Journal* Connie Tyrrell Burns dubbed Ant's narration "humorous, tongue-in-cheek, and as irreverent as her independent heroine," and *Booklist* critic Susan Dove Lempke called Choldenko's story "funny, moving, and completely believable."

In *Al Capone Does My Shirts* Choldenko returns to middle-grade angst, this time by exploring the trauma of moving to a new home. Set in 1935, the novel introduces twelve-year-old Moose Flanagan. Moose is less than enthused when he learns that his family is moving to Alcatraz, the notorious island prison located within sight of San Francisco. In order to afford the tuition to send Moose's autistic sister Natalie to a special boarding school, Mr. Flanagan is working as an electrician and prison guard on the island, where he oversees infamous criminals like mobster Al Capone, a man better known as Scarface. Moose has to leave his winning little-league baseball team behind to make the move, and he feels that his sacrifice has gone unnoticed. Now he sees very little of his busy father and his mom is almost totally involved with Natalie's illness and education. A new confidante is found in Piper, the warden's feisty daughter, who leads Moose into mischief as he learns to accept his family's situation and appreciate his parents' sacrifices.

Al Capone Does My Shirts was inspired by a newspaper article Choldenko read that discussed Alcatraz's evolution from prison to museum. It also discussed the little-known fact that, during its years as a prison, the island was home to the families of prison guards and officials. While researching her book, Choldenko served as a docent on Alcatraz island, immersing herself in the history of the institution, its inmates, and the prison support staff. She also took inspiration from her own sister, Gina, who suffered from autism. The book's title comes from a joke Moose and Piper make about the prison's

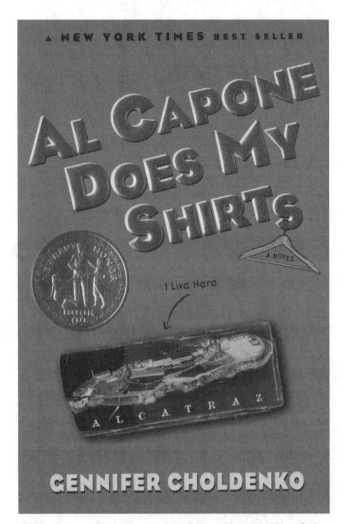

Choldenko's award-winning novel Al Capone Does My Shirts *finds a preteen living in very unusual—and very humorous—circumstances.* (Reproduced by permission of Puffin Books, a division of Penguin Young Readers Group, a member of Penguin Group (USA), Inc., 375 Hudson Street, New York, NY 10014. All rights reserved.)

famous inmate and his prison jobs. Capone worked in the prison laundry during his stay on Alcatraz, and military personnel stationed in San Francisco during World War II used to make a similar joke: "Al Capone does my shorts."

In *Booklist* Ed Sullivan praised *Al Capone Does My Shirts* as a "warm, engaging coming-of-age story," and a *Publishers Weekly* contributor recommended the "fast-paced and memorable" story due to Choldenko's ability to create "unusual characters and plot lines." According to *School Library Journal* reviewer Miranda Doyle, the novel is "told with humor and skill," and Paula Rohrlick wrote in *Kliatt* that the author couches with in her story a "sensitive portrait of autism and how it affects a family." In *Kirkus Reviews* a writer noted that Choldenko's "pacing is exquisite" and makes *Al Capone Does My Shirts* a "great read," and this was shared by the Newbery awards committee in according the novel Newbery Honor Book status.

Moose and Piper return in *Al Capone Shines My Shoes,* as the boy is required to make good on a debt to the notorious Scarface—maybe the worst of the over 270 criminal masterminds inhabiting Alcatraz—after Capone pulls the unwitting Natalie into his scheme. She is about to leave for boarding school when the cagey criminal reveals that he was the anonymous donor who helped pay for her schooling. Now Moose is left to make good on this debt, and when the prison break occurs he must wrestle with a difficult moral dilemma. Meanwhile, Moose also begins to look at Piper as more than just a friend, even though he sometimes questions her manipulative character. "Choldenko hits a grand slam with this richly rewarding sequel," proclaimed a *Kirkus Reviews* critic in appraising *Al Capone Shines My Shoes,* and *Horn Book* contributor Jonathan Hunt asserted that the author's inclusion of "historical details of daily life on Alcatraz . . . remain as interesting as ever." Citing Choldenko's "sprightly writing," Marilyn Taniguchi also praised the novel in *School Library Journal,* noting of *Al Capone Shines My Shoes* that the "comical and poignant plot twists" add up to an example of "superlative historical fiction."

Also taking place in California, *If A Tree Falls at Lunch Period* takes readers to an exclusive middle school where the friendship between two seventh graders is explored. Overweight Kirsten is the daughter of a doctor, and her weight is the result of dealing with many stresses in her tension-fraught family. Walker, a scholarship student and one of only three African-American children attending Mountain School, was raised by a single mom; he misses his old friends and does not share many of the experiences of his fellow students. Choldenko's novel is told through two alternating narratives: Kirstin's first-person drama as well as a third-person overview of Walker's struggle to fit in.

According to *Horn Book* contributor Susan Dove Lempke, *If a Tree Falls at Lunch Period* "explores themes of racism and wealth with subtlety and insight," while a *Kirkus Reviews* writer noted that "Choldenko's talent for characters and conversation brings the two voices instantly to life." While the *Kirkus Reviews* critic suggested the novel's value in sparking "book-club or classroom discussion," *School Library Journal* critic Lillian Hecker cited *If a Tree Falls at Lunch Period* for its "sparkling characterization and touches of humor."

Choldenko turns from historical fiction to fantasy in *No Passengers beyond This Point,* which also finds a family on the move. For India, Finn, and Mouse Tompkins, hard economic times have caused their mother to lose the family home and she now sends the siblings to Colorado to live with their uncle Red. During the flight, the children;s plane encounters some strange turbulence, and when it finally touches down, it is not in Colorado but in a surreal land called Falling Bird. Met at the airport by a strange man, the three children are each sent to a separate home. Although their first day allows each to fulfill his or her dreams, after this day of bliss each receives a clock marking a twenty-four-hour countdown to a forbidding deadline. Suddenly, India, Finn, and

Mouse find themselves part of a larger puzzle, and they must discover what to make of the three clues they have been given.

Describing this strange new world as a "lightly Kafkaesque dreamland," Ian Chipman added in *Booklist* that *No Passengers beyond This Point* "is delivered with an unusually thoughtful dose of weirdness" and draws readers into "a fast-paced mind-bender" of a story. Choldenko crafts a first-person narrative in triplicate in detailing the adventures of the three siblings, and she "shines in her characterization of children and their idiosyncratic kidspeak," according to a *Kirkus Reviews* writer. Noting that the Tompkins children's "homeless existence" in Falling Bird "mirrors their real-world limbo," Emma Burkhart added in her *School Library Journal* appraisal that Choldenko's imaginative story takes fantasy fans on "a fun ride . . . full of adventure, suspense, and good characterizations."

Although Choldenko has focused predominately on middle-grade novels since writing *Moonstruck,* she returns to the picture-book format on occasion. In *How to*

Cover of Choldenko's young-adult novel No Passengers beyond This Point, *featuring artwork by Tyson Mangelsdorf.* (Jacket cover art copyright © 2011 by Tyson Mangelsdorf. Reproduced by permission of Dial Books for Young Readers, a division of Penguin Young Readers Group, a member of Penguin Group (USA), 375 Hudson Street, New York, NY 10014. All rights reserved.)

Make Friends with a Giant, which features cartoon illustrations by Amy Walrod, first grader Jake worries that he is too short of stature until he makes a friend of Jacomo, the new boy next door. Jacomo is practically a giant and at school he is bullied due to his clumsy strength and cumbersome size. Jake becomes Jacomo's protector, learning to accept his own differences in the process. In *Horn Book* Christina M. Hepperman dubbed *How to Make Friends with a Giant* a "perceptive portrait of . . . friendship" illustrating that "the best way to get over your own insecurities is to help someone else with theirs." A *Kirkus Reviews* writer also praised the story, calling Jake an "inventive" friend, while in *School Library Journal* Grace Oliff described Choldenko's picture book as "a quirky tale of two opposites."

Artist S.D. Schindler captures the humor of Choldenko's picture-book text in *Louder Lily,* which focuses on a young girl who is so quiet that even her teacher forgets that she is there. When a class project requires that students pair up, Lily team up with Cassidy Clummer, an overbearing bully who trusts that her new partner's shyness will let her get away with misbehaving. When the safety of a class pet is threatened by Cassidy's meanness, however, Lily's values overcome her self-consciousness in a story that a *Publishers Weekly* critic described as a "perceptive classroom drama" enriched by "restrained but deeply empathetic writing."

With illustrations by Melissa Sweet, *A Giant Crush* finds Jackson the Rabbit wrestling with another kind of shyness common to young school-goers: shyness around a classmate he has a special affection for. With Valentine's Day approaching, Jackson plans a special gift for Cami, but he becomes discouraged when loud-mouth classmate Carter also seems to view Cami as his favorite. Fortunately, Jackson's best friend Cooper is there to encourage his buddy to follow his heart and also to recount his story. Sweet's "bright-hued" illustrations "capture the nuances of the interpersonal dynamics at play" in Choldenko's "entertaining" story, wrote a *Kirkus Reviews* writer, and in *Booklist* Diane Foote asserted that, while "a Valentine's Day story about cute bunnies has the potential to be saccharine sweet," *A Giant Crush* "hits just the right note."

Biographical and Critical Sources

PERIODICALS

Booklist, March 1, 1997, Ilene Cooper, review of *Moonstruck: The True Story of the Cow Who Jumped over the Moon,* p. 1169; April 15, 2001, Susan Dove Lempke, review of *Notes from a Liar and Her Dog,* p. 1550; February 1, 2004, Ed Sullivan, review of *Al Capone Does My Shirts,* p. 976; August, 2007, Gillian Engberg, review of *Louder, Lili,* p. 84; September 1, 2009, Andrew Medlar, review of *Al Capone Shines My Shoes,* p. 88; February 1, 2011, Ian Chipman, review of *No Passengers beyond This Point,* p. 80; December 1, 2011, Diane Foote, review of *A Giant Crush,* p. 66.

Horn Book, March-April, 2005, "Newbery Medal," p. 235; September-October, 2006, Christine M. Heppermann, review of *How to Make Friends with a Giant,* p. 563; July-August, 2007, Susan Dove Lempke, review of *If a Tree Falls at Lunch Period;* September-October, 2009, Jonathan Hunt, review of *Al Capone Shines My Shoes,* p. 555; January-February, 2011, Susan Dove Lempke, review of *No Passengers beyond This Point,* p. 90.

Kirkus Reviews, March 1, 2004, review of *Al Capone Does My Shirts,* p. 220; June 1, 2006, review of *How to Make Friends with a Giant,* p. 570; August 15, 2007, review of *If a Tree Falls at Lunch Period;* September 1, 2007, review of *Louder, Lili;* August 1, 2009, review of *Al Capone Shines My Shoes;* December 15, 2010, review of *No Passengers beyond This Point;* December 1, 2011, review of *A Giant Crush.*

Kliatt, March 1, 2004, review of *Al Capone Does My Shirts,* p. 220.

Publishers Weekly, February 10, 1997, review of *Moonstruck,* p. 83; May 14, 2001, review of *Notes from a Liar and Her Dog,* p. 82; July 7, 2003, review of *Notes from a Liar and Her Dog,* p. 74; February 2, 2004, review of *Al Capone Does My Shirts,* p. 78; August 7, 2006, review of *How to Make Friends with a Giant,* p. 58; July 15, 2007, review of *If a Tree Falls at Lunch Period,* p. 167; September 17, 2007, review of *Louder, Lili,* p. 53; August 17, 2009, review of *Al Capone Shines My Shoes,* p. 63; December 6, 2010, review of *No Passengers Beyond This Point,* p. 49.

School Library Journal, April, 1997, Patricia Pearl Doyle, review of *Moonstruck,* p. 91; April, 2001, Connie Tyrrell Burns, review of *Notes from a Liar and Her Dog,* p. 139; March, 2004, Miranda Doyle, review of *Al Capone Does My Shirts,* p. 203; July, 2006, Grace Oliff, review of *How to Make Friends with a Giant,* p. 70; August, 2007, Lillian Hecker, review of *If a Tree Falls at Lunch Period;* September, 2007, Barbara Katz, review of *Louder, Lili,* p. 161; September, 2009, Marilyn Taniguchi, review of *Al Capone Shines My Shoes,* p. 152; February, 2011, Emma Burkhart, review of *No Passengers beyond This Point,* p. 104.

Times Educational Supplement, August 6, 2004, Jan Mark, review of *The Rock and a Hard Case,* p. 25.

Voice of Youth Advocates, February, 2005, review of *Al Capone Does My Shirts,* p. 441; April, 2011, Lynn Evarts, review of *No Passengers Beyond This Point,* p. 77.

ONLINE

Gennifer Choldenko Home Page, http://www.choldenko.com (March 1, 2012).

Quercus Web site, http://www.windingoak.com/quercus/ (July, 2006), interview with Choldenko.

University of Connecticut/Teachers for a New Era Web site, http://www.tne.uconn.edu/ (September 15, 2008), Susan Raab, interview with Choldenko.

CLINE, Eric H. 1960-

Personal

Born September 1, 1960, in Washington, DC; married; children. *Education:* Dartmouth College, B.A. (classical archaeology), 1982; Yale University, M.A. (Near Eastern languages and literatures), 1984; University of Pennsylvania, Ph.D. (ancient history), 1991.

Addresses

Home—Washington DC. *Office*—Phillips Hall 302, The George Washington University, Washington, DC 20052. *E-mail*—ehcline@gwu.edu.

Career

Educator, archaeologist, and historian. George Washington University, Washington, DC, associate professor of ancient history and archaeology, chair of Department of Classical and Semitic Languages and Literatures (now Near Eastern Languages and Civilizations), beginning 2004, and director of Capitol Archaeological Institute. Archaeologist; associate U.S. director of excavations at Megiddo; co-director of excavations at Tel Kabri, Israel. American Schools of Oriental Research, former vice president and member of various committees, now member, board of trustees; American School of Classical Studies in Athens, secretary/treasurer, 1997-99. Member of editorial board of periodicals, including *Near Eastern Archaeology,* 1997-2001, 2008—, *Archaeological Odyssey,* 1998-2001, *AIA Newsletter,* 1998-2002, *National Geographic,* 2007—, and *Journal of Mediterranean Archaeology and Archaeometry,* 2008—. Has appeared on radio and television and in documentary films; lecturer at Smithsonian Institution, Metropolitan Museum of Art, Skirball Museum, and other institutions.

Member

Archaeological Institute of America (trustee and member of board), American Oriental Society, American Research Center in Egypt, Association of Ancient Historians.

Awards, Honors

Best Popular Book on Archaeology Award, Biblical Archaeology Society, 2001, for *The Battles of Armageddon,* 2009, for *From Eden to Exile,* and 2011, for *Biblical Archaeology*; Morton Bender Excellence in Undergraduate Teaching Award, George Washington University, 2004; Excellence in Undergraduate Teaching Award, Archaeological Institute of America, 2005; Oscar and Shoshana Trachtenberg Award for Faculty Scholarship, George Washington University, 2011.

Writings

Sailing the Wine-Dark Sea: International Trade and the Late Bronze Age Aegean (dissertation), British Archaeological Reports (Oxford, England), 1994, reprinted, 2009.

The Battles of Armageddon: Megiddo and the Jezreel Valley from the Bronze Age to the Nuclear Age, University of Michigan Press (Ann Arbor, MI), 2000.
Jerusalem Besieged: From Ancient Canaan to Modern Israel, University of Michigan Press (Ann Arbor, MI), 2004.
(With Jill Rubalcaba) *The Ancient Egyptian World,* Oxford University Press (New York, NY), 2005.
From Eden to Exile: Unraveling Mysteries of the Bible, National Geographic (Washington, DC), 2007.
Biblical Archaeology: A Very Short Introduction, Oxford University Press (New York, NY), 2009.
(With Jill Rubalcaba) *Digging for Troy: From Homer to Hisarlik,* illustrated by Sarah S. Brannen, Charlesbridge (Watertown, MA), 2010.
(With Mark W. Graham) *Ancient Empires: From Mesopotamia to the Rise of Islam,* Cambridge University Press (New York, NY), 2011.

EDITOR

(With David O'Connor) *Amenhotep III: Perspectives on His Reign,* University of Michigan Press (Ann Arbor, MI), 1998.
(With David O'Connor) *Thutmose III: A New Biography,* University of Michigan Press (Ann Arbor, MI), 2006.
The Oxford Handbook of the Bronze Age Aegean (ca. 3000-1000 BC), Oxford University Press (New York, NY), 2010.
(With David O'Connor) *Ramesses III: The Life and Times of Egypt's Last Hero,* University of Michigan Press (Ann Arbor, MI), 2011.

Contributor of over 100 articles to journals and periodicals. Editor of symposia; general editor of *The Ancient World,* Sharpe Reference (Armonk, NY), 2007.

Author's work has been translated into Croatian.

Sidelights

Well known in his field through his scholarship, field work, and role as a go-to source for media documentaries, Eric H. Cline is also a professor of archaeology at George Washington University, where he chairs the Department of Classical and Near-Eastern Languages and Civilizations. Cline's primary expertise is in the military history of Mediterranean empires and his excavations and survey work have taken him to Greece, Crete, Egypt, and Israel, among other countries. His dedication to making modern archaeology of interest to the general public has led to his appearance on numerous television documentaries—including broadcasts on the History Channel, the National Geographic Channel, the Discovery Channel, and public television stations in the United States and United Kingdom—as well as his authorship of books for a range of reading levels and interests.

Published by the National Geographic Society, Cline's *From Eden to Exile: Unraveling Mysteries of the Bible* allows the general reader to put biblical stories in an

Professor Eric H. Cline teams up with author Jill Rubalcaba to introduce young readers to archaeological history in **Digging for Troy: From Homer to Hisarlik.** (Illustration copyright © 2011 by Sarah S. Brannen. Reproduced by permission of Charlesbridge Publishing, Inc., Watertown, MA. All rights reserved.)

historic context. Cline addresses several of the Bible's most-compelling mysteries—including the location of the Garden of Eden, the ultimate resting place of Noah's Ark, the truth about the Ark of the Covenant, and the fate of Israel's ten lost tribes—by recounting the relevant biblical history and then tcomparing it with the relevant facts gleaned from archaeologists, historians, and religious scholars. While some stories are disproved or proved by factual evidence, others are relegated to the possible as Cline sets forth his own and others' conjectures. Reviewing *From Eden to Exile* in *Booklist*, Ilene Cooper praised the work as "an accessibly written introduction that will likely prompt readers to dig deeper," while Fred Rhodes concluded in *Middle East* that Cline "discloses fascinating possibilities for each mystery and proposes provocative solutions" that sometimes part company with traditional scholarship." Dubbing Cline's work "surprisingly intriguing beach reading," Dan Vergano added in his *USA Today* review of *From Eden to Exile:* "Who doesn't love a good mystery, especially one that is thousands of years old?"

Cline teams up with nonfiction author Jill Rubalcaba to share his knowledge and enthusiasm for ancient cultures with middle-grade readers in the books *The Ancient Egyptian World* and *Digging for Troy: From Homer to Hisarlik.* Part of Oxford University Press's "The World in Ancient Times" series, *The Ancient Egyptian World* takes readers over 4,000 years into the past, then follows the course of Egypt's rise to power along the banks of the Nile as pharaoh follows pharaoh and the civilization gains in technology and military might. In *School Library Journal* Coop Renner noted that the

clearly presented information in *The Ancient Egyptian World* makes the book of particular use to report writers, and the "complexities of archaeology and . . . the unraveling and reassembling of information are . . . simplified" for the layman.

Digging for Troy focuses on the history of one of archaeology's most amazing discoveries, a search inspired by Homer's Iliad that ultimately located the site of the ancient city of Troy (now located in Turkey and called Hisarlik) in the late nineteenth century. After his discovery, eccentric German businessman Heinrich Schliemann dug around the site of Troy with little understanding of how he was destroying archaeological evidence. Fortunately, the site of Troy has ultimately yielded much to scientists and historians in the years since. Praising *Digging for Troy* in *School Library Journal*, Paula Willey noted that the book is "extraordinarily readable," well illustrated and designed, and "speckled with lines from The Iliad," and *Booklist* contributor Carolyn Phelan recommended Cline and Rubalcaba's work to "readers intrigued by archaeology in general or ancient Troy."

Biographical and Critical Sources

PERIODICALS

Booklist, June 1, 2007, Ilene Cooper, review of *From Eden to Exile: Unraveling Mysteries of the Bible,* p. 9; March 1, 2011, Carolyn Phelan, review of *Digging for Troy: From Homer to Hisarlik,* p. 41.

Choice, November, 2010, review of *The Oxford Handbook of the Bronze Age,* p. 568.

Middle East, June, 2008, Fred Rhodes, review of *From Eden to Exile,* p. 65.

Publishers Weekly, June 28, 2004, review of *Jerusalem Besieged: from Ancient Canaan to Modern Israel,* p. 38.

School Library Journal, January, 2006, Coop Renner, review of *The Ancient Egyptian World,* p. 148; April, 2008, review of *Encyclopedia of Society and Culture in the Ancient World,* p. 88; March, 2011, Paula Willey, review of *Digging for Troy,* p. 185.

Time, April 29, 2010, Ishaan Tharoor, "Has Noah's Ark Been Discovered in Turkey?"

USA Today, July 15, 2007, Dan Vergano, review of *From Eden to Exile,* p. D7.

ONLINE

Eric H. Cline Academic Home Page, http://home.gwu.edu/~ehcline (February 28, 2012).

* * *

COHEN, Deborah Bodin 1968-

Personal

Born 1968, in Columbia, MD; married Dave Cohen (a journalist); children: Arianna, Jesse, Ezra. *Education:*

University of Michigan, B.A. (English); Hebrew Union College, ordained, 1997. *Religion:* Jewish.

Addresses
Home—Potomac, MD. *E-mail*—DeborahBCohen@gmail.com.

Career
Rabbi and writer. Religious Action Center of Reform Judaism, Washington, DC, legislative assistant; Advocacy Institute, Washington, DC, former program associate; Beth Shalom, Cary, NC, rabbi and education director, 1997-2000; Temple Emanuel, Cherry Hill, NJ, rabbi, beginning 2000; Har Shalom, Potomac, MD, currently director of congregational learning.

Awards, Honors
Sydney Taylor Book Award Notable Book designation, Association of Jewish Libraries, 2005, for *The Seventh Day;* National Jewish Book Award for Family Literature, and Notable Book for Teens selection, American Library Association, both 2006, both for *Lilith's Ark;* Notable Book for Younger Readers selection, Association of Jewish Libraries, 2007, for *Papa Jethro;* Sydney Taylor Honor Book selection, 2008, for *Engineer Ari and the Rosh Hashanah Ride;* National Jewish Book Award finalist, Sugarman Award, and Sydney Taylor Book Award Honor Book selection, all 2009, all for *Nachshon Who Was Afraid to Swim.*

Writings

The Seventh Day, illustrated by Melanie Hall, Kar-Ben (Minneapolis, MN), 2005.
Lilith's Ark: Teenage Tales of Biblical Women, Jewish Publication Society (Philadelphia, PA), 2006.

Jago's illustration assignments include creating the unique artwork for Deborah Bodin Cohen's Nachson Who Was Afraid to Swim. (Illustration copyright © 2009 by Jago. Reprinted with the permission of Kar-Ben Publishing, a division of Lerner Publishing Group, Inc. All rights reserved. No part of this excerpt may be used or reproduced in any manner whatsoever without the prior written permission of Lerner Publishing Group, Inc.)

Papa Jethro: A Story of Moses' Interfaith Family, illustrated by Jane Dippold, Kar-Ben (Minneapolis, MN), 2007.

Engineer Ari and the Rosh Hashanah Ride, illustrated by Shahar Kober, Kar-Ben (Minneapolis, MN), 2008.

Nachshon Who Was Afraid to Swim: A Passover Story, illustrated by Jago, Kar-Ben (Minneapolis, MN), 2009.

Engineer Ari and the Sukkah Express, illustrated by Shahar Kober, Kar-Ben (Minneapolis, MN), 2010.

Engineer Ari and the Hanukkah Mishap, illustrated by Shahar Kober, Kar-Ben (Minneapolis, MN), 2011.

Sidelights

An ordained rabbi and educator in the Reform Judaism tradition, Deborah Bodin Cohen is also the author of books that share faith-based stories with new generations. "Through my Jewish picture books and Jewish novels, I hope to share the traditions and joy of Judaism and to foster a love of Jewish literature," Cohen noted on her home page. *The Seventh Day,* her retelling of the creation story, was named a Sydney Taylor Notable Book in 2005 and marked the start of Cohen's second career as an author for children. In the years since, she has produced several other picture books as well as engaging older readers with *Lilith's Ark: Teenage Tales of Biblical Women.* Reviewing *The Seventh Day,* a *Publishers Weekly* critic wrote that "Cohen's text expresses a joyous mood of appreciating wonders provided by God and . . . giving thanks for such gifts," while in *School Library Journal* Amy Lilien-

Harper recommended the prayerful story to parents in both "Reform and Conservative Jewish communities."

Cohen celebrates a well-known Jewish holiday in *Nachshon Who Was Afraid to Swim: A Passover Story.* Because Nachshon is the son of Egyptian slaves, he is raised to expect to spend his life in service. However, Moses's talk of giving freedom to the Jewish slaves of Pharaoh's kingdom inspires the boy. Following the older man in his flight from Egyptian troops, Nachshon reaches the shores of a vast body of water that threatens to block their escape. As revealed in the Torah, his total belief in Moses' words allows Nachshon to be the first to follow the prophet into the parting waters and across the sea to safety. Praising the "stylized art" contributed by illustrator Jago, a *Kirkus Reviews* writer described *Nachshon Who Was Afraid to Swim* as "a stirring tale of courage and faith." In *Publishers Weekly,* a contributor also recommended the picture book, writing that Cohen shifts "the Exodus story to a personal scale without robbing it of significance."

Cohen teams up with artist Shahar Kober in creating a trio of books featuring a train engineer living in nineteenth-century Israel. Based on an actual incident that took place in 1892, *Engineer Ari and the Rosh Hashanah Ride* finds Engineer Ari guiding the first train from Jaffa to the holy city of Jerusalem only days before the Jewish New Year, although he regrets the way he departed from his friends in his home city. Along the route, Ari stops the train to load the food that will be

Shahar Kober creates the engaging artwork for Cohen's picture book Engineer Ari and the Sukkah Express. (Illustration copyright © 2010 by by Shahar Kober. Reproduced by permission of Kar-Ben Publishing, a division of Lerner Publishing Group, Inc. All rights reserved. No part of this except may be used or reproduced in any manner whatsoever without the prior written permission of Lerner Publishing Group, Inc.)

used during Jerusalem's Rosh Hashanah celebration, learning a valuable lesson about the true meaning of the holiday along the way. In *Engineer Ari and the Sukkah Express* the engineer joins friends Jesse and Nathaniel to construct a sukkah in preparation for their Sukkot celebration, using a train car to share this creation with new friends and old, while a wandering camel threatens to delay Ari's arrival at home for the family holiday. In *School Library Journal* Rachel Kamin praised *Engineer Ari and the Rosh Hashana Ride* as a "delightful" story that comes to life in "cheerful illustrations" that capture the historic setting "with nostalgia and charm." Cohen's "easy, flowing text with patterned repetitive phrases" makes the second "Engineer Ari" book a "smooth, predictable" story-hour selection, according to a *Kirkus Reviews* writer, while a *Publishers Weekly* critic recommended *Engineer Ari and the Hanukkah Mishap* as an "imaginative" tale that will capture the interest of "train-loving children."

Winner of the National Jewish Book Award for Family Literature in 2006, *Lilith's Ark* collects a group of stories that are based in the bible and detail the challenges that faced Jewish women of ancient times: Lilith, Eve, Sarah, Rachel, Leah, Tamar, Rebekah, and Asenath. Along with each story, Cohen includes appropriate selections from the Hebrew Bible and augments each story with historical information and discussion questions that highlight the universal aspects of each young woman's unique challenge. Praised by *Kliatt* critic Maureen Griffin as "beautifully written," *Lilith's Ark* "speaks of heroism and creative spirit in a way that is attractive and encouraging," the critic added.

Biographical and Critical Sources

PERIODICALS

Booklist, October 1, 2007, Stephanie Zvirin, review of *Papa Jethro: A Story of Moses' Interfaith Family,* p. 72; September 1, 2008, Ilene Cooper, review of *Engineer Ari and the Rosh Hashanah Ride,* p. 103; September 19, 2011, review of *Engineer Ari and the Hanukkah Mishap,* p. 63.

Kirkus Reviews, January 15, 2009, review of *Nachshon Who Was Afraid to Swim: A Passover Story;*; July 15, 2010, review of *Engineer Ari and the Sukkah Express;* September 1, 2011, review of *Engineer Ari and the Hanukkah Mishap.*

Kliatt, January, 2007, Maureen Griffin, review of *Lilith's Ark: Teenage Tales of Biblical Women,* p. 34.

Publishers Weekly, February 14, 2005, review of *The Seventh Day,* p. 78; December 22, 2008, review of *Nachson Who Was Afraid to Swim,* p. 51; July 12, 2010, review of *Engineer Ari and the Sukkah Express,* p. 46; September 1, 2011, review of *Engineer Ari and the Hanukkah Mishap.*

School Library Journal, August, 2005, Amy Lilien-Harper, review of *The Seventh Day,* p. 86; October, 2007, Rachel Kamin, review of *Papa Jethro,* p. 110; September, 2008, Rachel Kamin, review of *Engineer Ari and the Rosh Hashanah Ride,* p. 142; March, 2009, Rachel Kamin, review of *Nachshon Who Was Afraid to Swim,* p. 108.

ONLINE

Congregation Har Shalom Web site, http://www.harshalom. org/ (February 28, 2012), "Deborah Bodin Cohen."
Deborah Bodin Cohen Home Page, http://deborahbodin cohen.com (March 1, 2012).*

*   *   *

COOK, Kristi
(Kristi Astor, Kristina Cook)

Personal

Born June 29; married; children: two daughters. *Education:* University of Southern Mississippi, degree.

Addresses

Home—Riverdale, NY. *E-mail*—AuthorKristiCook@aol. com.

Career

Writer. Former nursery-school teacher and grant writer.

Writings

Haven, Simon Pulse (New York, NY), 2011.
Mirage, Simon Pulse (New York, NY), 2012.

AS KRISTINA COOK

Unlaced, Zebra Books (New York, NY), 2004.
Unveiled, Zebra Books (New York, NY), 2005.
Undressed, Zebra Books (New York, NY), 2006.
To Love a Scoundrel, Zebra Books (New York, NY), 2007.

AS KRISTI ASTOR

A Midnight Clear, Zebra Books (New York, NY), 2010.

Contributor to fiction anthologies.

Sidelights

Haven, Kristi Cook's first novel for a young-adult audience, has earned comparisons to Stephanie Meyer's wildly popular "Twilight" series of paranormal romances. In *Haven* Cook (who also writes for adults under a variety of pseudonyms) introduces Violet McKenna, the newest student at Winterhaven, an exclusive

Kristi Cook (Photograph by Tara Kearney. Reproduced by permission.)

boarding school located in New York state. Violet has a history of seizures, and she now realizes that she is actually experiencing precognitive visions, which always concern people she loves and—sadly and perhaps significantly—always end in violence.

Once enrolled at Winterhaven, Violet learns from her roommate, Cece, that the school caters to a special breed of student: those who possess psychic abilities. As her gifts flourish in this new environment, the teen finds herself drawn to an engaging and attractive schoolmate named Aidan. Their relationship blossoms, and eventually Violet learns that Aidan is actually a vampire who hopes to use Winterhaven's facilities to discover a cure for his condition. After his research is mysteriously sabotaged, Violet has a strange vision of Aidan covered in blood, and she worries that she might now be his preordained killer.

In a review of *Haven*, Amy Sisson remarked in Voice of Youth Advocates that Cook's prose is natural and smooth, and the boarding school setting is enjoyable. *School Library Journal* contributor Samantha Larsen Hastings observed of the novel that the author "uses well-known vampire lore and twists it a little to create her own vampire/psychic world." "With a brooding, almost hypnotic atmosphere," according to *Booklist* contributor Melissa Moore, "the story's pace is relentless."

Biographical and Critical Sources

PERIODICALS

Booklist, January 1, 2011, Melissa Moore, review of *Haven,* p. 96.
Bulletin of the Center for Children's Books, February, 2011, Kate Quealy-Gainer, review of *Haven,* p. 274.
School Library Journal, March, 2011, Samantha Larsen Hastings, review of *Haven,* p. 158.
Voice of Youth Advocates, April, 2011, Amy Sisson, review of *Haven,* p. 77.

ONLINE

Kristi Cook Home Page, http://kristi-cook.com (March 1, 2012).
Simon & Schuster Web site, http://authors.simonandschuster.com/ (March 1, 2012), "Kristi Cook Revealed."*

* * *

COOK, Kristina
See COOK, Kristi

* * *

COOPER, Rose 1978-

Personal
Born 1978; stepfather a mortician; married; husband's name Carl; children: three sons. *Hobbies and other interests:* Chocolate.

Addresses
Home—Sacramento, CA. *Agent*—Rosemary Stimola, Stimola Literary Studio, 308 Livingston Ct., Edgewater, NJ 07020. *E-mail*—Email@Rose-Cooper.com.

Career
Author and illustrator. *Exhibitions:* Work exhibited at galleries in Northern CA.

Member
Society of Children's Book Writers and Illustrators.

Writings

SELF-ILLUSTRATED; "BLOGTASTIC" MIDDLE-GRADE NOVEL SERIES

Gossip from the Girls' Room, Delacorte Press (New York, NY), 2011.

Rumors from the Boys' Room, Delacorte Press (New York, NY), 2011.

Secrets from the Sleeping Bag, Delacorte Press (New York, NY), 2012.

Author's work has been translated into several languages, including Chinese, Greek, Hebrew, Portuguese, Spanish, and Vietnamese.

OTHER

Contributor of humor articles and columns to periodicals.

Sidelights

A self-taught artist who is based in California, Rose Cooper weaves her own illustrations through the text of her "Blogtastic" series of middle-grade novels. Cooper honed her quirky sense of humor while growing up as a mortician's daughter, and she took her first publishers' rejection in stride by the time she hit her teens. She eventually hit her stride writing humorous articles and columns for the periodical market, but still she continued to dream of seeing her byline adorning the cover of a novel. Shifting her intended audience to younger teens did the trick, and since producing her first novel, *Gossip from the Girls' Room,* Cooper has let her irrepressible preteen heroine dictate her further adventures in *Rumors from the Boys' Room* and *Secrets from the Sleeping Bag.*

Sixth grader Sofia Becker keeps a secret notebook, and her scribblings there are the source of Cooper's humorous story in *Gossip from the Girls' Room.* A chronicle of the ups and downs of life at Middlebrooke Middle School, the novel also chronicles Sophia's efforts at making it into the school's popular clique and besting arch rival Mia St. Claire, an attempt that yields more downs than ups. Hoping to be noticed by the girls she calls the Pretties, she and best friend Nona take the class they take and play the sports they play, all to no avail. Now that her mom begins work as the school's substitute Spanish teacher, Sophia fears that she will wander Middlebrooke's social wasteland forever, or at least until ninth grade. However, being a nobody has its benefits: Because Sandy is socially invisible, private conversations between more-popular classmates do not end when she enters the room. All sorts of juicy gossip is transcribed in her notebook and then exposed in an anonymous post on the school blog, making Sophia the talk of Middlebrooke even though nobody knows her identity. Gossip can take on a life of its own, as the preteen soon discovers, and trying to take back a hurtful remark posted on the Internet is pretty much impossible.

Comparing *Gossip from the Girls' Room* to Jeff Kinney's "Diary of a Wimpy Kid" books, Shauna Yusko added in *Booklist* that Cooper's "humorous take on trying to fit in will find wide appeal." The novel "keenly captures Sofia's quintessential preteen voice," asserted a

Kirkus Reviews writer, and her "spunky" albeit self-involved commentary teams well with Cooper's "hilarious sketches" of stick-figured classmates and what a *Publishers Weekly* critic characterized as "her feeble attempts at matchmaking."

Biographical and Critical Sources

PERIODICALS

Booklist, January 1, 2011, Shauana Yusko, review of *Gossip from the Girls' Room,* p. 104.

Bulletin of the Center for Children's Books, January, 2011, Hope Morrison, review of *Gossip from the Girls' Room,* p. 231.

Kirkus Reviews, December 15, 2010, review of *Gossip from the Girls' Room.*

Publishers Weekly, December 6, 2010, review of *Gossip from the Girls' Room,* p. 49.

School Library Journal, March, 2011, Brenda Kahn, review of *Gossip from the Girls' Room,* p. 158.

ONLINE

Rose Cooper Home Page, http://www.rose-cooper.com (March 1, 2012).*

*   *   *

COULOUMBIS, Audrey

Personal

Born in Springfield, IL; married Akila Couloumbis (an actor and director; died, 2009); children: Nikki, Zachary.

Addresses

Home—NY; and FL. *Agent*—Jill Grinberg Literary Management, 244 5th Ave., 11th Fl., New York, NY 10001.

Career

Writer. Worked variously as a housekeeper, sweater designer, and school custodian.

Awards, Honors

Newbery Honor Book citation, American Library Association, 2000, for *Getting Near to Baby.*

Writings

NOVELS

Just before Daybreak, St. Martin's Press (New York, NY), 1987.

Getting Near to Baby, Putnam (New York, NY), 1999.

Say Yes, Putnam (New York, NY), 2002.

Summer's End, Putnam (New York, NY), 2005.

The Misadventures of Maude March; or, Trouble Rides a Fast Horse, Random House (New York, NY), 2005.

Maude March on the Run; or, Trouble Is Her Middle Name, Random House (New York, NY), 2007.

Love Me Tender, Random House (New York, NY), 2008.

(With Akila Couloumbis) *War Games: A Novel Based on a True Story,* Random House (New York, NY), 2009.

Jake, Random House (New York, NY), 2010.

Lexie, illustrated by Julia Denos, Random House (New York, NY), 2011.

Not Exactly a Love Story, Random House Children's Books (New York, NY), 2012.

Sidelights

Audrey Couloumbis writes novels for both young teens and 'tween, among them the acclaimed young-adult novel *Getting Near to Baby* and middle-grade fiction such as *Say Yes, Jake,* and *Lexie.* "Everything you want to know about a person will be in their books," Cou-

Featuring an illustration by Ian Schoenherr, Audrey Couloumbis's award-winning novel Getting Near to Baby, was published in 1999. (Illustration copyright © 1999 by Ian Schoenherr. Reproduced by permission of G.P. Putnam's Sons, a division of Penguin Young Readers Group, a member of Penguin Group (USA) Inc., 375 Hudson Street, New York, NY 10014. All rights reserved.)

loumbis told *Teacher Librarian* interviewer Teri S. Lesesne in discussing the inspiration for her stories. "Even when the characters and the events resemble nothing of their actual life, you are reading the approach they take to life, their path. Writers bring all that they meet on the road to their work."

Born in Illinois, Couloumbis developed an early interest in storytelling, often creating "serial stories that I told myself, like a kind of internal radio program complete with different voices and an assortment of subplots," as she related to Lesesne. Around age twelve she "finally make the connection to putting stories on paper, just in time to thoroughly mortify my mother with uncensored accounts of what life was like at our house. Writing was then forbidden, but it was too late; I'd already discovered the joy of creating and recreating happy endings for anything life threw at me."

Published in 1987, Couloumbis's debut novel *Getting Near to Baby* was described as "an exquisitely crafted story of loss, family love, and new beginnings" by *School Library Journal* critic Barbara Wysocki. The story concerns two young girls whose lives are changed by tragedy. Following the death of their baby sister and their mother's subsequent bout of depression, twelve-year-old Willa Jo and Little Sister reluctantly move in with their loving but controlling Aunt Patty. Events come to a head one day when Patty discovers the sisters sitting on the roof of her house, steadfastly refusing to come down. "The author's plainly worded but evocative descriptions give life to the characters and tender poignancy to even simple observations," noted *Horn Book* contributor Lauren Adams in a review of *Getting Near to Baby,* and a *Publishers Weekly* critic concluded that "the combined strength of [Couloumbis's] . . . unforgettable cast of characters leaves a lasting and uplifting impression."

A twelve year old arrives home from school to find that her stepmother has abandoned her in Couloumbis's *Say Yes,* another novel for middle graders. Frightened, alone, and penniless, Casey enlists the aid of Paulie, the son of her apartment's superintendent, but he ends up involving her in a burglary. "Rather than drawing clear lines between villains and heroes in this modern-day survival tale, Couloumbis invents realistically complex characters, whose morals are tested by fear and desperation," observed a reviewer discussing *Say Yes* in *Publishers Weekly.*

Other troubled families are a feature of Couloumbis's novels *Love Me Tender, Lexie,* and *Jake.* In *Love Me Tender* Elvira lives in a tense family where affection is very rare, and she competes with younger sister Kerrie for any scrap of love that her constantly quarreling parents might throw their way. Mel has not spoken to her own family in years. When her mom becomes pregnant, Elvira's father escapes from the situation and heads to Las Vegas for a break from the drama. Then Elvira's mom gets a phone call with news that her own mother may be dying. A sudden road trip to Tennessee and the healing that follows rebuild generational relationships as well as strengthening the sibling bonds between Elvira and Kerrie. Predicting that preteens "will enjoy the humor" in *Love Me Tender,* Ilene Cooper added in *Booklist* that Elvira's first-person narration "will carry many of them through the story," and a *Kirkus Reviews* critic cited "Couloumbis's rich realistic dialogue" as well as the "happy ending [that] is never in doubt" as among the novel's strengths. Reviewing *Love Me Tender* in *Publishers Weekly,* a contributor asserted that the story's "winning, witty portrayal of a slightly neurotic American family encapsulates universal truths about family relationships."

In *Jake* a ten year old realizes what it takes to be a grown up when his widowed mother accidentlaly breaks her leg and goes to the hospital. With no one else to call, Jake's paternal grandfather travels to Jake's home to take care of the boy, bringing along his misbehaving dog Max. Worried that his gruff grandpa will be hard to live with, the boy is relieved to find out otherwise. Because it is the holiday season, neighbors and casual friends also extend a caring hand to the boy and his

Cover of Couloumbis's middle-grade coming-of-age novel Jake, *featuring artwork by Antonio Javier Cáparo.* (Jacket cover copyright © 2010 by Yearling. Reproduced by permission of Yearling, an imprint of Random House Children's Book, a division of Random House, Inc.)

mom, creating a supportive wall that helps Jake experience security for the first time. Writing in *Booklist,* Hazel Rochman predicted that Couloumbis's story "about the meaning of family will touch readers," and a *Kirkus Reviews* writer noted that *Jake* features "the sort of kind, supportive people young readers should know in life as in literature." "A slice-of-life novel filled with warmth and quiet humor," according to a *Publishers Weekly* critic, *Jake* "confirms that . . . family love can overcome obstacles."

Another ten year old is the focus of *Lexie,* and this time Couloumbis's story focuses on a family's changing dynamic as the consequence of divorce. While she traditionally spends part of her summer at the beach, this year Lexie is joining her father and Vicky, his new girlfriend, while Mom vacations elsewhere. Having to share her father's attention with Vicky is bad enough, but the woman has two sons of her own who will also be sharing the family's summer house. Couloumbis's "precisely worded story explores the nuances of Lexie's feelings" about her changing world," wrote Phelan in *Booklist,* and a *Kirkus Reviews* writer noted that the "convincing characters and solid dialogue" in the novel "enhance the credible plot" that reflects the girl's confusion, betrayal, and gradual acceptance. Avoiding a pert and happy ending, the author shows all three children recognizing that they "are caught in an inevitable situation and might just make the best of it," according to *Horn Book* reviewer Betty Carter, and Faith Brautigam wrote in *School Library Journal* that *Lexie* benefits from a "keenly observant narrator" who "makes a fine reporter as the two families work toward creating a new kind of normal."

In *Summer's End* Couloumbis examines the effects of the Vietnam War on an American family. When Grace's older brother, Collin, burns his draft card at an anti-war protest, he enrages his stepfather, who throws the teenager out of the house. When Grace's mother speaks out in support of Collin's decision, it creates such a rift in the family that Grace retreats to her grandmother's farm. Paula Rohrlick, writing in *Kliatt,* stated that *Summer's End* "adeptly captures the confusion of the times," and *Booklist* contributor Gillian Engberg noted that Couloumbis's story explores "a family's complex sorrow, anger, and love with incisive clarity and honesty."

In *War Games: A Novel Based on a True Story* Couloumbis collaborated with husband Akila Couloumbis to recall a story from his experiences growing up in a small town in Greece during World War II. Twelve-year-old Petros and older brother Zola watch as Nazi troops arrive at their town, and soon a German officer is garrisoned with their family. The brothers have reason to fear the officer's presence in their home: older cousin Landros is active in the Greek underground and the brothers are actually citizens of the United States, which is about to enter the war on the side of the Allied powers. "A gripping story that's also a fine introduction to a complex time," according to *Horn Book* critic

Joanna Rudge Long, *War Games* is "lively with dialogue." A *Publishers Weekly* contributor recommended the Couloumbiss' novel as a "poignant and plainspoken account of the everyday impacts of a vast war and the importance of small victories." Sadly, *War Games* would be the couple's only collaboration: it was published in 2009, the year of Akila Couloumbis's death.

A pair of orphaned sisters creates havoc in the Old West in Couloumbis's historical novel *The Misadventures of Maude March; or, Trouble Rides a Fast Horse*. While heading to Missouri to locate their last remaining relative, eleven-year-old Sallie March and older sister Maude become the object of sensational newspaper stories after they inadvertently steal some horses, rob a bank, and gun down an outlaw. Their adventures continue in *Maude March on the Run!; or, Trouble Is Her Middle Name*, as Sallie and Maude continue their search for Uncle Arlen while also evading the law. Joined by con man Joe Harden, the sisters successfully keep a low profile until Maude's fame catches up with them in the form of a "Wanted" poster with a hefty reward. "Sallie's narration is delightful, with understatements that are laugh-out-loud hilarious," remarked Connie Tyrrell Burns in her *School Library Journal* review of *The Misadventures of Maude March*, and a contributor to *Kirkus Reviews* noted of Couloumbis's novel that "adventure and humor add up to great family entertainment." "Descriptive details . . . are woven seamlessly into the lively story" in *Maude March on the Run!*, noted *School Library Journal* critic Quinby Frank, "and provide [readers with] a real feel for the flavor of the Old West." Calling the second "Maude March" novel "a natural for reading aloud," a *Kirkus Reviews* writer sized up the story's attributes: "humor, rollicking adventure and heroines to root for."

Biographical and Critical Sources

PERIODICALS

Booklist, November 1, 1999, Michael Cart, review of *Getting Near to Baby,* p. 515; May 1, 2002, Hazel Rochman, review of *Say Yes,* p. 1518; July, 2005, Gillian Engberg, review of *The Misadventures of Maude March; or, Trouble Rides a Fast Horse,* p. 1922; February 15, 2008, Ilene Cooper, review of *Love Me Tender,* p. 82; October 1, 2009, Ian Chipman, review of *War Games: A Novel Based on a True Story,* p. 38; September 1, 2010, Hazel Rochman, review of *Jake,* p. 105; July 1, 2011, Carolyn Phelan, review of *Lexie,* p. 60.

Bulletin of the Center for Children's Books, November, 1999, review of *Getting Near to Baby,* p. 88; January, 2006, Loretta Gaffney, review of *The Misadventures of Maude March,* pp. 224-225.

Horn Book, November, 1999, Lauren Adams, review of *Getting Near to Baby,* p. 736; July-August, 2002, Jennifer Brabander, review of *Say Yes,* p. 456; July-August, 2005, Lauren Adams, review of *Summer's End,* p. 468; September-October, 2005, Anita L. Burkam, review of *The Misadventures of Maude March,* p. 575; November-December, 2009, Joanna Rudge Long, review of *War Games,* p. 665; July-August, 2011, Betty Carter, review of *Lexie,* p. 146.

Kirkus Reviews, April 15, 2002, review of *Say Yes,* p. 565; April 15, 2005, review of *Summer's End,* p. 470; September 1, 2005, review of *The Misadventures of Maude March,* p. 970; December 15, 2006, review of *Maude March on the Run!, or Trouble Is Her Middle Name;* April 1, 2008, review of *Love Me Tender;* September 1, 2009, review of *War Games;* August 15, 2010, review of *Jake;* May 1, 2011, review of *Lexie.*

Kliatt, July, 2005, Paula Rohrlick, review of *Summer's End,* p. 10.

New York Times Book Review, January 17, 2010, Julie Just, review of *War Games,* p. 13.

Publishers Weekly, September 13, 1999, review of *Getting Near to Baby,* p. 85; May 6, 2002, review of *Say Yes,* p. 59; August 15, 2005, review of *The Misadventures of Maude March,* pp. 58-59; March 3, 2008, review of *Love Me Tender,* p. 47; October 26, 2009, review of *War Games,* p. 58; August 30, 2010, review of *Jake,* p. 53.

School Library Journal, December, 1999, review of *Getting Near to Baby,* p. 40; July, 2002, B. Allison Gray, review of *Say Yes,* p. 118; June, 2005, Connie Tyrrell Burns, review of *Summer's End,* p. 153; September, 2005, Connie Tyrrell Burns, review of *The Misadventures of Maude March,* pp. 202-203; January, 2007, Quinby Frank, review of *Maude March on the Run!,* p. 126; April, 2008, Jennifer Ralston, review of *Love Me Tender,* p. 139; October, 2009, Kathleen Isaacs, review of *War Games,* p. 124; October, 2010, Eva Mitnick, review of *Jake,* p. 70; July, 2011, Faith Brautigam, review of *Lexie,* p. 64.

Teacher Librarian, June, 2003, Teri S. Lesesne, interview with Couloumbis, pp. 46-48.

ONLINE

Audrey Couloumbis Home Page, http://www.audrey couloumbis.com (March 1, 2012).*

D-F

DAVIS, Rebecca Fjelland 1956-

Personal

Born 1956, in IA; married Terry Davis (an author; divorced); children. *Education:* Waldorf College, associates degree; St. Cloud State University, B.A. (English); Minnesota State University, M.F.A. (creative writing). *Hobbies and other interests:* Cycling, dogs, spending time with friends and family.

Addresses

Home—Good Thunder, MN. *Agent*—Sterling Lord Literistic, 65 Bleeker St., New York, NY 10012. *E-mail*—rfd@rebeccafjellanddavis.com.

Career

Author and educator. South Central College, Mankato, MN, instructor in composition, literature and film, and humanities.

Awards, Honors

Artist Initiative grant, Minnesota State Arts Board; Blue Ribbon in Fiction selection, *Bulletin of the Center for Children's Books,* 2003, for *Jake Riley: Irreparably Damaged;* Loft Awards for Children's Literature honorable mention, 2007, for *Chasing AllieCat.*

Writings

Rebecca Fjelland Davis (Photograph by Steve Deger. Reproduced by permission.)

SELF-ILLUSTRATED

Jake Riley: Irreparably Damaged, HarperCollins (New York, NY), 2003.

Beaches and Bicycles: A Summer Counting Book, Capstone Press (Mankato, MN), 2006.

Flowers and Showers: A Spring Counting Book, Capstone Press (Mankato, MN), 2006.

Footballs and Falling Leaves: A Fall Counting Book, Capstone Press (Mankato, MN), 2006.

Snowflakes and Ice Skates: A Winter Counting Book, Capstone Press (Mankato, MN), 2006.

10, 9, 8 Polar Animals!: A Counting Backward Book, Capstone Press (Mankato, MN), 2007.

Counting Pets by Twos, Capstone Press (Mankato, MN), 2007.

More or Less: A Rain Forest Counting Book, Capstone Press (Mankato, MN), 2007.

Zoo Animals 1, 2, 3, Capstone Press (Mankato, MN), 2007.

Woof and Wag: Bringing Home a Dog, illustrated by Andi Carter, Picture Window Books (Minneapolis, MN), 2009.

Chasing AllieCat, Flux (Woodbury, MN), 2011.

Girl Meets Boy: There Are Two Sides to Every Story, Chronicle Books (San Francisco, CA), 2012.

Contributor to anthology *Girl Meets Boy,* Chronicle Books (San Francisco, CA), 2012.

Author's work has been translated into Spanish.

Biographical and Critical Sources

PERIODICALS

Booklist, September 1, 2003, Michael Cart, review of *Jake Riley: Irreparably Damaged,* p. 112; January 1, 2011, Karen Cruze, review of *Chasing AllieCat,* p. 92.

Bulletin of the Center for Children's Books, July, 2003, review of *Jake Riley,* p. 441.

Kirkus Reviews, May 15, 2003, review of *Jake Riley,* p. 749.

Publishers Weekly, June 30, 2003, review of *Jake Riley,* p. 81; January 10, 2011, review of *Chasing AllieCat,* p. 51.

School Library Journal, July, 2003, Francisca Goldsmith, review of *Jake Riley,* p. 128; January, 2009, Kara Schaff Dean, review of *Woof and Wag: Bringing Home a Dog,* p. 89; March, 2011, Carol A. Edwards, review of *Chasing AllieCat,* p. 158.

Voice of Youth Advocates, October, 2003, review of *Jake Riley,* p. 302; December, 2010, Lucy Schall, review of *Chasing AllieCat,* p. 450.

ONLINE

Book Cellar Web log, http://thebookcellarx.com/ (February 2, 2012), Kelly Millner Halls, interview with Davis.

Rebecca Fjelland Davis Home Page, http://www.rebecca fjellanddavis.com (March 3, 2012).

Rebecca Fjelland Davis Web log, http://rebeccafjelland ddavis.blogspot.com (March 3, 2012).

*　　*　　*

DEVLIN, Ivy
See SCOTT, Elizabeth

*　　*　　*

EVANS, Shane W.

Personal

Married Yukie Heard (an accountant), 2006; children: Yurie (daughter). *Education:* Syracuse University, B.A., 1993. *Hobbies and other interests:* Playing guitar, songwriting, traveling.

Addresses

Home—MO. *Office*—Dream Studio, 711 E. 31st St., Kansas City, MO 64110.

Career

Children's book illustrator and graphic and Web designer. Hallmark Cards, Kansas City, MO, card designer, for seven years; freelance illustrator; Dream Studio, Kansas City, owner and founder, 2009—. Contributor to Disney Channel animated television series *Homemade Love.* Beans and Rice Productions (MCA Records), creative director and musician, 2001-02. Designer of furniture and clothing; photographer. Presenter at schools, conferences, workshops, and festivals.

Awards, Honors

Boston Globe/Horn Book Honor Book designation, and Orbis Pictus Honor Book Award for nonfiction, both 2000, both for *Osceola,* edited by Alan Govenar; honored at National Book Festival, 2002; International Reading Association Children's Book Award Notable Book designation; Lee Bennett Hopkins Honor Book designation, Pennsylvania Center for the Book, 2004, for *The Way a Door Closes* by Hope Anita Smith; named Volunteer of the Year, American Civil Liberties Union (KS and Western MO chapter), 2009; NAACP Image Award for literature, National Association for the Advancement of Colored People, 2011, for *My Brother Charlie* by Holly Robinson Peete, Ryan Elizabeth Peete, and Denene Millner; Coretta Scott King Book Award, American Library Association, 2012, for *Underground.*

Writings

SELF-ILLUSTRATED

Olu's Dream, Katherine Tegen Books (New York, NY), 2009.

Underground: Finding the Light to Freedom, Roaring Brook Press (New York, NY), 2011.

We March, Roaring Brook Press (New York, NY), 2012.

ILLUSTRATOR

Angela Johnson, *Gone from Home,* DK Ink (New York, NY), 1998.

Shaquille O'Neal, *Shaq and the Beanstalk and Other Very Tall Tales,* Scholastic (New York, NY), 1999.

Quincy Troupe, *Take It to the Hoop, Magic Johnson,* Jump at the Sun (New York, NY), 2000.

Angela Johnson, *Down the Winding Road,* DK Ink (New York, NY), 2000.

Alan Govenar, editor, *Osceola: Memories of a Sharecropper's Daughter,* Hyperion (New York, NY), 2000.

Sylviane A. Diouf, *Bintou's Braids,* Chronicle Books (San Francisco, CA), 2001.

Doreen Rappaport, *No More! Stories and Songs of Slave Resistance,* Candlewick Press (Cambridge, MA), 2002.

bell hooks, *Homemade Love,* Hyperion (New York, NY), 2002.

Alice McGill, *Here We Go Round,* Houghton Mifflin (Boston, MA), 2002.

Hope Anita Smith, *The Way a Door Closes,* Henry Holt (New York, NY), 2003.

Andrea Davis Pinkney, *Fishing Day,* Jump at the Sun (New York, NY), 2003.

Doreen Rappaport, *Free at Last! Stories and Songs of Emancipation,* Candlewick Press (Cambridge, MA), 2004.

Deloris Jordan with Roslyn M. Jordan, *Did I Tell You I Love You Today?,* Simon & Schuster (New York, NY), 2004.

Catherine Clinton, *Hold the Flag High,* Katherine Tegen Books (New York, NY), 2005.

Carol Maillard, *Still the Same Me,* Simon & Schuster (New York, NY), 2005.

Doreen Rappaport, *Nobody Gonna Turn Me 'Round: Stories,* Candlewick Press (Cambridge, MA), 2006.

Nikki Grimes, *When Gorilla Goes Walking,* Orchard Books (New York, NY), 2007.

Catherine Clinton, *When Harriet Met Sojourner,* Katherine Tegen Books (New York, NY), 2007.

Kathy Whitebread, *Art from Her Heart: Folk Artist Clementine Hunter,* G.P. Putnam's Sons (New York, NY), 2008.

Holly Robinson Peete, Ryan Elizabeth Peete, and Daneine Miller, *My Brother Charlie,* Scholastic Press (New York, NY), 2010.

Charles R. Smith, *Black Jack: The Ballad of Jack Johnson,* Roaring Brook Press (New York, NY), 2010.

Donna L. Washington, *Li'l Rabbit's Kwanzaa,* Katherine Tegen Books (New York, NY), 2010.

Taye Diggs, *Chocolate Me!,* Feiwel & Friends (New York, NY), 2011.

ILLUSTRATOR; "SHANNA'S FIRST READERS" SERIES BY JEAN MARZOLLO

Shanna's Princess Show, Jump at the Sun (New York, NY), 2001.
Shanna's Doctor Show, Jump at the Sun (New York, NY), 2001.
Shanna's Ballerina Show, Jump at the Sun (New York, NY), 2002.
Shanna's Teacher Show, Jump at the Sun (New York, NY), 2002.

Adaptations

Jean Marzollo's "Shanna's First Readers" series, featuring Evans's art, was adapted as both a Disney cartoon and the television program *Shanna's Kindergarten Countdown.* Marzollo's 2004 beginning readers *Shanna's Animal Riddles* and *Shanna's Party Surprise,* with illustrations by Maryn Roos, are also based on Evans's artwork.

Sidelights

A recipient of the prestigious Coretta Scott King Book Award, Missouri-based illustrator and graphic artist Shane W. Evans has garnered acclaim for his contribu-

tions to dozens of books for children. Known primarily for his bold, stylized, mixed-media artwork, Evans has collaborated on book projects with celebrity authors that include *Shaq and the Beanstalk and Other Very Tall Tales* by basketball star Shaquille O'Neal, as well as with actress Holly Robinson Peete. He also brings elements of African-American history to life in his pictures for Catherine Clinton's *When Harriet Met Sojourner* and Charles R. Smith's *Black Jack: The Ballad of Jack Johnson.*

Recalling his transition from graphic design to book illustration, Evans explained to interviewer Don Tate for the *Brown Bookshelf* Web site: "From . . . child[hood] I was fascinated by the art and as an adult I could see the creative diversity in books for children." He continued, "My illustrating of books actually came from showing a body of work that I created after I got back from West Africa. It was a very expressive body of work that had an interesting story-telling element to it."

Described by a *Horn Book* contributor as "formally composed paintings that gently evoke [the] character of both people and place," Evans' work for Alan Govenar's award-winning *Osceola: Memories of a Share-*

Here We Go Round, *Alice McGill's picture-book story about a close-knit multigenerational family, comes to life in Shane W. Evans' line art.* (Illustration copyright © 2002 by Shane W. Evans. Reprinted by permission of Houghton Mifflin Harcourt Publishing Company. All rights reserved.)

Nikki Grimes' story of a housecat with attitude is brought to life in Evans' artwork for **When Gorilla Goes Walking.** (Illustration copyright © 2007 by Shane W. Evans. Reprinted by permission of Scholastic, Inc.)

cropper's Daughter open a window onto the long life of ninety-one-year-old Texas native Osceola Mays. Reviewing Doreen Rappaport's *Free at Last! Stories and Songs of Emancipation* for *Kirkus Reviews,* a writer cited the "passion and power" created by the Rappaport/Evans collaboration, noting that Evans' "glowing, almost monumental oils convey the pent-up anger and sadness" of blacks during the Reconstruction era. In *Booklist* Hazel Rochman praised the individual portraits in the book, writing that they "celebrate the courage of people who helped break the color line," and Joanna Rudge Long asserted in *Horn Book* that the artist's "powerful, page-filling paintings of stalwart figures of serious mien, lend . . . drama to the simply described events." An imagined meeting between former slaves and abolitionists Harriet Tubman and Sojourner Truth is the subject of *When Harriet Met Sojourner,* a picture book in which "Evans's dramatic collage-style illustrations evoke the quilts the women worked on, piecing together their history," according to Rochman.

Evans also focuses on the mid-nineteenth century in two books by Catherine Clinton: *Hold the Flag High* and *When Harriet Met Sojourner.* A story of the Massachusetts 54th, an all-black regiment that fought for the Union Army during the U.S. Civil War, *Hold the Flag High* centers on the close relationships that existed among the members of this ill-fated fighting force, es-

pecially between Ned, the drummer boy, and Sergeant William H. Carney, the first African American to received the Congressional Medal of Honor. In his oil paintings, Evans "capture[s] the mood and action of the battle in a powerful and effective manner," according to *School Library Journal* contributor Lucinda Snyder Whitehurst, the critic adding that "the illustrations convey pain and confusion but [avoid] . . . graphic violence."

Among Evans' other illustration projects are picture books such as *Gorilla Goes Walking,* with a text by Nikki Grimes, and *Bintou's Braids,* Sylviane A. Diouf's story about a young African girl who looks forward to the time when her hair is long enough to be styled like that of the women in her village. *Did I Tell You I Love You Today?,* by the mother-daughter team of Deloris Jordan and Roslyn Jordan, features Evans' bright paintings alongside a text that illustrates the unconditional love of a mother for her child. Reviewing *Did I Tell You I Love You Today?* for *Publishers Weekly,* a contributor wrote that the story's "warmly portrayed characters, generous rounded shapes and velvety, saturated palette will draw readers into . . . the affection and bustle of family life."

In *Bintou's Braids* African girls and women "with their large expressive eyes and warm demeanor . . . gracefully move through Evans's . . . oil paintings in abundant earth tones and bright African batiks," wrote a

Holly Robinson Peete and daughter Ryan Elizabeth Peete share a story about Ryan's autistic brother in **My Brother Charlie,** *featuring artwork by Evans.* (Illustration copyright © 2010 by Shane W. Evans. Reproduced by permission of Scholastic, Inc.)

Publishers Weekly contributor, while in *School Library Journal* Marian Drabkin maintained that the artist's "oil paintings glow in rich tones of gold, sand, and blue." Evans' art has also appeared in several installments of Jean Marzollo's popular "Shanna's First Readers" picture-book series. Geared for elementary-grade girls, books such as *Shanna's Princess Show* and *Shanna's Doctor Show* were also adapted as animated cartoons featuromg Evans' art.

Kathy Whitebread's picture-book biography *Art from Her Heart: Folk Artist Clementine Hunter* chronicles the life of a woman who documented and interpreted the then-vanished world of Southern plantation life. Too poor to afford quality paper, Hunter applied her water-colors to whatever she had on hand—paper bags, window shades, milk jugs, even pieces of wood. According to *School Library Journal* critic Barbara Elleman, Evans' collage illustrations "portray Hunter in hard times and in good. He often focuses on her hands and face, bringing strength and vitality to the pictures."

Peete teams with her daughter, Ryan Elizabeth Peete, on *My Brother Charlie,* a picture book based on their experiences with Holly's son and Ryan's twin brother, RJ, who is autistic. In the story, sister Callie describes the joys and frustrations of living with a sibling who has autism. Evans' mixed-media illustrations for this book earned praise from *School Library Journal* critic Laura Butler, who stated that they "skillfully depict the family's warmth and concern," while *Booklist* contributor Rochman reported that the pictures "show the loving connections in Callie's African American family, as well as the tension and anger." A writer in *Kirkus Reviews* observed that Evans' art for *My Brother Charlie* "employs a lot of texture, adding patterning and interest to the simple, uncluttered design."

Smith tells the story of the first African-American heavyweight boxing champion in *Black Jack.* Jack Johnson, the son of a former slave, won the title in 1908, defeating Canadian Tommy Burns after reigning champion Jim Jeffries refused to fight him because of his race. "Evans . . . draws forms that press forward out of the pages," a reviewer in *Publishers Weekly* noted, and Mary Landrum explained in *School Library Journal* that the illustrator employs "bold colors and strong brushstrokes to convey the athlete's larger-than-life personality." *Booklist* critic Ian Chipman also applauded the "lithe and swaggering artwork" in *Black Jack,* noting that it lends a tremendous visual charisma, grace, and grandeur to" its subject.

In *Li'l Rabbit's Kwanzaa,* a work for younger readers by Donna L. Washington, a young bunny makes a special contribution to a wondrous celebration. Feeling left out of his family's Kwanzaa preparations, Li'l Rabbit decides to make himself useful by informing the neighbors of his grandmother's illness, an action that results in a great surprise. "Evans' fanciful paintings feature a host of helpful animal characters," Roger Sutton com-

Andrea Davis Pinkney teams up with Evans to share a story of friend-ship in **Fishing Day.** (Illustration copyright © 2003 by Shane W. Evans. Reprinted by permission of Disney-Hyperion, an imprint of Disney Book Group, LLC. All rights reserved.)

mented in *Horn Book,* and Rochman concluded that the artist's "playful, textured pictures capture the spirit of community that is the essence of the holiday."

With *Olu's Dream* Evans released his first self-illustrated title. In a *Brown Bookshelf* online interview with Kelly Starling Lyons, he recalled: "The idea for *Olu's Dream* was truly seeded out of life. I was recognizing the blessings in my life and how all of the love that has been around me since I was a child has helped me to live my dreams, not only live them but realize the importance of having them." Ten years in the making, the picture book centers on a rambunctious youngster who lets his imagination soar after his father interrupts his play and sends him to bed. After the lights go out, Olu visualizes himself grappling with monsters, gorging on pizza, and whizzing through space with his trusty sidekick, his teddy bear. A writer in *Kirkus Reviews* noted that Evans' "anime-influenced illustrations depict the spunky protagonist as a wide-eyed, cute-as-a-button child of mixed-race descent."

Evans honors the bravery of the rescuers on the Underground Railroad in another self-illustrated work, *Underground: Finding the Light to Freedom.* Narrated by a group of escaping slaves, the work follows their perilous nighttime journey from the plantation to the freedom of a safe house. "Telling the story without overwhelming readers is a delicate task, but Evans walks the line perfectly," a contributor asserted in *Publishers Weekly.* The "minimalist text is intense," Rochman observed, and Jayne Damron commended the artwork in *School Library Journal,* writing that Evans' "collaged nocturnal paintings shimmer with an arresting luminescence." A writer in *Kirkus Reviews* maintained that, although numerous texts explore the Underground Railroad, "few if any portray the experience with such compelling immediacy" as *Underground.*

Evans' work in children's books is only one facet of his career. In addition to book illustration, he is a graphic artist and Web designer, and he has also been involved in animated film and music production. His Dream Studio, a studio space and art gallery that also serves as a music venue and gathering space for friends and neighbors, is located in Evans's Kansas City, Missouri, neighborhood. "My commitment is to help people dream and not feel bound by race, jobs, relationships or politics," the artist remarked to Jeneé Osterheldt in the *Kansas City Star.*

Biographical and Critical Sources

PERIODICALS

Booklist, February 15, 2000, Michael Cart, review of *Down the Winding Road,* p. 1118; November 15, 2001, Hazel Rochman, review of *Bintou's Braids,* p. 580; May 1, 2003, Hazel Rochman, review of *The Way a Door Closes,* p. 1590; November 15, 2003, Hazel Rochman, review of *Fishing Day,* p. 602; February 15, 2004, Hazel Rochman, review of *Free at Last!: Stories and Songs of Emancipation,* p. 1076; April 15, 2005, Carolyn Phelan, review of *Hold the Flag High,* p. 1451; April 15, 2007, Gillian Engberg, review of *When Gorilla Goes Walking,* p. 44; October 15, 2007, Hazel Rochman, review of *When Harriet Met Sojourner,* p. 50; September 1, 2008, Hazel Rochman, review of *Art from Her Heart: Folk Artist Clementine Hunter,* p. 92; March 1, 2010, Hazel Rochman, review of *My Brother Charlie,* p. 78; April 1, 2010, Ian Chipman, review of *Black Jack,* p. 40; November 1, 2010, Hazel Rochman, review of *Li'l Rabbit's Kwanzaa,* p. 77; February 1, 2011, Hazel Rochman, review of *Underground: Finding the Light to Freedom,* p. 74.

Childhood Education, fall, 2009, Kimberly Bridy, review of *When Harriet Met Sojourner,* p. 54.

Horn Book, March, 2000, review of *Osceola: Memories of a Sharecropper's Daughter,* p. 212; January-February, 2002, Anita L. Burkam, review of *Bintou's Braids,* p. 67; March-April, 2002, Joanna Rudge Long, review of *No More! Stories and Songs of Slave Resistance,* p. 231; May-June, 2004, Joanna Rudge Long, review of *Free at Last!,* p. 346; July-August, 2005, Susan P. Bloom, review of *Hold the Flag High,* p. 483; July-August, 2010, Susan Dove Lempke, review of *Black Jack: The Ballad of Jack Johnson,* p. 137; November-

December, 2010, Roger Sutton, review of *Li'l Rabbit's Kwanzaa,* p. 68; January-February, 2011, Betsy Hearne, review of *Underground,* p. 111.

Kansas City Star (Kansas City, MO), November 15, 2009, Edward M. Eveld, "Award-Winning Illustrator Shane Evans Is Living His Dream"; January 23, 2012, Jeneé Osterheldt, "Book by Artist Shane Evans Earns Coretta King Award."

Kirkus Reviews, December 1, 2002, review of *Homemade Love,* p. 1769; December 15, 2003, review of *Free at Last!,* p. 1454; May 15, 2005, review of *Hold the Flag High,* p. 585; October 15, 2007, review of *When Harriet Met Sojourner;* August 15, 2009, review of *Olu's Dream;* January 15, 2010, review of *My Brother Charlie;* November 15, 2010, review of *Underground.*

Publishers Weekly, October 29, 2001, review of *Bintou's Braids,* p. 63; December 17, 2001, review of *No More!,* p. 91; November 18, 2002, review of *Homemade Love,* p. 59; May 19, 2003, review of *The Way a Door Closes,* p. 74; December 23, 2003, review of *Free at Last!,* p. 62; December 6, 2004, review of *Did I Tell You I Love You Today?,* p. 58; December 3, 2007, review of *When Harriet Met Sojourner,* p. 70; January 25, 2010, review of *My Brother Charlie,* p. 119; June 21, 2010, review of *Black Jack,* p. 45; November 29, 2010, review of *Underground,* p. 47; July 25, 2011, review of *Chocolate Me!,* p. 53.

School Library Journal, May, 2000, Jody McCoy, review of *Down the Winding Road,* p. 146, and Coop Renner, review of *Osceola,* p. 182; December, 2000, Jeffrey A. French, review of *Take It to the Hoop, Magic Johnson,* p. 137; January, 2002, Marian Drabkin, review of *Bintou's Braids,* p. 97; April, 2002, Lauralyn Persson, review of *Here We Go Round,* p. 117; December, 2002, Amy Lilien-Harper, review of *Homemade Love,* p. 97; May, 2003, Mary N. Oluonye, review of *The Way a Door Closes,* p. 177; February, 2004, Tracy Bell, review of *Free at Last!,* p. 168; October, 2004, Mary N. Oluonye, review of *Fishing Day,* p. 65; December, 2004, Tracy Bell, review of *Did I Tell You I Love You Today?,* p. 112; July, 2005, Lucinda Snyder Whitehurst, review of *Hold the Flag High,* p. 88; October, 2006, Mary N. Oluonye, review of *Nobody Gonna Turn Me 'Round,* p. 182; May, 2007, Andrea Tarr, review of *When Gorilla Goes Walking,* p. 97; April, 2008, Robin L. Gibson, review of *When Harriet Met Sojourner,* p. 159; September, 2008, Barbara Elleman, review of *Art from Her Heart,* p. 170; September, 2009, Maryann H. Owen, review of *Olu's Dream,* p. 120; March, 2010, Laura Butler, review of *My Brother Charlie,* p. 129; July, 2010, Mary Landrum, review of *Black Jack,* p. 76; October, 2010, Joanna K. Fabicon, review of *Li'l Rabbit's Kwanzaa,* p. 77; January, 2011, Jayne Damron, review of *Underground,* p. 88.

ONLINE

Brown Bookshelf Web site, http://thebrownbookshelf.com/ (February 26, 2008), Don Tate, interview with Evans; (September 21, 2009) Kelly Starling Lyons, interview with Evans.

Shane W. Evans Home Page, http://www.shaneevans.com (March 1, 2012).*

FEASEY, Steve

Personal

Born in Hertfordshire, England; married; wife's name Zoe; children: one son, one daughter.

Addresses

Home—Hertfordshire, England. *Agent*—Sam Copeland, Rogers, Coleridge & White, 20 Powis Mews, London W11 1JN, England. *E-mail*—steve@stevefeasey.com.

Career

Author. Formerly worked in photographic industry. Coach of rugby leagues; presenter at schools.

Awards, Honors

Waterstone's Children's Book Prize shortlist, 2009, for *Changeling*.

Writings

"CHANGELING"/"WERELING" NOVEL SERIES

Changeling, Macmillan Children's Books (London, England), 2009, published as *Wereling*, Feiwel & Friends (New York, NY), 2010.
Dark Moon, Macmillan Children's Books (London, England), 2009, Feiwel & Friends (New York, NY), 2011.
Blood Wolf, Macmillan Children's Books (London, England), 2009.
Demon Games, Macmillan Children's Books (London, England), 2010.
Zombie Dawn, Macmillan Children's Books (London, England), 2011.

Adaptations

The "Changeling" novels were adapted as e-books.

Sidelights

In his career as an author, Steve Feasey will readily admit that he is a "late starter" he noted on his home page that he began writing only after turning thirty years old. Tapping his childhood love of adventure novels, as well as his interest in Greek mythology and monster lore, Feasey decided to balance the scales of teen horror fiction in his "Changeling" series of novels for teen readers. The author has worked in the photographic industry for many years, and his ability to succinctly capture visual—and often visceral—imagery has helped his "Changeling" books—*Wereling, Dark Moon, Blood Wolf,* among them—engage even reluctant readers.

Because vampire stories have proliferated, often morphing into paranormal romances in the wake of Stephenie Meyer's popular "Twilight" series, other creatures

of the night—namely werewolves—have become underrepresented. The werewolf's extreme transformation from human to animal is a dramatic one, and it is something that fourteen-year-old orphan Trey Laporte never imagined he would actually experience. However, when he meets Lucien Charron, Trey learns about his strange destiny and finally makes sense of the strange bouts of amnesia he has recently experienced. Lucien is a vampire who vowed to Trey's father that he would watch over his son and teach him to tame the transforming power which revealed itself at puberty. A werewolf through heredity, Trey now feels his wolf side fighting for release, even as Lucien hopes to control it so that the teen can help him in his ongoing battle against creatures of evil intent. With the help of his vampiric mentor as well as Lucien's sorceress daughter Alexa and human friend Tom O'Callahan, Trey focuses his animal aggression against Lucian's evil brother Caliban and his dark army.

Published in Feasey's native England as *Changeling*, *Wereling* was described by *Booklist* critic Daniel Kraus as a "propulsive blend of action and myth" fueled by

Cover of Steve Feasey's paranormal mystery Wereling, *which introduces a teen dealing with an unsettling genetic legacy.* (Jacket cover photograph © 2010 by Gary Spector. Reproduced by permission of Feiwel & Friends Book, an imprint of Macmillan Children's Books, a division of Macmillan Publishers, Ltd.)

descriptive language "a notch above" that typical of the genre. "Feasey kicks off a gripping new series" in *Wereling,* asserted a *Publishers Weekly* contributor, the reviewer adding that the story's "world building is solid, the characters believable, and the action genuine." In *School Library Journal* Samantha Larsen Hastings noted the "technological twist" Feasey gives to the werewolf tradition while predicting that both "paranormal fans and reluctant readers will feast on this fast-paced . . . tale."

Feasey's "Changeling" series continues in *Dark Moon,* as the werewolf mythology is further refined. While some werewolves transform into brutal beasts lusting for blood, Trey remains half-human in his wolfen shape and can both sense and act on his emotions. As the battle with Caliban comes to a close, Lucien is seriously injured, leaving Trey and his friends searching for a way to restore the vampire's power. In *Blood Wolf* Trey faces a new challenge, teaming up with Alexa and Tom to battle a plague of supernatural creatures that includes a parasitic demon called a necrotroph. Alexa is kidnaped in *Demon Games,* forcing Trey to search for her in the shadowy Netherworld, where a battle to the death awaits him, and the young werewolf's adventures conclude in *Zombie Dawn.*

Writing in *Booklist,* Kraus recommended *Dark Moon* as "solid, boycentric fantasy fare," while for *School Library Journal* reviewer Donna Rosenblum Feasey's second "Changeling" novel draws readers into "an intriguing world full of mystery and suspense" where the "heart-racing" plot leads directly to a "cliff-hanger ending."

Biographical and Critical Sources

PERIODICALS

Booklist, May 15, 2010, Daniel Kraus, review of *Wereling,* p. 51; February 1, 2011, Daniel Kraus, review of *Dark Moon,* p. 78.
Publishers Weekly, April 5, 2010, review of *Wereling,* p. 63.
School Library Journal, August, 2010, Samantha Larsen Hastings, review of *Wereling,* p. 98; February, 2011, Donna Rosenblum, review of *Dark Moon,* p. 106.
Voice of Youth Advocates, August, 2010, Kathleen Beck, review of *Wereling,* p. 265.

ONLINE

Just Imagine Story Centre Web site, http://www.justimagine storycentre.co.uk/ (March 1, 2012), Nicki Gamble, interview with Feasey.
Steve Feasey Home Page, http://www.stevefeasey.com (March 1, 2012).

FREYTES, Silvio 1971-

Personal

Born 1971, in Córdoba, Argentina.

Addresses

Home—Córdoba, Argentina.

Career

Author, director, and filmmaker. Creative director in advertising.

Awards, Honors

Numerous film awards, including from Festival Iberoamericano de Publicidad, Ojo de Iberoamérica, and Lápiz de Oro; Daniel Gil Design Award for Best Children's Book, 2009, for *In Just One Second.*

Writings

Solo un segundo, illustrated by Flavio Morais, Kalandraka Ediciones Andalucia (Argentina), 2007, translated as *In Just One Second,* Wilkins Farago (Albert Park, Victoria, Australia), 2009.

Author of children's books published in Argentina. Author of script for short film *Disparos bajo tierra,* 2005.

Biographical and Critical Sources

PERIODICALS

Kirkus Reviews, October 15, 2010, review of *In Just One Second.*
Magpies, July, 2009, Jo Goodman, review of *In Just One Second,* p. 28.
Publishers Weekly, October 25, 2010, review of *In Just One Second,* p. 48.
Revista la Central, July 6, 2010, Iván Lomascov, interview with Freytes.

ONLINE

Kalandraka Web site, http://www.kalandraka.com/ (March 5, 2012), "Silvio Freytes."*

*   *   *

FRIESNER, Esther 1951-
(Esther M. Friesner)

Personal

Born July 16, 1951, in New York, NY; daughter of David R. (a teacher) and Beatrice (a teacher) Friesner; married Walter Stutzman (a software engineer), December 22, 1974; children: Michael Jacob, Anne Elizabeth. *Education:* Vassar College, B.A. (cum laude; Spanish and drama), 1972; Yale University, M.A. (Spanish), 1975, Ph.D. (Spanish), 1977.

Addresses

Home—Madison, CT. *E-mail*—efriesner@cshore.com.

Career

Writer. Yale University, New Haven, CT, instructor in Spanish, 1977-79, 1983.

Member

Science Fiction Writers of America.

Awards, Honors

Named Outstanding New Fantasy Writer, *Romantic Times,* 1986; Best Science Fiction/Fantasy Titles citation, *Voice of Youth Advocates,* 1988, for *New York by Knight;* Skylark Award, 1994; Nebula Award finalist for Best Novelette, 1995, for *Jesus at the Bat;* Nebula Award for Best Short Story, 1995, for "Death and the Librarian"; Hugo Award finalist, and Nebula Award for Best Short Story, both 1996, both for "A Birthday."

Writings

FICTION

(As Esther M. Friesner) *Harlot's Ruse,* Popular Library (New York, NY), 1986.
(As Esther M. Friesner) *The Silver Mountain,* Popular Library (New York, NY), 1986.
(As Esther M. Friesner) *Druid's Blood,* New American Library (New York, NY), 1988.
(As Esther M. Friesner) *Yesterday We Saw Mermaids,* Tor (New York, NY), 1992.
Wishing Season (young-adult novel), Atheneum (New York, NY), 1993.
(With Laurence Watt-Evans; as Esther M. Friesner) *Split Heirs,* Tor (New York, NY), 1993.
(As Esther M. Friesner) *The Psalms of Herod,* White Wolf Publishing (Stone Mountain, GA), 1995.
The Sherwood Game, Pocket Books (New York, NY), 1995.
Child of the Eagle: A Myth of Rome, Baen (Riverdale, NY), 1996.
The Sword of Mary, White Wolf Publishing (Stone Mountain, GA), 1996.
(With Robert Asprin) *E. Godz,* Baen (Riverdale, NY), 2003.
Temping Fate, Dutton (New York, NY), 2006.
Threads and Flames (historical fiction), Viking (New York, NY), 2010.

"CHRONICLES OF THE TWELVE KINGDOMS" FANTASY SERIES; AS ESTHER M. FRIESNER

Mustapha and His Wise Dog, Avon (New York, NY), 1985.
Spells of Mortal Weaving, Avon (New York, NY), 1986.
The Witchwood Cradle, Avon (New York, NY), 1987.
The Water King's Laughter, Avon (New York, NY), 1989.

"NEW YORK BY KNIGHT" FANTASY SERIES; AS ESTHER M. FRIESNER

New York by Knight, New American Library (New York, NY), 1986.
Elf Defense, New American Library (New York, NY), 1988.
Sphynxes Wild, New American Library (New York, NY), 1989.

"DEMONS" SERIES; FANTASY NOVELS

Here Be Demons, Ace (New York, NY), 1988.
Demon Blues, Ace (New York, NY), 1989.
Hooray for Hellywood, Ace (New York, NY), 1990.

"GNOME MAN'S LAND" FANTASY SERIES

Gnome Man's Land (first volume in trilogy), Ace (New York, NY), 1991.
Harpy High (second volume in trilogy), Ace (New York, NY), 1991.
Unicorn U (third volume in trilogy), Ace (New York, NY), 1992.

"MAJYK" FANTASY SERIES

Majyk by Accident, Ace (New York, NY), 1993.
Majyk by Hook or Crook, Ace (New York, NY), 1994.
Majyk by Design, Ace (New York, NY), 1994.

"PRINCESSES OF MYTH" SERIES

Nobody's Princess, Random House (New York, NY), 2007.
Nobody's Prize, Random House (New York, NY), 2008.
Sphinx's Princess, Random House (New York, NY), 2009.
Sphinx's Queen, Random House (New York, NY), 2010.
Spirit's Princess, Random House (New York, NY), 2012.

"CHICKS IN CHAINMAIL" SERIES; EDITOR AND CONTRIBUTOR

Chicks in Chainmail, Baen (Riverdale, NY), 1995.
Did You Say "Chicks"?!, Baen (Riverdale, NY), 1998.
Chicks 'n' Chained Males, Baen (Riverdale, NY), 1999.
The Chick Is in the Mail, Baen (Riverdale, NY), 2000.
Turn the Other Chick, Baen (Riverdale, NY), 2004.
Chicks Ahoy!, Baen Books (Riverdale, NY), 2010.

SCIENCE FICTION

Warchild ("Star Trek: Deep Space Nine" series), Pocket Books (New York, NY), 1994.

To Storm Heaven ("Star Trek: The Next Generation" series) Pocket Books (New York, NY), 1997.

OTHER

(Editor, with Martin H. Greenberg; as Esther M. Friesner) *Alien Pregnant by Elvis,* DAW (New York, NY), 1994.

(Editor, with Martin H. Greenberg; as Esther M. Friesner) *Blood Muse: Timeless Tales of Vampires in the Arts,* Donald I. Fine (New York, NY), 1995.

(As Esther M. Friesner) *Men in Black II* (based on the screenplay by Robert Gordon and Barry Fanaro), Del Rey (New York, NY), 2002.

Death and the Librarian and Other Stories, Five Star (Waterville, ME), 2002.

(Editor) *Witch Way to the Mall,* Baen (Riverdale, NY), 2009.

(Editor) *Strip Mauled,* Baen (Riverdale, NY), 2009.

Fiction published in anthologies, sometimes under name Esther M. Friesner, including *Elsewhere III,* Ace, 1984; *Afterwar,* Baen, 1985; *Werewolves,* Harper & Row, 1988; *Arabesques II,* Avon, 1989; *Carmen Miranda's Ghost Is Haunting Space Station Three,* Baen, 1990; *Cthulthu 2000,* edited by Jim Turner, Arkham House, 1995; *Newer York,* Roc, 1991; *The Ultimate Frankenstein,* Dell, 1991; *What Might Have Been,* Bantam, 1992; *Snow White, Blood Red,* Morrow, 1993; *Alternate Warriors,* Tor, 1993; *Bet You Can't Read Just One,* edited by Alan Dean Foster, Ace, 1993; *Weird Shakespeare,* edited by Kitt Kerr, DAW Books, 1994; *Excalibur,* edited by Richard Gilliam, Ed Kramer, and Martin H. Greenberg, Warner Books, 1995; *Fantastic Alice,* edited by Margaret Weis, Ace, 1995; *Gothic Ghosts,* edited by Charles Grant and Wendy Webb, Tor, 1997; *The Mammoth Book of Comic Fantasy,* edited by Mike Ashley, Carroll & Graf, 1998; *Black Cats and Broken Mirrors,* edited by Greenberg and Helfers, DAW Books, 1998; *Streets of Blood: Vampire Stories from New York City,* edited by Lawrence Schimel and Greenberg, Cumberland House, 1998; *Merlin,* edited by Greenberg, DAW Books, 1999; *Black Heart, Ivory Bones,* edited by Ellen Datlow and Terri Windling, Avon, 2000; *Single White Vampire Seeks Same,* edited by Brittany A. Koren, DAW Books, 2001; *Knight Fantastic,* edited by Greenberg and John Helfers, DAW Books, 2002; *Murder by Magic,* edited by Rosemary Edghill, Warner Aspect, 2004; *You Bet Your Planet,* edited by Greenberg and Koren, DAW Books, 2005; *My Big Fat Supernatural Wedding,* edited by P.N. Elrod, St. Martin's Griffin, 2006; *Heroes in Training,* edited by Jim Hines, DAW Books, 2007; *Something Magic This Way Comes,* edited by Greenberg and Sarah Hoyt, DAW Books, 2008; and *Full Moon City,* edited by Daryl Schweitzer and Greenberg, Simon & Schuster, 2010. Contributor of short fiction and poetry, sometimes under name Esther M. Friesner, to periodicals, including *Isaac Asimov's Science-Fiction Magazine, Fantasy and Science Fiction, Marion Zimmer Bradley's Fantasy Magazine, Amazing Stories, Fantasy Book, H.P. Lovecraft's Magazine of Horror,* and *Pulphouse.*

Sidelights

Called by Fred Lerner in *Voice of Youth Advocates* "one of the most prolific writers of fantasy fiction, and one of the funniest," Esther Friesner overturns many of the conventions of the fantasy genre. A prolific novelist, Friesner's works include her "New York by Knight" novel series, in which a dragon and his armored pursuer bring their ages-old battle to the streets of modern-day New York, and the "Gnome Man's Land" trilogy, which finds high schooler Tim Desmond forced to cope not only with adolescence, but also with everything from a plague of "little people" to exotic monsters and gods. Other works of fiction find her experimenting with science fiction, while in her "Princesses of Myth" stories she taps teens' fascination with historical figures by imagining the adolescence of famous women in ancient Greece, Egypt, and Japan. Friesner has also flaunted fantasy tradition through her editorship of the multivolume "Chicks in Chainmail" anthologies, which collect penned-by-invitation short stories in which amazons co-opt the heroic role traditionally reserved for

Cover of Split Heirs, *a fantasy coauthored by Esther Friesner and Lawrence Watt-Evans and featuring cover art by Walter Velez.* (Copyright © 1993 by Lawrence Watt-Evans and Esther M. Friesner. Reproduced by permission of St. Martin's Press.)

macho men. "I can't say that there's one particular sort of writing I prefer over another," Friesner remarked to Lazette Gifford in an interview in *Vision: A Resource for Writers.* "Funny, serious, what-you-will, as long as I'm deriving satisfaction from the work at hand, it's good for me."

Born and raised in Brooklyn, New York, Friesner took an early interest in literature. As she once recalled to *SATA:* "My mother told me long stories when we were going on car trips—stories from the works of Washington Irving, for instance. She'd tell me 'The Legend of Sleepy Hollow,' and I kept saying, 'I want another story, I want another story.' Finally she said, 'Look, learn to read and you can have all the stories you want.' So I thought 'That sounds like a good idea,' and I learned to read. Instead of bedtime stories, my father would sit down and read me collections of the 'Pogo' comic strip by Walt Kelly. That was wonderful. It totally warped my sense of humor in just the right way."

Friesner attended Vassar College, studying Spanish and drama, and Yale University, where she earned her master's and doctoral degrees in classical Spanish literature, specializing in the works of playwright Lope de Vega. While attending Yale, she got to know Shariann Lewitt, a published science-fiction author who was then at work on a fantasy novel. "We saw her building a whole world," Friesner once recalled to *SATA,* "working out all the details on a big legal pad she had. This was quite different from writing a short story. I thought, 'Oh, building a world. I get to be God! How nice. I'm going to try that.'"

Friesner's first published novel, *Spells of Mortal Weaving,* became the second volume in her "Chronicles of the Twelve Kingdoms" series. The chronicle begins with the Arabian Nights-styled adventure novel *Mustapha and His Wise Dog,* which is "enlivened by an exotic and evocative fantasy setting, and a pair of captivating characters," according to Don D'Ammassa in *Twentieth-Century Science-Fiction Writers.* The series, which also includes *The Witchwood Cradle* and *The Water King's Laughter,* follows the struggles of various mortals through several generations as they attempt to overthrow Morgeld, an evil demigod. "Although Friesner followed traditional forms for the most part in this series," D'Ammassa concluded, "her wry humor and gift for characterization marked her early as someone to watch."

Friesner's original short fiction has won several awards, and examples are collected in her anthology *Death and the Librarian and Other Stories.* This group of a dozen tales includes the Nebula-winning title story as well as a haunting response to 9/11 titled "Ilion," the poignant "All Vows," and the humorous "True Believer" and "Jesus at the Bat." Praising the title story as "darkly humorous," Jackie Cassada added in *Library Journal* that *Death and the Librarian and Other Stories* "illustrate[s] the author's acutely sensitive vision of wonder in the

everyday world," and *Booklist* critic Paula Luedtke wrote that the collected tales "fearlessly explore the depths and breadths of feeling and experience exquisitely well." Noting the range of emotions that the author skillfully calls forth with her tales, Luedtke added that Friesner "writes boldly, and her wit is sharp, funny, and often wry."

Temping Fate and *Thread and Flames* are among Friesner's standalone novels geared for teens. The first, a humorous story, centers on sardonic, unconventional Ilana Newhouse as she sets about finding a summer job. With help from the Divine Relief Temp Agency, Ilana is sent to work at Tabby Fabricant Textiles, where she soon discovers herself attending to a most unusual task: typing death receipts for the Fates: Clotho, Lachesis, and Atropos. "Teens familiar with Greek mythology will have the most fun with this book," Ginny Gustin noted in *School Library Journal,* and Gillian Engberg maintained in *Booklist* that "the clever, brash concept will easily draw teens."

Far more serious in its approach, *Threads and Flames* is based on an actual incident: the 1911 Triangle Shirtwaist Factory Fire in New York City. As Friesner's story opens, thirteen-year-old Raisa has just arrived in New York City after traveling alone from her home in rural Poland. Hoping to stay with her sister, Henda, and now caring for a toddler orphaned during the trip, Raisa instead finds herself all alone in the strange city, but through resourcefulness she lands a job as a stitcher at the Triangle Shirtwaist Factory, which takes its name from the popular button-down blouse that was popular at the turn of the twentieth century. Over the next few months Raisa begins to build a life in her new home, even makes friends of coworkers who speak Yiddish and becoming part of the city's ethnic community. When the fire breaks out on March 25, 1911, readers share Raisa's terror as she fights for survival in a tragedy where 146 workers would be killed. *Threads and Flames* may inspire comparison to readers' experiences of the September 11, 2001 attacks in the same city, observed a *Kirkus Reviews* writer, and Friesner's "rich" descriptive language makes the story's characters more than "mere trajectories toward tragedy." In *Booklist* Ann O'Malley also praised the author's writing, noting that the "sparkling prose" in *Threads and Flames* "makes the immigrant experience in New York's Lower East Side come alive," while Amanda McFadden predicted in her *Voice of Youth Advocates* review that Friesner's "fast-moving and engrossing" tale will appeal to teens "interested in fictional history coupled with a romantic theme."

The first book in Friesner's "Princesses of Myth" series, *Nobody's Princess* blends myth and fantasy in an entertaining teen-centered story. The story focuses on Helen of Troy, who as a young girl lives in Sparta, where she rejects the life of a princess. Instead, Helen trains to be a warrior alongside her brothers, learning how to wield weapons, hunt and kill game, and ride a horse. Setting her heroine's story against the rich culture of ancient

Greece, with its colorful gods and mythology, Friesner continues Helen's story in *Nobody's Prize,* as the young woman disguises herself as a young man in order to follow Jason and his crew aboard the *Argo* in their quest to find the Golden Fleece.

Cheri Dobbs, reviewing *Nobody's Princess* for *School Library Journal,* predicted that fans of mythology "will enjoy this lively tale," while Claire Rosser claimed in *Kliatt* that Friesner's novel "will please readers interested in ancient Greek legends." Also appraising *Nobody's Prize,* Rosser wrote that the author "clearly is gifted at weaving myth, history, and adventure into an exciting YA novel," and *School Library Journal* critic Beth L. Meister recognized that the "characters are given depth and flaws" while "details about food and customs of the time are woven into the story."

Friesner moves from Greece to Egypt as she continues her "Princesses of Myth" series with *Sphinx's Princess* and *Sphinx's Queen.* Here her focus is Nefertiti, the woman who would one day rule Egypt but who comes from a prosperous merchant family. Curious and courageous, Nefertiti secretly learns to read, and as she grows

Cover of **Nobody's Princess,** *a novel by Friesner that features artwork by Larry Rostant.* (Jacket cover copyright © 2007 by Random House Children's Books. Reproduced by permission of Random House Children's Books, a division of Random House, Inc.)

in beauty she is used by her aunt, Queen Tiye, as an ally and spy at the royal court. In *Sphinx's Queen* the young woman must rebuild her world after her betrothal to Pharaoh's eldest son, Thutmose, is undone by a false accusation of treason. Now a fugitive, Nefertiti is aided by Amenophis, the prince she truly loves, as well as by her faithful slave girl Nara, in making her way home to her family in the hope that they can clear her name before she is captured by Pharaoh's army.

In *Sphinx's Princess* the author melds fact and the work of historians together with her "definite sense of contemporary 'tween/teen princess fantasies," according to a *Kirkus Reviews* writer, and in *Booklist* Kristen McKulski cited the "dramatic plot twists, . . . powerful female subject, and engrossing details of life in ancient Egypt" as elements that should attract readers. The vivid descriptive detail in *Sphinx's Queen* allows Friesner's fans to "learn about and experience an ancient culture," according to *Voice of Youth Advocates* critic Karen Sykeny, while in *School Library Journal* Corinne Henning-Sachs observed that the novel's "fine prose" depicts teen characters engaging in "the questioning of religion that most young people experience as they approach maturity." Noting that the author dramatizes *Sphinx's Queen* to make its impact more vivid, a *Kirkus Reviews* contributor concluded that teens "with a predilection for ancient mythology viewed through the lens of modern mores may enjoy this fantastical read."

Aside from her series work, Friesner is also the author of several stand-alone novels. In *Split Heirs,* which was coauthored with Laurence Watt-Evans, she tells the tale of Gorgonan marauders who take over the city of Hydrangea. The leader of the marauders, Gudge, crowns himself king and forcibly marries the princess of Hydrangea, Artemesia. The couple has triplets, yet the siblings are raised separately, with only one remaining in the palace. According to a *Publishers Weekly* contributor, this plot, peppered with "mistaken identities," results in "a lighthearted fantasy."

Friesner has also teamed up with fellow writer Robert Asprin on *E. Godz,* which follows a successful business woman's efforts to make her children worthy of inheriting her business empire. Edwina Godz is CEO of E.Godz, which supports the nonprofit efforts of magic-related organizations. Because the Godz offspring, Peez and Dov, are more concerned with battling each other than advancing the family business, Edwina feigns a fatal illness and devises a contest through which the siblings learn to deal with each other. Reviewing the novel, *Kliatt* contributor Sherry Hoy dubbed the Friesner-Asprin collaboration "light fun with a touch of Carlos Castaneda."

Ideas for Friesner's fiction can come from overheard conversations, family vacations, newspaper accounts, favorite comics such as Walt Kelly's "Pogo"—just about anywhere, in fact. "Finding ideas for stories has never been a problem for me," she remarked to *Suite101* online interviewer Lynne Jamneck. "They're everywhere! Finding the time to get them all down on paper . . . that's the problem. But it's so satisfying when I get the initial inspiration and am—finally—able to tame it to the point where I'm successfully communicating it to readers."

Friesner views humor as an important ingredient in her works, but not necessarily the defining one. As she mentioned in an *Intergalactic Medicine Show* interview with Darrell Schweitzer, "My reputation seems to still be very much about the comedy. And yet I have almost a shadow-reputation of being able to write very dark things, or certainly serious, if not dark things. Both of my Nebula Award stories were dark stories, especially 'A Birthday.'" Friesner's refusal to pigeonhole her writing is a key to her success, as she told Gifford. "I'm not a funny writer or a serious writer or a fantasy writer or a poet or a playwright. I'm a writer. Either I write in the vein that a particular story demands or I wind up writing a less than satisfactory (for me) story."

"When I write," Friesner once explained to a *SATA* interviewer, "I try to make the story so interesting that I wouldn't mind rereading it myself. . . . It's important

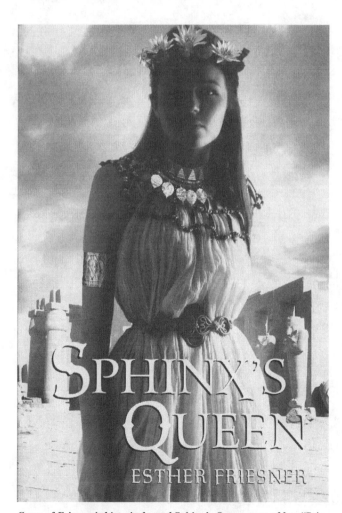

Cover of Friesner's historical novel **Sphinx's Queen,** *part of her "Princesses of Myth" series.* (Jacket cover copyright © 2010 by Random House Children's Books. Reproduced by permission of Random House Children's Book, a division of Random House, Inc.)

to interest your readers because if you don't you won't have readers anymore. But if you don't interest yourself in what you're writing. . . . Well, the process of going from the first draft to the published book takes an awfully long time. You will have to look at that story and those characters a lot—you'll have to do another draft, perhaps even a third, then the editor will go over it, then the copy editor. Every time you're going to be reading the same words. If they aren't good words, you're going to get the feeling of being trapped at a party with people you don't like."

Biographical and Critical Sources

BOOKS

Twentieth-Century Science-Fiction Writers, 3rd edition, St. James Press (Detroit, MI), 1991.

PERIODICALS

Booklist, December 1, 1995, Roland Green, review of *Blood Muse: Timeless Tales of Vampires in the Arts,* p. 609; December 1, 2002, Paula Luedtke, review of *Death and the Librarian and Other Stories,* p. 651; November 1, 2004, Roland Green, review of *Turn the Other Chick,* p. 472; May 15, 2006, Gillian Engberg, review of *Temping Fate,* p. 53; March 15, 2007, Frances Bradburn, review of *Nobody's Princess,* p. 42; February 1, 2008, Frances Bradburn, review of *Nobody's Prize,* p. 42; September 15, 2009, Kristen McKulski, review of *Sphinx's Princess,* p. 52; October 15, 2010, Anne O'Malley, review of *Threads and Flames,* p. 51; November 1, 2010, Shauna Yusko, review of *Sphinx's Queen,* p. 62.

Intergalactic Medicine Show, July, 2008, Darrell Schweitzer, interview with Friesner.

Journal of Adolescent & Adult Literacy, March, 2007, Jennifer Michalicek, review of *Nobody's Princess,* p. 512.

Kirkus Reviews, August 15, 2009, review of *Sphinx's Princess*; August 15, 2010, review of *Sphinx's Queen.*

Kliatt, September, 2005, Sherry Hoy, review of *E. Godz,* p. 23; May, 2007, Claire Rosser, review of *Nobody's Princess,* p. 10; March, 2008, Claire Rosser, review of *Nobody's Prize,* p. 12.

Library Journal, December, 2002, Jackie Cassada, review of *Death and the Librarian and Other Stories,* p. 185.

Publishers Weekly, June 21, 1993, review of *Split Heirs,* p. 90; November 1, 1993, review of *Wishing Season,* p. 81; October 9, 1995, review of *Blood Muse,* p. 77; April 30, 2007, review of *Nobody's Princess,* p. 161.

School Library Journal, September, 2002, Pam Johnson, review of *Men in Black II,* p. 256; August, 2006, Ginny Gustin, review of *Temping Fate,* p. 120; July 1, 2007, Cheri Dobbs, review of *Nobody's Princess,* p. 101; June, 2008, Beth L. Meister, review of *Nobody's*

Prize, p. 140; November, 2009, Paula Willey, review of *Sphinx's Princess,* p. 106; November, 2010, Corinne Henning-Sachs, review of *Sphinx's Queen,* p. 114; January, 2011, Renee Steinberg, review of *Threads and Flames,* p. 104.

Voice of Youth Advocates, December, 1991, Fred Lerner, "The Newcomer," p. 294; December, 2010, Amanda McFadden, review of *Threads and Flames,* p. 452, and Karen Sykeny, review of *Sphinx's Queen,* p. 469.

ONLINE

Baen Books Web site, http://www.baen.com/ (November 1, 2009), interview with Friesner.

Esther Friesner Home Page, http://www.sff.net/people/e. friesner (March 1, 2012).

Vision: A Resource for Writers Web site, http://www.lazette. net/vision/ (January 1, 2002), Lazette Gifford, interview with Friesner.

Suite101.com, http://scififantasyfiction.suite101.com/ (August 25, 2009), Lynne Jamneck, interview with Friesner.

Suvudu Web site, http://www.suvudu.com/ (October 20, 2009), Shawn Speakman, interview with Friesner.

Weekly Reader Online, http://www.weeklyreader.com/ readandwriting/ (September 10, 2009), interview with Friesner.*

*   *   *

FRIESNER, Esther M.
See FRIESNER, Esther

G

GIDWITZ, Adam 1982-

Personal
Born 1982, in San Francisco, CA. *Education:* B.A. (English literature), 2004; Bank Street College of Education, degree.

Addresses
Home—Brooklyn, NY. *Agent*—Sarah Burnes, Gernert Company, 136 E. 57th St., New York, NY 10022.

Career
Educator and author. Saint Ann's School, Brooklyn, NY, part-time teacher of elementary and high school.

Awards, Honors
Notable Children's Books selection, American Library Association, 2010, for *A Tale Dark and Grimm.*

Writings

A Tale Dark and Grimm, Dutton Children's Books (New York, NY), 2010.

Contributor to periodicals, including London *Times.*

Adaptations
A Tale Dark and Grimm was adapted for audiobook by Recorded Books, 2011.

Sidelights
Adam Gidwitz taps the ancient roots of fairy tales in his children's book *A Tale Dark and Grimm,* and the picture his stories paint is not a pretty one. No cute and colorful talking-animal friends find their way into the

pages of Gitwitz's stories, no benign fairy godmothers appear to guide children safely through the dark, threat-

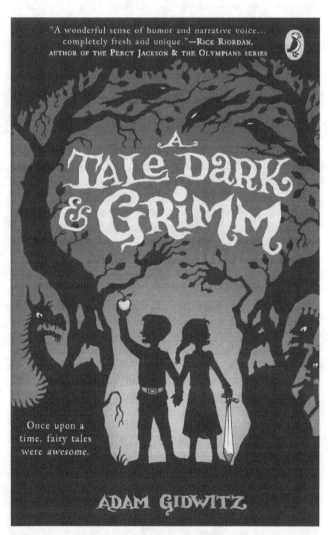

Adam Gidwitz introduces a new generation to the real voice of the Brothers Grimm in his novel A Tale Dark and Grimm, *a book featuring cover art by Hugh D'Andrade.* (Jacket cover art © 2010 by Hugh D'Andrade. Reproduced by permission of Puffin Books, a division of Penguin Young Readers Group, 345 Hudson Street, New York, NY 10014.)

ening landscape of these time-honored tales. Describing his book's approach as "scary, and gory, and grim" in a London *Times* article, Gidwitz explained that *A Tale Dark and Grimm* taps the true roots of the stories collected by Wilhelm and Jacob Grimm during the early 1800s. In the *New York Times Book Review*, Marjorie Ingall recalled discovering the Grimms' stories as a child. "I felt both thrilled and duped," the critic recalled. "Why had no one told me that fairy tales were creepily delicious?" In *A Tale Dark and Grimm* Gidwitz recrafts these "creepily delicious" stories into what Ingall described as "a completely postmodern creation." He sends Hansel and Gretel on a quest that "wends through all the tales like a trail of bread crumbs" and touches on medievalesque horrors via a narration that "ricochets [in tone] between lyrical and goofy."

Born in California and raised in Baltimore, Gidwitz eventually studied English literature in college. Although intending to write a novel for adults, he became interested in a younger readership after he got a teaching job at a private school in Brooklyn, New York, where he now makes his home. Gidwitz took a sabbatical in order to write but kept in touch with his students by hosting storytelling sessions at the school library, and one day he decided to read from the Brothers Grimm. While tackling a particularly strange story titled "Faithful Johannes," he leavened the most horrific moments with humorous asides, and by the story's end his audience was begging for more.

It was not long before Gidwitz had shelved his adult novel in favor of working on the manuscript that would become *A Tale Dark and Grimm*. In crafting his book, he worked hard to capture the spontaneity of that library storytelling experience. "When I'm writing, I literally pretend I'm telling the story to children," he explained on his home page, "leaning in here or out there, trying to create for the reader the experience that I would create for my kids in the classroom. I try to love my readers as much as I love my students, and make them happy and make them feel cared for, just as I do for my students."

While on a quest for a stable family in *A Tale Dark and Grimm*, Hansel and Gretel find their traditional fate as the prey of a forest-dwelling witch multiplied eightfold as they are cast in a succession of eight Grimm tales that includes "Faithful Johannes" and "The Seven Swallows." Along the way, they are "beheaded . . . , dismembered, hunted, killed, brought back to life, [and] sent to hell," noted Ian Chipman in an enthusiastic *Booklist* review of Gidwitz's child-friendly narrative. Characterizing *A Tale Dark and Grimm* as a "darkly humorous chapter book," Susan Dove Lempke added in *Horn Book* that the author's "commentary" relieves the tension of the tales and is "set off in bold type." "With disarming delicacy and unexpected good cheer," the author compiles these classic tales "into a novel that's almost addictively compelling," noted *School Library Journal* contributor Miriam Lang Budin, while a *Kirkus*

Reviews writer characterized the storytelling style employed in *A Tale Dark and Grimm* as "wicked smart and wicked funny."

Biographical and Critical Sources

PERIODICALS

Booklist, November 15, 2010, Ian Chipman, review of *A Tale Dark and Grimm,* p. 49.
Bulletin of the Center for Children's Books, December, 2010, Karen Coats, review of *A Tale Dark and Grimm,* p. 185.
Horn Book, January-February, 2011, Susan Dove Lempke, review of *A Tale Dark and Grimm,* p. 93.
Kirkus Reviews, October 15, 2010, review of *A Tale Dark and Grimm.*
New York Times Book Review, Marjorie Ingall, review of *A Tale Dark and Grimm,* p. 26.
Publishers Weekly, November 8, 2010, review of *A Tale Dark and Grimm,* p. 34; December, 20, 2010, "Flying Starts," p. 18.
School Library Journal, November, 2010, Miriam Lang Budin, review of *A Tale Dark and Grimm,* p. 114; December, 2010, Rick Margolis, interview with Gidwitz, p. 19; July, 2011, Maria Salvadore, review of *A Tale Dark and Grimm,* p. 53.
Times (London, England), August 24, 2011, Adam Gidwitz, "The Grimm Truth," p. 17.

ONLINE

Adam Gidwitz Home Page, http://www.adamgidwitz.com (March 3, 2012).*

* * *

GOLDIN, David 1963-

Personal

Born January 28, 1963, in Ridgewood, NJ; son of Allan and Felicia (a lyricist) Goldin. *Education:* Rhode Island School of Design, B.F.A., 1985. *Hobbies and other interests:* Travel, book binding, toy making.

Addresses

Home—Woodstock, NY. *E-mail*—david@davidgoldin.com.

Career

Illustrator and animator. Ink Tank, New York, NY, animator, 1985-87; freelance editorial illustrator, beginning 1987. Occasional lecturer at Parsons School of Design and School of Visual Arts. *Exhibitions:* Work exhibited at New York Illustration Gallery, New York, NY, 1989-93; and at galleries in Los Angeles, CA, Tokyo, Japan, and Prague, Czech Republic.

David Goldin (Photograph by Ella Goldin. Reproduced by permission.)

Awards, Honors

Spot Illustration Competition winner, Society of Publication Designers, 1992; honors from AIGA, American Illustration, and Art Director's Club.

Writings

(Self-illustrated) *Go-Go-Go!,* Abrams (New York, NY), 2000.

ILLUSTRATOR

Meg F. Schneider, *Help, My Teacher Hates Me: How to Survive Poor Grades, a Friend Who Cheats Off You, Oral Reports, and More,* Workman Publishing (New York, NY), 1994.

Tad Hardy, *The Lost Cat,* Houghton Mifflin (Boston, MA), 1995.

Laurel Snyder, *Baxter, the Pig Who Wanted to Be Kosher,* Tricycle Press (Berkeley, CA), 2010.

Contributor to *Blab 11,* edited by Monte Beauchamp, Fantagraphics, 2000. Also illustrator of posters, CD covers, and book covers.

ILLUSTRATOR; "SCIENCE FAIR WINNERS" SERIES BY KAREN ROMANO YOUNG

Bug Science: Twenty Projects and Experiments about Arthropods: Insects, Arachnids, Algae, Worms, and Other Small Creatures, National Geographic (Washington, DC), 2009.

Crime Scene Science: Twenty Projects and Experiments about Clues, Crimes, Criminals, and Other Mysterious Things, National Geographic (Washington, DC), 2009.

Experiments to Do on Your Family: Twenty Projects and Experiments about Sisters, Brothers, Parents, Pets, and the Rest of the Gang, National Geographic (Washington, DC), 2010.

Junkyard Science: Twenty Projects and Experiments about Junk, Garbage, Waste, Things We Don't Need Anymore, and Ways to Recycle or Reuse It—or Lose It, National Geographic (Washington, DC), 2010.

Sidelights

An award-winning artist, David Goldin has provided the illustrations for a range of children's books, among them Tad Hardy's *The Lost Cat* and Laurel Snyder's *Baxter, the Pig Who Wanted to Be Kosher.* Although his work for Karen Romano Young's "Science Fair Winners" books have helped build his reputation as an illustrator, Goldin also has an original, self-illustrated picture book to his credit: *Go-Go-Go!,* a humorous, action-packed tale about a zany bicycle race.

A stray kitty with a mischievous personality elicits very different reactions from its owner and its rescuer in Hardy's *The Lost Cat.* After a pet owner discovers that his beloved feline is missing, he designs a series of

Goldin's humorous retro-styled art is a feature of Laurel Snyder's picture book **Baxter, the Pig Who Wanted to Be Kosher.** (Illustration copyright © 2010 by David Goldin. Reproduced by permission of Tricycle Press, an imprint of Random House Children's Books, a division of Random House, Inc.)

Goldin's illustration projects include Karen Romano Young's "Science Fair Winners" series, which includes **Junkyard Science.** (Illustration copyright © 2010 by David Goldin. Reproduced by permission of National Geographic Society.)

"Lost Cat" posters that highlights the creature's most adorable features and behaviors. Meanwhile, the individual who finds the lost cat creates his own set of posters, imploring its owner to take the troublemaking feline off his hands. "Goldin's amiable cartoons suit Hardy's classified-ad-style choppy sentences and easy rhymes," a critic wrote in *Publishers Weekly*. "Both text and illustrations show an understanding of the lovable and annoying aspects of any cat's personality," Lolly Robinson noted of the same work in *Horn Book*.

In *Baxter, the Pig Who Wanted to Be Kosher* Snyder introduces a well-meaning porker who hopes to share some holiday spirit. When Baxter hears about Shabbat, the Jewish Sabbath, he can not wait to join in the fun. Unfortunately, the pig is told that he will not be part of the festive dinner because he is not kosher, so Baxter makes a futile attempt to reach that goal by gorging on kosher dills and challah and learning how to moo. "The delightfully expressive and comical pen-and-ink illustrations are digitally enhanced with photographs of storefronts, deli counters, pickle jars, and traditional Jewish foods," Rachel Kamin stated in her *School Library Journal* review of *Baxter, the Pig Who Wanted to Be Kosher*. A *Publishers Weekly* contributor applauded the combination of Snyder's text and Goldin's illustra-

tions, remarking that "the bright, daffy prose and ebulliently goofy cartoon and photo collages" will appeal to readers of any religious persuasion.

A bicycle racer must overcome a series of obstacles to defeat his hated rival in Goldin's original picture book *Go-Go-Go!* Determined to capture the crown this year, Maurice dons his lucky helmet, boards his trusty bike, and pedals to the starting line where his trash-talking nemesis, Stinky, awaits. When the race begins, however, the biker veers wildly off course and winds up splashing through a pond and flying through the sky. He also ventures into the zoo, where he picks up a host of unwelcome—and quite heavy—passengers. With the finish line in sight, the race appears to be hopelessly lost, until the crowd's chant of "Go-Go-Go!" rallies Maurice's flagging spirits.

In the words of a *Publishers Weekly* reviewer, in *Go-Go-Go!* "Goldin packs a comic wallop of obstacles in Maurice's quest for the gold," and Michael Cart remarked in his *Booklist* appraisal that the author/illustrator's "cartoon illustrations comically expand this postmodern celebration of the power of positive persistence."

Biographical and Critical Sources

PERIODICALS

American Biology Teacher, April, 2011, Elizabeth Cowles, review of *Experiments to Do on Your Family: Twenty Projects and Experiments about Sisters, Brothers, Parents, Pets, and the Rest of the Gang,* p. 248, and April Falkosky and Andrea Redinger, review of *Junkyard Science: Twenty Projects and Experiments about Junk, Garbage, Waste, Things We Don't Need Anymore, and Ways to Recycle or Reuse It—or Lose It,* p. 248.

Booklist, March 15, 1995, Stephanie Zvirin, review of *Help, My Teacher Hates Me: How to Survive Poor Grades, a Friend Who Cheats off You, Oral Reports, and More,* p. 1321; December 1, 2000, Michael Cart, review of *Go-Go-Go!,* p. 720; October 1, 2009, Daniel Kraus, review of *Crime Scene Science: Twenty Projects and Experiments about Clues, Crimes, Criminals, and Other Mysterious Things,* p. 53; December 1, 2010, Miriam Aronin, review of *Experiments to Do on Your Family,* p. 42.

Horn Book, July-August, 1996, Lolly Robinson, review of *Lost Cat,* p. 449; September-October, 2010, Elissa Gershowitz, review of *Baxter, the Pig Who Wanted to Be Kosher,* p. 65.

Kirkus Reviews, July 15, 2010, review of *Baxter, the Pig Who Wanted to Be Kosher.*

Publishers Weekly, March 11, 1996, review of *Lost Cat,* p. 63; September 4, 2000, review of *Go-Go-Go!,* p. 107; June 28, 2010, review of *Baxter, the Pig Who Wanted to Be Kosher,* p. 127.

School Library Journal, September, 2000, Meghan R. Malone, review of *Go-Go-Go!,* p. 198; March, 2010, Christine Markley, reviews of *Bug Science: Twenty Projects and Experiments about Arthropods: Insects, Arachnids, Algae, Worms, and Other Small Creatures* and *Crime Scene Science,* both p. 182; August, 2010, Rachel Kamin, review of *Baxter, the Pig Who Wanted to Be Kosher,* p. 86.

ONLINE

David Goldin Home Page, http://www.davidgoldin.com (March 1, 2012).*

*   *   *

GUIBORD, Maurissa 1961-

Personal

Born 1961; married; children: triplets. *Education:* M.D.

Addresses

Home—Scarborough, ME. *Agent*—Ted Malawer, Upstart Crow Literary Agency, P.O. Box 25404, Brooklyn, NY 11202.

Career

Writer. Formerly worked as a doctor of internal medicine.

Awards, Honors

Agatha Award nomination, 2006, for short story "Yankee Swap."

Writings

Warped (novel), Delacorte Press (New York, NY), 2011.

Contributor to periodicals, including *Ellery Queen's Mystery Magazine.*

Sidelights

A visit to her local library to research fiber crafts provided the impetus for Maurissa Guibord's debut novel *Warped,* a critically acclaimed fantasy tale. While researching patterns for an afghan she planned to crochet, Guibord ran across a book describing "The Oak King, the Holly King, and the Unicorn," a set of seven medieval tapestries housed in the Cloisters museum in New York City. The textiles, which depict the hunt for a unicorn, the creature's slaying, and its resurrection, are

Cover of Maurissa Guibord's novel Warped, *a fantasy romance that revolves around a magical tapestry.* (Jacket cover copyright © 2011 by Delacorte Press. Reproduced by permission of Delacorte Press, an imprint of Random House Children's Books, a division of Random House, Inc.)

rich in symbolism and prompted Guibord to ponder whether a supernatural being could be trapped with the threads of such a tapestry.

Warped opens as Tessa Brady, a Maine teenager, discovers an ancient text and a mysterious unicorn tapestry concealed within a box her father recently purchased at auction. When Tessa pulls on a loose thread of the tapestry she frees Will de Chauncy from captivity. Her action infuriates Gray Lily, the witch who imprisoned Will in the tapestry centuries earlier and needs his vitality to ensure her immortality. Tessa also finds herself at odds with the Norns, or Fates, who want to regain possession of the life-giving threads that were stolen from them.

"This absorbing and mesmerizing read has it all—fantasy, romance, witchcraft, life-threatening situations, detective work, chase scenes, and a smattering of violence," Genevieve Gallagher commented in her *School Library Journal* review of *Warped*. Other reviewers applauded Guibord's fully realized portrait of her teen protagonist. "Tessa does provide a realistic and likeable character, as she juggles love, friendship, and family loyalty," Kaitlin Connors noted in *Voice of Youth Advocates,* and *Horn Book* critic Rachel Smith described Tessa as "a charismatic heroine in a story that is suspenseful, romantic, and—in Will's earnest reactions to twenty-first-century inventions and language—very funny."

Biographical and Critical Sources

PERIODICALS

Booklist, January 1, 2011, Cindy Welch, review of *Warped,* p. 100.

Horn Book, March-April, 2011, Rachel Smith, review of *Warped,* p. 117.

Kirkus Reviews, December 15, 2010, review of *Warped.*

Publishers Weekly, November 15, 2010, review of *Warped,* p. 58.

School Library Journal, March, 2011, Genevieve Gallagher, review of *Warped,* p. 162.

Voice of Youth Advocates, April, 2011, Kaitlin Connors, review of *Warped,* p. 81.

ONLINE

Maurissa Guibord Home Page, http://maurissaguibord. com (March 1, 2012).

Maurissa Guibord Web log, http://mguibord.livejournal. com/ (March 1, 2012).

Scarborough Leader Online (Scarborough, ME), http:// blog.scarboroughleader.com/ (January 14, 2011), Dan Aceto, interview with Guibord.*

H

HARMON, Kari Lee
See TOWNSEND, Kari Lee

* * *

HARTT-SUSSMAN, Heather

Personal

Born in Montreal, Quebec, Canada; married Peter Sussman (an entertainment executive), September 30, 1993; children: Scotty, Jack, Anthony (deceased). *Education:* Brandeis University, degree; Attended Sorbonne, University of Paris. *Hobbies and other interests:* Yoga.

Addresses

Home—Toronto, Ontario, Canada.

Career

Broadcast journalist and author. BCP (advertising firm), Montreal, Quebec, Canada, copywriter until 1991; *Hollywood Reporter,* Los Angeles, CA, reporter and associate international editor, 1991-93; *TV Guide* (French-Canada edition), editor in chief of international news, beginning 1993; *E!* (television program), correspondent, then host, for two years; host of *TV Guide Television;* appeared on numerous television programs.

Awards, Honors

Blue Spruce Award nomination, Ontario Library Association, 2011, for *Noni Says No.*

Writings

Nana's Getting Married, illustrated by Georgia Graham, Tundra Books of Northern New York (Plattsburgh, NY), 2010.

Noni Says No, illustrated by Genèvieve Côté, Tundra Books of Northern New York (Plattsburgh, NY), 2011.

Here Comes Hortense! (sequel to *Nana's Getting Married*), illustrated by Georgia Graham, Tundra Books of Northern New York (Plattsburgh, NY), 2012.

Author of column "Heather Hartt in Hollywood" for French-Canadian edition of *TV Guide* for five years.

Author's work has been translated into French and Braille.

Sidelights

Heather Hartt-Sussman began writing stories for young children after enjoying a successful career as an entertainment journalist that led her from Los Angeles and work as a reporter and editor for *Hollywood Reporter* to editorship of the French-Canadian edition of *TV Guide* and a television host on the E! network. Now returned with her family to her native Canada, Hartt-Sussman has earned the appreciation of a younger audience through her picture books. In addition to creating engaging multigenerational stories for the companion books *Nana's Getting Married* and *Here Comes Hortense!,* she also introduces readers to a feisty young heroine in *Noni Says No,* a story illustrated by Genèvieve Côté.

The star of *Noni Says No* is a little girl with amazing abilities: Noni can help her mother by entertaining her baby brother, can tie her own shoelaces, and is responsible enough to walk to a nearby friend's house without supervision. However, as she has gotten older, Noni has become fearful of saying "No" to things she really does not want to do, and this makes her grow silently frustrated with strong-minded best-friend Susie. When Noni finally decides to assert her own views after Susie's demands push too far, a surprising thing happens: her worries prove unfounded and the girls' friendship survives.

Noting that "Susie's reaction" will "reassure children who find themselves in a similar predicament," Kathy Piehl added in her *School Library Journal* review that *Noni Says No* "could generate good discussions" between parents and children. Complimenting Côté's energetic and sketchy illustrations for the story, Susan Perren added in the Toronto *Globe & Mail* that "Hartt-Sussman's perfectly paced and pitched text carries the story forward in a most engaging fashion."

In *Nana's Getting Married* and its sequel, Hartt-Sussman broaches a common occurrence that often affects young children but is seldom the topic of picture books. In the first story, a six-year-old boy is taken aback when his loving grandmother starts dating Bob. Nana used to knit and snuggle up with a storybook and bake cookies, but now her focus is less on the narrator and more on impressing Bob with her pretty clothes and makeup and a large does of her time and attention. Although the boy first attempts to derail the budding love affair, both adults soon make clear that, as their wedding looms, they will both make ample room for him in their future together. They make good on these intentions in *Here Comes Hortense!,* although the boy's

trip to Wonder World with Nana and Bob now involves competing for attention with Bob's energetic granddaughter.

The first-person narration in *Nana's Getting Married* "is exactly right to convey to young readers the emotional devastation that the [boy] . . . is feeling as he perceived his grandmother's dereliction of duty," wrote Valerie Neilsen in her appraisal of the entertaining picture book for *Canadian Review of Materials.* Hartt-Sussman's "message about open-mindedness and acceptance hits its mark," asserted a *Publishers Weekly* critic in reviewing *Nana's Getting Married,* and Graham's "brassy chalk-pastel" art captures the boy's quizzical view of his grandmother's changing world. "The illustrations are wonderfully whimsical," wrote *Resource Links* contributor Lorie Battershill, the critic calling the same book "a two-sided winner." Praising *Here Comes Hortense!* for also featuring "playful, quirky, colourful and action-packed artwork," Reesa Cohen added in her *Canadian Review of Materials* appraisal that Hartt-Sussman's sequel "should be . . . welcomed" by adults "seeking stories that explore intergenerational relationships."

Heather Hartt-Sussman introduces a girl who learns a lesson in assertiveness in **Noni Says No,** *a story illustrated by Genèvieve Côté.* (Illustration copyright © 2011 by Genèvieve Côté. Reproduced by permission of Tundra Books.)

Biographical and Critical Sources

PERIODICALS

Canadian Review of Materials, December 18, 2009, Valerie Nielsen, review of *Nana's Getting Married;* April 29, 2011, Aileen Wortley, review of *Noni Says No;* Reesa Cohen, review of *Here Comes Hortense!*

Globe & Mail (Toronto, Ontario, Canada), April 2, 2011, Susan Perren, review of *Noni Says No.*

Publishers Weekly, January 25, 2010, review of *Nana's Getting Married,* p. 117.

Quill & Quire, January, 2011, Shannon Ozirny, review of *Noni Says No.*

Resource Links, December, 2009, Lorie Battershill, review of *Nana's Getting Married,* p. 3.

School Library Journal, April, 2010, Amy Lilien-Harper, review of *Nana's Getting Married,* p. 126.

ONLINE

Heather Hartt-Sussman Home Page, http://www.heatherhartt.com (February 28, 2012).

Open Book Toronto Web site, http://www. openbooktoronto. com/ (February 9, 2010), Ashley Person, interview with Hartt-Sussman.*

*   *   *

HATKE, Ben 1977-

Personal

Born 1977; married; wife's name Anna; children: Angelica, Zita, Julia, Ronia. *Education:* Attended Charles Cecil Studios (Florence, Italy). *Hobbies and other interests:* Juggling, playing tin whistles.

Addresses

Home—Front Royal, VA. *E-mail*—ben@househatke. com.

Career

Author, illustrator, and comics artist.

Writings

SELF-ILLUSTRATED GRAPHIC NOVELS

Zita the Spacegirl: Far from Home, First Second (New York, NY), 2010.

Legends of Zita the Spacegirl, First Second (New York, NY), 2012.

Creator of Web comics.

ILLUSTRATOR

Regina Doman, *Angel in the Waters,* Sophia Institute Press (Manchester, NH), 2004.

Neal Lozano, *Will You Bless Me?,* Maple Corners Press (Clinton Corners, NY), 2006.

Neal Lozano, *Can God See Me in the Dark?,* Maple Corners Press (Clinton Corners, NY), 2007.

Elizabeth Marie DeDomenico, *Saint John Vianney: A Priest for All People,* Pauline Books & Media (Boston, MA), 2008.

Neal Lozano, *What Can I Give God?,* Maple Corners Press (Clinton Corners, NY), 2008.

Ethel Pochocki, *Around the Year Once upon a Time Saints,* Bethlehem Books (Bathgate, ND), 2009.

Contributor to periodicals, including *Flight;* work included in anthology *Flight Explorer,* Villard, 2008.

Sidelights

Inspired by "Calvin & Hobbes," "Garfield," and "Elf Quest" comics, as well as by fantasy novels such as Madeline L'Engle's *A Wrinkle in Time,* sequential artist Ben Hatke created the "Zita the Spacegirl" series of children's graphic novels. "I was interested in . . . keeping the illustration style and the cartooning very open and readable," Hatke noted of his upbeat adventure saga in a *School Library Journal* online interview with Scott Robins. "I wanted to make a book that almost anyone could pick up and follow and find something entertaining or interesting. It's my attempt to draw in as many different types of readers as possible and especially readers who maybe haven't read a graphic novel before." In addition to his work on "Zita the Spacegirl," the cartoon artist produces Web comics and book illustrations and has had his work included in the popular *Flight* anthologies edited by Kazu Kibuishi.

The adventure begins in *Zita the Spacegirl: Far from Home,* where readers first meet spunky young Zita and her friend Joseph. While exploring a crater, the two children discover a strange object with a bright red control button. True to his nature, Joseph urges caution but Zita impulsively pushes the button, revealing an intergalactic portal. A tentacled creature reaches out and grabs Joseph, pulls the surprised boy through the portal, and both disappear. The plucky Zita pursues her friend, winding up in an alien world inhabited by robots and other strange creatures and where whimsical solutions are often found to seemingly dire problems. As the girl sets about tracking down her friend with plans to save him from his future as an alien sacrifice, she shoulders the responsibilities of an epic hero, vanquishing threats, portents and prophecies, and a host of odd and suspicious characters. Zita's adventures continue in *Legends of Zita the Spacegirl.*

Dubbing *Zita the Spacegirl* "plenty funny," Ian Chipman recommended Hatke's story for its "increasingly looney and charming" cast of "aliens, robots, and unclassifiable blobs and hairy things." The story's "characters are richly imagined and portrayed," noted a *Kirkus Reviews* writer, the critic predicting that *Zita the Spacegirl* will be "sure to captivate young graphic-novel aficionados." In her *School Library Journal* Web log review, Elizabeth Bird discussed Hatke's cartooning style, citing his "penchant for combining the cute with the weird" and adding that he "isn't afraid to include wordless sequences to set the pace, or to switch up the panel size and jump cuts . . . in an action scene." While grown ups will "enjoy the subtle humor and inside jokes" in Hatke's high-spirited tale, the "charming, well-told story has a timeless 'read to me' quality that makes it perfect for one-on-one sharing," according to *School Library Journal* critic Barbara M. Moon. *Zita the Spacegirl* "is definitely something you can hand to your kids, boys and girls alike, secure in the knowledge that they'll take a lot of enjoyment out of the experience," concluded Bird, dubbing Hatke's graphic-novel debut "a sweet tale."

Biographical and Critical Sources

PERIODICALS

Booklist, December 15, 2010, Ian Chipman, review of *Zita the Spacegirl: Far from Home,* p. 37.
Bulletin of the Center for Children's Books, January, 2011, April Spisak, review of *Zita the Spacegirl,* p. 237.
Kirkus Reviews, February 1, 2008, review of *Flight Explorer*; December 15, 2010, review of *Zita the Spacegirl.*
Publishers Weekly, May 29, 2006, review of *Flight,* p. 43.
School Library Journal, January, 2011, Barbara M. Moon, review of *Zita the Spacegirl,* p. 132.

ONLINE

Ben Hatke Home Page, http://www.househatke.com (March 1, 2012).
Ben Hatke Web site, http://letflythecannons.blogspot.com (March 1, 2012).
Graphic Novel Reporter Online, http://graphicnovelreporter.com/ (February 28, 2012), John Hogan, interview with Hatke.
School Library Journal Web log, http://blog.schoollibraryjournal.com/ (February 15, 2011), Elizabeth Bird, review of *Zita the Spacgirl;* (May 20, 2011) Scott Robins, interview with Hatke.*

*   *   *

HEASLEY, Gwendolyn

Personal

Born in MN. *Education:* Davidson College, B.A. (English), 2005; University of Missouri, Columbia, M.A. (journalism), 2009. *Hobbies and other interests:* Travel.

Gwendolyn Heasley (Photograph by Elizabeth Cryan. Reproduced by permission.)

Addresses

Home—New York, NY. *E-mail*—gwendolyn.heasley@gmail.com.

Career

Educator and author. Artists & Artisans, New York, NY, literary agent until 2011; Keene University, Union, NJ, adjunct professor in children's and young-adult literature, beginning 2009. Teaching artist at The Loft, Minneapolis, MN.

Member

Society of Children's Book Writers and Illustrators.

Writings

Where I Belong, HarperTeen (New York, NY), 2011.
A Long Way from You, HarperTeen (New York, NY), 2012.

Sidelights

Like many girls of her age, Gwendolyn Heasley grew up reading Ann M. Martin's phenomenally popular "Baby-Sitter's Club" novels. Unlike many of Martin's fans, Heasley was inspired to both read and write, and as she grew up she concidered being an author a reasonable career choice. After studying both English and journalism in college, Heasley moved to New York City and worked as a literary agent while beginning her writing career. With the publication of her first teen novel, *Where I Belong,* she shifted her "day job" from literary agent to adjunct professor, sharing her enthusiasm for writing with college students while continuing her own writing career.

Part of a sub-genre that some critics have dubbed "recessionary fiction,' *Where I Belong* is set in the wake of the economic downturn of the late 2000s. Sixteen-year-old Corrinne Corcoran has grown up in a wealthy Manhattan family, living in a posh downtown apartment and hanging out with her similarly affluent, trend-spotting, and somewhat snobbish friends. All that changes, however, when the Corcoran family's savings are lost in a risky investment scheme and Corrinne's father is laid off from his job and must relocate to Dubai to find work. While her mom gets the apartment ready for a quick sale in a tough real-estate market, Corrinne and her brother are sent south to rural Broken Spoke, Texas, to spend some time with their maternal grandparents. Although the teen feels constrained now that she no longer has free use of a credit card, there is not much for sale in Broken Spoke that she would even want: the stores cater to farm girls rather than fashionistas, and who has time to use the latest techno-gadgets when they are either attending the local public school or working a part-time job shoveling manure? Although Corrinne first channels her resentment into finding a way back to the city, she begins to view her new life in a new way after she gets to know a cute coworker, makes a good friend, and helps out at a local rodeo. While things continue to trend upward in her social life in Broken Spoke, a visit from a snobbish New York friend gives Corrinne the chance to weigh city and country life and ultimately embrace her "recessionista" lifestyle.

Praising *When I Belong* as a good choice for "readers looking for the comfortingly familiar riches-to-rags story," Lynn Rashid added in *School Library Journal* that Heasley's heroine "is witty and appropriately bratty" in her role as narrator. A *Publishers Weekly* critic dubbed the same novel "a sweet, by-the-numbers romance with a substantial dose of corning humor," and in *Voice of Youth Advocates* Teri Lesesne recommended Heasley's debut as an entertaining read serving up "equal doses of romance and teen angst."

Biographical and Critical Sources

PERIODICALS

Bulletin of the Center for Children's Books, April, 2011, Karen Coats, review of *Where I Belong,* p. 374.

Heasley's novel **Where I Belong** *follows an upscale teen on her ride down the economic ladder.* (Jacket cover photograph © 2011 by Mark Tucker/ MergeLeft Reps., Inc. Reproduced by permission of HarperTeen, an imprint of HarperCollins Children's Books, a division of HarperCollins Publishers.)

Publishers Weekly, December 20, 2010, review of *Where I Belong,* p. 54.
School Library Journal, March, 2011, Lynn Rashid, review of *Where I Belong,* p. 162.
Voice of Youth Advocates, April, 2011, Teri Lesesne, review of *Where I Belong,* p. 59.

ONLINE

Gwendolyn Heasley Home Page, http://www.gwendolyn heasley.com (March 12, 2012).*

*   *   *

HISCHE, Jessica 1984-

Personal

Born 1984, in Charleston, SC. *Education:* Temple University, B.F.A. (graphic and interactive design), 2006. *Hobbies and other interests:* Designing Web sites.

Addresses

Home—San Francisco, CA; Brooklyn, NY. *Agent*—Frank Sturges, Artist Representative; Frank@sturgesreps.com. *E-mail*—hello@jessicahische.com.

Career

Illustrator, letterer, and typeface designer. Headcase Design, Philadelphia, PA, designer, 2006-07; Louise Fili, Ltd., New York, NY, senior designer, 2007-09; freelance designer. Member of board of directors, Type Directors Club. *Exhibitions:* Work included in exhibitions at Gallery Nucleus, Los Angeles, CA; Lucky Gallery, Brooklyn, NY; and Somerset House, London, England, as well as in Australia and Ireland.

Awards, Honors

Named among *Print* Magazine New Visual Artists; 30 under 30 in Art and Design inclusion, *Forbes* magazine; named among "Young Guns," Art Directors Club; GDUSA Person to Watch selection; Person of the Year selection, Lettercult, 2010.

Illustrator

Candace Fleming, *Amelia Lost: The Life and Disappearance of Amelia Earhart,* Random House (New York, NY), 2010.

Tara Duggan, *Cake Stencils: Recipes and How-to Decorating Ideas for Cakes and Cupcakes: 8 Food-safe Plastic Stencils,* photographs by Angie Cao, Chronicle Books (San Francisco, CA), 2011.

Contributor to numerous periodicals, including *Atlantic Monthly, Boston Globe, Cincinnati Monthly, Entertainment Weekly, Gentleman's Weekly, New York Magazine, New York Times, Nickelodeon, O, Plan Sponsor, Village Voice,* and *Wired.*

Biographical and Critical Sources

PERIODICALS

Booklist, December 1, 2010, Kay Weisman, review of *Amelia Lost: The Life and Disappearance of Amelia Earhart,* p. 41.

Publishers Weekly, January 17, 2011, review of *Amelia Lost,* p. 51.

ONLINE

Jessica Hische Home Page, http://www.jessicahische.is (March 15, 2012).

Jessica Hirsche Web log, http://www.the accidental hipster.com (March 15, 2012).

HOFFMAN, Nina Kiriki 1955-

Personal

Born March 20, 1955, in San Gabriel, CA; daughter of Hallock Brown Hoffman (an educator) and Gene Knudsen (a writer and peaceworker). *Education:* Santa Barbara City College, A.A., 1977; University of Idaho, B.A., 1980.

Addresses

Home—Eugene, OR. *Agent*—Matthew Bialer, Trident Media Group LLC, Carnegie Hall Tower, 152 W. 57th St., 16th Fl., New York, NY 10019.

Career

Writer. Instructor in writing at community colleges; B. Dalton bookstore, bookseller until 2008. *Magazine of Science Fiction and Fantasy,* member of production staff.

Member

Phi Beta Kappa.

Awards, Honors

World Fantasy Award nomination, World Fantasy Convention, 1992, for novella "Unmasking", 1999, for *A Red Heart of Memories*; Nebula Award nomination, Science Fiction Writers of America, 1993, for novella "The Skeleton Key"; Bram Stoker Award for Superior Achievement in a First Novel, 1994, for *The Thread That Binds the Bones;* Nebula Award finalist, and World Fantasy Award finalist, both 1995, both for *The Silent Strength of Stones;* Nebula Award nomination, World Fantasy Award nomination, World Fantasy Convention, and Theodore Sturgeon Award shortlist, University of Kansas Center for the Study of Science Fiction, all 1995, all for novelette "Home for Christmas"; Endeavor Award finalist, 2000, for *A Red Heart of Memories,* 2001, for *Past the Size of Dreaming,* 2004, for *A Stir of Bones,* 2007, for *Spirits That Walk in Shadow;* Philip K. Dick Award finalist, 2006, for *Catalyst;* numerous award nominations, including for *Locus,* HOMer, Mythopoeic, James Tiptree, Jr., and Bram Stoker awards.

Writings

Legacy of Fire (short stories), Pulphouse (Eugene, OR), 1990.

Courting Disasters, and Other Strange Affinities (short stories), Wildside Press (Newark, NJ), 1991.

(With Tad Williams) *Child of an Ancient City,* illustrated by Greg Hildebrandt, Atheneum (New York, NY), 1992.

The Thread That Binds the Bones, Avon (New York, NY), 1993.

The Silent Strength of Stones, Avon (New York, NY), 1995.

Body Switchers from Outer Space ("Ghosts of Fear Street" series), Minstrel Books (New York, NY), 1996.

Why I'm Not Afraid of Ghosts ("Ghosts of Fear Street" series), Minstrel Books (New York, NY), 1997.

(With Kristine Kathryn Rusch and Dean Wesley Smith) *Echoes* ("Star Trek Voyager" series), Pocket Books (New York, NY), 1998.

(With R.L. Stine) *I Was a Sixth-Grade Zombie* ("Ghosts of Fear Street" series), Golden Books (New York, NY), 1998.

A Fistful of Sky, Berkley/Ace (New York, NY), 2002.

Time Travelers, Ghosts, and Other Visitors (short stories), Five Star (Waterville, ME), 2003.

Spirits That Walk in Shadow, Viking (New York, NY), 2006.

Fall of Light (sequel to *A Fistful of Sky*), Ace (New York, NY), 2009.

Contributor to periodicals, including *Amazing Stories, Magazine of Science Fiction and Fantasy,* and *Weird Tales.* Work included in anthologies *Flights: Extreme Visions of Fantasy,* edited by Al Sarrantonio, NAL/Roc, 2004; *Children of Magic,* edited by Martin H. Greenberg and Kerrie Hughes, DAW; *Year's Best Fantasy 7,* edited by David G. Hartwell and Kathryn Cramer, Tachyon, 2007; *The Lone Star Stories Reader,* edited by Eric T. Marin, LSS, 2008; *The Dimension Next Door,* edited by Greenberg and Hughes, DAW, 2008; *Magic in the Mirrorstone: Tales of Fantasy,* edited by Steve Berman, Mirrorstone, 2008; and *Troll's-Eye View: A Book of Villainous Tales,* edited by Ellen Datlow and Terri Windling, Viking, 2009.

"RED HEART OF MEMORIES"/"MATT BLACK" SERIES

Unmasking, Axolotl Press (Eugene, OR), 1992.

A Red Heart of Memories (adult novel), Berkley/Ace (New York, NY), 1999.

Past the Size of Dreaming (adult novel), Berkley/Ace (New York, NY), 2000.

A Stir of Bones (prequel; for teens), Viking (New York, NY), 2003.

Several short stories, novelettes, and novellas are included in the "Red Heart of Memories" series, including "Home for Christmas," published in 1995.

"MAGIC NEXT DOOR" MIDDLE-GRADE NOVEL SERIES

Thresholds, Viking (New York, NY), 2010.

Meeting, Viking (New York, NY), 2011.

Adaptations

Several of Hoffman's novels have been adapted as audiobooks, including *A Stir of Bones,* 2003.

Sidelights

Nina Kiriki Hoffman writes novels and short stories that span the genres of fantasy, science fiction, and horror. Critically praised for her imaginative plots and realistic characters, Hoffman achieved acclaim early in her career when she was awarded the Bram Stoker Award for Superior Achievement in a First Novel for *The Thread That Binds the Bones.* Among her more-recent works, she has focused on young-adult readers, producing *Spirits That Walk in Shadows, A Fistful of Sky,* and her "Magic Next Door" middle-grade novel series.

Hoffman grew up in California and started writing as a preteen. "I often wrote about gifted kids trying to blend," she later recalled to interviewer Karen Meisner in *Strange Horizons.* "I didn't envision these stories as extending into a connected series of novels. I didn't even realize I was writing novel-like objects. I just kept writing about the same characters and their friends and eventually their children because I liked my established worlds." She began submitting stories to magazines such as *Weird Tales* and *Amazing Stories* beginning in her late twenties, often drawing on these established worlds. Many of these short stories fall into the horror genre, and Hoffman explained to a *Locus* interviewer that this was "because I was doing a lot of psychological work at the time and there's so much cool scary stuff in that." *Legacy of Fire,* and *Courting Disasters, and Other Strange Affinities,* collect many of these early tales.

Containing nine stories, *Time Travelers, Ghosts, and Other Visitors* moves beyond horror to include science fiction and fantasy. Here Hoffman deals with such subjects as time travelers looking for comic books, ghosts hoping to save a woman from a serial killer, alien invasions, and dancing princesses. Many of these tales, like those published in her previous collections, originally appeared in periodicals such as the *Magazine of Science Fiction and Fantasy.* Roland Green, reviewing the collection for *Booklist,* praised *Time Travelers, Ghosts, and Other Visitors* as "contemporary short fantasy at its best."

Hoffman's first longer work, a collaboration between Hoffman and Tad Williams, was the fantasy novel *Child of an Ancient City.* In this story, a group of lost soldiers is challenged to a story-telling contest by a vampire who offers to free the man who tells the saddest story. The stories told during the challenge are contained in the last part of the book and brought to life in black-and-white illustrations by fantasy artist Greg Hildebrandt. Reviewing this work, Sally Estes wrote in *Booklist* that *Child of an Ancient City* is "a colorful variation on the *Arabian Nights* theme" that results in "a haunting fantasy."

Described by *Science Fiction Chronicle* contributor Don D'Ammassa as "very strange and disturbing," Hoffman's novella *Unmasking* takes place in the small town of Linden, where residents confront painful, repressed memories that are made to surface by a scientist who adds a foreign enzyme to the local water supply. Matilda "Matt" Blackaver, a homeless woman with psychic powers, lives in Linden and is known for conversing with houses, cars, and doors. While she sees beyond the effects of the enzyme, most residents can not and revenge, suicide, and other tragic efforts figure heavily in the novella's plot. Tom Easton, writing in *Analog Science Fiction and Fact,* called *Unmasking* "a beautifully executed story," while Edward Bryant wrote in *Locus* that Hoffman's work "is cut from a bolt of classic science fiction fabric" to render up "a perfect therapeutic metaphor for the me decade." Bryant compared *Unmasking* to George Romero's classic "B" horror film *Night of the Living Dead,* calling it "first-rate story-telling" in which the author "tosses off fascinating sparks that ought to be fanned into flames."

Hoffman has reprised Matt Black as the central character in several other novels, thus constructing her "Red Heart of Memories" series. Matt's "dream-eyes" allow her to visualize what others are thinking, and she can also communicate with in inanimate objects. In *A Red Heart of Memories* she joins fellow wanderers Edmund Reynolds and Susan "Suki" Backstrom on a journey to discover the hidden pieces of their pasts. The plot reveals that each of their gifts was the result of trauma. "Hoffman handles the interconnected solutions to the trio's problems with skill, as each solution leads subtly to greater understanding and compassion," noted a *Publishers Weekly* reviewer in reviewing the novel, while *Library Journal* contributor Jackie Cassada commended *A Red Heart of Memories* for its combination of "graceful storytelling and down-to-earth magic."

Along with Edmund, Suki, and Matt, *Past the Size of Dreaming* introduces several new characters, including Julio, who was abducted by a wizard as a child. After taking ownership of a haunted house with its own distinct personality, the troupe members cast spells and work to combat the darkness within themselves. Although a *Publishers Weekly* critic described Hoffman's premise as "a fuzzy concern with spiritual union with all the universe," Cassada wrote in *Library Journal* that the author's "sensuous prose and gentle humor add a graceful charm" to *Past the Size of Dreaming.* In *Booklist* Roberta Johnson also praised the "beautifully precise writing" in the novel while concluding that the entire "Red Heart of Memories" series stands as "a lasting addition to the urban fantasy canon."

Hoffman directly addresses a young-adult readership in *A Stir of Bones*, a prequel of sorts to her "Red Heart of Memories" series. Returning to Susan and Edmund's first meeting as teens, she uses Susan's perspective to reveal an adolescence characterized by physical abuse at the hand of her father. Susan resorts to dishonesty in order to spend time with Edmund and the other chosen friends who will later appear in *Past the Size of Dreaming.* They meet at an abandoned house which turns out to be haunted by Nathan, a teenaged ghost. Unhappiness prompts Susan to consider suicide in the house so that she can spend eternity with Nathan, but ultimately her friends convince her to otherwise transform her life.

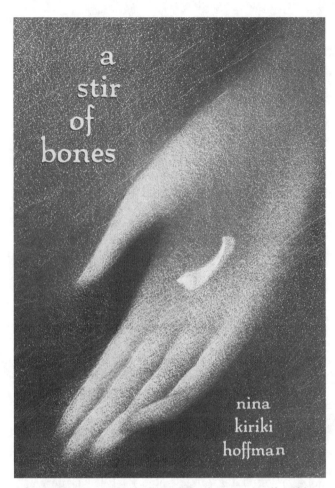

A haunted house provides the key to bolstering a teen's self-confidence in Hoffman's novel A Stir of Bones, *featuring cover art by Leonid Gore.* (Jacket illustration copyright © 2003 by Leonid Gore. Reproduced by permission of Viking Children's Books, a division of Penguin Young Readers Group, a member of Penguin Group (USA) Inc., 375 Hudson Street, New York, NY 10014. All rights reserved.)

A Stir of Bones "deals with the complexities of child abuse admirably, without offering pat answers or unrealistic resolutions," Tim Pratt noted in his review of Hoffman's novel for *Strange Horizons.* John Peters, writing in *Booklist,* described the same work as "richly endowed with complex relationships, a strange and subtle brand of magic, evocative language, and suspenseful storytelling," while Kathleen Whalin pointed out in *School Library Journal* that in Susan's narrative voice "everything . . . seems matter-of-fact and dispassionate, which draws readers in and intensifies the horror." Describing Hoffman's prose as "controlled and effective," a *Kirkus Reviews* writer judged *A Stir of Bones* to be "the best of the three" novels in the "Red Heart of Memories" series.

Drawing on her own adolescence in the companion novels *A Fistful of Sky* and *Fall of Light,* Hoffman introduces readers to the LaZelles, a Southern California family in which teens "transition," thereby gaining magical powers. In *A Fistful of Sky* Gypsum LaZelle has graduated from high school but has yet to "transition." Pitied by her family, Gypsum finds comfort in her father, who is nonmagical, as well as through her job and her love of food. Eventually, the teen falls extremely ill and recovers, only to discover that she has finally transitioned and now has the power to communicate with inanimate objects. Gypsum's sister Opal is the focus of *Fall of Light,* as she uses her skill in transforming humans into mythical beings while working in up in Oregon as part of the production staff of a horror film. When her costume for the actor cast as the film's Dark God causes the young man to subtly transform, Opal must exorcize whatever evil creature she has aided in possessing his spirit.

In a review for *Booklist,* Roberta Johnson noted that the "real attractions" in *A Fistful of Sky* are "its portrait of family dynamics and its sympathetic heroine." In *Booklist* Krista Hutley noted the "frequent touches of droll humor" in *Fall of Light,* while a *Publishers Weekly* critic remarked on the "tension" that threads through an otherwise "entertaining supernatural thriller." *A Fistful of Sky* will appeal to mature teens due to its themes of "reawakening and personal growth," the critic added.

Hoffman also focuses on adolescent transformation in *Catalyst: A Novel of Alien Contact,* but here she employs a distant planet as her setting. Kaslin is a young teen when he joins his parents in migrating to Chuudoku, a planet wherein the native species lives underground and possess three eyes. In addition to being a dysfunctional couple, Kaslin's parents have always been social misfits, and that stigma makes him the target of Histly, a well connected, bullying rich girl at his new school on Chuudoku. Pursued by Histly, Kaslin flees into a cave where he and his nemesis both make contact with the native Chuudokuans. While he develops a rapport with the cave dwellers, Histly does not. When she becomes dependent upon him for survival, Kaslin has many of his frustrated-teen fantasies fulfilled. Calling the teen characters in *Catalyst* "vibrant creations" within an imaginative story, Ray Olson added in his *Booklist* review that "their psychology" will seem "utterly credible for smart adolescents" in a novel that he recommended for mature teens due to its sexual content.

First-year college students Kim and Jaimie have been assigned to the same dormitory room when readers first meet them in *Spirits That Walk in Shadow.* Their incompatibilities quickly surface: Jaimie comes from a close-knit family steeped in Magic while Kim is deeply depressed over a recent rejection by a close friend. Jaimie's ability to sense the supernatural becomes useful, however, when she realizes that a *yuri,* a malevolent demon, is forcing Kim to remain in a state of despair. Only with the help of her talented cousins is Jaimie able to help vanquish the creature feeding off Kim's soul in a story *Kliatt* critic Chara Chancellor dubbed "an enchanting read that is impossible to put down." Kim and Jaimie's dual narratives help Hoffman keep her storyline "tight and exciting," according to a *Kirkus Review* writer, and the inclusion of "romance, mysterious vampirism and college students solving problems on their own will appeal . . . to teens." Re-

viewing *Spirits That Walk in Shadow* for *Booklist,* Holly Koelling described the work as "an intriguing and well-paced story that will appeal to those who enjoy both fantasy and mystery," while *School Library Journal* contributor Emily Rodriguez praised Hoffman's style, with its "light, witty exchanges" and its "quirky tone and colorful imagery."

Hoffman turns to middle-grade readers in her "Magic Next Door" series, which includes *Thresholds* and *Meeting.* Artistic-minded Maya Andersen is about to start seventh grade at her new home in Oregon when readers first meet her in *Thresholds.* The Idaho native puts worries about fitting in out of her mind when she meets neighbors Travis, Benjamin, and Gwenda and learns that the Janus House Apartments, where her new friends live, is built atop a maze of portals leading to alternate worlds. The supernatural spill-over from Janus House reaches Maya's room and she is tricked into raising an extraterrestrial, Fortunately, this alien as actually a *sissimi;* or protector, named Rimi, and Maya will need protection as she is drawn into the fantastic reality of her new friends. Further adventures spill forth in *Meeting* as Maya and Rimi help the Janus House portal-

Cover of Thresholds, *the first volume in Hoffman's middle-grade "Magic Next Door" series.* (Jacket cover art © 2010 by Joshua Middleton. Reproduced by permission of Viking, a division of Penguin Young Readers Group, a member of Penguin Group (USA), 375 Hudson Street, New York, NY 10014. All rights reserved.)

keepers locate members of the Krithi, aliens hoping to take over the universe, starting with Earth.

Reviewing *Thresholds* in *School Library Journal,* Laurie Slagenwhite Waiters called Hoffman's fanciful storyline "intriguing" because Maya's experiences allow her to deal with her recent relocation and begin "to see hope for the future." "Fantasy fans will find plenty to enjoy here," predicted *Booklist* critic Carolyn Phelan, while a *Kirkus Reviews* writer noted that the mix of "fantasy and science fiction" in *Thresholds* makes it "well positioned to explore the opportunities each [genre] presents." "Lovely worldbuilding, an appealing heroine, and [fantastic] detail that's refreshingly practical . . . make this one stand out," concluded another *Kirkus Reviews* critic in appraising Hoffman's follow-up adventure, *Meeting.*

While much of Hoffman's fiction continues to focus on teens, she features adult characters in both *The Thread That Binds the Bones* and *The Silent Strength of Stones.* In the first, a janitor with magical powers uses his gifts to prevent the suicides of two youths in Portland, then retires to a small town where he meets and marries the daughter of a well-connected family. Bryant noted in *Locus* that the novel's cast of characters "would do [Victorian novelist Charles] Dickens proud, in terms both of number and of character traits." Another original fantasy, *The Silent Strength of Stones,* prompted Tim Pratt to hail Hoffman as "a genius" in his review of the work for *Strange Horizons.*

Biographical and Critical Sources

BOOKS

Science Fiction & Fantasy Literature, 1975-1991, Gale (Detroit, MI), 1992.

PERIODICALS

Booklist, March 15, 2001, Roberta Johnson, review of *Past the Size of Dreaming,* p. 1360; October 1, 2002, Roberta Johnson, review of *A Fistful of Sky,* p. 308; May 1, 2003, Roland Green, review of *Time Travelers, Ghosts, and Other Visions,* p. 1586; October 1, 2003, John Peters, review of *A Stir of Bones,* p. 310; September 15, 2006, Ray Olson, review of *Catalyst,* p. 33; November, 2006, Holly Koelling, review of *Spirits That Walk in Shadow,* p. 42; December 1, 2006, Frieda Murray, review of *Short Work,* p. 33; May 15, 2009, Krista Hutley, review of *Fall of Light,* p. 27; August 1, 2010, Carolyn Phelan, review of *Thresholds,* p. 56.

Bulletin of the Center for Children's Books, January, 2007, April Spisak, review of *Spirits That Walk in Shadow,* p. 217; September, 2010, Kate Quealy-Gainer, review of *Thresholds,* p. 24.

Horn Book, July-August, 2009, Claire E. Gross, review of *Firebirds Soaring.*

Kirkus Reviews, February 15, 2001 review of *Past the Size of Dreaming,* p. 224; August 1, 2003, review of *A Stir of Bones,* p. 1018; October, 1, 2006, review of *Spirits That Walk in Shadow,* p. 1015; July 15, 2010, review of *Thresholds;* June 15, 2011, review of *Meeting.*

Kliatt, November, 2006, Cara Chancellor, review of *Spirits That Walk in Shadow,* p. 11.

Library Journal, October 15, 1999, Jackie Cassada, review of *A Red Heart of Memories,* p. 110; March 15, 2001, Jackie Cassada, review of *Past the Size of Dreaming,* p. 110.

Locus, June, 2002, interview with Hoffman.

Publishers Weekly, September 20, 1999, review of *A Red Heart of Memories,* p. 79; January 29, 2001, review of *Past the Size of Dreaming,* p. 70; March 23, 2009, review of *Fall of Light,* p. 51.

Register-Guard (Eugene, OR), April 26, 2009, Bob Keefer, "Tales of Magic," p. E3.

School Library Journal, December, 2003, Kathleen Whalin, review of *A Stir of Bones,* p. 152; January, 2007, Emily Rodriguez, review of *Spirits That Walk in Shadow,* p. 129; September, 2010, Laurie Slagenwhite Waiters, review of *Thresholds,* p. 155.

Voice of Youth Advocates, December, 2006, Ann Welton, review of *Spirits That Walk in Shadow,* p. 442; August, 2009, Lisa Martincik, review of *Fall of Light,* p. 237.

ONLINE

Locus Online, http://www.locusmag.com/ (December 30, 2009), "Nina Kiriki Hoffman."

Strange Horizons Web site, http://www.strangehorizons.com/ (November 24, 2003), Tim Pratt, "The Birth of Damage: Nina Kiriki Hoffman's *A Stir of Bones;*" Karen Meisner, interview with Hoffman.*

J-K

JOSEPHUS JITTA, Ceseli 1952-

Personal
Born 1952, in Wassenaar, Netherlands. *Education:* Attended Académie Julien (Paris, France), 1970-71; Rietveld Academie (Amsterdam, Netherlands), degree, 1978; attended Rijksacademie.

Addresses
Home—Amsterdam, Netherlands. *E-mail*—ceseli@ceseli.nl.

Career
Illustrator, author, and puppeteer, beginning 1982. Teacher at university level. Designer for theatrical performances. *Exhibitions:* Work exhibited at Galerij Lenten, Epse, Netherlands, 1982; Israel Galerie, Amsterdam, Netherlands, 1986; Biennale Bratislava, 1993, 1995; Galerie 2001, Badhoevedorp, Netherlands, 1995; Galerie Lughien, Amsterdam, 1995; Achter de Zuilen, Bloemendall, Netherlands, 1995; Asian Pacific Cultural Center/UNESCO, Tokyo, Japan, 1995; Gassan Diamonds, Amsterdam, 1997; Spui 28 gallery, The Hague, Netherlands, 1998; Atelier 48, Amsterdam, 2001; and Stedelijk Museum, Amsterdam, 2001.

Awards, Honors
Vlag en Wimpel award, 1999, for *Jan Jappie en de Veelvraat;* Gouden Uil prize nomination, and Gouden Penseel prize nomination, both 2007, both for *Loa en de Leasecat;* other honors.

Writings

SELF-ILLUSTRATED

Wat is er toch met Lola Fink?, Zirkoon (Amsterdam, Netherlands), 2001.

De Wolkenfabriek, Zirkoon (Amsterdam, Netherlands), 2002.

De Diamant van Opa, Zirkoon (Amsterdam, Netherlands), 2004.

Lola en de Leasekat, Zirkoon (Amsterdam, Netherlands), 2006, translated as *Lola and the Rent-a-Cat,* Frances Lincoln Children's Books (London, England), 2010.

Mihn Tekendagboek, Nieuw Amsterdam (Amsterdam, Netherlands), 2009.

ILLUSTRATOR

Marga Smits, *Sinterklass,* Kimio (Blaricum, Netherlands), 1986.

Kerstmis, Kimio (Naarden, Netherlands), 1987.

Henri van Daele, *Tijger,* Harlekijn (Westbroek, Netherlands), 1987.

Bies van Ede (pen name of Willem Johannes Franciscus van Ede) *Geloof je het zelf? en andere Verhalen,* Harlekijn (Westbroek, Netherlands), 1990.

Marianne van Delft, *Anna waait weg,* Harlekijn (Westbroek, Netherlands), 1991.

Rosalie Purvis, *Jana's Nachtreis,* Kimio (Naarden, Netherlands), 1992.

Ton van Reen, *De Circusprinses,* Wildeboer (Amsterdam, Netherlands), 1994.

Greet Beukenkamp, *Bonje om de Boomhut,* Sjaloom (Amsterdam, Netherlands), 1994.

Biggeltrijn en Pandjesman, Kimio (Naarden, Netherlands), 1994.

Ton van Reen, *Barbara, Bas, Boris, Beer,* Wildeboer (Amsterdam, Netherlands), 1994.

Ton van Reen, *De Meermeermin* (sequel to *Barbara, Bas, Boris, Beer*), Wildeboer (Amsterdam, Netherlands), 1995.

Joke Kranenbarg, *Kete op het Dak,* Sjaloom (Amsterdam, Netherlands), 1995.

Ton van Reen, *De Elfenkoning* (sequel to *De meermeermin*), Wildeboer (Amsterdam, Netherlands), 1996.

Geertje Gort, *Toen Duifje ging zwemmen,* Kimio (Naarden, Netherlands), 1996.

Moni-Nilsson-Brännstroöm, *Tsatsiki* (translated from the Swedish), Piramide (Amsterdam, Netherlands), 1997.

Moni-Nilsson-Brännstroöm, *Tsatsiki in Griekenland* (translated from the Swedish), Piramide (Amsterdam, Netherlands), 1998.

Karel Eykman, *Als er een God is,* Piramide (Amsterdam, Netherlands), 1998.

Moni-Nilsson-Brännstroöm, *De Wereld van Tsatsiki* (translated from the Swedish), Piramide (Amsterdam, Netherlands), 1998.

Karel Eykman, *David,* Piramide (Amsterdam, Netherlands), 1998.

Geertje Gort, *Jan Jappie en de Veelvraat,* Zirkoon (Amsterdam, Netherlands), 1999.

Harm de Jonge, *De Prinses uit het Sparrenbos,* Zwijsen (Tilburg, Netherlands), 2000.

Moni-Nilsson-Brännstroöm, *Tsatsiki en Retzina* (translated from the Swedish), Piramide (Amsterdam, Netherlands), 2000.

Karel Eykman, *Waar het om Gaat: 7 x7 bijbelse gedichten,* De Fontein (Baarn, Netherlands), 2004.

Nico ter Linden, *Koning op een Ezel: verhalen uit het Nieuwe Testament* (also see below), Balans (Amsterdam, Netherlands), 2005.

Marita de Sterck, *Tasjes,* Zwijsen this (Tilburg, Netherlands), 2006.

Nico ter Linden, *Het land onder de Regenboog: Verhalen uit het Oude Testament* (also see below), Balans (Amsterdam, Netherlands), 2006.

Karel Eykman, *Met open ogen: 100 Bijbelse gedichten,* De Fontein (Baarn, Netherlands), 2007.

Nico ter Linden, *De Profeet in de vis: Verhalen uit het Oude Testament* (also see below), Balans (Amsterdam, Netherlands), 2007.

Nico ter Linden, *De Kinderbijbel van Nico ter Linden compleet* (includes *Het Land onder de Regensboog, De Profeet in de vis,* and *Koning op een Ezel*), Balans (Amsterdam, Netherlands), 2008.

Thérèse Major, *Mam, kom terug!,* Nieuw Amsterdam (Amsterdam, Netherlands), 2008.

Marita de Sterck, *Schatjepatatje,* De Eenhoorn (Wielsbeke, Netherlands), 2009.

Ienne Biemans, *Rosa en de Wonderschoenen,* Nieuw Amsterdam (Amsterdam, Netherlands), 2010.

Karen Eykman, *Was ik een Schaap, dan wist ik het wel: Bijbelse figuren in Gedichten en Verhalen,* Van Gennep (Amsterdam, Netherlands), 2011.

Elseline Knuttel, selector, *Leesletters: Gedichten,* De Inktvis (Dordrecht, Netherlands), 2011.

Books featuring Josephus Jitta's art have been translated into Danish and Swedish.

Biographical and Critical Sources

PERIODICALS

Booklist, November 15, 2010, Daniel Kraus, review of *Lola and the Rent-a-Cat,* p. 51.

Kirkus Reviews, November 15, 2010, review of *Lola and the Rent-a-Cat.*

School Librarian, winter, 2010, Trevor Dickinson, review of *Lola and the Rent-a-Cat,* p. 220.

ONLINE

Ceseli Josephus Jitta Home Page, http://www.ceseli.nl (March 3, 2012).

De Eenhoorn Web site, http://www.eenhoorn.be/ (March 3, 2012), "Ceseli Josephus Jitta."

Nederlands Letterenfonds Web site, http://www.nlpvf.nl/ (March 3, 2012), "Ceseli Josephus Jitta."

* * *

KLISE, James 1967-

Personal

Born 1967, in Peoria, IL; partner's name Mike. *Education:* Attended Catholic University of America; University of Missouri, M.A.; Bennington College, M.F.A. (creative writing).

Addresses

Home—Chicago, IL. *Office*—CICS Northtown Academy, 3900 W. Peterson Ave., Chicago, IL 60659-3162. *E-mail*—jamesklise@gmail.com.

Career

Writer and librarian. CICS Northtown Academy, Chicago, IL, librarian and adviser. Has taught writing at Columbia College, Chicago, and University of Missouri, Columbia.

Awards, Honors

Stonewall Book Awards Honor Book selection, and Rainbow Books list inclusion, both American Library Association, and Lambda Literary Award finalist, all 2011, all for *Love Drugged.*

Writings

Love Drugged (young-adult novel), Flux (Woodbury, MN), 2010.

Contributor of short stories to periodicals, including *Ascent, Story Quarterly, New Orleans Review,* and *Southern Humanities Review.* Contributor of essays and reviews to periodicals, including *Chicago Sun-Times, Booklist,* and *Readerville Journal.*

Sidelights

In his debut novel, *Love Drugged,* James Klise presents "a thoughtful story about identity, sexuality, and learning to accept oneself," in the words of a *Publishers*

James Klise (Photograph by John Coffey. Reproduced by permission.)

Weekly critic. The plot of *Love Drugged* centers on a closeted gay teenager who takes an experimental drug designed to "cure" homosexuality. The themes Klise addresses in his novel are close to his heart: the author, who is gay, works as a librarian at a charter high school in Chicago, Illinois. "I am the GSA (Gay-Straight Alliance) adviser at my school," Klise explained to *Chicago Tribune* reporter Courtney Crowder. "And working with young people who are LGBTQ made me remember all that fear and confusion I had when I was a gay teen. I wanted to write something about that."

The protagonist of *Love Drugged,* fifteen-year-old Jamie Bates, is slowly coming to terms with his homosexuality. When a classmate discovers that Jamie is gay, the teen becomes terrified at the thought of being outed at school. In a desperate attempt to deny his sexuality, Jamie begins dating Celia Gamez, a beautiful and intelligent student who has expressed an interest in him. Coincidentally, Celia's father, a wealthy pharmaceutical scientist, has recently developed an experimental drug called Rehomoline which suppresses homosexual desires in the male brain. Jamie makes a fateful decision to steal some of the pills, which not only fail to increase his desire for Celia but also cause nasty side

effects. When Jamie goes to Dr. Gamez for help, the teen learns that he has been serving as a human guinea pig for the manipulative scientist.

In his *Booklist* review of *Love Drugged,* Michael Cart observed that Klise "succeeds in capturing the terrible anxiety of a teen discovering the truth of his sexual identity," and *Voice of Youth Advocates* contributor Angie Hammond commented that "the issues presented are very real for many teens." Through Jamie's experiences, as David Purse remarked on the Lambda Literary Web site, Klise "shows that the most damaging lies can be the ones that we tell ourselves and that after we come to terms with who we really are, there is an opportunity for things to get better."

Klise notes that his work as a high-school librarian has benefited his writing. "I see check-out trends in the library, and it's always interesting to see what prompts a student to take out a book, and why they may reject it after reading—or scanning—only a page or two," he told *Cynsations* online interviewer Cynthia Leitch Smith. "They are passionate, demanding readers, impatient for story, and they always remind me what matters: vivid characters and compelling, well-paced plotting."

Cover of Klise's novel Love Drugged, *in which focuses on a gay teen's efforts to pass for straight in high school.* (Jacket cover photograph © Amanda Rohde/iStockphoto.com. Reproduced by permission of Flux, an imprint of Llewellyn Worldwide, Ltd.)

Biographical and Critical Sources

PERIODICALS

Booklist, November 1, 2010, Michael Cart, review of *Love Drugged,* p. 64.

Chicago Tribune, May 28, 2011, Courtney Crowder, "Tales for the Young at Heart" (profile of Klise); November 1, 2010, Rex W. Huppke, "North Side Librarian's First Novel Explores How Difficult It Is to Be Gay in High School."

Kirkus Reviews, August 1, 2010, review of *Love Drugged.*

Publishers Weekly, September 6, 2010, review of *Love Drugged,* p. 42.

School Library Journal, May, 2011, Betty S. Evans, review of *Love Drugged,* p. 116.

Voice of Youth Advocates, August, 2010, Angie Hammond, review of *Love Drugged,* p. 249.

ONLINE

Cynsations Web log, http://cynthialeitichsmith.blogspot.com/ (November 19, 2010), Cynthia Leitich Smith, interview with Klise.

James Klise Home Page, http://www.jamesklise.com (March 1, 2012).

Lambda Literary Web site, http://www.lambdaliterary.org/ (August 16, 2011), David Purse, review of *Love Drugged.*

Story Siren Web log, http://www.thestorysiren.com/ (August 17, 2010), "Guest Post: James Klise."

*   *   *

KRUG, Nora 1977-

Personal

Born 1977, in Karlsruhe, Germany. *Education:* Liverpool Institute for Performing Arts, B.A.; Universität der Künste Berlin, master's degree; School of Visual Arts, M.F.A., 2004.

Addresses

Office—Parsons The New School for Design, 2 W. 13th St., Rm. 807, New York, NY 10011. *E-mail*—norakrug@gmx.net.

Career

Illustrator, animator, and educator. Muthesius University for Fine Arts and Design, Kiel, Germany, former professor of illustration; Parsons The New School for Design, New York, NY, associate professor of illustration. Creator of animated short films, including *How-to-Bow. Exhibitions:* Animated works exhibited at Ars Electronica, Linz, Austria; Ogaki Biennale, Gifu, Japan; and Sundance Film Festival, Park City, UT.

Awards, Honors

Deutscher Akademischer Austausch Dienst scholarship; Fulbright scholarship; New York Art Director's Club honor, Digital Sparks Competition winner, and *CMYK* magazine Digital Competition winner, all for animation *How-to-Bow.com;* gold medal, Society of Illustrators, 2007, for biographical comic "Fukutsu," and 2011, for biographical comic "Kamikaze."

Writings

SELF-ILLUSTRATED

Red Riding Hood Redux (five volumes), Briese (Borgerhout, Belgium), 2011.

Also creator of comics, including "Fukutsu" and "Kamikaze."

ILLUSTRATOR

Molly Rausch, *My Cold Went on Vacation,* G.P. Putnam's Sons (New York, NY), 2011.

Nora Krug creates the cartoon art that captures the whimsy in Molly Rausch's picture book My Cold Went on Vacation. (Illustration copyright © 2011 by Nora Krug. Reproduced by permission of G.P. Putnam's Sons, a division of Penguin Group (USA), Inc.)

Contributor of editorial illustrations to periodicals, including the *New York Times,* the London *Guardian, Le Monde diplomatique, Playboy, Vanity Fair,* and the *Wall Street Journal.*

Sidelights

Nora Krug studied performance design, documentary film, and illustration in her native Germany as well as in England and New York City in the course of developing her career as an award-winning animator and illustrator. Honored by New York's prestigious Society of Illustrators and exhibiting her work internationally, Krug is also a professor at New York's Parson's The New School for Design. In addition to creating a number of award-winning comics, she has also won young fans through her work illustrating Molly Rausch's humorous picture book *My Cold Went on Vacation.*

My Cold Went on Vacation sidesteps the cold, hard facts of medical science in imagining how sniffles, coughs, and other assorted symptoms make their way through the human population. Told that his cold is caused by a germ, a little boy personifies this germ as a guest in his body and imagines where the creature will go after spending time with him. In the boy's whimsical imagination, this particular germ—depicted in Krug's artwork as a green, red-nosed monster with bright pink eyes—hops off the boy to start his next adventure during a ride on the boy's school bus. After climbing a mountain, crossing an ocean, and eventually making its way around the world, the germ chooses its next human host: the narrator's sister!

Reviewing *My Cold Went on Vacation* in *Booklist,* Hazel Rochman predicted that "young children . . . will enjoy the global adventures and comical nonsense" in the illustrated story while adult readers will "get the parody" running through Rausch's text. A *Publishers Weekly* contributor dubbed the picture-book collaboration as "an idiosyncratic meditation about a germ on the move" and added that Krug's "quirky, electric-hued pictures combine folk art and cartoon" elements. Susanne Myers Harold also recommended the Rausch/Krug collaboration in *School Library Journal,* citing the mix of a "lighthearted, absurdist" story and "bold, whimsical art."

Biographical and Critical Sources

PERIODICALS

Booklist, January 1, 2011, Hazel Rochman, review of *My Cold Went on Vacation,* p. 113.
Publishers Weekly, November 15, 2010, review of *My Cold Went on Vacation,* p. 56.
School Library Journal, March, 2011, Suzanne Myers Harold, review of *My Cold Went on Vacation,* p. 132.

ONLINE

Illostribute Web site, http://illostribute.com/ (September 7, 2011), Toby Thane Neighbors, interview with Krug.
Nora Krug Home Page, http://www.nora-krug.com (March 1, 2012).
Parsons The New School for Design Web site, http://www. newschool.edu/ (March 1, 2012), "Nora Krug."*

*   *   *

KUNZE, Lauren

Personal

Born in Piedmont, CA. *Education:* Harvard University, B.A. (English), 2008. *Hobbies and other interests:* Reading, running, theater.

Addresses

Home—Piedmont, CA.

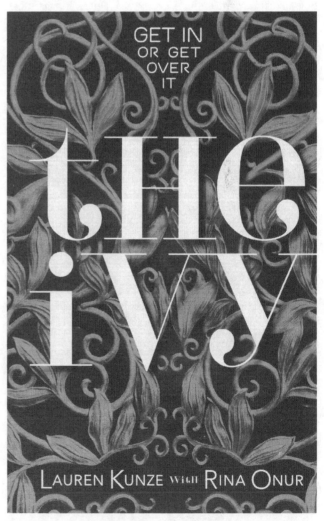

Cover of Lauren Kunze and Rina Onur's novel The Ivy, *the first part of a series about competitive college life.* (Jacket cover © 2010 by Christy Hale. Reproduced by permission of Greenwillow Books, an imprint of HarperCollins Children's Books, a division of HarperCollins Publishers.)

Career
Writer.

Writings

"IVY" NOVEL SERIES; WITH RINA ONUR

The Ivy, Greenwillow Books (New York, NY), 2010.
Secrets, Greenwillow Books (New York, NY), 2011.
Rivals, Greenwillow Books (New York, NY), 2012.

Sidelights
Lauren Kunze and fellow Harvard University graduate Rina Onur revisit their college days in the "Ivy" series of young-adult novels, which center on an ambitious teenager's freshman year at the prestigious Ivy League school. Kunze believes that the "Ivy" books offer a departure from the norm, noting that most novels for teens feature protagonists who are still attending middle-school or high school. "There are almost no books . . . that take place in college," she told *Thirteen.org* interviewer Leon Neyfakh. "It's sort of this off-the-map area—it's this uncharted territory. So [the series] is unique in its Harvard setting, but I think overall the experience of a young girl going off [to] college and going into a vastly new environment and encountering all these different people is very universal."

In *The Ivy,* the first installment in the series, Kunze and Onur introduce Callie Andrews, a California transplant who must rely on her more sophisticated roommates to help her navigate the often difficult-to-decipher East Coast social scene. As the semester progresses, Callie falls for an upperclassman whose jealous ex-girlfriend, Alexis, will decide if Callie can join an exclusive club as well be part of the staff of the *Harvard Crimson,* the school newspaper. A *Publishers Weekly* critic described *The Ivy* as "a guilty pleasure," while *School Library Journal* critic Tracy Glass dubbed the novel "a light-hearted and quirky read."

Secrets, the second work in the series, focuses on Callie's attempts to keep Alexis from spilling news about a sex tape Callie's high-school boyfriend made without her permission. In *School Library Journal,* Jessie Spalding applauded the authors' portrayal of Cassie, noting that the protagonist "is intelligent and aware, and the roadblocks to her finding happiness and love are logical." In *Rivals* Callie is torn between two suitors while trying to cement her positions at both the *Harvard Crimson* and the Hasty Pudding Club. "Smoothly continuing intrigues from earlier novels," as a writer for *Kirkus Reviews* stated, *Rivals* "tantalizes with tension and drama."

Biographical and Critical Sources

PERIODICALS

Booklist, September 1, 2010, Jennifer Hubert, review of *The Ivy,* p. 99.
Kirkus Reviews, August 1, 2010, review of *The Ivy;* May 15, 2011, review of *Secrets;* February 15, 2012, review of *Rivals.*
Publishers Weekly, September 6, 2010, review of *The Ivy,* p. 42.
School Library Journal, December, 2010, Traci Glass, review of *The Ivy,* p. 116; September, 2011, Jessie Spalding, review of *Secrets,* p. 160.

ONLINE

HarperTeen Web site, http://www.harperteen.com/ (March 1, 2012), "Lauren Kunze."
Ivy Web site, http://www.ivybookseries.com/ (March 1, 2012).
Thirteen.org, http://www.thirteen.org/ (September 20, 2010), Leon Neyfakh, interview with Kunze.*

L

LARSON, Kirby 1954-

Personal
Born August 17, 1954, in Seattle, WA; daughter of David Neil (a mechanical contractor) and Donna Marie (a bookkeeper) Miltenberger; married Neil Edwin Larson (a certified public accountant), September 6, 1975; children: Tyler Kenton, Quinn Lois. *Education:* Western Washington State College, B.A., 1976; University of Washington, M.A., 1980. *Hobbies and other interests:* Gardening, bird watching, traveling, visiting with friends.

Addresses
Home and office—Kenmore, WA.

Career
Children's book author. Whidbey Island Writers Workshop, Whidbey Island, WA, former member of creative-writing faculty. Northshore Performing Arts Center Foundation, cofounder. Moorlands Elementary Parent-Teacher Association, co-president, 1991-94; Northshore School District, member of board of directors, 1994-2001.

Member
Author's Guild, Society of Children's Book Writers and Illustrators, PEN.

Awards, Honors
Golden Acorn Award for PTA Service, 1994; Oppenheim Platinum Award, CYBILS Award finalist, *Seattle Times* Best Book designation, Borders Original Voice designation, Montana Book Award, and Book Links Lasting Connections designation, all 2006, and Newbery Honor designation and several children's choice awards, all 2007, all for *Hattie Big Sky;* Henry Bergh Children's Book Award, American Society for the Pre-

Kirby Larson (Photograph by Shawn Jezerinac. Reproduced by permission.)

vention of Cruelty to Animals, Teachers' Choice selection, International Reading Association (IRA), Children's Choice selection, IRA/Children's Book Council (CBC), Notable Social Studies Trade Book for Young People designation, National Council for the Social Studies/CBC, and Best Children's Books of the Year designation, Bank Street College of Education, all 2008, all for *Two Bobbies;* (with Mary Nethery and Brian Dennis) Christopher Medal, and Gold Award, National Parenting Publication Awards, both 2009, both for *Nubs.*

Writings

FICTION; FOR CHILDREN

Second-Grade Pig Pals, illustrated by Nancy Poydar, Holiday House (New York, NY), 1994.
Cody and Quinn, Sitting in a Tree, illustrated by Nancy Poydar, Holiday House (New York, NY), 1996.
The Magic Kerchief, illustrated by Rosanne Litzinger, Holiday House (New York, NY), 2000.
Hattie Big Sky (young-adult novel), Delacorte Press (New York, NY), 2006.
The Fences between Us: The Diary of Piper Davis ("Dear America" series), Scholastic (New York, NY), 2010.
The Friendship Doll (middle-grade novel), Delacorte Press (New York, NY), 2011.

NONFICTION; FOR CHILDREN

(With Mary Nethery) *Two Bobbies: A True Story of Hurricane Katrina, Friendship, and Survival,* illustrated by Jean Cassels, Walker (New York, NY), 2008.

Cover of Larson's entertaining chapter book Cody and Quinn, Sitting in a Tree, *featuring artwork by Nancy Poydar.* (Illustration copyright © 1996 by Nancy Poydar. Reproduced by permission of Holiday House, Inc.)

(With Mary Nethery and Brian Dennis) *Nubs: The True Story of a Mutt, a Marine, and a Miracle,* Little, Brown (New York, NY), 2009.

"SWEET VALLEY KIDS" CHAPTER-BOOK SERIES

Scaredy-Cat Elizabeth, Bantam Doubleday Dell (New York, NY), 1995.
Elizabeth Hatches an Egg, Bantam Doubleday Dell (New York, NY), 1996.

Adaptations

Hattie Big Sky was adapted as an audiobook narrated by Kirsten Potter, Listening Library, 2007.

Sidelights

Kirby Larson has gained critical praise for creating good-humored chapter books that accurately reflect the concerns of children, works of historical fiction that explore turbulent eras in U.S. history, and gratifying and comforting nonfiction tales. Larson's young-adult novel *Hattie Big Sky* earned the author a prestigious Newbery Honor designation, and her coauthored *Two Bobbies: A True Story of Hurricane Katrina, Friendship, and Survival* garnered the Henry Bergh Children's Book Award from the American Society for the Prevention of Cruelty to Animals.

Larson's first two chapter books, *Second-Grade Pig Pals* and *Cody and Quinn, Sitting in a Tree,* introduce a second grader named Quinn. In addition to worries about celebrating a holiday devoted to swine in *Second-Grade Pig Pals,* Quinn finds herself with friend problems when her efforts to befriend Manuela, a new student, are foiled by more-aggressive classmate Annie May. Quinn's solution to her dilemma, which involves both girls working together to compose a limerick about pigs, gives the book a "whole-hoggedly satisfying ending," in the opinion of *School Library Journal* contributor Janet M. Bair. Susan Dove Lempke, reviewing Larson's first book for the *Bulletin of the Center for Children's Books,* predicted that young readers will enjoy following Quinn's "travails as she agonizes, in true-to-life second-grade fashion, over the pigs and Manuela."

The class bully, with his relentless taunting, tries to ruin Quinn's friendship with a boy in *Cody and Quinn, Sitting in a Tree.* Here Quinn & Company "act out this typical school story with a generous measure of humor and sensitivity," wrote Pat Mathews in a *Bulletin of the Center for Children's Books* review, and Kay Weisman declared in *Booklist* that "Larson has an accurate sense of seven-year-olds' preoccupations and a good ear for dialogue."

Turning to younger children in *The Magic Kerchief,* Larson tells the story of a crabby old woman named Griselda, whose terse and insulting remarks win her

Cover of Larson's young-adult novel Hattie Big Sky, *featuring artwork by Jonathan Barkat.* (Jacket cover copyright © 2006 by Delacorte Press. Reproduced by permission of Delacorte Press, an imprint of Random House Children's Books, a division of Random House, Inc.)

few friends in her small village. When the sharp-tongued woman's kindness toward a traveling stranger earns her the gift of a magic scarf, however, Griselda gains the ability to speak in a way that matches her generosity of heart. Featuring pastel-toned illustrations by Rozanne Litzinger, *The Magic Kerchief* was praised by *School Library Journal* reviewer Sheilah Kosco for its "simple, humorous prose." In *Publishers Weekly* a critic wrote that Larson's "buoyant original folktale bristles with lively description," and a *Horn Book* critic concluded that the "lighthearted" picture book "offers a humorous take on the theme of kindness being its own reward."

Larson honors the life of her own great-grandmother, Hattie Inez Brooks Wright, in her teen novel *Hattie Big Sky.* Readers meet Hattie Brooks when she is sixteen years old and an orphan living in Arlington, Iowa. When she receives word that she has inherited a homesteading claim from her uncle Chester, Hattie makes the journey west to Montana and attempts to improve the claim despite the wartime hardships of the years 1917 to 1919 and the efforts of a nearby rancher to take over her land. Noting that the young woman's first year is con-

sumed by her need to survive the harsh conditions and also do the fence-mending, planting, and harvesting required to maintain her claim, *Booklist* reviewer Kathleen Odean wrote that Larson's "richly textured" novel features "figurative language . . . that draws on the "sounds, smells, and sights of the prairie." In *Kliatt,* Claire Rosser predicted that *Hattie Big Sky* would appeal to fans of Laura Ingalls Wilder's "Little House" series, and wrote that the "strength and intelligence, . . . courage and loyal friendship" of Larson's protagonist "make her a real hero." Dubbing the book "heartwarming yet poignant," *School Library Journal* reviewer Sharon Morrison praised the author's ability to paint, for teens, "a masterful picture of the homesteading experience and the people who persevered," and a *Kirkus Reviews* writer called *Hattie Big Sky* a "fine offering [that] may well inspire readers to find out more about their own family histories."

Larson's contribution to the "Dear America" series, *The Fences between Us: The Diary of Piper Davis,* is set weeks before the devastating attack on Pearl Harbor that occurred in December of 1941. Thirteen-year-old Piper lives quietly with her family in Seattle, Washington, where her father is pastor of a Baptist church. After the bombing raid on Pearl Harbor, everything changes: Piper grows concerned for her older brother, who recently joined the Navy, as well as for her Japanese friends and neighbors, who are routinely harassed, beaten, and arrested. When members of her father's predominately Japanese congregation are sent to the Minidoka War Relocation Center, an internment camp in Idaho, the pastor decides to follow. First angry at having to leave her family home, Piper comes to respect her father's courageous stance, and she eventually develops a close friendship with a Japanese-American girl living at the camp. "Larson does an excellent job recreating the tension Piper feels," Ann Reddy noted in her review of *The Fences between Us* for *Voice of Youth Advocates,* and Kim Dare observed in *School Library Journal* that "Piper's convincing narration allows readers to appreciate the dilemma that occurs when individual rights seem to clash with national security."

Another work of historical fiction, Larson's *The Friendship Doll,* is based on a true story. In 1927 fifty-eight exquisitely crafted Friendship Dolls arrived in the United States, a gift from Japanese children. The dolls—each about three feet tall and dressed in richly colored kimonos—proved so popular with the American public that they were exhibited around the nation. Many of them were eventually placed on permanent display in museums, although a number went missing, presumed destroyed, during World War II. Larson's middle-grade novel focuses on one of the dolls, Miss Kanagawa, who also helps narrate the tale. During her travels across the decades, Miss Kanagawa helps change the lives of several young girls, in the process becoming more human herself. "The well-developed characters are appealing and distinct," remarked *Booklist* reviewer Lynn Rutan, who also praised the "deftly handled historical detail"

Cover of Larson's The Fences between Us, *part of the "Dear America" diary series and featuring cover art by Tim O'Brien.* (Jacket cover photographs © Tim O'Brien. Cover illustration copyright © 2010 by Scholastic, Inc. Reproduced by permission of Scholastic, Inc.)

in the story. According to *School Library Journal* critic Allison Tran, Larsen's "story is not solely lighthearted . . .; heavy topics such as death, grief, and aging are addressed in a straightforward yet remarkably affecting manner."

Larson has collaborated with friend and fellow writer Mary Nethery on two well-received works of nonfiction. *Two Bobbies* centers on the unlikely relationship between a blind cat and its loyal companion, a stray dog, both which were found wandering the streets of New Orleans, Louisiana, months after Hurricane Katrina devastated the Gulf Coast region in 2005. Rescued and taken to a rescue shelter, Bob Cat and Bobbi (so named because of their bobbed tails) garnered national attention, and eventually found a new home on an Oregon ranch. Writing in *School Library Journal*, Judith Constantinides called *Two Bobbies* a "touching animal tale" in which the coauthors "concentrate on the 'feel good' aspect of the two Bobbies." "The descriptive, sometimes folksy prose . . . accessibly convey[s] the Bobbies' experiences," Shelle Rosenfeld commented in her *Booklist* appraisal of Larson and Nethery's animal-centered tale.

Larson and Nethery teamed up with U.S. Marine Brian Dennis on *Nubs: The True Story of a Mutt, a Marine, and a Miracle,* another heart-warming animal tale. While serving at a border fort in Iraq during his tour of duty, Dennis began caring for a feral dog he called "Nubs," a reference to the dog's ears, which had been docked. As their bond grew, Nubs tried, unsuccessfully, to follow Dennis's unit on its missions. When Dennis was relocated to Jordan, the canine endured a treacherous seventy-mile journey through the freezing desert to reunite with his caregiver. Ordered to get rid of the dog, Dennis raised enough money to transport Nubs across the world to his San Diego home, where friends cared for the dog until the marine returned stateside. Writing in *Booklist,* Daniel Kraus applauded the "hugely inspirational" story, and a critic in *Publishers Weekly* predicted that *Nubs* would appeal to readers who enjoy "stories of animals that triumph against the odds."

"Once upon a time, there was a little girl with a funny name and blue cats-eye glasses," Larson once told *SATA.* "Her family moved around a lot; nearly every fall, she was the new kid in school. Sometimes she was lonely but she never worried about making friends—she had two brothers and a sister to play with and hundreds of companions in the books she read. When she wasn't reading, the girl liked to build cushion forts in the living room or put on plays for her parents. She never broke any bones or world records, except maybe for reading. The girl loved to read so much that sometimes even her teachers complained!

"When the little girl grew up, she did many things—went to college, worked at a radio station; she even made those annoying sales calls people hang up on. Along the way, she met a handsome prince (maybe not a prince, but definitely handsome), got married and had two children, a boy and a girl. Those babies loved being read to! Which was good because, even though she was grown up, the girl still loved to read. She especially loved to read about George and Martha, Frog and Toad, dear little Frances, and anything by Betsy Byars. The girl loved these children's books so much that she wanted to write one herself. So she did.

"And it was awful. She wrote another one and it was worse. And no fairy godmother showed up to help her, either. She kept writing. Some of it was still bad, but some of it was getting better! The girl didn't give up and, one day, one of her stories was published.

"You've no doubt guessed that this fairy tale is about me. Everything's absolutely true—except for the part about not having a fairy godmother. Actually, I have many! They are fellow children's book writers who tell me when my story needs work and give me good ideas about how to fix it, as well as illustrators and designers who make the books look lovely and publicists and booksellers who tell the world about them. That is why I so treasure all my fairy godmothers.

"Just because your books are published doesn't necessarily mean you've arrived. The truth is writers have to start over again with each new book they write—at least I do. After my third book, *The Magic Kerchief,* debuted, I didn't sell anything for five depressing years. One day I was sitting with my grandmother, who'd been overcome by age and Alzheimer's. We were folding kitchen towels and she said the oddest thing: 'The only time Mom was ever afraid was in the winter when the wild horses stampeded.' I had no idea what the remark referred to, nor if it was even true, but I had to find out.

"Despite hating history, I immersed myself in genealogy files, national archives, newspapers, and old photos to learn more about my great grandmother, Hattie Inez Brooks, who had homesteaded by herself in eastern Montana. Eventually her story became the inspiration for what I soon realized was my first novel. I wrote and wrote and wrote—through the bad stuff—until I began to find some good stuff. I kept writing. Three years later, thanks to the encouragement of my family and dear writing friends, I sold *Hattie Big Sky* to Delacorte Press. Even if *Hattie Big Sky* hadn't received a 2007 Newbery Honor award, I would feel successful. I am proud of it not because of any awards or reviews, but because it touches other people just like the books I read as a child and budding writer had touched me."

Biographical and Critical Sources

PERIODICALS

Booklist, November 1, 1994, Mary Harris Veeder, review of *Second-Grade Pig Pals,* p. 497; April 1, 1996, Kay Weisman, review of *Cody and Quinn, Sitting in a Tree,* p. 1366; August, 2000, Shelle Rosenfeld, review of *The Magic Kerchief,* p. 2148; September 1, 2006, Kathleen Odean review of *Hattie Big Sky,* p. 126; September 1, 2008, Shelle Rosenfeld, review of *Two Bobbies: A True Story of Hurricane Katrina, Friendship, and Survival,* p. 102; October 1, 2009, Barbara A. Ward and Terrell A. Young, "Compassion through Friendship" (profile), p. S31; October 1, 2009, Daniel Kraus, review of *Nubs: The True Story of a Mutt, a Marine, and a Miracle,* p. 42; July 1, 2010, Gillian Engberg, review of *The Fences between Us: The Diary of Piper Davis,* p. 60; July 1, 2011, Lynn Rutan, review of *The Friendship Doll,* p. 60.

Bulletin of the Center for Children's Books, December, 1994, Susan Dove Lempke, review of *Second-Grade Pig Pals,* p. 1334; September, 1996, Pat Mathews, review of *Cody and Quinn, Sitting in a Tree,* p. 19; March, 2007, Elizabeth Bush, review of *Hattie Big Sky,* p. 299.

Horn Book, September, 2000, review of *The Magic Kerchief,* p. 551.

Kirkus Reviews, September 1, 2006, review of *Hattie Big Sky,* p. 906; August 15, 2008, review of *Two Bobbies*; August 15, 2010, review of *The Fences between Us.*

Kliatt, September, 2006, Claire Rosser, review of *Hattie Big Sky,* p. 14.

Publishers Weekly, September 18, 2000, review of *The Magic Kerchief,* p. 111; September 22, 2008, Matthew Thornton, "A Soldier's Best Friend," p. 18; November 9, 2009, review of *Nubs,* p. 45.

School Library Journal, November, 1994, Janet M. Bair, review of *Second-Grade Pig Pals,* p. 84; April, 1996, Cheryl Cufari, review of *Cody and Quinn, Sitting in a Tree,* p. 113; November, 2006, Sharon Morrison, review of *Hattie Big Sky,* p. 140; July, 2007, Charli Osborne, review of *Hattie Big Sky,* p. 56; September, 2008, Judith Constantinides, review of *Two Bobbies,* p. 166; December, 2009, Kara Schaff Dean, review of *Nubs,* p. 97; December, 2010, Kim Dare, review of *The Fences between Us,* p. 118; August, 2011, Allison Tran, review of *The Friendship Doll,* p. 110.

Seattle Times, January 27, 2007, "A Plucky Legacy," p. C1.

Voice of Youth Advocates, October, 2010, Ann Reddy, review of *The Fences between Us,* p. 352.

ONLINE

*Bildungsroman Web log,*http://slayground.livejournal.com/ (January 6, 2007), interview with Larson.

Kirby Larson Home Page, http://www.kirbylarson.com (March 1, 2012).

Kirby Larson Web log, http://kirbyslane.blogspot.com (March 1, 2012).

Random House Web site, http://www.randomhouse.com/ (March 1, 2012), "Author Spotlight: Kirby Larson."*

* * *

LAVAU, Alexandra
See WATTS, Frances

* * *

LENG, Qin
(Qin Chin Leng)

Personal

Born in Shanghai, China; immigrated to Canada; father an artist. *Education:* Mel Hoppenheim School of Cinema, B.A. (film animation), 2006. *Hobbies and other interests:* Travel, food.

Addresses

Home—Toronto, Ontario, Canada. *E-mail*—qinchin@ hotmail.com.

Career

Illustrator, animator, and designer. Film work includes projects for National Film Board of Canada, Montreal,

Qin Leng (Reproduced by permission.)

Quebec, Canada; Fluorescent Hill; Le Sens de la Culture Chinoise (performance event), Montreal; CORE; Yowza Animation; and 95Story, Toronto, Ontario, Canada.

Awards, Honors

Numerous awards for animated short films; Blue Spruce Award nomination, Ontario Library Association, Best Books for Kids and Teens selection, Canadian Children's Book Centre, and *ForeWord* Book of the Year Award finalist, all c. 2011, all for *A Flock of Shoes* by Sarah Tsiang.

Illustrator

Anrenee Englander, *Dear Diary, I'm Pregnant,* Annick Press (Toronto, Ontario, Canada), 2009, revised edition, 2010.

Anne Dublin, *The Orphan Rescue,* Second Story Press (Toronto, Ontario, Canada), 2010.

Sarah Tsiang, *A Flock of Shoes,* Annick Press (Toronto, Ontario, Canada), 2010.

Andrée Poulin, *Cent bonshommes de neige,* Dominique et Cie. (Saint-Lambert, Québec, Canada), 2011.

Sarah Tsiang, *Dogs Don't Eat Jam, and Other Things Big Kids Know,* Annick Press (Toronto, Ontario, Canada), 2011.

Cheryl Foggo, *Dear Baobab,* Second Story Press (Toronto, Ontario, Canada), 2011.

Jennifer Lloyd, *The Best Thing about Kindergarten,* Simply Read Books (Vancouver, British Columbia, Canada), 2011.

Rebecca Hainnu and Anna Ziegler, *A Walk on the Tundra,* Inhabit Media (Iqaluit, Nunavut, Canada), 2011.

Matthew Price, *Catch That Puppy,* Matthew Price, 2011.

Russell Punter, *The Goose Girl,* Usborne Publishing (London, England), 2012.

Sarah Tsiang, *Stone Hatchlings,* Annick Press (Toronto, Ontario, Canada), 2012.

Contributor to periodicals, including *Chirp, Highlights for Children,* and *Owl* magazine, and to educational publications.

Works featuring Leng's illustrations have been translated into Chinese, French, German, Italian, and Korean.

Sidelights

Qin Leng has a truly international perspective in her work as an illustrator and animator. Born in China, she lived in France and French-speaking Quebec, Canada, before settling in English-speaking Toronto, Ontario, where she now works. As the daughter of an artist, Leng was able to pursue her natural creativity with confidence, knowing that it was possible for her to meld it into a successful career. In addition to her film work, which includes credits at both the National Film Board of Canada and Yowza Animation, she has also found success in the arena of children's books, a longtime interest. In reviewing Leng's illustrations for Cheryl Foggo's African-themed story in *Dear Baobab,* a *Kirkus Reviews* writer noted that her "watercolors with pleasantly loose ink lines" bring to life Foggo's "gentle, purposeful story."

A Walk on the Tundra, a picture book by Rebecca Hainnu and Anna Ziegler, introduces children to the ecology of the Arctic region by following a girl named Inuujaq and her Inuktituk grandmother as they take a walk around their home one spring day. While noting that the work "is more of an educational reference book than a storybook," Stacey Matson added in her *Canadian Review of Materials* review that Leng's "simple and colourful" images "help . . . to liven up the informational text with active, flowing illustrations."

Leng has collaborated with Canadian poet and author Sarah Tsiang on several picture-book projects. Tsiang casts her daughter Abby as the central character in *A Flock of Shoes,* which finds a little shoe lover convinced by her mother that her favorite summer sandals have migrated south as part of a flock of flying shoes when they are replaced by boots in the fall. "Washed with cheerful colors," according to *Booklist* contributor Carolyn Phelan, "Leng's cartoon-style drawings interpret the story with originality and wit." Catharine Callegari wrote in her *School Library Journal* review of *A Flock of Shoes* that the story's "drawings are a satisfying mix of color, action, and white space." Noting that

Leng's work as an illustrator includes the energy-filled "Saturday Market." (Courtesy of Qui Leng.)

"Tsiang's flight of fancy is delightfully captured in Leng's cartoon-style illustrations," a *Kirkus Reviews* writer predicted of the same book that the "whimsical tale is sure to beguile."

Biographical and Critical Sources

PERIODICALS

Booklist, October 15, 2010, Carolyn Phelan, review of *A Flock of Shoes,* p. 55.
Canadian Review of Materials, February 17, 2012, Stacey Matson, review of *A Walk on the Tundra.*
Children's Bookwatch, November, 2010, review of *The Orphan Rescue.*
Kirkus Reviews, November 15, 2010, review of *A Flock of Shoes*; August 15, 2011, review of *Dear Baobab.*
School Library Journal, March, 2011, Catherine Callegari, review of *A Flock of Shoes,* p. 137.

ONLINE

Herman Agency Web site, http://www.hermanagencyinc.com/ (March 1, 2012), "Qin Leng."
Qin Leng Home Page, http://qinleng.com (March 1, 2012).

*   *   *

LENG, Qin Chin
See LENG, Qin

*   *   *

LIWSKA, Renata

Personal

Born in Warsaw, Poland; immigrated to Canada; married Mike Kerr (an illustrator). *Education:* Attended Alberta College of Art and Design. *Hobbies and other interests:* Watching pandas.

Addresses

Home—Calgary, Alberta, Canada. *E-mail*—rliwska@telusplanet.net.

Career

Author and illustrator. *Exhibitions:* Work included in group shows staged at B42 Gallery, Oakville, Ontario, Canada; Uppercase Gallery, New York, NY; and Original Art Show, Society of Illustrators, New York, NY, 2008.

Awards, Honors

Governor General's Literary Award for Illustration finalist, and Gold Medal, Society of Illustrators New York, both 2010, both for *The Quiet Book* by Deborah Underwood; Governor General's Award finalist, 2011, for *The Red Wagon.*

Writings

SELF-ILLUSTRATED

Little Panda, Houghton Mifflin (Boston, MA), 2008.
Red Wagon, Philomel Books (New York, NY), 2011.

ILLUSTRATOR

Barbara Joosse, *Orphanage Number One,* Philomel (New York, NY), 2005.
Barbara Joosse, *Nikolai, the Only Bear,* Philomel (New York, NY), 2005.
Mary Labatt, *A Puppy Is for Loving,* Orca Book Publishers (Victoria, British Columbia, Canada), 2007.
Mary Cuffe-Perez, *Skylar,* Philomel (New York, NY), 2008.
Deborah Underwood, *The Quiet Book,* Houghton Mifflin Books for Children (New York, NY), 2010.
Deborah Underwood, *The Loud Book!,* Houghton Mifflin Harcourt (Boston, MA), 2011.

Also illustrator of activity books.

Works featuring Liwska's art have been translated into several languages, including French, Japanese, Korean, Portuguese, and Spanish.

Sidelights

Renata Liwska, a Polish-born Canadian illustrator, has provided the artwork for stories by Barbara Joosse, Mary Cuffe-Perez, Mary Labatt, and Deborah Under-

Renata Liwska creates the colorful illustrations that bring to life Barbara Joosse's tender story in Nikolai, the Only Bear. (Illustration copyright © 2005 by Renata Liwska. Reproduced by permission of Philomel Books, a division of Penguin Group (USA), Inc.)

wood in addition to sharing her original, self-illustrated stories in the picture books *Little Panda* and *Red Wagon*. "My best work involves subjects that I can relate to personally," Liwska remarked on her home page. "I need to be able to get involved in my illustrations on an emotional level and I like to incorporate personal experience whenever possible."

Featuring a story by Joosse, *Nikolai, the Only Bear* centers on the efforts of a North American couple to adopt a Russian child named Nikolai. In the book's illustrations, Nikolai is portrayed as a lonely bear cub that no one wants until the American visitors decide to make him part of their family. "Joosse and . . . Liwska convey that no child is beyond the reach of love," noted a *Publishers Weekly* critic in appraising *Nikolai, the Only Bear*, while in *Kirkus Reviews* a critic praised the artist's depiction of Nikolai by noting that the bear's shifting emotions are "expressed in relatively subtle but clear shifts of head and posture."

Skylar, a story by Cuffe-Perez, finds a flock of pond geese agreeing to help a one-eyed heron migrate to its birthplace. In this book, "Liwska's shaded black-and-white pencil renderings work with the text to give readers a strong sense of place," wrote Susan Hepler in her *School Library Journal* review of the story.

The artist's creative collaboration with Underwood has produced two picture books that take young children from one extreme to the other. In *The Quiet Book* Underwood's simple text pairs with Liwska's animal-focuses art to illustrate the many forms quiet can take: from the soothing silence of falling snow to the muffled sounds heard under water to the momentary quiet while anticipating something terribly loud. *The Quiet Book* demonstrates "suspense, eloquence, and surprise" via Liwska's "digitally colored pencil illustrations," according to *Booklist* critic Hazel Rochman, and a *Publishers Weekly* critic dubbed the same work a "treasure of a book" in which "subtly engaging" images featuring "delicately furred animals . . . ably reflect the emotions that each type of quiet elicits."

Liwska and Underwood ramp up the energy level in *The Loud Book!*, which finds their menagerie of young characters demonstrating the different degrees of loud: from a burp in a quiet room to a ringing alarm and ear-piercing whistles to cheers to the bang of falling objects. Although the "colors are a bit brighter" in *The Loud Book!*, the companion volume "stars the same gang of fuzzy creatures and is every bit as charming," asserted another *Publishers Weekly* critic. "Eschewing noise lines and other dramatic visuals . . . , Liwska instead shows mouths open in loud roars, boisterous crowds and hands over tortured ears," noted a *Kirkus Reviews* in describing the colorful pencil art, and *School Library Journal* Blair Christolon ranked *The Loud Book!* as a "deliciously worthy companion" to *The Quiet Book*.

Little Panda, Liwska's self-illustrated picture-book debut, was inspired by a late-night television news report about the unusual bearlike creatures. Her interest

In addition creating art for other writers, Liwska has created the original self-illustrated picture book **Little Panda.**

piqued, the artist began researching pandas on the Internet, studying their behaviors and routines. "With this book," she wrote on her home page, "I hope to give the reader a little taste of the joy I get from observing these wonderful animals."

In *Little Panda* Grandfather Panda tells young Bao Bao a cautionary tale about a tiny panda who falls asleep in the branches of his favorite tree and awakens to find a hungry tiger climbing up after him. Using the lessons his mother has taught him, the tiny panda manages an unlikely escape. According to *Booklist* reviewer Margaret Bush, "Liwska's melange of the fanciful and the real is well crafted in the smooth telling and artwork." A critic for *Publishers Weekly* also complimented the artwork in *Little Panda,* remarking that the artist/author's digitally enhanced pencil drawings "evoke the simplicity of traditional Chinese art and underscore the intimacy" of her tale.

A little fox named Lucy is the star of *Red Wagon,* another original picture book by Liwska. Lucy is eager to spend time with her three best friends—a raccoon, a hedgehog, and a rabbit—and play with her shiny red wagon. When Mother Fox asks Lucy to go to the store to purchase some vegetables for dinner, the youngster cannot bear to leave her new toy behind. She also brings her playmates along and the four imaginative animals quickly transform the wagon-pulling errand into a fan-

Liwska combines an engaging story and original art in her picture book Red Wagon. (Copyright © 2011 by Renata Liwska. Reproduced by permission of Philomel Books, a division of Penguin Group (USA), Inc.)

tastical journey that includes trips on a sailing ship and a space ship as well as a circus adventure. As her "story moves between fantasy and reality," Liwska's "fluffy, soft, and friendly looking" animal characters engage young children, according to Roxanne Burg in her *School Library Journal* review, and a *Horn Book* critic Cynthia K. Ritter ranked *Red Wagon* as "an enjoyable story to read with creative little critters just like Lucy." "A mundane task fills with delicious thrills" in Liwska's art and story, according to a *Kirkus Reviews* writer, while in *Booklist* Gillian Engberg praised *Red Wagon* as "a winning story of imaginative play that makes a worthy partner" to Crockett Johnson's picture-book classic *Harold and the Purple Crayon*.

Biographical and Critical Sources

PERIODICALS

Booklist, January 1, 2008, Suzanne Harold, review of *Skylar*, p. 84; December 1, 2008, Shelle Rosenfeld, review of *Little Panda*, p. 56: February 15, 2010, Hazel Rochman, review of *The Quiet Book*, p. 81; January 1, 2011, Randall Enos, review of *The Loud Book!*, p. 113; February 15, 2011, Gillian Engberg, review of *Red Wagon*, p. 68.

Horn Book, January-February, 2005, Susan P. Bloom, review of *Nikolai, the Only Bear*, p. 79; January-February, 2009, Jennifer M. Brabander, review of *Little Panda*, p. 80; January-February, 2011, Cynthia K. Ritter, review of *Red Wagon*, p. 79.

Kirkus Reviews, March 1, 2005, review of *Nikolai, the Only Bear*, p. 288; January 15, 2008, review of *Skylar*; December 15, 2010, review of *Red Wagon*; March 1, 2011, review of *The Loud Book!*

Publishers Weekly, April 11, 2005, review of *Nikolai, the Only Bear*, p. 53; September 22, 2008, review of *Little Panda*, p. 57; February 15, 2010, review of *The Quiet Book*, p. 127; November 8, 2010, review of *The Quiet Book*, p. 32; February 21, 2011, review of *The Loud Book!*, p. 130.

School Library Journal, April, 2005, review of *Nikolai, the Only Bear*, p. 99; July, 2008, Susan Hepler, review of *Skylar*, p. 70; November, 2008, Margaret Bush, review of *Little Panda*, p. 92; February, 2011, Roxanne Burg, review of *Red Wagon*, p. 86; May, 2011, Blair Christolon, review of *The Loud Book!*, p. 90.

ONLINE

Little Panda Book Web site, http://www.littlepandabook.com/ (February 15, 2009).

Renata Liwska Home Page, http://www.wronghand.com (February 15, 2012).

Renata Liwska Web log, http://renataliwska.blogspot.com (February 15, 2012).*

*　　*　　*

LONDON, C. Alexander 1980-
(Charles London)

Personal

Born 1980, in Brooklyn, NY. *Education:* College degree. *Hobbies and other interests:* SCUBA diving, skeet shooting.

Addresses

Home—Brooklyn, NY.

Career

Author, journalist, and librarian. Worked variously as researcher in African refugee camps and assistant to a Hollywood talent agent; former librarian. Relief worker in Bosnia, 2004.

Writings

"ACCIDENTAL ADVENTURES" CHAPTER-BOOK SERIES

We Are Not Eaten by Yaks, illustrated by Jonny Duddle, Philomel Books (New York, NY), 2011.
We Dine with Cannibals, illustrated by Jonny Duddle, Philomel Books (New York, NY), 2011.

OTHER

(Under name Charles London) *One Day the Soldiers Came: Voices of Children in War,* HarperPerennial (New York, NY), 2007.
(Under name Charles London) *Far from Zion: In Search of a Global Jewish Community,* William Morrow (New York, NY), 2009.

Sidelights

C. Alexander London has led a life that seems full of contradictions. Although he has worked as a mild-mannered librarian, London's resume also includes a stint as a globe-hopping journalist who covered several civil wars as well as a volcanic eruption in the Democratic Republic of Congo. London's excursion to Burma occurred just in time to make him a witness a battle between Buddhist monks and a military government that shut down Burma's airports as well as television and the Internet.

Illustrated by Jonny Duddle, *We Are Not Eaten by Yaks* introduces Celia and Oliver Navel, eleven-year-old twins who dread adventures of any and all sorts. Unfortunately, their parents scour the globe in search of excitement, and the Navel children have spent their childhood either on the road or living at rooms in the Explorers Club, where they spend most of their time watching television. When Mrs. Navel disappears while searching for the location of the Lost Tablets of Alexandria, her husband packs up the twins and heads to Tibet, where the clues lead. It quickly becomes clear that rival adventurer Sir Edmund S. Tithletorpe-Schmidt III is behind the woman's disappearance, but that does not stop Celia and Oliver's father from wagering their freedom against the discovery of the lost city of Shangri-La. With their future hanging in the balance, the twins become actively involved in the hunt, and their journey takes them into secret caves and over waterfalls, moved along via several unfortunate forms of transportation, and eventually coming face to face with a mythical

creature in a novel that *Booklist* reviewer Todd Morning claimed "stands out for its funny take on the [adventure] theme." In a story that a *Publishers Weekly* critic characterized as "absurdly comical," London also tweaks time-honored parental caveats, writing that the twins' "TV expertise helps them outwit many bumbling adults." With each turn off the page in *We Are Not Eaten by Yaks,* "the adventures keep coming," concluded Patty Saidenberg in *School Library Journal,* and London fuels his story's "quick pace" with a double dose of "wit and humor."

While Mom eventually returns home safely, she does not stay long; the Navel family is off on another globe-trotting adventure in *We Dine with Cannibals.* During another summer in which they are destined to mourn the loss of television reception, Oliver and Celia travel to the rain forests of South America where their mother continues her search for the Lost Tablets, Dad decides to scout out clues to the whereabouts of El Dorado, and popular television host Corey Brandt taps the Navels' expertise while filming an episode of *The Celebrity Adventurist.* The lifestyle of the average cannibal Amazonian jungle dweller is not something the twins find appealing, and a secret organizations also threatens their safety in a sequel that "has more thrills and more mystery" than the first "Accidental Adventures" novel, according to a *Kirkus Reviews* writer. Noting that *We Dine with Cannibals* "features many goofy situations," Morning added in *Booklist* that London leaves his readers with a cliff-hanger ending that "promises more . . . adventures to come."

In addition to entertaining younger readers in his light-hearted "Accidental Adventures" chapter-book series, London also uses his talent for writing to share his more-thoughtful side. He meditates on his spiritual and ethnic roots in *Far from Zion: In Search of a Global Jewish Community* and addresses the tragedy of young people around the world whose lives have been destroyed by violence in *One Day the Soldiers Came: Voices of Children in War.*

Biographical and Critical Sources

PERIODICALS

Booklist, January 1, 2011, Todd Morning, review of *We Are Not Eaten by Yaks,* p. 111; November 1, 2011, Todd Morning, review of *We Dine with Cannibals,* p. 122.
Bulletin of the Center for Children's Books, March, 2011, Elizabeth Bush, review of *We Are Not Eaten by Yaks,* p. 334.
Kirkus Reviews, October 1, 2011, review of *We Dine with Cannibals.*
Publishers Weekly, January 3, 2011, review of *We Are Not Eaten by Yaks,* p. 51.

C. Alexander London chronicles the exploits of some reluctant adventurers in **We Are Not Eaten by Yaks,** *a book featuring artwork by Jonny Duddle.*

School Library Journal, April, 2011, Patty Saidenberg, review of *We Are Not Eaten by Yaks,* p. 179.

ONLINE

Boys and Literacy Web log, http://www.boystobooks.com/ (November 15, 2011), Trudy Zufelt, interview with London.

C. Alexander London Home Page, http://www.calexander london.com (March 2, 2012).*

*   *   *

LONDON, Charles
See LONDON, C. Alexander

M

MARCIANO, John Bemelmans 1970-

Personal
Born 1970; son of Barbara Bemelmans; grandson of Ludwig Bemelmans (a writer and illustrator). *Education:* Degree (art history).

Addresses
Home—Brooklyn, NY.

Career
Writer and illustrator.

Writings

SELF-ILLUSTRATED CHILDREN'S BOOKS

Madeline Says Merci: The Always-Be-Polite Book, Viking (New York, NY), 2001.
Delilah, Viking (New York, NY), 2002.
Harold's Tail, Viking (New York, NY), 2003.
There's a Dolphin in the Grand Canal!, Viking (New York, NY), 2005.
Madeline Loves Animals, Viking (New York, NY), 2005.
Madeline and the Cats of Rome, Viking (New York, NY), 2008.
Anonyponymous: The Forgotten People behind Everyday Words, Bloomsbury (New York, NY), 2009.
Toponymity: An Atlas of Words, Bloomsbury (New York, NY), 2010.
Madeline at the White House, Viking (New York, NY), 2011.
Madeline and Her Dog, Viking (New York, NY), 2011.

OTHER

(With grandfather, Ludwig Bemelmans) *Madeline in America, and Other Holiday Tales* (contains "The Count and the Cobbler," "Bemelmans' Christmas Memory," and "Sunshine"), Scholastic (New York, NY), 1999.

Bemelmans: The Life and Art of Madeline's Creator, edited by C. Hennessy, illustrated by Ludwig Bemelmans, Viking (New York, NY), 1999.

Sidelights
The grandson of award-winning writer Ludwig Bemelmans, John Bemelmans Marciano has earned accolades for creating self-illustrated children's books which extend his family legacy, such as *Madeline and the Cats of Rome* and *Madeline at the White House.* Marciano began his career in children's literature in an almost magical fashion: while rummaging through family memorabilia, he discovered an unfinished manuscript for a children's story by his grandfather that featured Bemelmans' beloved picture-book heroine Madeline. Although Marciano had never met his grandfather, who passed away in 1962, his mother introduced him to the six "Madeline" books with their engaging stories and art.

Madeline in America, and Other Holiday Tales is based on Bemelmans' unfinished manuscript, "Madeline's Christmas in Texas," completed and illustrated by Marciano. Basing his illustrations on the pencil sketches left by his grandfather, Marciano completes the story of Madeline who, with teacher Miss Clavel and the other eleven girls from her school in Paris, travels to Texas after she inherits a cattle ranch, along with several gold mines and oil wells. Including two other stories by Bemelmans, *Madeline in America, and Other Holiday Tales* also features an essay by Marciano's mother, Barbara Bemelmans, describing Christmas festivities in her artistic father's home.

In reintroducing Madeline to generations of new audiences, Marciano has cast the perky French schoolgirl in his original work, *Madeline Says Merci: The Always-Be-Polite Book,* in which Madeline is transformed into what *School Library Journal* contributor Carol Schene dubbed "a mini 'Miss Manners.'" Taking place in the streets of Paris, the book finds Madeline exhibiting proper behavior in a variety of situations, each captured in illustrations that, according to Schene, show that Bemelmans' "impish Parisian is still alive and well." In addition to reprising his grandfather's picture-book character, Marciano has produced *Bemelmans: The Life and Art of Madeline's Creator,* a study of the Caldecott Medal-winning author/illustrator and journalist that was praised by a *Horn Book* critic as "an entirely affectionate biography."

Marciano set his 2008 work—the first completely original "Madeline" tale in almost fifty years—in the city he once called home. In *Madeline and the Cats of Rome,* Miss Clavel and the girls decide to escape the cold, rainy Paris spring and vacation in the sunny Italian capital. After the group visits the Sistine Chapel, the Triton Fountain, and other wondrous sites, a young thief steals Miss Clavel's camera, prompting Madeline and friend Genevieve to give chase. Although the girls retrieve the pilfered item, they also find themselves under arrest (only briefly, however) and agree to help the bandit find homes for a gaggle of stray cats. Reviewing *Madeline and the Cats of Rome* for *Booklist,* Carolyn Phelan noted that "Marciano does a good job of recapturing the look and the verve of his grandfather's artwork," and a *Kirkus Reviews* writer maintained that the new work "does seamlessly extend the series."

Before writing *Madeline and the Cats of Rome,* Marciano diligently studied his grandfather's narrative and artistic techniques, realizing that critics and readers alike would carefully analyze his work. "I knew that people would really want it to look just like the original," he remarked to Brian Bethune in *Maclean's.* "And I also knew that was impossible." In the end, Marciano decided to imitate, not replicate, Bemelmans' style, bringing a personal touch to the work, such as the Italian setting. "My grandfather knew [Paris] so well: He knew every tree, every architectural detail," he told *Houston Chronicle* interviewer Scott Timberg. "I had lived in Rome on and off—and I have this lifetime love of cats."

Marciano's *Madeline at the White House* is based on an unfinished project Bemelmans had started before his death: a collaboration with former First Lady Jacqueline Kennedy. In the work, Penelope "Candle" Randall, the very lonely daughter of the president of the United States, receives an Easter visit from Madeline and her Parisian classmates. After participating in the annual Easter Egg Roll on the lawn of the White House and overindulging on sweets, most of the girls take to bed with stomach aches. Candle and Madeline, however, enjoy a late-night aerial tour of Washington, DC, courtesy of the fun-loving magician who first appeared in

John Bemelmans Marciano provides a fresh adventure for his grandfather's popular character in his self-illustrated picture book Madeleine at the White House.

Marciano joins his grandfather, beloved writer Ludwig Bemelmans, in the picture book **Madeleine in America, and Other Holiday Tales.** (Illustration copyright © 1999 by John Bemelmans Marciano. Reproduced by permission of Scholastic, Inc.)

Madeline's Christmas. Marciano's efforts again drew comparisons to his grandfather's "Madeline" stories. A writer in *Kirkus Reviews* observed that Marciano "pairs verse that channels his esteemed progenitor's in tone," and *Booklist* critic Kay Weisman wrote that he captures "the rhythms and artistic style of the originals." "Marciano's paintings are faithful to those of his grandfather," a *Publishers Weekly* contributor stated.

Marciano has gone on to expand his picture-book repertoire beyond the antics of Madeline. In *Delilah* he tells a tale of friendship between a farmer and a frisky lamb that soon becomes the farmer's constant companion. Enjoying the lamb—named Delilah—so much, the farmer acquires a whole flock of sheep, only to realize that the value of a thing is not always increased when it is acquired in large numbers. Calling *Delilah* "a charmer," Jeanne Clancy Watkins predicted that young readers "will not be able to resist these engaging friends," while a *Kirkus Reviews* critic suggested that the book might "become a bedtime favorite." Most critics praised Marciano's illustrations, a *Publishers Weekly* reviewer noting that the author/illustrator "draws faces with the evocative simplicity of his grandfather's draftsmanship." The *Kirkus Reviews* writer deemed the pencil and gouache artwork in *Delilah* "delightfully simple."

Other books by Marciano include *Harold's Tail,* about a Manhattan-dwelling squirrel that learns what life is like for the less fortunate when he takes a dare, shaves the fluff from his tail, and finds himself reviled due to his resemblance to a city rat. In *Booklist,* Julie Cummins described *Harold's Tail* as a "clever, urban animal survival tale," while a *Kirkus Reviews* contributor viewed Marciano's illustrated story as a "study of prejudice and elitism" disguised as a lively children's book.

Animals also star in *There's a Dolphin in the Grand Canal!,* as a boy living in Venice, Italy, discovers a dolphin splashing about in the city's canal but has a difficult time convincing his parents as to the truth of what he has seen. Noting that the Venice scenery, with its "meticulous painted brickwork and golden touches," is the author/illustrator's "strong suit," a *Publishers Weekly* critic wrote that *There's a Dolphin in the Grand Canal!* "makes for an entertaining introduction to Venice."

Harold the squirrel learns an important life lesson in Marciano's bittersweet picture book **Harold's Tail.** (Illustration copyright © 2003 by John Bemelmans Marciano. Reproduced by permission of Viking Children's Books, a division of Penguin Young Readers Group, a member of Penguin Group (USA) Inc., 375 Hudson Street, New York, NY 10014. All rights reserved.)

A little boy visiting Venice discovers more excitement than he expected in Marciano's **There's a Dolphin in the Grand Canal!** (Reproduced by permission of Viking Children's Books, a division of Penguin Young Readers Group, a member of Penguin Group (USA) Inc., 375 Hudson Street, New York, NY 10014. All rights reserved.)

School Library Journal critic Wendy Lukehart maintained that Marciano's picture-book "romp" effectively "capture[s] the grandeur and diversity of Venetian architecture and the magical quality of the liquid streets."

Biographical and Critical Sources

PERIODICALS

Booklist, August, 2002, Helen Rosenberg, review of *Delilah,* p. 1973; September 1, 2003, Julie Cummins, review of *Harold's Tale,* p. 119; June 1, 2005, Karin Snelson, review of *There's a Dolphin in the Grand Canal!,* p. 1822; September 1, 2008, Carolyn Phelan, review of *Madeline and the Cats of Rome,* p. 106; January 1, 2011, Kay Weisman, review of *Madeline at the White House,* p. 113.

Bulletin of the Center for Children's Books, April, 2000, review of *Bemelmans: The Life and Art of Madeline's Creator,* p. 297.

Horn Book, January, 2000, review of *Bemelmans,* p. 106.

Houston Chronicle, Scott Timberg, "Madeline's Back, but This Time She's in Rome with Cats," p. 2.

Kirkus Reviews, May 1, 2002, review of *Delilah,* p. 660; August 2, 2003, review of *Harold's Tale,* p. 1020; May 15, 2005, review of *There's a Dolphin in the Grand Canal!,* p. 592; July 15, 2008, review of *Madeline and the Cats of Rome;* November 15, 2010, review of *Madeline at the White House.*

Maclean's, October 20, 2008, Brian Bethune, review of *Madeline and the Cats of Rome,* p. 74.

Publishers Weekly, November 19, 2001, review of *Madeline Says Merci: The Always-Be-Polite Book,* p. 70; April 15, 2002, review of *Delilah,* p. 63; August 11, 2003, review of *Harold's Tale,* p. 280; June 27, 2005, review of *There's a Dolphin in the Grand Canal!,* p. 62; July 21, 2008, review of *Madeline and the Cats of Rome,* p. 158; January 3, 2011, review of *Madeline at the White House,* p. 48.

School Library Journal, December, 2001, Carol Schene, review of *Madeline Says Merci,* p. 124; February, 2000, Lisa Falk, review of *Madeline in America, and Other Holiday Tales,* p. 91; August, 2002, Jeanne Clancy Watkins, review of *Delilah,* p. 161; November, 2003, Susan Helper, review of *Harold's Tale,* p. 108; August, 2005, Wendy Lukehart, review of *There's a Dolphin in the Grand Canal!,* p. 102; November, 2008, Rachel Kamin, review of *Madeline and the Cats of Rome,* p. 94; March, 2011, Mary Hazelton, review of *Madeline at the White House,* p. 129.

USA Today, September 18, 2008, Bob Minzesheimer, review of *Madeline and the Cats of Rome,* p. D4.

Voice of Youth Advocates, August, 2000, review of *Bemelmans,* p. 206.

ONLINE

BookPage Web site, http://www.bookpage.com/ (June, 2002), Heidi Henneman, interview with Marciano.

Canadian Review of Materials Online, http://www.umanitoba.ca/cm/ (February 18, 2000), Dave Jenkinson, review of *Madeline in America, and Other Holiday Tales.*

Penguin Books Web site, http://us.penguingroup.com/ (March 1, 2012), interview with Marciano.

Reading Rockets Web site, http://www.readingrockets.org/ (March 1, 2012), "Meet John Bemelmans Marciano" (video interview and transcript).*

*   *   *

MARCUS, Kimberly

Personal

Born in MA; married; children: two. *Education:* B.S. (psychology); Boston University, M.S. (social work); Emerson College, graduate certificate (picture-book writing).

Addresses

Home—Darmouth, MA. *Agent*—Tracey Adams, Adams Literary; info@adamsliterary.com. *E-mail*—kimberly.marcus@mac.com.

Career

Therapist and author. Worked as a child therapist. Presenter at schools.

Member

Society of Children's Book Writers and Illustrators (New England region).

Awards, Honors

Ruth Landers Glass Memorial scholarship in writing, Society of Children's Book Writers and Illustrators (New England region); Quick Pick for Reluctant Readers selection, and YALSA Best Fiction for Young Adults selection, both American Library Association, both 2012, both for *Exposed.*

Writings

Exposed (young-adult novel), Random House (New York, NY), 2011.

Scritch-Scratch a Perfect Match (picture book), illustrated by Mike Lester, G.P. Putnam's Sons (New York, NY), 2011.

Sidelights

Although Kimberly Marcus enjoyed writing while growing up, she did not pursue it seriously until years later, after training as a social worker and establishing a career as a child therapist. When her own children reached preschool age, Marcus used her free time to take writing courses with an eye to publishing, and after many hours of writing and revising, many letters to editors, and almost as many polite rejections, she sold her first manuscript: the picture-book text for *Scritch-Scratch a Perfect Match.* Shortly thereafter, Marcus received another sign that her decision to become a writer was the right one when her young-adult free-verse novel *Exposed* found a home with another New York City publisher. "I love the balance I've found between creating longer works focusing on some tough issues tackled by teens, and wordplay and rhyme for younger readers," she noted on her home page. "I feel truly blessed to be doing what I do, and being able to work in my pajamas is a definite perk to this amazing job."

Cover of Kimberly Marcus's verse novel Exposed, *in which a teen must salvage her reputation in the wake of a terrible accusation.* (Jacket cover copyright © Random House Children's Books. Reproduced by permission of Random House Children's Books, a division of Random House, Inc.)

For sixteen-year-old Liz, the main character in *Exposed,* the view into the future seems positive. Her talent for photography, fueled by passion, will likely lead to a successful career, while her social standing at her Cape Cod high school is secure due to her close friendship with Kate, a talented dancer. However, things become uncomfortably unbalanced after Kate begins to avoid Liz at school as well as on weekends. When the teens finally have it out, Liz's world is left in tatters: Kate explains that she was raped by Liz's older brother Mike during the friends' most-recent sleep-over at Liz's house. Suddenly, she is left unsure of the two people anchoring her world: Should she believe her best friend, or does she dare think her brother capable of such violence?

As "the accusation splinters alliances among Liz's friends and family," noted Daniel Kraus in his *Booklist* review of *Exposed,* Marcus chronicles the dramatic situation with the "utmost naturalism." *Voice of Youth Advocates* contributor Ava Ehde wrote that in *Exposed* the author employs an "ingenious style" to explore "a huge topic . . . with honesty, innocence and courage," while in *Horn Book* Tanya D. Auger cited the novel's "strong sense of place" and "a conclusion that's painful and genuine."

Marcus demonstrates her versatility as a writer by moving from the serious subject of rape to the whimsical story of an adventurous flea in *Scritch-Scratch a Perfect Match.* Brought to life in colorful pencil-and-watercolor cartoon art by Mike Lester, the story follows a feisty flea as it bites a dog that consequently sends its owner tumbling into a mud puddle. When the flea is scratched from the dog's furry coat it finds a new home on a stray cat, and another flurry of activity is unleashed. Murphy's animated, onomatopoeic text is also highlighted with entertaining expressions, and her simple rhyme scheme makes the story a good choice for story hours. Citing the book's mix of "nicely accessible" rhymes and "highly exaggerated" comic art, a *Kirkus Reviews* writer suggested that *Scritch-Scratch a Perfect Match* yields "clever fun and lots of giggles," while in *School Library Journal* Susan Weitz wrote that Marcus's debut picture book "explodes with sound on every page."

Biographical and Critical Sources

PERIODICALS

Booklist, February 1, 2011, Daniel Kraus, review of *Exposed,* p. 76.
Horn Book, May-June, 2011, Tanya D. Auger, review of *Exposed,* p. 97.
Kirkus Reviews, March 1, 2011, review of *Scritch-Scratch a Perfect Match.*
Publishers Weekly, January 3, 2011, review of *Exposed,* p. 52.

School Library Journal, April, 2011, Susan Weitz, review of *Scritch-Scratch a Perfect Match,* p. 149, and Jill Heritage Maza, review of *Exposed,* p. 179.
Voice of Youth Advocates, April, 2011, review of *Exposed,* p. 11.

ONLINE

Kimberly Marcus Home Page, http://kimberlymarcus.com (February 28, 2012).*

*   *   *

McGUINESS, Dan

Personal

Born in Adelaide, South Australia, Australia. *Education:* Earned diploma (interactive multimedia); technical certificate. *Hobbies and other interests:* Video games, cartoons.

Addresses

Home—North Adelaide, South Australia, Australia. *Agent*—Carole Carroll; c.carroll@internode.on.net. *E-mail*—dan.s.mcguiness@gmail.com.

Career

Author and illustrator. Worked variously at a factory, as a film editor, and in a comic-book shop.

Writings

Pilot and Huxley: The First Adventure, Graphix/Scholastic (New York, NY), 2011.
Pilot and Huxley: The Next Adventure, Graphix/Scholastic (New York, NY), 2011.

Sidelights

Dan McGuiness is an Australian cartoonist whose success might be used by children to debunk parental assertions that a love of video games and comic books does not translate into a career. McGuiness did not just enjoy reading comics, however; he also enjoyed making up his own, and this talent earned him a measure of popularity in grade school. With no plans for college, he worked in a factory after graduating from high school until the opportunity came to start a small business with some friends. A diploma in multimedia studies allowed him to develop his creative abilities, and led McGuiness to work on various film and video projects. It was a job at a comic-book shop that helped him translate his visual storytelling into sequential art and led to his creation of the "Pilot and Huxley" graphic novels.

In *Pilot and Huxley: The First Adventure* readers meet two boys who are the best of friends. While playing a video game, they discover that they have somehow activated a terrible weapon that is in the possession of an alien race intent on invading Earth. When the aliens attempt to retrieve the game containing this activation code, they accidentally beam the two gamers into an alternate world where the game becomes uncomfortably real. On their way back to earth, Pilot and Huxley team up with a strange girl named Brett to tackle stinging bees, pirates, and a sea monster while also making their way out of a dragon's nostril, all while saving Earth for future generations and making it home in time for dinner.

"A graphic novel that keeps the madcap plot moving and the jokes coming," according to Travis Jonker in *School Library Journal, Pilot and Huxley: The First Adventure* also features brightly colored illustrations that will "certainly appeal to boy readers." "McGuiness's illustrations are colorful and kinetic, fitting the tale's many humorous twists," asserted a *Publishers Weekly* critic, while in *Kirkus Reviews* a critic recommended *Pilot and Huxley: The First Adventure* to fans of Dav Pilkey, describing the book as "a zany, gross-out graphic novel that reads like a madcap, G-rated *South Park* episode."

When McGuiness's quirky heroes return in *Pilot and Huxley: The Next Adventure,* they get a chance to see Santa on his day off, when the jolly gift-giver is not so jolly. In fact, it turns out that Santa Claus is downright evil every day of the year except one. When they run into the proverbial "Jolly Old Elf" on December 23rd while visiting a different dimension, Pilot and Huxley find themselves on another outlandish adventure, this one featuring giant elves, talking edibles, and a red-nosed reindeer packing heavy-duty heat.

Pilot and Huxley: The Next Adventure "is full of inspired nonsense," quipped a *Kirkus Reviews* writer, adding that McGuiness captures the rhythm of popular animated-cartoon speak with its "sarcastic comment, self-referential joke, [and] ridiculous occurrence that our heroes take perfectly in stride." In his quirky cartoon mix, McGuiness has created "just the thing" to cause grown-ups discomfort "while their kids delight in its semi-naught fun," concluded Jesse Karp in his *Booklist* review of the Aussie author's graphic-novel follow-up.

Biographical and Critical Sources

PERIODICALS

Booklist, December 15, 2010, Jesse Karp, review of *Pilot and Huxley: The First Adventure,* p. 37l; October 15, 2011, Jesse Karp, review of *Pilot and Huxley: The Next Adventure,* p. 37.

Bulletin of the Center for Children's Books, February, 2011, Kate Quealy-Gainer, review of *Pilot and Huxley: The First Adventure,* p. 285.

Kirkus Reviews, November 15, 2010, review of *Pilot and Huxley: The First Adventure;* July 15, 2011, review of *Pilot and Huxley: The Next Adventure.*

Publishers Weekly, November 1, 2010, review of *Pilot and Huxley: The First Adventure,* p. 47.

School Library Journal, March, 2011, Travis Jonker, review of *Pilot and Huxley: The First Adventure,* p. 189.

ONLINE

Dan McGuiness Home Page, http://danmcguiness.com.au (March 3, 2012).*

Dan McGuiness shares his quirky world view with preteen readers in his graphic novel Pilot and Huxley: The First Adventure. (Copyright © 2009 by Dan McGuiness. Reproduced by permission of Omnibus Books, a division of Scholastic Australia, Pty.)

MIKULSKI, Keri 1977-
(Nicole Leigh Shepherd)

Personal

Born 1977; married; children: one daughter. *Education:* Rutgers University, M.F.A. (creative writing). *Hobbies and other interests:* Sports.

Addresses

Home—New Jersey. *Agent*—3 Seas Literary Agency, P.O. Box 8571, Madison, WI 53708.

Career

Author and educator. Teacher of writing on the college level.

Writings

"PRETTY TOUGH" YOUNG-ADULT NOVEL SERIES

Head Games, Razorbill (New York, NY), 2011.
Stealing Bases, Razorbill (New York, NY), 2012.
(Under name Nicole Leigh Shepherd) *Making Waves,* Penguin Group (New York, NY), 2012.
And Fifteen Love, Razorbill (New York, NY), 2012.

Contributor to periodicals, including *Current Heath 2.*

Sidelights

Organized sports were a central part of Keri Mikulski's high-school experience, and she shares her passion for athletic competition in the novels she now writes for teen girls. A teacher of writing on the college level, Mikulski is also the author of several novels in Razorbill's "Pretty Tough" series, which find teenage athletes dealing with typical adolescent issues while also learning life lessons on the field, on the court, or even in the pool.

In *Head Games* Mikulski focuses on high-school freshman Taylor Thomas, whose height and talent have made her the obvious choice as center on her private school's basketball team. Competitive on the court, Taylor is farless assertive in social settings, where she naively hopes to make friends with everybody. Fashion-forward best friend Hannah is one person Taylor can count on to help her navigate life at her new school, but even Hannah can only help so far when Taylor attempts to befriend her new boyfriend's ex. Reviewing Mikulski's novel in *Voice of Youth Advocates,* Beth Karpas predicted that, with its focus on "a teenage girl trying to balance sports, school, boys, and friends," *Head Games* "is sure to be popular" with its intended audience, and a *Kirkus Reviews* critic dubbed the debut novel "a rather sweet if undemanding story."

Mikulski has continued to contributor to the "Pretty Tough" series, focusing on baseball in *Stealing Bases,* swimming competition in *Making Waves,* and tennis in

And Fifteen Love. Making Waves, which finds Abby sidetracked by romance while working at a posh country club and poised to win the summer lifeguarding competition, was published under Mikulski's pen name, Nicole Leigh Shepherd.

Biographical and Critical Sources

PERIODICALS

Kirkus Reviews, December 1, 2010, review of *Head Games.*
Voice of Youth Advocates, February, 2011, Beth Karpas, review of *Head Games,* p. 556.

ONLINE

Keri Mikulski Home Page, http://kerimikulski.com (March 8, 2012).
Pretty Tough Web site, http://www.prettytough.com/ (March 15, 2012).*

Cover of Keri Mikulski's teen-focused sports novel **Head Games.** (Jacket cover © 2011 by PrettyTOUGH Sports, LLC. Reproduced by permission of Penguin Young Readers Group, a member of Penguin Group (USA), 345 Hudson Street, New York, NY 10014.)

MORSE, Joe

Personal

Married Lorraine Tuson (an illustrator and designer); children: two. *Education:* Ontario College of Art and Design, degree (with honors); graduate study at Instituto Allende; also studied art in Europe and Japan.

Addresses

Office—Sheridan College, 1430 Trafalgar Rd., Oakville, Ontario L6H 2L1, Canada. *Agent*—Sally Heflin, Heflinreps; sally@helfinreps.com. *E-mail*—joe@joemorse.com.

Career

Artist, illustrator, and educator. Sheridan College, Oakville, Ontario, Canada, program coordinator and professor of illustration, 1990—. *Exhibitions:* Works included in private collections and in group show at Columbia College, Chicago, IL, 2008.

Awards, Honors

Two Elizabeth Greenshields Foundation grants; Notable Children's Books in Language Arts designation, National Council of Teachers of English, Books for the Teen Age selection, New York Public Library, Governor General's Award for Best Children's Book nomination, and Best Books for Young Adults designation, American Library Association, all 2007, and Young Adult Choices selection, International Reading Association, 2008, all for *Casey at the Bat* by Ernest L. Thayer; Governor General's Award for Best Children's Book, 2012, for *Play Ball, Jackie!* by Stephen Krensky; recipient of more than 150 international awards.

Joe Morse creates the energetic art for Stephen Krensky's picture book **Play Ball, Jackie!**, *the story of baseball great Jackie Robinson.* (Illustration copyright © 2011 by Joe Morse. Reproduced by permission of Millbrook Press, a division of Lerner Publishing Group, Inc. All rights reserved. No part of this excerpt may be used or reproduced in any manner whatsoever without the prior written permission of Lerner Publishing Group, Inc.)

Illustrator

Ernest L. Thayer, *Casey at the Bat,* KCP Poetry (Toronto, Ontario, Canada), 2006.

Stephen Krensky, *Play Ball, Jackie!,* Millbrook Press (Minneapolis, MN), 2011.

John Coy, *Hoop Genius: How a Desperate Teacher and a Rowdy Class Invented Basketball,* Carolrhoda Books (Minneapolis, MN), 2011.

Contributor to periodicals, including *Rolling Stone,* London *Times, Esquire, Gentleman's Quarterly,* and the *New York Times.*

Sidelights

A professor of illustration at Sheridan College, Joe Morse lives dangerously for his art. Morse, who works primarily with oil and acrylic, must wear a gas mask, gloves, and coveralls to protect himself from the toxic solvents he uses to thin his paints. His painstaking efforts have been well rewarded, however: he has earned more than 150 international honors during his career. He has also garnered critical accolades for his work on a number of children's books, including a contemporary version of Ernest L. Thayer's classic *Casey at the Bat* and *Play Ball, Jackie!,* a story by Stephen Krensky.

Since "Casey at the Bat" was first published in 1888, Thayer's poem about a revered slugger's failure to deliver a clutch hit for his baseball team, has been enjoyed by generations of readers. Morse gives the work a modern look, placing his multiracial ballplayers in an urban setting replete with metal fences and high rise buildings. As Marilyn Taniguchi observed in her *School Library Journal* review of the book, the athletes "are strikingly rendered in oils and acrylics, their features sharply limned in thick black lines and smudges of neutral color." According to Gregory Bryan in the *Canadian Review of Materials,* Morse's "illustrations bring a gritty, hard-edged, realism to the otherwise playful, light-hearted tale," and *Resource Links* contributor Laura Reilly sensed "a tough almost desperate feel to the illustrations."

In *Play Ball, Jackie!* Krensky depicts the major-league debut of baseball great Jackie Robinson, the first African American to cross the "color line" that existed in early twentieth-century professional sports. On April 15, 1947, Robinson started at first base for the Brooklyn Dodgers, and his appearance forever changed the sport. "Morse's dramatically grained, exaggerated artwork plays up the intensity of the era's racial tensions," a critic remarked in *Publishers Weekly,* and Ian Chipman, writing in *Booklist,* commended the "Dodger-blue-and-graphite kineticism of Morse's stylized, limber figures and dynamic layouts."

Biographical and Critical Sources

PERIODICALS

Booklist, February 1, 2011, Ian Chipman, review of *Play Ball, Jackie!,* p. 74.

Canadian Review of Materials, March 17, 2006, Gregory Bryan, review of *Casey at the Bat.*

Publishers Weekly, January 24, 2011, "Baseball Books Storm the Field," review of *Casey at the Bat,* p. 150.

Resource Links, June, 2006, Laura Reilly, review of *Casey at the Bat,* p. 10.

School Library Journal, June, 2006, Marilyn Taniguchi, review of *Casey at the Bat,* p. 186; March, 2011, Marilyn Taniguchi, review of *Play Ball, Jackie!,* p. 126.

ONLINE

Communication Arts Online, http://www.commarts.com/ (February 21, 2012), interview with Morse.

Cynsations Web log, http://cynthialeitichsmith.blogspot.com/ (May 31, 2006), Cynthia Leitich Smith, interview with Morse.

Joe Morse Home Page, http://www.joemorse.com (March 1, 2012).

Sheridan College Web site, http://www.sheridancollege.ca/ (March 1, 2012), "Joe Morse."

*   *   *

MURPHY, Yannick 1962-

Personal

Born 1962; married; husband a veterinarian; children: three. *Education:* Attended Hampshire College and New York University.

Addresses

Home—Reading, VT. *E-mail*—yannick@hughes.net.

Career

Writer. Has taught at New York University, Oberlin College, University of Southern California, and University of California at Los Angeles.

Awards, Honors

Whiting Writers' Award, Mrs. Giles Whiting Foundation, 1990, for *Stories in Another Language;* National Endowment for the Arts fellowship; MacDowell Artists' Colony fellowship; Chesterfield screenwriting fellowship (in conjunction with Amblin Studios).

Writings

ADULT NOVELS

The Sea of Trees, Houghton Mifflin (Boston, MA), 1997.

Here They Come, McSweeney's (San Francisco, CA), 2006.

Signed, Mata Hari, Little, Brown (New York, NY), 2007.

Yannick Murphy (Photograph by Clark Hsiao. Reproduced by permission.)

The Call, Harper Perennial (New York, NY), 2011.

CHILDREN'S PICTURE BOOKS

Ahwoooooooo!, illustrated by Claudio Munoz, Clarion
    Books (NewYork, NY), 2005.
Baby Polar, illustrated by Kristen Balouch, Clarion Books
    (New York, NY), 2009.
The Cold Water Witch, illustrated by Tom Lintern, Tricycle
    Press (Berkeley, CA), 2010.

OTHER

Stories in Another Language (short stories), Knopf (New
    York, NY), 1987.
In a Bear's Eye (short stories), Dzanc Books (Westland,
    MI), 2008.

Short fiction anthologized in *The O. Henry Prize Stories 2007: The Best Stories of the Year,* Anchor Books
(New York, NY), 2007. Contributor to periodicals, including *Antioch Review, McSweeney's, Agni Online,*
and *Southwest Review.*

Sidelights

Praised by *Booklist* contributor Donna Seaman as "both
incisive and imaginative," Yannick Murphy is known
for her acclaimed adult novels as well as for award-
winning short fiction that has been collected in *Stories
in Another Language* and *In a Bear's Eye.* Although
Murphy's fiction often focuses on young characters, it
resonates with adult themes. It is in her picture books
Ahwoooooooo!, Baby Polar, and *The Cold Water Witch*
that the author truly engages younger readers.

Illustrated by Claudio Munoz, *Ahwoooooooo!* revolves
around Little Wolf's efforts to learn how to howl at the
moon. Unfortunately, Little Wolf is on his own, since
his parents are too busy to coach him. After being taught
by other animals how to hoot, croak, and sing like a
whippoorwill, the cub's grandfather finally helps his
grandson learn to be perhaps the most vocal member of
the pack. "Themes of intergenerational bonding and
childhood milestones lend substance to this agreeable
picture book," wrote Jennifer Mattson in her *Booklist*
review of Murphy's first story for children. A *Kirkus
Reviews* contributor referred to *Ahwoooooooo!* as "a
tender, sometimes humorous journey that evokes the
yearning of childhood."

Illustrated with digital art by Kristen Balouch, *Baby
Polar* focuses on the special love between a mother and
child as Mama Polar Bear allows herself to become a
prop in Baby Polar's imaginative winter games. When
the snow falls however, the cub leaves the cave to play
and chase snowflakes. As the snowfall continues, Baby
Polar becomes lost and searches for refuge, only to find
his mother, who has secretly been keeping sight of him
all the while. "Murphy's skillful pacing creates just
enough suspense" to engage young audiences, noted a
Publishers Weekly, while in *Kirkus Reviews* a contributor noted the "warmth" and "humor" in the story's
"simple text." Praising Balouch's "subtly textured" images, Carolyn Phelan deemed *Baby Polar* a "nicely ca-
denced story of a mother lost and found."

The Cold Water Witch, illustrated by Tom Lintern, also
takes place in the winter, but this time Murphy focuses
on a little girl who is tucked safely in her cozy bed.
The cold of the night outside brings the Cold Water
Witch to the girl's room in hopes of enticing the child
to leave her world and travel to the witch's icy
homeland. Familiar with fairy tales, the little girl refuses to be tempted by the witchy-white woman, leading to "a satisfying battle of wits" between the two, according to a *Publishers Weekly* critic. Describing *The
Cold Water Witch* as "a frosty fairy tale," a *Kirkus Reviews* writer added that Lintern employs a cool artist's
palette in his digital illustrations evoking "the appropriate hoary atmosphere" for Murphy's tale. With its "con-
fident, sensible protagonist" and "cozy tone and cumu-
lation," Murphy's picture-book tale "draws loosely on
folktale motifs," noted Margaret Bush in her *School Library Journal* review of *The Cold Water Witch.*

Murphy's adult novel *Here They Come* features a young
teen narrator. The unnamed thirteen year old lives in
New York City with her precocious sisters, a suicidal
brother, a drunken grandmother, and a depressed mother
who is nevertheless full of resolve to make it. Able to
bend spoons with her mind, the girl attempts to keep
her family together as various dysfunctions pull it apart.
When her deadbeat father abandons the family and disappears, the narrator's brother goes off to Spain to look
for him while the rest of the family stays home to deal
with their myriad problems. Reviewing *Here They Come*
for *Publishers Weekly,* a contributor wrote that Murphy

Murphy's picture book-story in **The Cold Water Witch** *is brought to life in colorful artwork by Tom Lintern.* (Reproduced by permission of Tricycle Press, an imprint of Random House Children's Books, a division of Random House, Inc.)

"creates a world as magical and harrowing as the struggle to come to grips with maturity," and a *Kirkus Reviews* contributor cited her "skill for [evoking] lovely imagery." The story's "bizarre mixture of naturalism and surrealism is intriguing—and well written," wrote Michael Cart in his *Booklist* review of *Here They Come*, and Jim Coan concluded in *Library Journal* that, while "not intended as a realistic portrait of troubled family life, this readable work is . . . at once funny and sad."

In *Signed, Mata Hari* Murphy draws on the real-life experiences of Dutch citizen Margaretha Geertruida Zelle, the woman popularly known as Mata Hari. In addition to being a well-known exotic dancer and courtesan to many wealthy and powerful men in Europe, Zelle was also accused of being a spy during World War I, an allegation for which she was executed by firing squad in France in 1917. Murphy profiles a very different life in *The Call,* this time turning her attention to David, a veterinarian living in New England. As he continues to make his rounds treating the many animals in his rural region, David also searches for the person responsible for the tragic hunting accident that has left his son, Sam, in a coma. Praising *The Call* as "marvelous" and "a triumph," a *Kirkus Reviews* critic added that "Murphy is a subtle, psychologically perceptive writer, and the book has a wry humor that's laconic and surreal and shot through with the tender mysteries of family life."

Biographical and Critical Sources

PERIODICALS

Booklist, February 1, 2006, Michael Cart, review of *Here They Come,* p. 30; August 1, 2006, Jennifer Mattson, review of *Ahwooooooooo!,* p. 92; September 1, 2007, Margaret Flanagan, review of *Signed, Mata Hari,* p. 56; February 1, 2008, Donna Seaman, review of *In a Bear's Eye,* p. 27; November 15, 2009, Carolyn Phelan, review of *Baby Polar,* p. 41; August 1, 2011, Donna Seaman, review of *The Call,* p. 20.

Books, January 5, 2008, review of *Signed, Mata Hari,* p. 11.

Boston Globe, December 3, 2007, Renée Graham, review of *Signed, Mata Hari.*

Independent (London, England), September 19, 2007, Julie Wheelwright, review of *Signed, Mata Hari.*

Kirkus Reviews, March 1, 1997, review of *The Sea of Trees,* p. 329; January 1, 2006, review of *Here They Come,* p. 13; May 1, 2006, review of *Ahwooooooooo!,* p. 464; September 15, 2007, review of *Signed, Mata Hari;* October 15, 2009, review of *Baby Polar;* July 1, 2010, review of *Cold Water Witch;* August 1, 2011, review of *The Call.*

Library Journal, June 1, 1987, Mary Soete, review of *Stories in Another Language,* pp. 129-130; April 15, 1997, Francisca Goldsmith, review of *The Sea of Trees,* p. 118; April 1, 2006, Jim Coan, review of *Here They Come,* p. 85; August 1, 2007, Maureen Neville, review of *Signed, Mata Hari,* p. 72; June 1, 2011, Travis Fristoe, review of *The Call,* p. 93.

New York Times Book Review, June 7, 1987, Alida Becker, review of *Stories in Another Language,* p. 30; August 17, 1997, Catherine Bush, review of *The Sea of Trees,* p. 12; December 23, 2007, "Sleeping with the Enemy," p. 10.

Publishers Weekly, April 24, 1987, Sybil Steinberg, review of *Stories in Another Language,* p. 60; March 10, 1997, review of *The Sea of Trees,* p. 48; January 30, 2006, Craig Morgan Teicher, interview with Murphy, p. 38, and review of *Here They Come,* p. 40; July 23, 2007, review of *Signed, Mata Hari,* p. 40; November 19, 2007, review of *In a Bear's Eye,* p. 33; November 9, 2009, review of *Baby Polar,* p. 45; July 5, 2010, review of *The Cold Water Witch,* p. 40; April 18, 2011, review of *The Call,* p. 29.

Quill & Quire, August, 1987, Paul Stuewe, review of *Stories in Another Language,* p. 34.

School Library Journal, June, 2006, Marianne Saccardi, review of *Ahwooooooooo!,* p. 123; September, 2010, Margaret Bush, review of *The Cold Water Witch,* p. 132.

Times (London, England), September 15, 2007, Peter Millar, review of *Signed, Mata Hari.*

ONLINE

Emerging Writers Forum Web site, http://www.breaktech. net/emergingwritersforum/ (February 9, 2007), interview with Murphy.

L.A. Weekly Online, http://www.laweekly.com/ (March 8, 2006), Michelle Huneven, interview with Murphy.

Yannick Murphy Home Page, http://www.yannickmurphy. com (March 12, 2012).*

N

NASCIMBENI, Barbara 1969-

Personal
Born 1969, in Italy. *Education:* Attended schools in Milan, Italy, and Darmstadt, Germany.

Addresses
Home—Hamburg, Germany; Sorède, Italy. *E-mail*—barbara.nascimbeni@web.de.

Career
Illustrator. *Exhibitions:* Work included in Bologna Illustrators' Exhibition, 1995, 1996; and in galleries throughout Italy.

Writings

SELF-ILLUSTRATED

Alle einsteigen!, Peter Hammer (Wuppertal, Germany), 2007.
Animals and Their Families, Owlkids Books (Berkeley, CA), 2012.

SELF-ILLUSTRATED; "ANIMAL PARADE" BOARD-BOOK SERIES

Big Band, Campbell Books (London, England), 2000.
Party Fun, Campbell Books (London, England), 2001.
Play Time, Campbell Books (London, England), 2001.
Picnic Time, Campbell Books (London, England), 2001.

SELF-ILLUSTRATED; "TODDLER TALES" INTERACTIVE BOARD-BOOK SERIES

Bella and the New Baby, Campbell Books (London, England), 2003.

Phoebe Loves Flying, Campbell Books (London, England), 2003.
Sam Goes Swimming, Campbell Books (London, England), 2003.
Ben and the Babysitter, Campbell Books (London, England), 2003.

SELF-ILLUSTRATED; "FURRY FRIENDS" BOARD-BOOK SERIES

Shy Edward Campbell Books (London, England), 2002.
Messy Lulu, Campbell Books (London, England), 2002.
Helpful Clementine, Campbell Books (London, England), 2002.
Noisy Ralph, Campbell Books (London, England), 2002.

ILLUSTRATOR

Eckhard Mieder, *Die kichernde Kuh,* Elefanten Press (Berlin, Germany), 1998.
Peter Paul Zahl, *Ananzi ist schuld,* Elefanten Press (Berlin, Germany), 1998.
Charise Neugebauer, *Das schönste Weihnachtsgeschenk,* Neugebauer (Hamburg, Germany), 1999, translated as *Santa's Gift,* North-South Books (New York, NY), 1999.
David Grossman, *Un bambino e il suo papá* (originally published in Hebrew), Mondadori (Milan, Italy), 1999.
Jonathan Shipton, *What If?,* Dial Books for Young Readers (New York, NY), 1999.
Mike Gibbie, *Small Brown Dog's Bad Remembering Day,* Macmillan Children's (London, England), 1999, Dutton Children's Books (New York, NY), 2000.
Paul Shipton, *Scarabeo Holmes e il mostro del giardino* (translation of *Bug Muldoon and the Garden of Fear*), Mondadori (Milan, Italy), 2000.
Charise Neugebauer, *Wer gewinnt?,* Naugebauer (Hamburg, Germany), 2000, translated as *The Real Winner,* North-South Books (New York, NY), 2000.
Emanuela Nava, *La tigre con le scarpe da ginnastica,* Salani (Milan, Italy), 2001.
Karen Wallace, *Archie Hates Pink,* Campbell (London, England), 2001.

Karen Wallace, *Dilly the Dancing Duck,* Campbell (London, England), 2001.

Karen Wallace, *Max the Monster Mole,* Campbell (London, England), 2001.

Karen Wallace, *Patrick the Pirate Pig,* Campbell (London, England), 2001.

Karen Wallace, *Sylvester the Singing Sheep,* Campbell (London, England), 2001.

Pamela Duncan Edwards, *Rude Mule,* Henry Holt (New York, NY), 2002.

Roberto Piumini, *Storie per chi le vuole,* Edizioni E.L. (San Dorligo della Valle, Italy), 2003.

Seruya Shalev, *Il bambino della mamma* (originally published in Hebrew), Mondadori (Milan, Italy), 2004.

Stefano Bordiglioni, *Un attimo prima di dormire,* Edizioni E.L. (San Dorligo della Valle, Italy), 2004.

Sally Crabtree, *The Higgledy Piggledy Pigs,* Macmillan Children's (London, England), 2004.

Miyoko Matsutani, *I miei primi tre anni* (translation of *Chiisai momochan*), Salani (Milan, Italy), 2005.

Petter Lidbeck, *Vinni macht Ferien* (translated from the Swedish), Fischer-Tashenbuch (Frankfurt am Main, Germany), 2005.

Nick Turpin, *Out Went Sam,* Evans (London, England), 2005.

Sue Swallow, *Albert Liked Ladders,* Evand (London, England), 2005.

Petter Lidbeck, *Vinni im Winter* (translated from the Swedish), Fischer-Tashenbuch (Frankfurt am Main, Germany), 2006.

Charlie Gardner, *Turn off the Telly!,* Evans (London, England), 2007.

Daniela Prusse, *Diebstahl im Königreich Tangramino,* Ravensburger (Ravensburg, Germany), 2007.

Petter Lidbeck, *Vinni in Venedig* (translated from the Swedish), Fischer-Tashenbuch (Frankfurt am Main, Germany), 2007.

Susan Hood, *Little Elephant's Listening Ears,* Reader's Digest Children's Books (Pleasantville, NY), 2007.

David Grossman, *Itamar e il cappello magico* (translation of *Itamar we-Kova Ha-ksamim ha-shachor*), Mondadori (Milan, Italy), 2008.

Nastrin Siege, *Wenn der Löwe brüllt,* Peter Hammer (Wuppertal, Germany), 2009.

Roberto Piumini, reteller, Hans Christian Andersen, *Il brutto anatroccolo,* Edizioni E.L. (San Dorligo della Valle, Italy), 2009.

Diane Marwood, reteller, *The Fox and the Crow,* Franklin Watts (London, England), 2009.

David Grossman, *Le avventure di Itamar* (originally published in Hebrew), Mondadori (Milan, Italy), 2010.

Du leibst groß und klein: Kindergebete, Herder (Freiburg, Germany), 2010.

(With others) Ulrike Graumann, *Mein Mitmachbuch—die Bibel: Gesschichte, Ausmalbilder, Rätsel-und Stickerseiten,* Herder (Freiburg, Germany), 2010.

Marie-Hélène Delval, *Les visages de Dieu,* Bayard (Paris, France), 2010, translated as *The Faces of God for Young Children,* Eerdmans Books for Young Readers (Grand Rapids MI), 2011.

Gott wird immer bei dir sein: die schönsten Kindergebete, Herder (Freiburg, Germany), 2011.

David Grossman, *Itamar il cacciatore di sogni* (originally published in Hebrew), Mondadori (Milan, Italy), 2011.

Georg Bydlinski, *Warten auf Gustav,* Residenz-Verlag (St. Pölten, Germany), 2011.

Christine Merz, *Wir haben dich immer lieb,* Sauerländer (Mannheim, Germany), 2011.

Roberto Piumini, *The Tortoise and the Hare,* Picture Window Books (Mankato, MN), 2011.

Werner Holzwarth, *Kleiner Riese, großer Zwerg,* Peter Hammer (Wuppertal, Germany), 2011.

So ein schöner Tag war heute: die schönsten Gute-Nacht-Gebete, Herder (Freiburg, Germany), 2011.

Michel Piquemal, *Le rire de Jiha,* Escabelle (France), 2011.

Françoise Gerbaulet, *Quand Jules se ptrend la tête,* Le Bonhomme Vert (France), 2011.

Books illustrated by Nascimeni have been translated into several languages, including Dutch, French, German, and Polish.

Biographical and Critical Sources

PERIODICALS

Booklist, September 1, 1999, Ilene Cooper, review of *Santa's Gift,* p. 149; June 1, 2000, Gillian Engberg, review of *Small Brown Dog's Bad Remembering Day,* p. 1907.

Kirkus Reviews, July 1, 2002, review of *Rude Mule*; January 15, 2011, review of *Images of God for Young Children.*

Publishers Weekly, June 28, 1999, review of *What If?,* p. 77; June 12, 2000, review of *Small Brown Dog's Bad Remembering Day,* p. 71; June 17, 2002, review of *Rude Mule,* p. 64.

School Library Journal, July, 2000, Linda Ludke, review of *Small Brown Dog's Bad Remembering Day,* p. 72, and Barbara Buckley, review of *The Real Winner,* p. 84; August, 2002, Mary Mule, review of *Rude Mule,* p. 155; April, 2011, Linda L. Walkins, review of *Images of God for Young Children,* p. 158.

Sunday Times (London, England), Nicolette Jones, review of *Archie Hates Pink,* p. 46.

ONLINE

Barbara Nascimbeni Home Page, http://www.barbara nascimbeni.com (March 8, 2012).*

*   *   *

NETHERY, Mary

Personal

Born in Eureka, CA; daughter of Louis Dante and Helen Jane Scuri; married Harry Arthur Nethery III (an environmental health administrator); children: Harry Arthur

Mary Nethery (Photograph by Gina Caldwell. Reproduced by permission.)

IV. *Education:* Humboldt State University, B.A. (magna cum laude) and teaching credential; University of San Francisco, M.A. *Politics:* Democrat. *Hobbies and other interests:* Ballet, travel, animals, interior design, movies, theater, fashion.

Addresses

Home—Eureka, CA. *Agent*—Transatlantic Literary Agency, 2 Bloor St. E., Ste. 3500, Toronto, Ontario M4W 1A8, Canada. *E-mail*—mary@marynethery.com.

Career

Writer.

Member

Society of Children's Book Writers and Illustrators, Association of Supervision and Curriculum Development, National Staff Development Council, Humane Society of America.

Awards, Honors

Commendation, California State Board of Education, for curriculum work; Henry Bergh Children's Book Award, American Society for the Prevention of Cruelty to Animals, Teachers' Choice selection, International Reading Association (IRA), IRA/Children's Book Council (CBC) Children's Choice selection, Notable Social Studies Trade Book for Young People designation, National Council for the Social Studies/CBC, and Best Children's Books of the Year designation, Bank Street College of Education, all c. 2008, all for *Two Bobbies;* Christopher Medal, and Gold Award, National Parenting Publication Awards, both 2009, both for *Nubs;* numerous state-selected children's choice awards.

Writings

Hannah and Jack, illustrated by Mary Morgan, Atheneum Books for Young Readers (New York, NY), 1996.
Orange Cat Goes to Market, illustrated by Doug Cushman, Candlewick Press (Cambridge, MA), 1997.
Mary Veronica's Egg, illustrated by Paul Yalowitz, Orchard Books (New York, NY), 1999.
(With Kirby Larson) *Two Bobbies: A True Story of Hurricane Katrina, Survival, and Friendship,* illustrated by Jean Cassels, Walker (New York, NY), 2008.
(With Brian Dennis and Kirby Larson) *Nubs: The True Story of a Mutt, a Marine, and a Miracle,* Little, Brown (New York, NY), 2009.
The Famous Nini: A Mostly True Story of How a Plain White Cat Became a Star, illustrated by John Manders, Clarion Books (New York, NY), 2010.

Contributor to children's magazines, including *Ladybug* and *Spider.*

Adaptations

Two Bobbies was adapted as an audiobook.

Sidelights

A versatile author of fiction and nonfiction, Mary Nethery has earned numerous accolades for her children's books, among them *Two Bobbies: A True Story of Hurricane Katrina, Survival, and Friendship,* as well as joining U.S. Marine Brian Dennis and fellow author Kirby Larson to create the bestselling *Nubs: The True Story of a Mutt, a Marine, and a Miracle.* "I seem to create universes populated with animals, chocolate, spunky characters, and a sense of the exotic and the adventurous," Nethery remarked in a *California Readers* interview with Bonnie O'Brian. "I tend to gravitate towards the themes of love, friendship, courage, and nobility of character."

Nethery's picture-book debut, *Hannah and Jack,* centers on the loving relationship between a young girl and her pet cat. When Hannah's family makes a visit to her grandmother's home, Jack must stay behind, and the youngster grows more despondent each day that she is away. With her grandma's support and encouragement, Hannah devises a clever way to address her predicament. Writing in *Horn Book,* Hanna B. Zeiger noted that readers will appreciate "the fact that Hannah is able to solve her problem independently." As Nethery once told *SATA, Hannah and Jack* "is a story of how one small child empowers herself to deal with separation, as well as to luxuriate in a reunion that has them."

In *Mary Veronica's Egg* a girl carefully nurtures an abandoned egg that she finds at the edge of a pond, believing that it contains something wondrous. Nethery's "affectionate homage to the rewards of patience and perseverance is an altogether agreeable outing," observed a *Publishers Weekly* contributor in reviewing the picture book, and Kathy Broderick applauded the "tender yet funny text" in her *Booklist* review of *Mary Veronica's Egg.*

Set in late-nineteenth-century Venice, Italy, *The Famous Nini: A Mostly True Story of How a Plain White Cat Became a Star* follows a stray cat's incredible rise to social prominence. After famed composer Giuseppe Verdi draws inspiration from the pitch-perfect meow of Nini, a white tomcat that finds shelter at a small café, the feline becomes an overnight sensation. Soon, the cat is receiving visitors from all over the world, including artists, royalty, and religious leaders. "Nethery has a lot of fun with Nini's story, creating characters openhearted enough to be touched by a purr," Kara Schaff Dean remarked in her *School Library Journal* review of the work.

Nethery has collaborated with Larson on a pair of critically acclaimed works of nonfiction. In *Two Bobbies* the authors chronicle the heartwarming tale of a dog and cat who became inseparable friends after surviving Hurricane Katrina in 2005. The animals, both of which had bobbed tails, were found wandering the streets of New Orleans, Louisiana, months after the disaster. After being taken to a rescue shelter, workers discover that Bob Cat is blind and relies on Bobbi to navigate the city streets. After the animals' story made the national news, they were adopted by a woman living in Oregon. "An excellent introduction to Katrina for young chil-

Nethery's story in **Hannah and Jack** *is accompanied by artwork by* **Mary Morgan.** (Illustration copyright © 1996 by Mary Morgan. Reproduced by permission of Atheneum Books for Young Readers, an imprint of Simon & Schuster Children's Publishing Division.)

dren," according to *School Library Journal* reviewer Judith Constantinides, *Two Bobbies* "memorializes a modern catastrophe."

Nethery and Larson also joined forces with Dennis, a Marine stationed in Iraq, for *Nubs,* "a feel-good" story, according to Dean. While serving in Iraq, Dennis befriended and cared for a feral dog he named "Nubs" because the animal's ears had been docked. Their bond grew stronger over the ensuing months, and each time Dennis's unit departed for a mission, Nubs attempted to follow. When Dennis was relocated to Jordan, the dog made a perilous seventy-mile journey through the war-torn region to find his human friend. As dogs are note welcome during military operations, Dennis was ordered to remove the canine, so the marine raised the funds needed to transport Nubs to his Southern California home, where they now live. A *Publishers Weekly* contributor predicted that *Nubs* will appeal to readers who enjoy "stories of animals that triumph against the odds."

"I've always loved to write," Nethery once told *SATA.* "In junior high school, my friend Katy and I wrote adventure and romance stories during math class, then compared them, chapter by chapter. It was much more fun than fumbling around with numbers. But it wasn't until my son was born that I became intrigued with children's literature. Reading him stories by such writers as James Marshall, Tomi Ungerer, Graham Oakley, Daniel Pinkwater, Jane Yolen, James Howe, Steven Kellogg, and Dr. Seuss gave us so many moments of joy and laughter, as well as insights. I came to admire the extraordinary skill and brilliance of these writers.

"I have had the good fortune to work with and learn from other authors, such as Nancy Farmer, Tricia Gardella, Barbara Kerley, Helen Ketteman, Kirby Larson, Ann Paul, Dian Curtis Regan, Vivian Sathre, Aaron Shephard, Jane Yolen, Tasha Wing, and magazine editor Kim Griswell. They've inspired me with their talent and skill and have generously shared their knowledge with me.

"My goal is to write books that children will read with a flashlight under the bed covers, long after their parents have kissed them goodnight. If they wake up the next morning with my characters still in their heads, then I am in heaven."

Biographical and Critical Sources

PERIODICALS

Booklist, July, 1999, Kathy Broderick, review of *Mary Veronica's Egg,* p. 1953; September 1, 2008, Shelle Rosenfeld, review of *Two Bobbies: A True Story of Hurricane Katrina, Friendship, and Survival,* p. 102; October 1, 2009, Barbara A. Ward and Terrell A. Young, "Compassion through Friendship," profile of Nethery, p. S31; October 1, 2009, Daniel Kraus, review of *Nubs: The True Story of a Mutt, a Marine, and a Miracle,* p. 42.
Kirkus Reviews, August 15, 2008, review of *Two Bobbies*; May 15, 2010, review of *The Famous Nini: A Mostly True Story of How a Plain White Cat Became a Star.*

Publishers Weekly, January 25, 1999, review of *Mary Veronica's Egg,* p. 95; September 28, 2008, Matthew Thornton, "A Soldier's Best Friend," p. 18; November 9, 2009, review of *Nubs,* p. 45.

School Library Journal, September, 2008, Judith Constantinides, review of *Two Bobbies,* p. 166; December, 2009, Kara Schaff Dean, review of *Nubs,* p. 97; August, 2010, Kara Schaff Dean, review of *The Famous Nini,* p. 82.

ONLINE

California Readers Web site, http://californiareaders.org/ (March 1, 2012), Bonnie O'Brian, "Meet Mary Nethery."

Mary Nethery Home Page, http://www.marynethery.com (March 1, 2012).

***John Manders creates the colorful art for Nethery's feline-centered story in* The Famous Nini.** (Illustration copyright © 2010 by John Manders. Reproduced by permission of Clarion Books, an imprint of Houghton Mifflin Harcourt Publishing Company. All rights reserved.)

NEWMAN, Barbara Johansen

Personal

Married; husband's name Phil; children: Dave, Mike, Ben. *Education:* B.F.A. with art education certification. *Hobbies and other interests:* Painting and drawing, collecting, thrift-store shopping.

Addresses

Home—Needham, MA. *Agent*—Andrea Cascardi, Transatlantic Literary Agency, Inc., 72 Glengowan Rd., Toronto, Ontario M4N 1G4, Canada; acascardi@optonline.net. *E-mail*—barbara@johansennewman.com.

Career

Illustrator, author, and textile designer. Freelance illustrator, beginning 1982; creator of art for calendars, greeting cards, and advertising. Puppeteer, performing, with husband, for Moonberry Puppet Theatre, c. 1970s. *Exhibitions:* Fiber sculptures exhibited at shows and galleries, including Kenan Center, 1974-90, and Rhinebeck, NY, 1975-80.

Awards, Honors

Various awards for illustration, puppetry, and soft sculpture.

Writings

SELF-ILLUSTRATED

Tex and Sugar: A Big City Kitty Ditty, Sterling Publishing (New York, NY), 2007.
Glamorous Glasses, Boyds Mills Press (Honesdale, PA), 2012.

ILLUSTRATOR

Chad Merkley, *Too Many Me's,* Raintree Steck-Vaughn (Austin, TX), 1999.
Natasha Wing, *The Night before the Tooth Fairy,* Grosset & Dunlap (New York, NY), 2003.
Louis G. Grambling, *Shoo! Scat!,* Marshall Cavendish (New York, NY), 2004.
Kelly Terwilliger, *Barnyard Purim,* Kar-Ben (Minneapolis, MN), 2012.

Contributor to periodicals, including *Boston Magazine, Boston Globe, Chicago Magazine, Cooking Light, Providence Journal, Miami Herald, Ms., Kiplingers' Report, Soap Opera Digest, Wall Street Journal,* and *Working Mother.*

ILLUSTRATOR; "DOYLE AND FOSSEY, SCIENCE DETECTIVES" READER SERIES BY MICHELE TORREY

The Case of the Gasping Garbage, and Other Super-Scientific Cases, Dutton (New York, NY), 2000.

Barbara Johansen Newman and her dog Bitty. (Photograph by Philip H. Newman. Courtesy of Barbara Johansen Newman.)

The Case of the Mossy Lake Monster, and Other Super-Scientific Cases, Dutton (New York, NY), 2002.
The Case of the Graveyard Ghost, and Other Super-Scientific Cases, Dutton (New York, NY), 2002.
The Case of the Barfy Birthday, and Other Super-Scientific Cases, Dutton (New York, NY), 2003.
The Case of the Terrible T. Rex, and Other Super-Scientific Cases, Sterling (New York, NY), 2010.
The Case of the Crooked Carnival, and Other Super-Scientific Cases, Dutton (New York, NY), 2011.

ILLUSTRATOR; "BONES" BEGINNING-READER SERIES BY DAVID A. ADLER

Bones and the Dog Gone Mystery, Viking (New York, NY), 2004.

Bones and the Big Yellow Mystery, Viking (New York, NY), 2004.

Bones and the Dinosaur Mystery, Viking (New York, NY), 2005.

Bones and the Cupcake Mystery, Viking (New York, NY), 2005.

Bones and the Birthday Mystery, Viking (New York, NY), 2007.

Bones and the Math Test Mystery, Viking (New York, NY), 2008.

Bones and the Roller Coaster Mystery, Viking (New York, NY), 2009.

Bones and the Clown Mix-up Mystery, Viking (New York, NY), 2010.

Sidelights

Massachusetts-based artist Barbara Johansen Newman began her creative career as a fiber artist and puppeteer with Moonberry Puppet Theatre before turning to graphic illustration. In addition to contributing art to dozens of books for children, including beginning readers by David A. Alder and the "Doyle and Fossey"

Newman's illustration projects include creating artwork for David A. Adler's **Bones and the Dog Gone Mystery.** (Jacket cover copyright © 2004 by Barbara Johansen Newman. Reproduced by permission of Viking Children's Books, a division of Penguin Young Readers Group, a member of Penguin Group (USA), Inc., 375 Hudson Street, New York, NY 10014. All rights reserved.)

Newman's illustration projects include creating the artwork for Michele Torrey's quirky mystery **The Case of the Crooked Carnival.** (Illustration copyright © 2010 by Barbara Johansen Newman. Reproduced by permission of Sterling Publishing Co., Inc.)

mystery series by Michele Torrey, Newman had created the original self-illustrated picture books *Tex and Sugar: A Big City Kitty Ditty* and *Glamorous Glasses.*

Praising Newman's contribution to Adler's *Bones and the Big Yellow Mystery, Booklist* contributor Gillian Engberg wrote that her "expressive acrylics reinforce the meaning in the words while extending the sense of silliness" in Adler's easy-reading story. The other seven "Bones" beginning readers continue the creative collaboration with similar success. Reviewing *Bones and the Birthday Mystery,* Erika Qualls asserted in *School Library Journal* that the artist's "bright and cheerful illustrations" pair with Adler's "easy-to-read and humorous text" to "once again" treat budding readers to "an enjoyable story."

Writing in *Booklist,* John Peters noted that Newman's "ink-and-wash" art "adds comic details" to Torrey's *The Case of the Gasping Garbage, and Other Super-Scientific Cases,* the first book in her ongoing "Doyle and Fossey, Science Detectives" series. In an appraisal of *The Case of the Mossy Lake Monster, and Other Super-Scientific Cases, School Library Journal* contributor Kay Bowes maintained that the artist's pencil drawings add "the right touch of zaniness" to Torrey's humorous story about the fifth-grade sleuths, and Nicole Waskie-Laura wrote in the same periodical that the "cartoon illustrations" in *The Case of the Crooked Carnival, and Other Super-Scientific Cases* "punctuate the text nicely" and echo the author's "tongue-in-cheek" humor.

Drawing on her talent for creating unique, animated characters from cloth, Newman brings a love of developing expressive characters to her illustration work for *Tex and Sugar.* In her story, readers meet a pair of larger-than-life small-town kitties with big dreams. Country singers Tex Mex Rex and Sugar Lee Snughead are each determined to find fame in the big city. Although their careers make slow starts separately, after the two country crooners team up while singing to the moon on a summer night, their shared affection for their music—and for each other—inspires their performance and makes them stars.

In *School Library Journal* Wanda Meyers-Hines praised the "rich, vibrant illustrations" in *Tex and Sugar,* adding that Newman's use of "meticulous detail depicts the all-animal cast and a wide range of expressions." Noting that the book's rhyming text, with its encouraging story about following one's dreams, "is unobtrusive," a *Kirkus Reviews* writer concluded of Newman's authorial debut: "It's the illustrations . . . that star."

Biographical and Critical Sources

PERIODICALS

Booklist, January 1, 2002, Shelle Rosenfeld, review of *The Case of the Mossy Lake Monster, and Other Super-*

Newman serves as both author and illustrator of the award-winning picture book **Tex and Sugar.** (Illustration copyright © 2007 by Barbara Johansen Newman. All rights reserved. Reproduced by permission.)

Scientific Cases, p. 860; August, 2002, John Peters, review of *The Case of the Gasping Garbage, and Other Super-Scientific Cases,* p. 2122; October 15, 2004, Gillian Engberg, review of *Bones and the Big Yellow Mystery,* p. 409; October 1, 2005, Connie Fletcher, review of *Bones and the Dinosaur Mystery,* p. 60; May 1, 2007, Carolyn Phelan, review of *Bones and the Birthday Mystery,* p. 49; March 1, 2008, Carolyn Phelan, review of *Bones and the Math Test Mystery,* p. 70; February 15, 2009, Carolyn Phelan, review of *Bones and the Roller Coaster Mystery,* p. 73.

Kirkus Reviews, July 15, 2002, review of *The Case of the Graveyard Ghost, and Other Super-Scientific Cases,* p. 1046; March 15, 2007, review of *Tex and Sugar: A Big City Kitty Ditty;* July 1, 2010, review of *The Case of the Crooked Carnival.*

School Library Journal, February, 2002, Kay Bowes, review of *The Case of the Mossy Lake Monster, and Other Super-Scientific Cases,* p. 114; December, 2003, Debbie Whitbeck, review of *The Case of the Barfy Birthday, and Other Super-Scientific Cases,* p. 114; November, 2004, John Sigwald, review of *Shoo! Scat!,* p. 104; December, 2004, Corrina Austin, review of

Bones and the Dog Gone Mystery, p. 96; October, 2005, Be Astengo, review of *Bones and the Dinosaur Mystery,* p. 102; May, 2007, Erika Qualls, review of *Bones and the Birthday Mystery,* p. 84; August, 2007, Wanda Meyers-Hines, review of *Tex and Sugar,* p. 86; April, 2008, Linda M. Kenton, review of *Bones and the Math Test Mystery,* p. 102; January, 2011, Nicole Waskie-Laura, review of *The Case of the Crooked Carnival, and Other Super-Scientific Cases,* p. 84; February, 2011, Terry Ann Lawler, review of *The Case of the Terrible T. Rex, and Other Super-Scientific Cases,* p. 91.

ONLINE

Barbara Johansen Newman Home Page, http://www.johansennewman.com (March 1, 2012).

Barbara Johansen Newman Studio Web log, http://johansennewman.typepad.com (March 1, 2012).

Tex and Sugar Web site, http://www.texandsugar.com/ (June 4, 2008).

O-P

OLIVER, Jana
    See OLIVER, Jana G.

*   *   *

OLIVER, Jana G.
    (Jana Oliver)

Personal

Born in IA; married. *Education:* College degree (nursing). *Hobbies and other interests:* Travel.

Addresses

Home—Atlanta, GA. *Agent*—Meredith Bernstein Literary Agency, 2095 Broadway, Ste. 505, New York, NY 10023.

Career

Novelist. Formerly worked as a registered nurse.

Awards, Honors

Gold Medal in Science Fiction/Fantasy category, Independent Publishers Book Awards, and *ForeWord* magazine Book of the Year selection, both 2007, both for *Sojourn;* Gold Medal in Science Fiction/Fantasy category, Independent Publishers Book Awards, and *ForeWord* magazine Book of the Year Honorable Mention selection, 2008, both for *Virtual Evil;* Silver Medal in Science Fiction/Fantasy category, Independent Publishers Book Awards, 2008, for *Madman's Dance;* numerous Romance Writers of America chapter awards.

Writings

FANTASY FICTION

The Summoning Stone, MageSpell Press (Atlanta, GA), 2002.

The Circle of the Swan, MageSpell Press (Atlanta, GA), 2004.

Contributor to anthologies, including *Nyx in the House of Night,* Smart Pop.

"TIME ROVERS" NOVEL SERIES

Sojourn, Dragon Moon Press (Calgary, Alberta, Canada), 2006.
Virtual Evil, Dragon Moon Press (Calgary, Alberta, Canada), 2007.
Madman's Dance, Dragon Moon Press (Calgary, Alberta, Canada), 2008.

"DEMON TRAPPERS" NOVEL SERIES

The Demon Trapper's Daughter, St. Martin's Griffin (New York, NY), 2010.
Soul Thief, St. Martin's Griffin (New York, NY), 2011.
Forgiven, St. Martin's Griffin (New York, NY), 2012.

Author's work has been translated into German, Portuguese, and Russian.

Sidelights

A native of Iowa, Jana G. Oliver earned her nursing degree, traveled, and worked as a subsistence farmer before beginning her career as a young-adult novelist specializing in urban fantasy. After self-publishing her first two books, Oliver attracted the attention of a Canadian-based fantasy publisher and led to her "Time Rovers" series, which includes *Sojourn, Virtual Evil,* and *Madman's Dance.* Her "Demon Trappers" novels move the author further into the paranormal genre due to their focus on a near-future world overrun by a scourge of fiends emanating from hell.

Oliver's "Time Rovers" series begins with *Sojourn,* which transports modern readers back to Victorian London and the year 1888. This London is not the city of

Charles Dickens, however; it is a city of shape shifters and secret-keepers. Twenty-first-century Time Rover Jacynda Lassiter has been transported here and tasked with locating a time tourist who must be returned to 2057 before he can meddle in history. Scouring London's WhiteChapel district, Jacynda knows enough of history to be on the look out for the legendary murderer Jack the Ripper, while anarchist's bombs also make the volatile epoch a threat. In *Virtual Evil* Jacynda goes in search of a fellow Time Rover but does not find him before his actions derail the path of history and send England down a course that the nation may not survive. Her adventures conclude in *Madman's Dance,* as shape shifters take advantage of Britain's social and political upheavals to claim power. Jacynda's dire warnings of time shifts and evil beings eventually land her in a nineteenth-century madhouse, leaving a physician and a detective from Scotland Yard to stop a megalomaniacal anarchist from creating an explosion that will destroy the historic city. Reviewing the first "Time Rovers" novel in *Small Press Bookwatch,* a contributor cited Oliver as "a gifted storyteller and a master of the [time-travel] genre."

Set in 2018, Oliver's "Demon Trappers" series takes readers to Atlanta, Georgia,. The southern city is being overrun by Hellspawn, Deaders, and other unsavory creatures that have been summoned forth by powerful necromancers doing Lucifer's bidding. At age seventeen, Riley Blackthorne is determined to follow in the footsteps of her father, legendary Demon Trapper Paul Blackthorne. While dedicated to her work, Riley is also looking forward to a future that will hopefully include a romance with apprentice Demon Trapper Simon. When Paul is killed in a battle with a vicious demon, Riley finds her future approaching faster than she imagined, but her first goal must be to prevent her dad from being resurrected as a zombie.

Joined by her father's partner—and the novel's co-narrator—Denver Beck as well as by best friend Peter and the enthusiastic Simon, Riley returns in *Soul Thief,* as a battle at the city's Tabernacle leaves the trappers' ranks in tatters. Now attracting the interest of the very-attractive demon hunter Ori, Riley is more preoccupied with the location of her father's corpse that with romance. She becomes more optimistic after reinforcements arrive from the Roman Catholic Church's home base at the Vatican, but soon it becomes clear that something is stalking her in particular. In *Forgiven* Riley learns that no good deed goes unpunished as the jealous Simon accuses her of being in league with Lucifer. With the final war between good and evil approaching, the teen finds herself the target of both sides. Whatever she does now will affect the war's outcome, but how?

Praising *The Demon Trapper's Daughter* as a "successful urban fantasy," a *Publishers Weekly* critic added that the novel's "strong female heroine, . . . fascinating setting, and a complex, thrill-soaked story" shows Oliver's "Demon Trappers" series to be "off to a strong start."

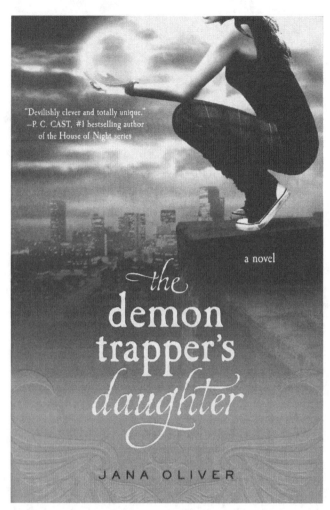

Cover of Jana G. Oliver's paranormal fantasy **The Demon Trapper's Daughter.** (Jacket cover photographs © by Morgan Norman (young woman); Colin Anderson/Getty Images (scene). Reproduced by permission of St. Martin's Press.)

The book presents an "inventive twist on the story of a girl breaking into a man's career field," noted *Booklist* contributor Cindy Welch, while Michelle Young cited the novel's mix of "paranormal adventure with a dash of romance and the promise of suspense" in her *Voice of Youth Advocates* review. For one *Kirkus Reviews* contributor, Oliver "successfully sets up a series with interesting chracters and a detailed world" in *The Demon Trapper's Daughter,* while another noted of *Soul Thief* that the story's focus shifts from actual "butt-kicking" to "detecting" as Riley moves behind the scenes "into the shadowy world of zombie summoners and witches."

Biographical and Critical Sources

PERIODICALS

Booklist, February 15, 2011, Cindy Welch, review of *The Demon Trapper's Daughter,* p. 70.
Kirkus Reviews, January 15, 2011, review of *The Demon Trapper's Daughter;* August 15, 2011, review of *Soul Thief.*

Publishers Weekly, December 20, 2010, review of *The De-mon Trapper's Daughter,* p. 55.
School Library Journal, February, 2011, Jake Pettit, re-view of *The Demon Trapper's Daughter,* p. 116.
Small Press Bookwatch, June, 2006, review of *Sojourn.*
Voice of Youth Advocates, February, 2011, Michelle Young, review of *The Demon Trapper's Daughter,* p. 574.

ONLINE

BookLoons Web site, http://www.bookloons.com/ (April, 2007), Martina Bexte, interview with Oliver.
Jana G. Oliver Home Page, http://www.janaoliver.com (March 2, 2012).
Smartpop Web site, http://www.smartpopbooks.com/ (March 10, 2011), Heather Butterfield, interview with Oliver.*

*　　　*　　　*

PERKINS, Stephanie

Personal

Born c. 1980, in CA; married; husband's name Jarrod. *Education:* B.A. (creative writing).

Addresses

Home—Asheville, NC. *Agent*—Kate Schafer Testerman, KT Literary; kate@ktliterary.com. *E-mail*—steph@ stephanieperkins.com.

Career

Novelist. Worked as a bookseller and librarian.

Awards, Honors

CYBILS Award for Young-Adult Fiction finalist, 2010, for *Anna and the French Kiss.*

Writings

YOUNG-ADULT NOVELS

Anna and the French Kiss, Dutton (New York, NY), 2010.
Lola and the Boy Next Door, Dutton Books (New York, NY), 2011.
Isla and the Happily Ever After, Dutton (New York, NY), 2013.

Sidelights

Stephanie Perkins took a methodical approach to her writing career: she started as a bookseller and then worked as a librarian before publishing her first young-adult novel, *Anna and the French Kiss.* The first part of a trilogy of teen romances, *Anna and the French Kiss* has been followed by *Lola and the Boy Next Door* and *Isla and the Happily Ever After,* both which show young women finding love in surprising places. "I've always loved telling stories," Perkins noted on her home page, "but it took years before I tried to make it my living. Even after I received a degree in creative writing, I worked hard to convince myself to do something else. To get a REAL job. I'm thankful the writing gods persisted. Still, I've always worked with books. . . . I love the way they smell, the weight of their pages in my hands, the Once Upon a Time of escape. I cannot imagine a life without literature."

In *Anna and the French Kiss* Perkins' heroine is Anna Oliphant, a high-schooler who anticipates smooth sail-ing through senior year due to her steady job, fantastic friends, and a romance-in-the-making with cute class-mate Toph. When her novelist father announces that he is shipping her off to attend an English-language board-ing school in Paris, Anna is despondent, but the magic of the city quickly works its charm. Soon she has four new friends to share time with, one of which is hand-some Brit Étienne St. Clair. Although Étienne has a

Cover of Stephanie Perkins' upbeat teen romance **Anna and the French Kiss,** *which takes readers on a trip to Paris.* (Jacket cover photography © by Michael Frost. Reproduced by permission of Dutton Children's Books, a division of Pen-guin Young Readers Group, a member of Penguin Group (USA), 345 Hudson Street, New York, NY 10014. All rights reserved.)

steady girlfriend, it is clear to Anna that they, too, share a connection. This romantic tension mounts over the coming months until an unwelcome bit of news regarding her crush from back home results in a seismic shift in their relationship.

In *Kirkus Reviews* a contributor commended *Anna and the French Kiss* as better than "the usual chick-lit fare," citing its mix of "smart dialogue, fresh characters and plenty of tingly interactions." Anna's narrative voice is "likeable" and "introspective," wrote *Booklist* reviewer Shelle Rosenfeld, while in *School Library Journal* Kimberly Castle praised Perkins' story as a "delightful debut novel with refreshingly witty characters." While noting the "predictable" romantic outcome, Charla Hollingsworth recommended Perkins' debut to fans of Sarah Dessen and Simone Elkeles in her *Voice of Youth Advocates* appraisal by asserting that "most teen girls will . . . root for Anna and St. Clair to finally make their infatuation official."

Love also comes to Lola Nolan, the central character in *Lola and the Boy Next Door,* but as the title suggests, this time the teen finds romance much closer to home. A native of San Francisco, Lola loves to design costumes, the more outré and theatrical the better, and she is known to everyone at her high school for her outrageous wardrobe. Her goals for junior year include keeping up her image at school; meanwhile, her top challenge on the home front is convincing her father to accept her equally outrageous relationship with twenty-two-year-old rock musician Max. Then twins Callipe and Cricket, childhood friends and neighbors, return from a two-year-long absence and Lola's romantic feelings for Cricket return. While dating a rock star certainly keeps Lola in the limelight she loves, Cricket's intelligence taps something far deeper. The author's "skill at capturing Lola's seesawing emotions make for a lively romance," wrote a *Publishers Weekly* critic in reviewing *Lola and the Boy Next Door,* while a *Kirkus Reviews* critic allerted fans of *Anna and the French Kiss* that the title character also returns from her year in Paris to "help" Lola "confront her renewed feelings for the boy next door."

Biographical and Critical Sources

PERIODICALS

Booklist, November 15, 2010, Shelle Rosenfeld, review of *Anna and the French Kiss,* p. 41.

Kirkus Reviews, November 1, 2010, review of *Anna and the French Kiss*; August 15, 2011, review of *Lola and the Boy Next Door.*

Mountaineer (Waynesville, NC), May 9, 2011, Stina Sieg, profile of Perkins.

Publishers Weekly, July 25, 2011, review of *Lola and the Boy Next Door,* p. 55.

School Library Journal, December, 2010, Kimberly Castle, review of *Anna and the French Kiss,* p. 122.

Voice of Youth Advocates, December, 2010, Charla Hollingsworth, review of *Anna and the French Kiss,* p. 458.

ONLINE

Stephanie Perkins Home Page, http://www.stephanie perkins.com (February 28, 2012).

*   *   *

PREBLE, Joy

Personal

Born in Chicago, IL; married; husband's name Rick; children: one son. *Education:* Northwestern University, degree.

Addresses

Home—Houston, TX. *Agent*—Jennifer Rofé, Andrea Brown Literary Agency; jennifer@andreabrownlit.com. *E-mail*—joypreble@gmail.com.

Career

Writer. English teacher at Cypress Creek High School, Houston, TX, and Oak Ridge High School, Conroe, TX.

Member

Society of Children's Book Writers and Illustrators.

Writings

"DREAMING ANASTASIA" NOVEL SERIES

Dreaming Anastasia: A Novel of Love, Magic, and the Power of Dreams, Sourcebooks Jabberwocky (Naperville, IL), 2009.

Haunted, Sourcebooks Fire (Naperville, IL), 2011.

Anastasia Forever, Sourcebooks Fire (Naperville, IL), 2012.

The Sweet Dead Life, Sourcebooks Fire (Naperville, IL), 2013.

OTHER

Contributor to newspapers and magazines.

Sidelights

Joy Preble combines fantasy, historical fiction, romance, and Russian folklore in her "Dreaming Anastasia" series of young-adult novels. A former high-school

Joy Preble (Toppell Photography. Reproduced by permission.)

English teacher, Preble drew inspiration for the series from her maternal grandmother, who was born in Russia, as well as from her lifelong interest in Russian literature, especially the fairytales collected by nineteenth-century writer Aleksandr Afanas'ev. One of the keys to the success of the "Dreaming Anastasia" series, Preble believes, is her courageous protagonist, Anne Michaelson, a teenager with supernatural powers. As the author stated to *Authors Unleashed* online interviewer Jen Wardrip, "I do come from a family—on both sides—with very strong, determined women who have always inspired me to never give up. . . . I wanted a story with a main character who was an amazing, strong female, and I wanted to be able to throw her all sorts of curves to see how she'd react."

In *Dreaming Anastasia: A Novel of Love, Magic, and the Power of Dreams* Preble introduces Anne, a high-school student living in Chicago, Illinois. Anne suffers from recurring dreams about Anastasia Romanov, the youngest daughter of Tsar Nicholas II, Russia's last emperor. Anastasia and her family members are believed to have been murdered by Communist forces in 1918, following the October Revolution. Through her dreams, Anne learns that Anastasia actually survived the massacre and is being held captive by Baba Yaga,

the fearsome witch of Russian lore. Then, an attractive and mysterious stranger named Ethan Kozninsky enters Anne's life, informing her that she holds the key to Anastasia's safety. Ethan, an immortal member of a secret brotherhood, has waited for Anne for decades; she has been chosen to rescue Anastasia because of her role in the Romanov legacy. "Preble's overall concept is interesting," a *Publishers Weekly* critic stated in a review of *Dreaming Anastasia.*

Haunted, the sequel to *Dreaming Anastasia,* finds Anne trying to restore her life to a sense of normalcy in the wake of her first adventure, relying on support from boyfriend Ben and best friend Tess. Soon, however, a crazed, wild-haired woman begins appearing to Anne, and she must turn for help to Ethan, who sacrificed his immortality to save Anastasia. Anne and Ethan identify the troubled woman as a *rusalka,* a demonic water nymph, and they learn that the creature has a connection to Anne's family. Complicating matters further, Baba Yaga has returned to Anne's dreams, and the teen becomes convinced that the witch wants something from her. "Themes of destiny, loss, and sacrifice run heavily" throughout *Haunted,* Christi Esterle remarked

Cover of Joy Preble's novel **Haunted,** *which finds a teen shaken by a strange spectre with malicious intent.* (Jacket cover photographs © by Elisa Lazo de Valdez/Corbis; Zena Holloway/Corbis. Reproduced by permission of Sourcebooks, Inc.)

in *School Library Journal.* "Suspenseful scenes fly by quickly as Anne tries to make sense of unexplained events," a writer stated in *Kirkus Reviews.*

Asked if she had any advice for budding authors, Preble remarked to Wardrip, "Don't ever let anyone tell you that you're too young or too old to do whatever your passion may be. I think it's amazing that I have met phenomenal writers in YA who are in their 20's and equally phenomenal writers who are much older. It's about the craft, not your age, and I think that applies to almost everything."

Biographical and Critical Sources

PERIODICALS

Booklist, April 15, 2011, Cindy Welch, review of *Haunted,* p. 56.

Houston Chronicle, April 28, 2011, Kim Morgan, "Words Come Easy to Woodlands Woman" (profile of Preble), p. 2.

Kirkus Reviews, January 15, 2011, review of *Haunted.*

Publishers Weekly, October 5, 2009, review of *Dreaming Anastasia: A Novel of Love, Magic, and the Power of Dreams,* p. 52.

School Library Journal, January, 2010, Renee Steinberg, review of *Dreaming Anastasia,* p. 111; May, 2011, Christi Esterle, review of *Haunted,* p. 122.

Voice of Youth Advocates, April, 2011, Lauri J. Vaughan, review of *Haunted,* p. 85.

ONLINE

Authors Unleashed Web log, http://authorsunleashed. blogspot.com/ (August 21, 2009) Jen Wardrip, interview with Preble.

Joy Preble Home Page, http://joypreble.com (March 1, 2012).

Joy Preble Web log, http://joysnovelidea.blogspot.com (March 1, 2012).

* * *

PRICE, Mara

Personal

Born in Mexico; immigrated to United States.

Addresses

Home—Southern CA. *Agent*—Adriana Dominguez, Full Circle Literary, Ste. 500, 7676 Hazard Ctr. Dr., San Diego, CA 92108. *E-mail*—mara@maraprice.com.

Career

Children's book author/illustrator and educator. Museum of Latin-American Art, teacher at workshops; presenter at schools and libraries.

Mara Price (Reproduced by permission.)

Member

Society of Children's Book Writers and Illustrators.

Awards, Honors

International Latino Book Award for Best Bilingual Children's Picture Book, San Diego Book Award for Best Children's Picture Book selection, and Paterson Prize for Books for Young People Special Recognition, all 2011, all for *Grandma's Chocolate/El chocolate de Abuelita.*

Writings

Grandma's Chocolate/El chocolate de abuelita, Spanish translation by Gabriela Baeza Ventura, illustrated by Lisa Fields, Piñata Books (Houston, TX), 2010.

Contributor of short fiction to periodicals, including *Iguana.* Cofounder of *Bloguitos* Web log.

Biographical and Critical Sources

PERIODICALS

Children's Bookwatch, January, 2011, review of *Grandma's Chocolate/El chocolate de abuelita.*

Kirkus Reviews, October 15, 2010, review of *Grandma's Chocolate/El chocolate de abuelita.*

Publishers Weekly, October 25, 2010, review of *Grandma's Chocolate/El chocolate de abuelita,* p. 46.

School Library Journal, January, 2011, Rebecca Alcala, review of *Grandma's Chocolate/El chocolate de abuelita,* p. 98.

ONLINE

Mara Price Home Page, http://www.maraprice.com (February 28, 2012).

Latinoteca Web site, http://www.latinoteca.com/ (March 1, 2012), Mara Price, "Writing Historical Fiction for Children."

School Library Journal Online, http://www.schoollibrary journal.com/ (April 5, 2011), Freda Mosquera, "El día de los niños/el día de los libros: Honoring Children, Language, and Literature."

R

RAUSCH, Molly

Personal

Born in MD. *Education:* State University of New York, New Paltz, M.F.A. (painting), 2003. *Hobbies and other interests:* Collecting typewriters, the alphabet.

Addresses

Home—P.O. Box 402, New Paltz, NY 12561. *Agent*—Van Brunt Projects, Box 793, Beacon, NY 12508. *E-mail*—engine.snipe@gmail.com.

Career

Writer and painter. Artist in residence at Anderson Ranch Arts Center, Snowmass Village, CO, 1998; The Artist House at St. Mary's College of Maryland, St. Mary's City, MD, 2003; and Roos Arts Gallery, Rosendale, NY, 2010.

Writings

My Cold Went on Vacation, illustrated by Nora Krug, G.P. Putnam's Sons (New York, NY), 2011.

Sidelights

Although Molly Rausch trained as a fine-art painter, she has not let her chosen medium confine her creativity to a traditional palette. In fact, it could be said that Rausch uses her neighborhood as her canvas. During August of 2009, for example, she erected a "Lost & Found Drawing Booth" in downtown New Paltz, New York, where patrons could file written descriptions of things they had lost or misplaced. From each description, Rausch created and mailed out a unique colored drawing, which she then mailed back to its original "owner." She received over seventy-five responses and compiled the results in a book. In another example of out-of-the-box creativity, Rausch began her "Postage Stamp Paintings" project, inspired by an envelope of used stamps her father had collected and then sent her way. Glued on a small piece of paper, each stamp became the starting point for an expanded scene painted in gouache with tiny brushstrokes and often containing whimsical elements.

Rausch's characteristic whimsy extends to storytelling in her picture book *My Cold Went on Vacation,* although here she hands off the illustration duties to Nora Krug. In the story she ignores medical science in imagining how sniffles, coughs, and other assorted cold symptoms might make their way through the human population. Told that his cold is caused by a germ, her story's young narrator personifies this germ—depicted in Krug's artwork as a green, red-nosed creature with glowing pink eyes—as a visitor and imagines where it will go after visiting him. A true adventurer, the germ hops off the boy and onto the school bus, ultimately making its way over a mountain, across a vast ocean, and all the way around the world before hoping aboard another child, which in this case turns out to be the narrator's sister.

Reviewing Rausch's story in *Booklist,* Hazel Rochman predicted that "young children . . . will enjoy the global adventures and comical nonsense" while adult readers will "get the parody" running through *My Cold Went on Vacation.* A *Publishers Weekly* contributor dubbed the picture-book collaboration as "an idiosyncratic meditation about a germ on the move" in which Krug's "quirky, electric-hued pictures combine folk art and cartoon" elements, while a *Kirkus Reviews* writer deemed the work "quirky and unusual, with a touch of multiculturalism." Recommending the book's pairing of a "light-

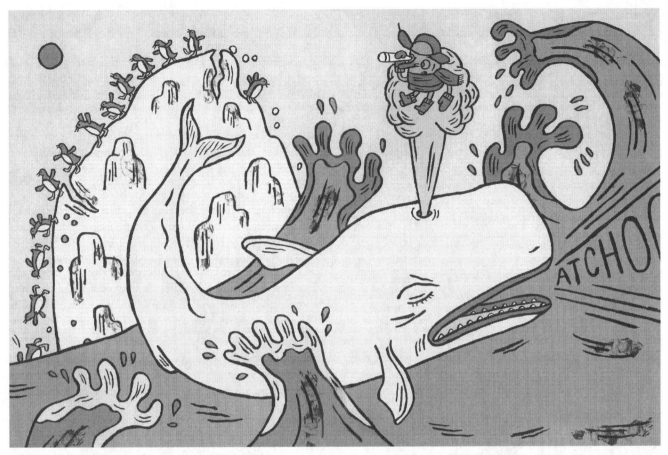

Molly Rausch's quirky story in **My Cold Went on Vacation** *comes to life in Nora Krug's comic-book-style graphics.* (Illustration copyright © 2011 by Nora Krug. Reproduced by permission of G.P. Putnam's Sons, a division of Penguin Group (USA), Inc.)

hearted, absurdist" story and "bold, whimsical art," Susanne Myers Harold concluded in *School Library Journal* that *My Cold Went on Vacation* is the "perfect choice" for an under-the-weather audience of young snifflers and sneezers.

Biographical and Critical Sources

PERIODICALS

Booklist, January 1, 2011, Hazel Rochman, review of *My Cold Went on Vacation*, p. 113.
Kirkus Reviews, December 1, 2010, review of *My Cold Went on Vacation*.
Publishers Weekly, November 15, 2010, review of *My Cold Went on Vacation*, p. 56.
School Library Journal, March, 2011, Suzanne Myers Harold, review of *My Cold Went on Vacation*, p. 132.

ONLINE

Molly Rausch Home Page, http://www.mollyrausch.com (February 28, 2012).
Postage Stamp Paintings Web site, http://www.postage stamppaintings.com/ (March 1, 2012).

Van Brunt Projects Web site, http://www.vanbruntgallery. com/ (March 1, 2012), "Molly Rausch."

*   *   *

REINHARDT, Dana 1971-

Personal
Born March 11, 1971, in Los Angeles, CA; married Daniel Sokatch; children: Noa, Zoe (daughters). *Education:* Attended law school. *Religion:* Jewish.

Addresses
Home—San Francisco, CA. *E-mail*—info@danarein hardt.net.

Career
Novelist. Worked variously as a waitress, fact checker for a film magazine, reader for a publishing company, and associate producer for television news programming.

Awards, Honors
CYBILS Awards finalist in young-adult fiction category, 2006, for *A Brief Chapter in My Impossible Life;* California Book Award, and Sydney Taylor Book Award, Association of Jewish Libraries, both 2010, both for *The Things a Brother Knows.*

Writings

A Brief Chapter in My Impossible Life, Wendy Lamb Books (New York, NY), 2006.
Harmless, Wendy Lamb Books (New York, NY), 2007.
How to Build a House, Wendy Lamb Books (New York, NY), 2008.
The Things a Brother Knows, Wendy Lamb Books (New York, NY), 2010.
The Summer I Learned to Fly, Wendy Lamb Books (New York, NY), 2011.

Adaptations

Harmless and *A Brief Chapter in My Impossible Life* were both adapted as audiobooks, Listening Library, 2006.

Sidelights

In her writing for young adults, Dana Reinhardt draws on an array of career experiences, among them her time as a waitress, law student, social worker, crisis hotline

Cover of Dana Reinhardt's debut novel, **A Brief Chapter in My Impossible Life,** *in which a teen's world turns upside down upon learning that she is adopted.* (Jacket cover copyright © 2006 by Wendy Lamb Books. Reproduced by permission of Wendy Lamb Books, an imprint of Random House Children's Books, a division of Random House, Inc.)

employee, and documentary film producer. Reinhardt brings the same grounded realism to her fiction, penning compelling novels such as *A Brief Chapter in My Impossible Life, Harmless, How to Build a House,* and *The Things a Brother Knows,* all which have been praised for their ability to speak plainly to adolescent readers.

Praised by a *Publishers Weekly* reviewer as a "moving first novel" that "celebrates family love and promotes tolerance of diverse beliefs," *A Brief Chapter in My Impossible Life* introduces sixteen-year-old Simone. Simone always knew she was different than her adopted family—she is olive skinned and has dark hair while her adopted parents are fair—but she takes deep pride in her family's agnostic beliefs. A grudging meeting with her birth mother, Rivka, ultimately changes the teen's perspective when she learns about the woman's devout Jewish faith. As Simone is exposed to the traditions of Orthodox Judaism, her relationship with her mother deepens and she ultimately gains tolerance while also developing a sense of her unique ethnic heritage.

While religion is a major theme in *A Brief Chapter in My Impossible Life,* Reinhardt weaves other facets of teen culture into her story, among them drinking, sex, and romance. A *Kirkus Reviews* critic noted that the balance the author strikes between seriousness—Rivka is dying of ovarian cancer—and humor is successful; the seriousness is interjected "in very realistic doses," then leavened "with a sense of humor and a sense of hope." In *Booklist,* Holly Koelling wrote that "both Simone and Rivka are strong, complicated characters who benefit greatly from each other," dubbing *A Brief Chapter in My Impossible Life* a story Reinhardt tells "with skill, attention to detail, and poignancy."

In *Harmless* fourteen-year-old best friends Anna, Emma, and Mariah decide to chance it one night and stay out late partying with a group of older boys. When they are caught by their parents, they cover by lying, claiming that one of the three was attacked and almost raped. Through each girl's narration, Reinhardt shows the damage that this lie causes as the girls' parents' effort to track down the attacker mobilizes law enforcement and ultimately leads an innocent man to jail. *Harmless* presents "a well-constructed object lesson in responsibility that will set teens thinking," concluded Frances Bradburn in her *Booklist* review of Reinhardt's novel, while in *Kliatt* Claire Rossner predicted that, while "it's hard to like these girls," some teens will be attracted to "just this topic: good girls behaving badly." Reinhardt's focus on family problems "add[s] depth and tension to the story," noted a *Publishers Weekly* contributor, and a *Kirkus Reviews* writer concluded of *Harmless* that the author "successfully avoids a sanctimonious tone" in her morally centered cautionary tale.

Family problems also plague Harper, the sixteen-year-old protagonist in Reinhardt's *How to Build a House.* For Harper, her father's pending divorce from her longtime stepmom means that she will lose the three most important people in her life: her stepmom, Jane, and her stepsisters Rose and Tess. While her family is crumbling, Harper's high-school confidante proves he can not be trusted, leaving her with the desire to escape for a while. To clear her head, Harper flies from her home in California to small-town Tennessee, where she joins a group of volunteers building homes for tornado victims. In Reinhardt's text, Harper's experiences working in the hot sun while mastering the rudiments of home building—in addition to camping out in rustic accommodations at a local motel—alternate with vignettes that crystallize her emotions about all that has brought her family to its destructive state. As the nails and boards and concrete in Tennessee are slowly transformed into a home, so Harper learns to reconstruct her past and place responsibility where it belongs. A budding romance with Teddy, a fellow volunteer, leaven the seriousness of Reinhardt's story as the relationship exposes her to "new lessons about love and family life," according to Rosser in *Kliatt.* "Readers will find Harper absolutely charming, even at her most sardonic moments," predicted a *Kirkus Reviews* writer, while a *Publishers Weekly* critic praised *How to Build a House* as "a work as intimately and intelligently wrought as [Reinhardt's] . . . previous YA novels."

For Drew Solo, a young teen growing up in California during the mid-1980s, a new friend opens up a window to a new life in *The Summer I Learned to Fly.* A shy and cautious loner, thirteen-year-old Drew focuses her attention on her own small piece of life, gaining affection from her pet rat, connecting with her dead father through one of his old journals, and nursing a secret crush on Nick, the cashier at her mom's cheese shop. During the summer, Drew experiences a series of subtle hurts as Nick gets a girlfriend and her mom acts short-tempered due to stress. Then she meets Emmett Crane, a reticent teen whose life goal is to find a legendary hot springs said to exist near San Francisco that dispenses water with healing properties. As the two teens team up to search for this spring, Drew also gains insights about her own emotional world, insights that include "some bittersweet lessons about love and sacrifice," according to a *Publishers Weekly* contributor. "Drew's emotional progression . . . is pitch-perfect every step of the way," asserted *Voice of Youth Advocates* reviewer Timothy Capehart, and her story is one with which "young girls especially will identify." The young teen's metamorphosis "is not drastic or world-changing, but a natural emergence of independence," explained a *Kirkus Reviews* writer, and in *Horn Book* Jennifer M. Brabander characterized *The Summer I Learned to Fly* as "quietly compelling." Praising Reinhardt as a "true storyteller," Frances Bradburn added in *Booklist* that the author deftly crafts "a moving coming-of-age story" from "implausible elements . . . and touchingly mundane details."

The relationship between two brothers is Reinhardt's focus in *The Things a Brother Knows,* which finds a teen dealing with his brother's guilt and stress as a re-

Cover of Reinhardt's novel **The Summer I Learned to Fly,** *featuring cover art by Ericka ORourke.* (Jacket cover copyright © 2011 by Wendy Lamb Books. Reproduced by permission of Wendy Lamb Books, an imprint of Random House Children's Books, a division of Random House, Inc.)

sult of his decision to serve in the U.S. Marines. Despite excelling as a student, Boaz Katznelson opted for military service instead of college, and now that he has returned home from deployment in the Middle East he seems like a different person. Younger brother Levi has always found it difficult living under Boaz's shadow, but Boaz has become a loner, staying in his room and hardly interacting with anyone. Suddenly, out of the blue, he announces his plan to hike the Appalachian Trail. Levi suspects that his brother is not being truthful, and when the older teen leaves home on this strange mission the younger boy commits an heroic act of his own, supported by his two best friends. Noting that *The Things a Brother Knows* "is not anchored in a specific war," Frances Bradburn added in *Booklist* that the novel "sensitively explores universal traumas that usurp the lives" of both those in active military and their families. "Levi's growing comprehension of Boaz's internal turmoi is gracefully and powerfully evoked" in Reinholdt's "timely novel," according to a *Publishers Weekly* contributor, and in *Horn Book* Jonathan Hunt noted that "the family dynamic is drawn with a deft and subtle hand." Remarking on the resonance of *The Things a*

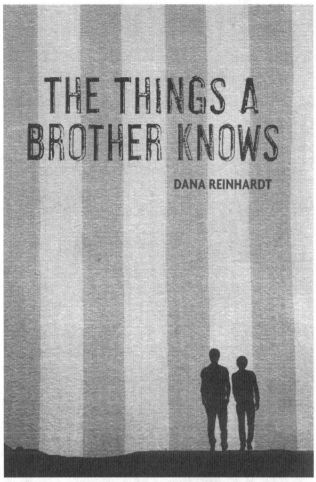

Cover of Reinhardt's coming-of-age novel **The Things a Brother Knows,** *which takes place during the Vietnam War era.* (Jacket cover copyright © 2010 Wendy Lamb Books. Reproduced by permission of Wendy Lamb Books, an imprint of Random House Children's Books, a division of Random House, Inc.)

Brother Knows, Amy Cheney praised Reinhardt's work in *School Library Journal* as "a powerful and timely portrait of young men trying to make sense of their lives."

Biographical and Critical Sources

PERIODICALS

Booklist, January 1, 2006, Holly Koelling, review of *A Brief Chapter in My Impossible Life,* p. 85; December 1, 2006, Frances Bradburn, review of *Harmless,* p. 39; April 15, 2008, Gillian Engberg, review of *How to Build a House,* p. 40; October 1, 2010, Frances Bradburn, review of *The Things a Brother Knows,* p. 81; June 1, 2011, Frances Bradburn, review of *The Summer I Learned to Fly,* p. 89.

Bulletin of the Center for Children's Books, February, 2006, Deborah Stevenson, review of *A Brief Chapter in My Impossible Life,* p. 283.

Horn Book, July-August, 2008, Jennifer M. Brabander, review of *How to Build a House,* p. 456; November-

December, 2010, Jonathan Hunt, review of *The Things a Brother Knows,* p. 102; July-August, 2011, Jennifer M. Bradburn, review of *The Summer I Learned to Fly,* p. 158.

Kirkus Reviews, January 15, 2006, review of *A Brief Chapter in My Impossible Life,* p. 88; February 1, 2007, review of *Harmless,* p. 128; April 15, 2008, review of *How to Build a House;* August 15, 2010, review of *The Things a Brother Knows;* June 1, 2011, review of *The Summer I Learned to Fly.*

Kliatt, January, 2006, Claire Rosser, review of *A Brief Chapter in My Impossible Life,* p. 10; January, 2007, Claire Rosser, review of *Harmless,* p. 18; May, 2008, Claire Rosser, review of *How to Build a House,* p. 16.

Publishers Weekly, January 2, 2006, review of *A Brief Chapter in My Impossible Life,* p. 63; January 15, 2007, review of *Harmless,* p. 53; April 7, 2008, review of *How to Build a House,* p. 61; August 30, 2010, review of *The Things a Brother Knows,* p. 55; May 23, 2011, Claire Rosser, review of *The Summer I Learned to Fly,* p. 16.

School Library Journal, February, 2006, Rich Margolis, interview with Reinhardt, p. 39; March, 2006, Janet Hilbun, review of *A Brief Chapter in My Impossible Life,* p. 228; March, 2007, Kelly Czarnecki, review of *Harmless,* p. 218; June, 2008, Kathleen E. Gruver, review of *How to Build a House,* p. 148; December, 2010, Amy Cheney, review of *The Things a Brother Knows,* p. 125; June, 2011, Susanne Roush, review of *The Summer I Learned to Fly,* p. 131.

Voice of Youth Advocates, April, 2006, Sarah Cofer, review of *A Brief Chapter in My Impossible Life,* p. 51; October, 2010, Cheryl Clark, review of *The Things a Brother Knows,* p. 356; June, 2011, Timothy Capehart, review of *The Summer I Learned to Fly,* p. 172.

ONLINE

Dana Reinhardt Home Page, http://www.danareinhardt.net (March 2, 2012).

Random House Web site, http://www.randomhouse.com/ (November 29, 2006), "Dana Reinhardt."*

*   *   *

REVIS, Beth

Personal

Born in NC; married. *Education:* North Carolina State University, B.A. (English education), M.A. (English literature). *Hobbies and other interests:* Travel.

Addresses

Home—North Carolina. *Agent*—Merrilee Heifetz, Writers House, 21 W. 26th St., New York, NY 10010. *E-mail*—bethrevis@gmail.com.

Career

Author and educator. Teacher in North Carolina public school until 2010.

Writings

"ACROSS THE UNIVERSE" YOUNG-ADULT NOVEL SERIES

Across the Universe, Razorbill (New York, NY), 2011.
A Million Suns, Razorbill (New York, NY), 2012.

Sidelights

A former teacher and North Carolina native, Beth Revis entertains teen readers with stories that mix fantasy and science fiction. Her debut novel, *Across the Universe,* was also intended as the first novel in her similarly named series and has been followed by *A Million Suns.*

In *Across the Universe* Revis introduces the central character in her trilogy. A passenger on the space ship Godspeed, seventeen-year-old Amy is in a cryogenically frozen state and traveling light years away to settle the planet Centauri-Earth, along with her parents. She awakens 250 years into her 300-year trip when her cryogenic unit is disabled and she barely survives the experience. From Elder, a fellow teen and one of 2,312

Cover of Beth Revis's science-based fantasy Across the Universe, *the first novel in a series about a teen's adventures in a near-future world.*
(Jacket cover copyright © 2011. Reproduced by permission of Razorbill, a division of Penguin Young Readers Group, a member of Penguin Group (USA), 375 Hudson Street, New York, NY 10014. All rights reserved.)

inhabitants who will live out their entire lives aboard the transport ship, she learns that the passengers' presence has been hidden from almost everyone by the captain, Eldest. If this is so, then who is methodically unplugging these frozen settlers, thereby risking their lives? Exploring the ship, Amy comes to understand the strange, robotic culture of the ship's space-bound crew, a culture that discourages independent thought in favor of mechanized behaviors that will sustain their long isolation within the ship's confined, artificial environment. As she attempts to stop more frozen passengers from being terminated, the teen also begins to have feelings for Elder, and both teens share their perspective on the mystery and their relationship in Revis's dual narrative.

Dubbed a "cunningly executed thriller" by *Booklist* contributor Daniel Kraus, *Across the Universe* serves up a "something's-wrong-aboard-this-spaceship" adventure that is also "a compulsively readable crowd-pleaser." In *Horn Book* Anita L. Burkam noted that "Revis establishes the setting and . . . constraints in such a pressing way that readers truly feel the characters' plight." For Amy, it is "grief and fear," according to Heather M. Campbell in *School Library Journal;* for Elder, he "begins to experience a coming-of-age that is convincingly written." "Wherever the series goes from here, this opener leaves an indelible imprint," asserted a *Kirkus Reviews* writer, calling the setting of *Across the Universe* both "credible and palpably claustrophobic." While noting that the first "Across the Universe" installment "hits all of the standard dystopian notes," a *Publishers Weekly* critic added that Revis melds "a believable romance and a series of tantalizing mysteries that will hold readers' attention."

Three months have passed since Amy was released from her cryogenic frozen sleep in *Across the Universe*, and in *A Million Suns* she has begun to reconcile herself to the fact that she may well spend the rest of her life as part of the strange society inhabiting the Godspeed. With the Eldest now gone, Elder leads the shipboard society as it travels toward Centauri-Earth and he hopes to make some positive changes. While he grapples with the chaos that results as he attempts to ween inhabitants from the old ways, Elder also discovers new challenges in a cryptic message left to Amy. The answer to this riddle may alter the course of everyone aboard the Godspeed.

While recommending that readers begin with *Across the Universe,* Ed Goldberg added in his *Voice of Youth Advocates* review that *A Million Suns* "does stand on its own" and has "plenty of action." "Setting and plot are the heart and soul of this ripping space thriller," asserted a *Kirkus Reviews* contributor, and Kraus deemed the sequel "a crackerjack read." Looking forward to the concluding volume of the "Across the Universe" series, Kraus concluded his *Booklist* review by noting that "Revis just might make straight-up sci-fi cool again."

Biographical and Critical Sources

PERIODICALS

Booklist, December 15, 2010, Daniel Kraus, review of *Across the Universe,* p. 47; December 1, 2011, Daniel Kraus, review of *A Million Suns,* p. 62.

Horn Book, March-April, 2011, Anita L. Burkam, review of *Across the Universe,* p. 123.

Kirkus Reviews, December 1, 2010, review of *Across the Universe*; December 15, 2011, review of *A Million Suns.*

Publishers Weekly, November 22, 2010, review of *Across the Universe,* p. 57.

School Library Journal, February, 2011, Heather M. Campbell, review of *Across the Universe,* p. 118.

Voice of Youth Advocates, February, 2012, Ed Goldberg, review of *A Million Suns,* p. 614.

ONLINE

Beth Revis Home Page, http://www.bethrevis.com (March 2, 2012).*

S

SCHARSCHMIDT, Sherry 1957-

Personal

Born 1957, in CA. *Education:* Attended University of California at Berkeley; Art Center College of Design, B.A. (advertising and design).

Addresses

Home—W. Chicago, IL. *E-mail*—catsdogswords@gmail.com.

Career

Illustrator, creative director, and artist. Ogilvy & Mather, senior art director, 1982-88; Leo Burnett Advertising, Tokyo, Japan, then Chicago, IL, associate creative director, 1991-97; Rapp Collins Worldwide, associate creative director, 1997-2001; Cramer Krasselt, Chicago, IL, creative director and vice president, beginning 2001.

Awards, Honors

Notable Children's Book for Younger Readers selection, American Library Association, 2011, for *Tuck Me In!* by Dean Hacohen.

Illustrator

Dean Hacohen, *Tuck Me In!*, Candlewick Press (Somerville, MA), 2010.

Sidelights

Sherry Scharschmidt embarked on a career in advertising after graduating from the prestigious Art Center College of Design, and her job has taken her to several major U.S. cities as well as allowing her to spend two years in Tokyo, Japan. Now settled in the Chicago area, Scharschmidt has also returned to her love of art by creating colorful dog-and cat-centered paintings incorporating found objects such as lettering salvaged from old signs. A collaboration with former colleague Dean Hacohen has also resulted in her first illustration project: the children's book *Tuck Me In!*

Described by a *Publishers Weekly* critic as "tailormade for bedtime," Hacohen's story for *Tuck Me In!* finds a range of young animals ready to settle down for the night. In each turn of the page, readers can play parent to an alligator, mouse, peacock, pig, zebra, and hedgehog as the lift-the-flap format lets them cover each baby animal with a cozy blanket. To illustrate the story, Scharschmidt contributes computer-generated illustrations that combine "colorful basic shapes with quick brush strokes adding details," according to a *Kirkus Re-*

Sherry Scharschmidt teams up with friend and author Dean Hacohen to create the engaging bedtime story **Tuck Me In!** (Illustration copyright © 2010 by Sherry Scharschmidt. Reproduced by permission of Candlewick Press, Somerville, MA.)

views writer, and in *School Library Journal* Marge Loch-Wouters praised the artist's use of bold patterns and strong colors as well as her "sketchy, jazzy style." Hacohen's "gentle, rhythmic" text also earned a nod from Loch-Wouters, the critic predicting that *Tuck Me In!* will "be re-read endlessly as a comfy prelude to bedtime."

Biographical and Critical Sources

PERIODICALS

Kirkus Reviews, August 1, 2010, review of *Tuck Me In!*
Magpies, November, 2010, Tali Lavi, review of *Tuck Me In!,* p. 24.
Publishers Weekly, August 23, 2010, review of *Tuck Me In!,* p. 48.
School Library Journal, August, 2010, Marge Loch-Wouters, review of *Tuck Me In!,* p. 76.

ONLINE

Sherry Scharschmidt Home Page, http://www.catsdogswords.com (March 3, 2012).*

*   *   *

SCOTT, Elizabeth (Ivy Devlin)

Personal

Born in VA; daughter of high-school teachers; married. *Education:* College degree.

Addresses

Home—Manassas Park, VA. *E-mail*—Elizabeth@elizabethwrites.com.

Career

Writer. Has worked as an editor, an office manager, and in sales.

Awards, Honors

Lambda Literary Award, 2007, and Popular Paperbacks for Young Adults designation, American Library Association (ALA), 2008, both for *Bloom;* Best Book for Young Adults designation, ALA, and Best Children's Books of the Year, Bank Street College of Education, both 2009, both for *Stealing Heaven;* Books for the Teen Age selection, New York Public Library, and Quick Pick for Reluctant Young-Adult Readers and Best Book for Young Adults designation, both ALA, all 2009, and Popular Paperbacks for Young Adults designation, ALA, and Young Adults' Choices selection, In-

ternational Reading Association, both 2010, all for *Living Dead Girl;* Best Book for Young Adults designation, ALA, 2010, for *Love You, Hate You, Miss You;* Quick Picks for Reluctant Young-Adult Readers designation, ALA, 2010, for *The Unwritten Rule.*

Writings

Bloom, Simon Pulse (New York, NY), 2007.
Perfect You, Simon Pulse (New York, NY), 2008.
Stealing Heaven, HarperCollins (New York, NY), 2008.
Living Dead Girl, Simon Pulse (New York, NY), 2008.
Something, Maybe, Simon Pulse (New York, NY), 2009.
Love You, Hate You, Miss You, HarperCollins (New York, NY), 2009.
Grace, Dutton Books (New York, NY), 2010.
The Unwritten Rule, Simon Pulse (New York, NY), 2010.
(As Ivy Devlin) *Low Red Moon,* Bloomsbury (New York, NY), 2010.
Between Here and Forever, Simon Pulse (New York, NY), 2011.

Cover of Elizabeth Scott's novel Grace, *in which a teen runs from her fate in a terror-filled near-future earth.* (Jacket cover photographs © 2010 by Erit L. Ransmayr (girl); Stockbyte Photography/Veer/Corbis (explosion). Reproduced by permission of Dutton Books, an imprint of Penguin Young Readers Group, a member of Penguin Group (USA), 375 Hudson Street, New York, NY 10014. All rights reserved.)

As I Wake, Dutton Books (New York, NY), 2011.
Miracle, Simon Pulse (New York, NY), 2012.

Sidelights

In her award-winning young-adult novels, which include *Bloom, Grace, Stealing Heaven,* and *The Unwritten Rule,* Elizabeth Scott examines themes of self-identity, friendship, loyalty, sexuality, and independence. In her works, Scott creates female characters with recognizable personality traits, not all of them admirable. Writing, she noted on her home page, "has made my life broader, stronger. It lifts me up and out of myself, and lets me see things I've never seen before. It has made me ask questions I can answer, as well as ones I can't. It shows me things I don't understand, and makes me see the truth of them."

Lauren, the protagonist of Scott's debut novel *Bloom,* cannot quite understand why she has won the heart of the most popular boy in her school, especially since they seem to have nothing in common. When an old friend named Evan arrives in town, Lauren finds herself in a love triangle as she tries to figure out what qualities she values most in a relationship. Even as she deceives her boyfriend in order to spend time with Evan, Lauren wonders why her old friend's more-dangerous lifestyle appeals to her.

Reviewing *Bloom* for *Kliatt,* Amanda MacGregor called Lauren "a refreshingly complex character . . . trying to figure out how to be herself." According to *School Library Journal* contributor Sarah Krygier, the conflict Scott introduces in her novel "rings true," creating "enough drama to keep readers interested."

Perfect You explores the life of Kate, a character for whom everything seems to be falling apart. While Kate's best friend ditches her, her clueless father blissfully sells vitamins at the local mall. Meanwhile, Kate's grandmother keeps trying to run the teen's life, and her complicated relationship with her boyfriend is becoming mostly physical. In *School Library Journal* Natasha Forrester wrote that in *Perfect You* Scott "does a good job portraying a teen who is simultaneously self-centered and sympathetic."

In *Stealing Heaven* Scott introduces Danielle, an eighteen year old who lives a rootless existence, moving relentlessly from town to town with her mother, a professional thief. When the duo arrives in the picturesque New England resort town of Heaven, Danielle unexpectedly makes friends with Allison Donaldson, whose house she planned to rob. Feeling a sense of permanence for the first time in her life, Danielle realizes that she can no longer participate in her mother's crime spree. *Stealing Heaven* "is deceptively touching," Heather E. Miller commented in *School Library Journal,* and *Kliatt* reviewer Ashleigh Larsen observed that Scott's strong-willed protagonist "gives a new perspective full of hope to YAs who feel trapped between family and friends."

Scott enters much darker territory in *Living Dead Girl,* a "harrowing tale of abuse leavened only by lyric writing," noted a writer in *Kirkus Reviews.* When she was ten years old, Alice was abducted by Ray, a pedophile who has controlled her through psychological terror and physical violence. Now age fifteen, Alice realizes that Ray plans to replace her with a younger girl, and at her abuser's bidding she helps search for his next victim, even though she suspects that Ray will kill her once she succeeds. "Alice tells her story in a flat, curt voice that reflects her emptiness and despair," Patty Campbell related in *Horn Book,* and Larsen maintained of *Living Dead Girl* that "Scott's portrayal of an abducted child's experience and mindset is shockingly authentic."

Scott returns to lighter fare with *Something, Maybe,* a "good-natured entry in the which-boy-will-she-choose canon," according to *Booklist* critic Daniel Kraus. Seventeen-year-old Hannah prefers a quiet life, in contrast to her estranged father, an aging Hugh Hefner-like playboy, and her mother, a Web-chat hostess who poses in lingerie. Just when Hannah catches the eye of two eligible classmates—good-looking Josh and comical Finn—her father complicates matters by contacting her

Cover of Something, Maybe, *Scott's novel about a teen who attempts to avoid the limelight of her television-star parents.* (Simon & Schuster, 2010. Jacket cover photograph © 2010 by Laurence Mouton/Photo Alto/Jupiterimages.)

for the first time in years. "Hannah is neither too witty nor too empty but nicely normal," a critic in *Kirkus Reviews* noted, and a *Publishers Weekly* contributor deemed *Something, Maybe* "a satisfying, romantic coming-of-age story."

Love You, Hate You, Miss You centers on an alcoholic teenager's efforts to repair her life. As the novel opens, a grief-stricken Amy is being released from a rehab clinic, which she entered after the death of her best friend, Julia, in an automobile accident. Through a series of letters written to Julia, as well as Amy's conversations with her therapist, teachers, and parents, readers get a clearer understanding of the complex relationship between the two girls as well as the events of that tragic night. "Scott offers a satisfying story of an engaging heroine successfully naming and confronting her demons," *Booklist* contributor Debbie Carton related in her review of *Love You, Hate You, Miss You.*

The Unwritten Rule focuses on Sarah and Brianna, life-long friends who find themselves at odds after they fall for the same boy. When the brash Brianna begins dating Ryan, the quiet and sensitive Sarah is devastated: she has had a crush on Ryan since eighth grade. After Ryan secretly confesses that he has feelings for her, as well, Sarah is torn between her love for Ryan and her loyalty to Brianna, who she knows as a troubled and insecure girl. In her review of *The Unwritten Rule*, Carton applauded "Scott's realistic dialogue and empathetic view of symbiotic relationships," and a *Kirkus Reviews* writer noted that the author gives [the love triangle] extra dimension by adding a painful look at Sarah and Brianna's toxic friendship."

In *Between Here and Forever* Scott offers "an emotionally wrenching exploration of hope, acceptance, and pride," Frances Bradburn remarked in *Booklist.* Seventeen-year-old Abby has always played second fiddle to her successful and beautiful older sister, Tess, but now Tess is left comatose after a car accident. When Eli, an attractive nurse's aide, enters the girl's hospital room, Tess's eyes flutter, giving Abby hope that her sister can recover. Abby persuades Eli to visit Tess regularly, hoping that his charms can affect a miracle cure, even as she refuses to believe that Eli's interest in her is genuine. "Scott slowly unfolds Abby's damaged psyche as the girl grows in her understanding of both herself and of her sister," a *Kirkus Reviews* writer stated in appraising *Between Here and Forever*, and Lynn Rashin commented in *School Library Journal* that Abby's "sense of self-doubt and guilt she feels will be relevant to many teens."

Scott blends mystery, science fiction, and romance in *As I Wake,* a dystopian tale about an amnesiac who will regain her memories only if she agrees to perform surveillance work for the government. The author "succeeds in weaving an unpredictable course," explained a critic in reviewing the novel for *Publishers Weekly.* In *Grace,* another dystopian tale, a young woman trains as

a suicide bomber to help defeat a totalitarian regime. "Scott's precisely written novel offers a gritty, distressing look at what happens when people have no freedom," asserted *Voice of Youth Advocates* reviewer Rachelle Bilz.

Scott has also written a well-received paranormal thriller under the pen name Ivy Devlin. *Low Red Moon* concerns Avery Hood, a Woodville teenager who awakens in the forest next to her parents' mutilated bodies, with no memory of their brutal murder. Forced to live in town with her estranged grandmother, Avery attempts to recall the events of that night with little success until she meets Ben Dusic, a new classmate. Their powerful attraction leads to romance, and when Avery realizes that Ben is a werewolf, she wonders if he is responsible for the killings. A reviewer for *Publishers Weekly* noted of *Low Red Moon* that "the emotion pouring off the pages should sweep readers into this haunting story."

Biographical and Critical Sources

PERIODICALS

Booklist, April 15, 2008, Frances Bradburn, review of *Stealing Heaven,* p. 41; October 15, 2008, Lynn Rutan, review of *Living Dead Girl,* p. 40; February 15, 2009, Daniel Kraus, review of *Something, Maybe,* p. 72; April 1, 2009, Debbie Carton, review of *Love You, Hate You, Miss You,* p. 33; March 1, 2010, Debbie Carton, review of *The Unwritten Rule,* p. 64; September 1, 2010, Ian Chipman, review of *Grace,* p. 98; June 1, 2011, Kimberly Garnick, review of *Low Red Moon,* p. 58, and Frances Bradburn, review of *Between Here and Forever,* p. 79.

Bulletin of the Center for Children's Books, July-August, 2007, Deborah Stevenson, review of *Bloom,* p. 484.

Horn Book, November-December, 2008, Patty Campbell, review of *Living Dead Girl,* p. 716; July-August, 2009, Elissa Gershowitz, review of *Love You, Hate You, Miss You,* p. 431; November-December, 2010, Christine M. Heppermann, review of *Grace,* p. 103.

Kirkus Reviews, May 15, 2008, review of *Stealing Heaven*; August 15, 2008, review of *Living Dead Girl*; January 15, 2009, review of *Something, Maybe*; June 15, 2009, review of *Love You, Hate You, Miss You*; March 15, 2010, review of *The Unwritten Rule;* August 15, 2010, reviews of *Low Red Moon* and *Grace*; May 1, 2011, review of *Between Here and Forever*; August 15, 2011, review of *As I Wake.*

Kliatt, May, 2007, Amanda MacGregor, review of *Bloom,* p. 28; May, 2008, Ashleigh Larsen, review of *Stealing Heaven,* p. 16; July, 2008, Amanda MacGregor, review of *Perfect You,* p. 26; September, 2008, Ashleigh Larsen, review of *Living Dead Girl,* p. 21.

Publishers Weekly, September 8, 2008, review of *Living Dead Girl,* p. 52; January 26, 2009, review of *Something, Maybe,* p. 121; June 29, 2009, review of *Love You, Hate You, Miss You,* p. 130; August 23, 2010, review of *Low Red Moon,* p. 50; September 27, 2010, review of *Grace,* p. 63; May 2, 2011, review of *Between Here and Forever,* p. 59; July 4, 2011, review of *As I Wake,* p. 66.

School Librarian, summer, 2011, Elizabeth Finlayson, review of *Low Red Moon,* p. 116.

School Library Journal, June, 2007, Sarah Krygier, review of *Bloom,* p. 160; April, 2008, Natasha Forrester, review of *Perfect You,* p. 148; August, 2008, Heather E. Miller, review of *Stealing Heaven,* p. 132; October, 2008, Carolyn Lehman, review of *Living Dead Girl,* p. 159; June, 2009, Sue Lloyd, review of *Love You, Hate You, Miss You,* p. 137; November, 2010, Necia Blundy, review of *Grace,* p. 126; June, 2011, Lynn Rashid, review of *Between Here and Forever,* p. 134.

Voice of Youth Advocates, June, 2007, Angelica Delgado, review of *Bloom,* p. 152; October, 2010, Kristin Fletcher-Spear, review of *The Unwritten Rule,* p. 358; November, 2010, Melyssa Malinowski, review of *Low Red Moon,* p. 110; December, 2010, Elaine Gall Hirsch, review of *Low Red Moon,* p. 468; Rachelle Bilz, review of *Grace,* p. 475; June, 2011, Liz Sundermann, review of *Between Here and Forever,* p. 172.

ONLINE

Elizabeth Scott Home Page, http://elizabethwrites.com (March 1, 2012).

Elizabeth Scott Web log, http://blog.elizabethwrites.com (March 1, 2012).

Simon & Schuster Web site, http://www.simonandschuster.com/ (March 1, 2012), "Author Revealed: Elizabeth Scott."*

*   *   *

SEGOVIA, Carmen 1978-

Personal

Born 1978, in Cerdanyola, Spain. *Education:* Studied cinema, set-design, and art.

Addresses

Home—Barcelona, Spain. *Agent*—Marlena Agency; marlenamarlenaagency.com. *E-mail*—carmen@carmensegovia.net.

Career

Illustrator and graphic artist.

Awards, Honors

X Concurso de Album Ilustrado a la Orilla del Viento Honor designation, 2008, for *El cuento del pingüino* by Antonio Ventura; Banco del Libro de Venezuela para los Mejores Libros para Niños y Jóvenes selection, 2010, for *En el laberinto del viento* by Marina Colasanti.

Illustrator

Elza Pilgrim, *The China Doll,* Sterling Pub. (New York, NY), 2005.

Jean Pierre Kerloc'h, *Croc-Blanc* (based on *White Fang* by Jack London), P'titGlénat (France), 2008.

Marina Colasanti, *En el laberinto del viento,* Anaya (Madrid, Spain), 2008.

Antonio Ventura, *El cuento del pingüino,* Fondo de Cultura Económica (Mexico City, Mexico), 2008.

François David, *La fille dans le miroir,* Sarbacane (Paris, France), 2009.

Susan Blackaby, *Brownie Groundhog and the February Fox,* Sterling (New York, NY), 2010.

Luisa Fontán Bos, *Los bichos bola,* Cuatro Azules (Madrid, Spain), 2011.

Contributor to anthology *The Exquisite Book: 100 Artists Play a Collaborative Game,* Chronicle Books (San Francisco, CA), 2010.

Biographical and Critical Sources

PERIODICALS

Booklist, January 1, 2006, Jennifer Mattson, review of *The China Doll,* p. 118.

Kirkus Reviews, November 15, 2010, review of *Brownie Groundhog and the February Fox.*

Publishers Weekly, January 16, 2006, review of *The China Doll,* p. 64; November 8, 2010, review of *Brownie Groundhog and the February Fox,* p. 57.

School Library Journal, January, 2006, Kirsten Cutler, review of *The China Doll,* p. 112; February, 2011, C.J. Connor, review of *Brownie Groundhog and the February Fox,* p. 75.

ONLINE

Carmen Segovia Home Page, http://www.carmensegovia.net (February 28, 2012).*

*   *   *

SHEPHERD, Nicole Leigh
See MIKULSKI, Keri

*   *   *

SHEPPERSON, Rob 1957-

Personal

Born 1957, in LA; married; children: two daughters. *Education:* Kansas City Art Institute, degree.

Addresses

Home—Croton-on-Hudson, NY. *E-mail*—robshepperson@earthlink.net.

Career

Illustrator.

Illustrator

The Sandman, Farrar, Straus & Giroux (New York, NY), 1989.

Kenneth C. Davis, *Don't Know Much about George Washington,* HarperCollins (New York, NY), 2003.

Christina Allen, *Hippos in the Night: Autobiographical Adventures in Africa,* HarperCollins (New York, NY), 2003.

Carolyn Coman, *The Big House,* Front Street Books (Asheville, NC), 2004.

Kenneth C. Davis, *Don't Know Much about Abraham Lincoln,* HarperCollins (New York, NY), 2004.

Elizabeth Starr Hill, *Wildfire!,* Farrar, Straus & Giroux (New York, NY), 2004.

Kenneth C. Davis, *Don't Know Much about Thomas Jefferson,* HarperCollins (New York, NY), 2005.

Charlotte Pomerantz, *Thunderboom!: Poems for Everyone,* Front Street Books (Asheville, NC), 2005.

Carolyn Coman, *The Big House,* Puffin Books (New York, NY), 2007.

David L. Harrison, *Bugs: Poems about Creeping Things,* Wordsong (Honesdale, PA), 2007.

Carolyn Coman, *Sneaking Suspicions,* Front Street (Asheville, NC), 2007.

J. Patrick Lewis, *Under the Kissletoe: Christmastime Poems,* Wordsong (Honesdale, PA), 2007.

David Harrison, *Vacation: We're Going to the Ocean,* Wordsong (Honesdale, PA), 2009.

Phyllis Root, *Lilly and the Pirates,* Front Street (Honesdale, PA), 2010.

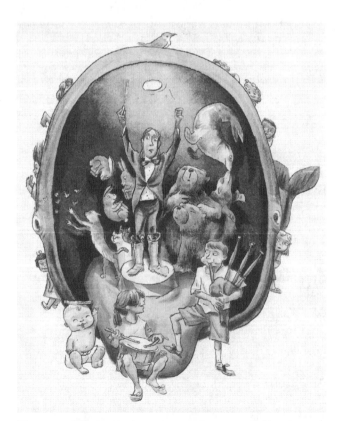

The sense of fun in Charlotte Pomerantz's poetry collection **Thunderboom!** *is echoed in Rob Shepperson's art.* (Front Street, an imprint of Boyds Mills Press, 2005. Illustration copyright © 2005 by Rob Shepperson. Reproduced by permission.)

Carolyn Coman, *The Memory Bank,* Arthur A. Levine Books (New York, NY), 2010.

Carolyn Coman, *Writing Stories: Ideas, Exercises, and Encouragement for Teachers and Writers of All Ages,* Stenhouse Publishers (Portland, ME), 2011.

Ron Rauss, *Can I Just Take a Nap?,* Simon & Schuster Books for Young Readers (New York, NY), 2012.

Contributor of artwork to periodicals, including *Advertising Age, INX, Newsweek, New York Times Book Review, Parenting, Radio Times, Reader's Digest, Soho Weekly News, Wall Street Journal,* and *Washington Post.*

Sidelights

The editorial illustrations created by Louisiana native Rob Shepperson have entertained readers of a number of high-profile publications, among them the *New York Times Book Review,* the *Wall Street Journal, Newsweek,* and the *Washington Post.* What these readers may not know is that Shepperson has also gained a following among young children through his work as a picture-book illustrator. His art work has brought to life poetry collections such as Charlotte Pomerantz's *Thunderboom!: Poems for Everyone* and J. Patrick Lewis's *Under the Kissletoe: Christmastime Poems* as well as picture books and chapter books that include Ron Rauss's *Can I Just Take a Nap?,* Phyllis Root's *Lilly and the Pirates,* and tales by Kenneth C. Davis, David Harrison, and Carolyn Coman, among others. Reviewing Harrison's *Bugs: Poems about Creeping Things,* a *Kirkus Reviews* contributor wrote that Shepperson's "amusing illustrations . . . are done in bold strokes of ink . . . , adding a sophisticated flair," while the "brightly shaded, borderline cartoon-y" images he contributes to Lewis's poetry collection "balance humor with warmth," according to *Horn Book* reviewer Claire E. Gross.

Shepperson's artwork for *Thunderboom!* is conveyed in pen-and-ink illustrations tinted with water color, a combination that adds "humor, charm and a sense of coherence to the collection," in the opinion of a *Kirkus Reviews* writer. Pomerantz's playful verse collection attempts to widen the literary horizons of young readers by presenting over fifty poems that encourage children to read aloud. Hazel Rochman, writing in *Booklist,* commented that Shepperson highlights the variety by creating illustrations that "reflect both rambunctious nonsense and the occasional quiet moments" in Pomerantz's work. A *Children's Bookwatch* reviewer noted that *Thunderboom!* is "nicely enhanced" with Shepperson's illustrations.

Shepperson's black-and-white illustrations have brought to life several tales by Coman. The first, the chapter book *The Big House,* centers on Ivy and Ray, two siblings whose parents have been sent to jail on charges of embezzlement. In an ironic turn of events, the pair is sent to live with wealthy Marietta Noland, the same woman who accused Ivy and Ray's parents of criminality. After arriving at Marietta's estate, La Grande Maison, the children hope to discover a way to

Shepperson's illustration projects include Phyllis Root's adventurous story in Lilly and the Pirates. *(Illustration copyright © 2010 by Rob Shepperson. Reproduced by permission of Boyds Mills Press.)*

free their parents. A critic for *Kirkus Reviews* described Shepperson's drawings as "splendid, Quentin Blake-style illustrations," adding that they "further enliven" Coman's energetic text. In a similar fashion, *School Library Journal* contributor B. Allison Gray commented of *The Big House* that "Shepperson's drawings make the story even more amusing."

A sequel to *The Big House, Sneaking Suspicions* finds Ivy and Ray reunited with their parents and heading on a family vacation to the Florida Everglades, where they hope to locate a long-lost relative. Shepperson's "wry illustrations feed the slapstick" of Coman's "tall-tale comedy" in *Sneaking Suspicions,* according to *Booklist* critic Rochman, and a *Kirkus Reviews* writer deemed the book's "comical and expressive pen-and-ink wash illustrations . . . a delight."

Another story by Coman, *The Memory Bank,* is more profusely illustrated, and the artwork helps tell the story of two sisters who are separated by their uncaring parents. While the younger sister, Honey, is abandoned, the older girl, Hope, is left in the care of the Memory Bank, a place where creativity, day dreams, and aspirations are stifled and controlled. "Is this book brilliant or bizarre?," asked Ilene Cooper in her *Booklist* review of

The Memory Bank. While equivocating in her answer, the critic was certain of Shepperson's contribution, writing that, "exuberantly alive," his drawings will inspire repeated readings. Steven Engelfried also applauded the artist's contribution to Coman's complex story in *The Memory Bank,* writing that Shepperson's "varied use of shading, line, and perspective makes each scene distinct as the plot progresses visually."

Biographical and Critical Sources

PERIODICALS

Booklist, April 15, 2003, Hazel Rochman, review of *Hippos in the Night: Autobiographical Adventures in Africa,* p. 1467; September 15, 2004, Carolyn Phelan, review of *Wildfire!,* p. 245; September 15, 2004, Ilene Cooper, review of *The Big House,* p. 242; April 1, 2006, Hazel Rochman, review of *Thunderboom!: Poems for Everyone,* p. 45; March 1, 2007, Hazel Rochman, review of *Bugs: Poems about Creeping Things,* p. 86; September 15, 2007, Hazel Rochman, review of *Sneaking Suspicions,* p. 66, and Carolyn Phelan, review of *Under the Kissletoe: Christmastime Poems,* p. 69; May 1, 2009, Carolyn Phelan, review of *Vacation: We're Going to the Ocean,* p. 76; September 15, 2010, Carolyn Phelan, review of *Lilly and the Pirates,* p. 67; November 1, 2010, Ilene Cooper, review of *The Memory Bank,* p. 52.

Children's Bookwatch, July, 2006, review of *Thunderboom!*

Horn Book, November-December, 2004, Roger Sutton, review of *Wildfire!,* p. 710; January-February, 2005, Christine M. Heppermann, review of *The Big House,* p. 91; November-December, 2007, Claire E. Gross, review of *Under the Kissletoe,* p. 632.

Kirkus Reviews, September 1, 2004, review of *The Big House,* p. 862; October 1, 2004, review of *Wildfire!,* p. 961; March 1, 2006, review of *Thunderboom!,* p. 237; February 15, 2007, review of *Bugs*; September 1, 2007, review of *Sneaking Suspicions*; April 15, 2009, review of *Vacation.*

Publishers Weekly, January 13, 2003, review of *Hippos in the Night,* p. 61; September 6, 2004, review of *The Big House,* p. 63.

School Library Journal, January, 2003, Sue Sherif, review of *Don't Know Much about George Washington,* p. 154; April, 2003, Patricia Manning, review of *Hippos in the Night,* p. 171; February, 2004, Patricia Ann Owens, review of *Don't Know Much about Abraham Lincoln,* p. 160; November, 2004, B. Allison Gray, review of *The Big House,* p. 138; December, 2004, Laura Scott, review of *Wildfire!,* p. 110; May, 2005, Susan Shaver, review of *Don't Know Much about Thomas Jefferson,* p. 146; May, 2006, Lee Bock, review of *Thunderboom!,* p. 116; June, 2007, Julie Roach, review of *Bugs,* p. 133; October, 2007, Wendy Smith-D'Arezzo, review of *Sneaking Suspicion,* p. 146; June, 2009, Kirsten Cutler, review of *Vacation,* p. 107; December, 2010, Steven Engelfried, review of *The Memory Bank,* p. 106.

ONLINE

Boyds Mills Press Web site, http://www.boydsmillspress. com/ (March 13, 2012).

Rob Shepperson Home Page, http://www.robshepperson. com (March 13, 2012).

Rob Shepperson Web log, http://robshepperson.blogspot. com (March 13, 2012).*

* * *

SHERRY, Maureen 1964(?)-

Personal

Born c. 1964, in New York, NY; married Steven Klinsky (a financial manager), 1995; children: two boys, two girls. *Education:* Cornell University, B.S.; Columbia University, M.F.A., 1986. *Hobbies and other interests:* Skiing, diving, swimming, ice skating, bike riding, yoga.

Addresses

Home—New York, NY. *E-mail*—maureen@maureen sherry.com.

Career

Writer. Bear Stearns (financial institution), New York, NY, managing director for twelve years. Volunteer in after-school programs in New York, NY.

Member

International Rescue Committee, Peconic Baykeeper.

Awards, Honors

Best New Voices listee, American Booksellers Association, 2010, for *Walls within Walls.*

Writings

Walls within Walls, illustrated by Adam Stower, Katherine Tegen Books (New York, NY), 2010.

Sidelights

Art imitates life for children's book author Maureen Sherry. In her debut title, *Walls within Walls,* Sherry depicts the adventures of the Smithfork children, who discover that their family's new Manhattan apartment is actually an elaborate puzzle designed by its previous owner, an eccentric multimillionaire. Although such a building might seem the stuff of fiction, Sherry's New York City home, which she shares with her husband and four children, holds its own set of mysteries.

After purchasing a furnished, 1920s-era Fifth Avenue apartment, Sherry hired architect Eric Clough to redesign and refurnish the space. "Some of that furniture and some of those walls conceal[ed] secrets—messages, games and treasures—that make up a Rube Goldberg maze of systems and contraptions," Penelope Green explained in profiling the restoration for the *New York Times.* The renovation, which took more than a year to complete, pleased the new owners. "You move into a place and you have your life there, and your memories, and it's all temporary," Sherry told Green. "Especially with apartments, which have such a fixed footprint. I like the idea of putting something behind a wall to wink at the next inhabitant and to wish them the good life hopefully that you have had there."

In *Walls within Walls* the good life awaits siblings CJ, Brid, and Patrick Smithfork after their father strikes it rich with his video-game company. Soon after moving into their Upper East Side apartment, the children discover a network of secret passageways and a host of clues that appear to reveal the whereabouts of a secret fortune belonging to Mr. Post, a former resident of the building. Using information gleaned from a volume of

Adam Stower created the eerie cartoon-style artwork for Maureen Sherry's Walls within Walls. (Illustration copyright © 2010 by Adam Stower. Reproduced by permission of Katherine Tegen Books, an imprint of HarperCollins Children's Books, a division of HarperCollins Publishers.)

Post's favorite poems, the Smithfork children crisscross the city in search of the lost treasure.

"This debut novel is a breathtaking romp," Caitlin Augusta noted in her *School Library Journal* review of *Walls within Walls*, adding that Sherry's obvious "passion will make readers fall in love with New York and the poems that portray its many personalities." A writer in *Kirkus Reviews* also enjoyed the novel, noting that the numerous puzzles and codes contained in *Walls within Walls* "challenge both characters and readers to look at the world with fresh eyes, humor and imagination."

Biographical and Critical Sources

PERIODICALS

Booklist, September 15, 2010, Ilene Cooper, review of *Walls within Walls,* p. 66.
Kirkus Reviews, August 1, 2010, review of *Walls within Walls.*
New York Times, June 12, 2008, Penelope Green, "Mystery on Fifth Avenue."
School Library Journal, October, 2010, Caitlin August, review of *Walls within Walls,* p. 126.

ONLINE

HarperCollins Web site, http://www.harpercollins.com/ (March 1, 2012), "Maureen Sherry."
Maureen Sherry Home Page site, http://maureensherry. com (March 1, 2012).*

*   *   *

SILBERBERG, Alan

Personal

Born in MA; married; wife's name Kalie (a singer/ songwriter and drama therapist); children: Zachary. *Education:* University of Massachusetts, B.A. (cartoon-communication education); Harvard University, M.Ed.

Addresses

Home—Montreal, Quebec, Canada. *E-mail*—alan@ silberbooks.com.

Career

Author, scriptwriter, and cartoonist. Creator and producer of television programming for the Public Broadcasting Service, Nickelodeon, the Disney Channel, FOX, and Kids WB. Author in residence at James Thurber House, Columbus, OH.

Awards, Honors

Sid Fleischman Humor Award, Society of Children's Book Writers and Illustrators, and Prize for Children's and Young-Adult Literature, Quebec Writers' Federation, both 2011, both for *Milo: Sticky Notes and Brain Freeze.*

Writings

SELF-ILLUSTRATED MIDDLE-GRADE NOVELS

Pond Scum, Hyperion Books for Children (New York, NY), 2005.
(Self-illustrated) *Milo: Sticky Notes and Brain Freeze,* Aladdin (New York, NY), 2010, published as *Milo and the Restart Button,* Simon & Schuster (London, England), 2010.

Author of television scripts, including for film *Dadnapped,* broadcast on the Disney Channel.

Adaptations

Dadnapped was adapted as a junior novel by Sarah Nathan, Disney Press (New York, NY), 2009.

Sidelights

Alan Silberberg had a long career writing for television before he switched to the more-traditional format of the printed book. His skill as a humorist, together with his ability to view the world from a child's perspective, made Silberberg's choice to write for middle graders an easy one. He showcases his varied talents in both *Pond Scum* and his self-illustrated *Milo: Sticky Notes and Brain Freeze,* the latter which earned its author the Sid Fleischman Humor Award. "Humor is important EVERYWHERE . . . ," Silberberg noted during an interview with Alice Pope for the Society of Children's Book Writers Web log. "When a book has something serious to say . . . humor can sometimes be the package that the message gets wrapped inside. And I'm all for that. Not that all books need messages or that all message books need humor. I just think kids need to laugh as much as humanly possible."

In *Pond Scum* readers meet Oliver, a troubled ten year old whose penchant for torturing defenseless insects is something that would make his newly divorced parents very concerned, only if they knew. Oliver's world changes after a move from the city to a run-down house by a pond in the middle of nowhere. There, magic enters the boy's life in the form of a gem that allows Oliver to transform into a range of different animals. He soon makes friends with Mooch, a salamander, and the always-singing crow Antoinne, His experiences as all sorts of creatures helps the boy learn that humans are powerful enough to help or harm the delicate balance of even a small ecosystem.

Alan Silberberg mixes humor with poignancy in his self-illustrated middle-grade novel Milo: Sticky Notes and Brain Freeze. (Copyright © 2011 by Alan Silberberg. Reproduced by permission of Aladdin, an imprint of Simon & Schuster Children's Publishing Division.)

Reviewing *Pond Scum* in *Booklist,* Todd Morning characterized Silberberg's tale as "frequently funny and exciting" as well as "suspenseful" and "vivid" in its evocation of the friction between humans and animal world. Featuring enough "snappy dialogue, . . . slime jokes, and body humor" to entice even reluctant preteen readers, *Pond Scum* achieves a good balance "of serious issues and funny moments," predicted Elaine E. Knight in her review of Siberberg's fiction debut for *School Library Journal.*

Published in the United Kingdom as *Milo and the Restart Button, Milo* was inspired by Silberberg's memories of his mother's death from brain cancer when he was nine years old. The novel was inspired, in part, by watching his own son reach the same age. "I was so aware of him being the age I was when my mum died," the author recalled to London *Guardian* reviewer Rebecca Abrams. "I saw how tender and young I'd been at that age, how life-wrenching and traumatic it is to lose a parent at that age." In the novel, Milo Cruikshank has mourned his mom for two years, and his family has been unstable ever since her death. Milo's father deals with the tragedy by relocating the family repeatedly, and his older sister is equally reluctant to talk about the loss. As Milo explains through his first-person narrative and drawings, his growing interest in girls also leads to problems when a girl he really likes is out of his league. Meanwhile, quirky next-door neighbor Hillary makes it plain that she really likes him. Fortunately, once the preteen begins to open up to his surroundings, new friends allow him to express and come to terms with his sadness over his mom's passing. If talking about things can help Milo, then it stands to reason that talking might help his dad and sister too, and the boy's efforts to promote family healing enrich Silberberg's coming-of-age story.

"Close to failing math, socially inept and awkward with girls," the young narrator in *Milo* "is easy to care about," wrote a *Kirkus Reviews* contributor, and Monica Edinger noted in *Horn Book* that his "voice is distinct and believable." Through Milo, Silberberg shares "a rich and real story of grief and growing up," Edinger added, while for *School Library Journal* contributor Tina Hudak, the author achieves a delicate balance by mixing "humor with poignancy to create a profound slice of one boy's life." "Silberberg has managed something that I would have deemed near impossible," Elizabeth Bird noted in her enthusiastic review of *Milo* for the *School Library Journal* Web log. "He's penned a funny novel that deals with the very real issue of how a family copes when one of its family members passes on and he's done it [by combining] . . . interstitial comics with a fun text and a gripping story." *Milo* "is a book that isn't afraid to get a little sad and serious once in a while," Bird added, deeming it "a dead mom book that kids will really gravitate towards."

Biographical and Critical Sources

PERIODICALS

Booklist, December 1, 2005, Todd Morning, review of *Pond Scum,* p. 49.
Bulletin of the Center for Children's Books, November, 2010, Karen Coats, review of *Milo: Sticky Notes and Brain Freeze,* p. 149.
Guardian (London, England), April 16, 2011, Rebecca Abrams, "Family" (profile), p. 5.
Horn Book, November-December, 2010, Monica Edinger, review of *Milo,* p. 104.
Kirkus Reviews, October 1, 2005, review of *Pond Scum*; August 1, 2010, review of *Milo.*
School Librarian, summer, 2011, Martin Axford, review of *Milo and the Restart Button,* p. 105.
School Library Journal, November, 2005, Elaine E. Knight, review of *Pond Scum,* p. 148; September, 2010, Tina Hudak, review of *Milo,* p. 164.

ONLINE

Alan Silberberg Home Page, http://www.silberbooks.com (March 8, 2012).
Alan Silberberg Web log, http://silberbook-blog.blogspot.com (March 8, 2012).
School Library Journal Web log, http://blog.schoollibraryjournal.com/afuse8production/ (July 2, 2010), Elizabeth Bird, review of *Milo.*
Society of Children's Book Writers and Illustrators Web log, http://scbwi.blogspot.com (March 4, 2011), Alice Pope, interview with Silberberg.

*   *   *

SMY, Pam

Personal

Born in England. *Education:* Anglia Ruskin University/ Cambridge School of Art, B.A. (illustration; with honours), M.A. (children's book illustration), 2001.

Addresses

Home—Cambridge, England. *E-mail*—Pam.Smy@anglia.ac.uk.

Career

Illustrator and educator. Anglia Ruskin University, Cambridge, England, senior lecturer in illustration.

Awards, Honors

Third Place, Macmillan Prize.

Illustrator

Sir Arthur Conan Doyle, *The Hound of the Baskervilles,* Candlewick Press (Cambridge, MA), 2006.

Bob Cattell and John Agard, *Shine on Butter-Finger,* Frances Lincoln (London, England), 2007.

Julia Donaldson, *Follow the Swallow,* Egmont (London, England), 2007.

Linda Newbery, *Lob,* David Fickling (Oxford, England), 2010.

Linda Newbery, *Lucy and the Green Man,* David Fickling Books (New York, NY), 2010.

Bob Cattell and John Agard, *Big City Butter-Finger,* Frances Lincoln (London, England), 2010.

Kathy Henderson, *Hush Baby, Hush! Lullabies from around the World,* Frances Lincoln (London, England), 2010.

Contributor to anthologies, including *Magical Tales of Ireland,* and to educational publications.

Books featuring Smy's illustrations have been translated into German.

Biographical and Critical Sources

PERIODICALS

Booklist, November 15, 2010, Sheele Rosenfeld, review of *Lucy and the Green Man,* p. 48.

Observer (London, England), April 4, 2010, Geraldine Brennan, review of *Follow the Swallow,* p. 44.

School Librarian, summer, 2010, Steve Hird, review of *Big City Butter-Finger,* p. 95, and Wendy Axford, review of *Lob,* p. 100; spring, 2011, Marzena Currie, refiew of *Hush Baby, Hush! Lullabies from around the World,* p. 26.

School Library Journal, January, 2011, Julie Roach, review of *Lucy and the Green Man,* p. 81.

ONLINE

Anglia Ruskin University Web site, http://www.anglia.ac.uk/ (March 1, 2012), "Pam Smy."

Pam Smy Web log, http://pamsmy.blogspot.com (January 30, 2012).*

STANLEY, Diane 1943-

Personal

Born December 27, 1943, in Abilene, TX; daughter of Onia Burton, Jr. (a U.S. Navy captain) and Fay (an author, playwright, and copywriter) Stanley; married Peter Zuromskis, May 30, 1970 (divorced, 1979); married Peter Vennema (a corporation president and editorial consultant), September 8, 1979; children: (first marriage) Catherine, Tamara; (second marriage) John Leslie. *Education:* Trinity University, B.A., 1965; attended Edinburgh College of Art, 1966-67; Johns Hopkins University, M.A., 1970. *Politics:* Democrat. *Religion:* Episcopalian *Hobbies and other interests:* Traveling, skiing, hiking, gardening.

Addresses

Home—Santa Fe, NM. *Agent*—Sheldon Fogelman Agency, 10 E. 40th St., Ste. 3205, New York, NY 10016.

Career

Author and illustrator of books for children. Freelance medical illustrator, 1970-74; Dell Publishing, New York, NY, graphic designer, 1977; G.P. Putnam's Sons and Coward, McCann & Geoghegan, New York, NY, art director of children's books, 1977-79; full-time author and illustrator, 1979—. *Exhibitions:* Works exhibited at Bush Galleries, Norwich, VT, 1987; National Center for Children's Illustrated Literature, Abilene, TX, 1998; National Museum of Women in the Arts, 2002, and others.

Awards, Honors

Children's Choice Award, American Reading Association, 1979, for *The Farmer in the Dell*; Notable Children's Trade Book in the Field of Social Studies designation, National Council for the Social Studies (NCSS), 1983, for both *The Month Brothers* by Samuil Yakovlevich Marshak and *The Conversation Club,* 1985, for *A Country Tale,* 1986, for both *Peter the Great* and *Captain Whiz-Bang,* 1988, for *Shaka: King of the Zulus,* 1990, for *Fortune,* 1991, for *The Last Princess* by Fay Grissom Stanley, and 1992, for *Bard of Avon*; Outstanding Science Trade Book for Children designation, National Science Teachers Association/Children's Book Council (CBC), 1985, for *All Wet! All Wet!* by James Skofield; Notable Book designation, American Library Association (ALA), 1986, and Golden Kite Award Honor Book selection, Society of Children's Book Writers and Illustrators (SCBWI), 1987, both for *Peter the Great;* Notable Book designation, ALA, and *Boston Globe/Horn Book* Honor Book for Nonfiction selection, both 1990, both for *Good Queen Bess*; Notable Book designation, ALA, 1991, and Children's Choices designation, International Reading Association (IRA)/CBC, and Carter G. Woodson Award, NCSS, both 1992, all for *The Last Princess*; Children's Choice Award, IRA/

Diane Stanley (Photograph courtesy of Diane Stanley.)

CBC, 1992, for *Siegfried;* Notable Book designation, ALA, and Orbis Pictus Award for Outstanding Nonfiction for Children nominee, National Council of Teachers of English (NCTE), both 1992, and Notable Children's Book in the Language Arts selection, 1993, all for *Bard of Avon*; Notable Book designation, ALA, 1994, for *Cleopatra,* 1998, for *Rumpelstiltskin's Daughter,* 2000, for *Raising Sweetness,* and 2002, for *Saladin, Noble Prince of Islam*; Orbis Pictus Award for Outstanding Nonfiction for Children, and Notable Book designation, ALA, both 1996, and *Boston Globe/Horn Book* Award for Nonfiction, 1997, all for *Leonardo da Vinci*; Golden Kite Award Honor Book selection, 1997, for *Saving Sweetness*; Notable Book designation, ALA, 1998, and Golden Kite Award nomination, 1999, both for *Joan of Arc*; Best Books for Young Adults designation, ALA, 1999, for *A Time Apart*; Oppenheim Toy Portfolio Gold Medal Book Award, 2004, for *Goldie and the Three Bears*; *Washington Post*/Children's Book Guild Nonfiction Award for body of work; Books for the Teen Age selection, New York Public Library, 2007, for *Bella at Midnight*; Mazza Medallion of Excellence for Artistic Diversity, University of Findlay, 2008, for body of work; Bank Street College of Education Best Book citation, and Arab American Award, both 2010, both for *Saving Sky.*

Writings

The Good-Luck Pencil, illustrated by Bruce Degen, Four Winds Press (New York, NY), 1986.

Siegfried, illustrated by John Sandford, Bantam (New York, NY), 1991.
Moe the Dog in Tropical Paradise, illustrated by Elise Primavera, Putnam (New York, NY), 1992.
The Gentleman and the Kitchen Maid, illustrated by Dennis Nolan, Dial (New York, NY), 1994.
Woe Is Moe, illustrated by Elise Primavera, Putnam (New York, NY), 1995.
Elena, Hyperion (New York, NY), 1996.
Saving Sweetness, illustrated by G. Brian Karas, Putnam (New York, NY), 1996.
Raising Sweetness, illustrated by G. Brian Karas, Putnam (New York, NY), 1999.
A Time Apart, Morrow (New York, NY), 1999.
The Mysterious Matter of I.M. Fine, HarperCollins (New York, NY), 2001.
Bella at Midnight, illustrated by Bagram Ibatoulline, HarperCollins (New York, NY), 2006.
The Mysterious Case of the Allbright Academy (sequel to *The Mysterious Matter of I.M. Fine*), HarperCollins (New York, NY), 2008.
Saving Sky, Harper (New York, NY), 2010.
The Silver Bowl, Harper (New York, NY), 2011.

SELF-ILLUSTRATED

(Adaptor) *Giambattista Basile, Petrosinella, a Neapolitan Rapunzel,* from the translation by John Edward Taylor, Warne (New York, NY), 1981, new edition, Dial (New York, NY), 1995.
The Conversation Club, Macmillan (New York, NY), 1983.
Birdsong Lullaby, Morrow (New York, NY), 1985.
A Country Tale, Macmillan (New York, NY), 1985.
Peter the Great, Four Winds Press (New York, NY), 1986.
Captain Whiz-Bang, Morrow (New York, NY), 1987.
(With husband, Peter Vennema) *Shaka: King of the Zulus,* Morrow (New York, NY), 1988.
Fortune, Morrow (New York, NY), 1990.
(With Peter Vennema) *Good Queen Bess: The Story of Elizabeth I of England,* Four Winds Press (New York, NY), 1990.
(With Peter Vennema) *Bard of Avon: The Story of William Shakespeare,* Morrow (New York, NY), 1992.
(With Peter Vennema) *Charles Dickens: The Man Who Had Great Expectations,* Morrow (New York, NY), 1993.
(With Peter Vennema) *Cleopatra,* Morrow (New York, NY), 1994.
The True Adventure of Daniel Hall, Dial (New York, NY), 1995.
Leonardo da Vinci, Morrow (New York, NY), 1996.
Rumpelstiltskin's Daughter, Morrow (New York, NY), 1997.
Joan of Arc, Morrow (New York, NY), 1998.
Michelangelo, HarperCollins (New York, NY), 2000.
Saladin, Noble Prince of Islam, HarperCollins (New York, NY), 2002.
Goldie and the Three Bears, HarperCollins (New York, NY), 2003.
The Giant and the Beanstalk, HarperCollins (New York, NY), 2004.

The Trouble with Wishes, HarperCollins (New York, NY), 2007.

Mozart: The Wonder Child: A Puppet Play in Three Acts, Collins (New York, NY), 2009.

"TIME-TRAVELING TWINS" NOVEL SERIES

Roughing It on the Oregon Trail, illustrated by Holly Berry, HarperCollins (New York, NY), 2000.

Joining the Boston Tea Party, illustrated by Holly Berry, HarperCollins (New York, NY), 2001.

Thanksgiving on Plymouth Plantation, illustrated by Holly Berry, Joanna Cotler Books (New York, NY), 2004.

ILLUSTRATOR

(Under name Diane Zuromskis) *The Farmer in the Dell,* Little, Brown (Boston, MA), 1978.

(Under name Diane Stanley Zuromskis) Verna Aardema, *Half-a-Ball-of-Kenki: An Ashanti Tale Retold,* Warne (New York, NY), 1979.

Fiddle-I-Fee: A Traditional American Chant, Little, Brown (Boston, MA), 1979.

Tony Johnston, *Little Mouse Nibbling,* Putnam (New York, NY), 1979.

M. Jean Craig, *The Man Whose Name Was Not Thomas,* Doubleday (New York, NY), 1981.

Toni Hormann, *Onions, Onions,* Crowell (New York, NY), 1981.

Jane Yolen, *Sleeping Ugly,* Coward (New York, NY), 1981.

Jean and Claudio Marzollo, *Robin of Bray,* Dial (New York, NY), 1982.

Joanne Ryder, *Beach Party,* Warne (New York, NY), 1982.

James Whitcomb Riley, *Little Orphan Annie,* Putnam (New York, NY), 1983.

Samuil Yakovlevich Marshak, reteller, *The Month Brothers: A Slavic Tale,* translated by Thomas P. Whitney, Morrow (New York, NY), 1983.

James Skofield, *All Wet! All Wet!,* Harper (New York, NY), 1984.

Fay Grissom Stanley, *The Last Princess: The Story of Princess Ka'iulani of Hawai'i,* Four Winds Press (New York, NY), 1991.

Adaptations

Moe the Dog in Tropical Paradise was released as a video by MCA/Universal Home Video, 1994, and was adapted as an animated segment of Bedtime Stories, Showtime Network; several of Stanley's works have been recorded as audiobooks.

Sidelights

An author and illustrator of fiction, nonfiction, and picture books as well as a re-teller of folktales from many cultures, Diane Stanley is regarded as an especially talented and versatile creator of literature for children. Her works have garnered a host of honors, including *Boston Globe/Horn Book* awards, a Carter G. Woodson award, and an Orbis Pictus award, and she has also received

the *Washington Post*/Children's Book Guild Nonfiction Award and the Mazza Medallion of Excellence for her work. "Perhaps the most striking aspect of my work is its variety," Stanley noted in an essay on the National Center for Children's Illustrated Literature Web site. "I have followed my own interests, especially history, never quite knowing where each project would take me and what would come next."

Stanley's picture books are written in a variety of styles, including humorous, gentle, and atmospheric, and feature children and animals, both real and anthropomorphic. She has also written longer stories, young-adult novels, and adaptations of familiar tales. As an illustrator, she uses a wide range of media, such as colored pencil and collage as well as her characteristic water color. Her images include miniature drawings, pastel-toned watercolors, and ornate, sumptuous paintings filled with light and intricate geometric shapes.

Although she has written and illustrated a variety of books for primary and middle graders, Stanley is perhaps best known for the self-illustrated biographies she creates for readers in the upper grades. These works, which are celebrated as appealing, balanced treatments that do justice to their subjects, profile warriors such as Russian tsar Peter the Great, Zulu king Shaka, and Saladin, the Muslim general; women rulers such as Cleopatra and Elizabeth I of England; and creators of art, music, and literature such as Williams Shakespeare, Leonardo da Vinci, Charles Dickens, and Wolfgang Amadeus Mozart. Sometimes collaborating with her husband, Peter Vennema, Stanley thoroughly researches each subject, weaving personalities and accomplishments into a form that resembles a story. In a review of *Joan of Arc* for *School Library Journal,* Shirley Wilton commended Stanley's "talent for historical research, skill in writing clear and interesting prose, and ability to adapt different art styles and techniques appropriate to her subjects."

Born in Abilene, Texas, Stanley is the only child of Burt Stanley, a U.S. Navy pilot, and Fay Grissom Stanley, a novelist, playwright, copywriter, and author of nonfiction. Her parents divorced not long after she was born and she went to live with her mother in her New York City brownstone.

After graduating from college in 1963, Stanley moved to Houston, where she worked as a lab technician in a hospital; she also took life-drawing classes at night. After studying abroad, she enrolled at the Johns Hopkins University College of Medicine in Baltimore, where she received her master's degree from Johns Hopkins in 1970. Shortly therafter, Stanley married Peter Zuromskis, a fellow classmate who had become a doctor. The couple would have two daughters, Catherine and Tamara.

Stanley read widely to her children when they were young, and in the process she discovered an interest in children's literature. While researching the field, she began experimenting with watercolors and pen-and-ink drawings; she also taught herself color-separation techniques. Stanley assembled a portfolio of illustrations for children's books while juggling full-time motherhood and freelance work as a medical illustrator, and after a trip to Boston-based Little, Brown & Company she received her first book contract.

In 1978, *The Farmer in the Dell* was published under Stanley's married name, Diane Zuromskis. In line drawings and pastel watercolors enclosed in circular frames that appear opposite the text of the familiar refrain, she depicts the farmer in his bachelor days, at his marriage, with his family, and with his animals. A reviewer in *Publishers Weekly* trumpeted that "Zuromskis's first book suggests that she has begun a rich career." A year later, Stanley illustrated Verna Aardema's *Half-a-Ball-of-Kenki: An Ashanti Tale Retold* and also produced *Fiddle-I-Fee: A Traditional American Chant.* Illustrated with lively four-color drawings, *Fiddle-I-Fee* depicts a red-haired, freckle-faced girl who has a dinner party in her tree house for all of the animals mentioned in the song. This book was the first of Stanley's books to be published as Diane Stanley; in the year of its publication, Stanley and Zuromskis were divorced.

In 1979, Stanley remarried and moved to Texas, where she became a full-time illustrator. She and second husband Peter Vennema had a son, John Leslie, in 1981; two years later, she produced *The Conversation Club,* a book she both wrote and illustrated. In this picture book, which features alternating spreads of watercolors and black-and-white drawings, Peter Fieldmouse is invited to a meeting of the Conversation Club, where everyone converses at once. Peter decides to form his own group, the Listening Club, where one mouse talks at a time. The club becomes a success when the mice experience the joys of both listening and being heard. Writing in *Booklist,* Ilene Cooper called *The Conversation Club* a "cozy little story with pictures to match," adding that, "as in other books, [Stanley's] patterning and design work are visual delights."

Stanley's first illustrated biography, *Peter the Great,* was inspired by her travels in the Soviet Union as well as her reading of Robert K. Massie's acclaimed biography of the Russian leader. She decided to condense the life of the Russian tsar, who opened communication between his backward country and the rest of Europe, into a standard thirty-two-page picture-book text. Beginning with his boyhood, Stanley's Peter emerges as a visionary and reformer as well as a tyrant. *Peter the Great* is illustrated with jewel-toned and intricately patterned watercolor-and-gouache images which draw on elements of both Asian and European art. Jean Fritz wrote in the *New York Times Book Review* that *Peter the Great* "stays close to the historical record and turns out to be the strongest story of all. . . . [Stanley] has the good sense not to embellish his extraordinary life and let it speak for itself." Fritz added that Stanley's "exquisite illustrations hang like framed pictures on her pages."

In the years since, Stanley has continued to create exceptional picture-books biographies. A critic in *Publishers Weekly* called *Leonardo da Vinci* a "virtuosic work," and in *School Library Journal,* Shirley Wilton deemed *Joan of Arc* a "magnificent picture book" as well as "a work of art, a good story, and a model of historical writing." Stanley received a *Boston Globe/Horn Book* Honor Book citation for *Good Queen Bess: The Story of Elizabeth I of England,* a book described as "a very human portrait of an important monarch" by *School Library Journal* contributor Nancy Mendaldi-Scanlon.

Saladin, Noble Prince of Islam concerns the twelfth-century Muslim ruler who united his people and battled against the Christian crusaders. According to *Booklist* critic Ilene Cooper, "the generally strong telling" in *Saladin, Noble Prince of Islam* "is more than matched by glorious paintings that mirror Islamic artwork of the times," and Kathleen T. Isaacs wrote in *School Library Journal* that the book presents "a fresh view of a conflict that still reverberates today."

Stanley examines the life of famed eighteen-century composer Wolfgang Amadeus Mozart, including his complicated relationship with his demanding father, in *Mozart: The Wonder Child: A Puppet Play in Three Acts.* Here her illustrations—in which the figures appear as puppets, complete with visible strings—were inspired by her visit to the Salzburg Marionette Theatre, which often performs versions of Mozart's operas. According to *School Library Journal* critic Wendy Lukehart, the "staged effects" in *Mozart* "are well suited to the story of a man who spent most of his life performing or composing."

Stanley's first book for young adults, the novel *A Time Apart,* was inspired by a British Broadcasting Corporation (BBC) miniseries about an actual Iron Age farm. In the novel, thirteen-year-old Ginny Dorris leaves Houston to stay in England with her professor father while her mother undergoes treatment for breast cancer. Her parents are divorced and her father is part of an experimental archaeological team replicating an Iron Age village. Battling homesickness and the primitive conditions of her new home, Ginny runs away from the experimental village and books a flight back to Houston with a credit card she has stolen from her father. After realizing how sick her mother is, she returns to England with her father, where she becomes immersed in the daily life of the community, discovers hidden strengths and learns to appreciate living a simpler lifestyle. Writing in *Booklist,* Sally Estes called *A Time Apart* a "very appealing novel" as well as an "enchanting 'time travel' into reality."

In her middle-grade novel *The Mysterious Matter of I.M. Fine,* Stanley "explores the power of the written word," according to *School Library Journal* critic Terrie Dorio. In the work, fifth-grader Franny Sharp notices that the bizarre ailments plaguing the children at her school bear a striking similarity to the events described in the plots of a wildly popular series of horror novels. Upon investigation, Franny and her friends discover that the reclusive Ida May Fine, author of the "Chiller" books, intends to use her works as part of a twisted revenge scheme. "Stanley cheerfully sends up horror series fiction," remarked a critic in *Publishers Weekly,* who added that *The Mysterious Matter of I.M. Fine* "should engage both ambitious readers and die-hard fans of the genre it satirizes."

In a sequel, *The Mysterious Case of the Allbright Academy,* Franny accepts an invitation to attend Allbright Academy, an elite boarding school founded by a pair of scientists. Soon she notices that her behavior has begun to mirror that of her brilliant, good-looking, and all-too-perfect classmates. When one of Franny's best friends leaves the academy under mysterious circumstances, the eighth grader decides to investigate and finds disturbing evidence that the school's famous chocolate brownies may contain a secret ingredient designed to control behavior. "With sympathetic Franny as narrator and a time-tested premise, Stanley hooks readers from the start," a *Publishers Weekly* critic observed, and *School Library Journal* reviewer Elaine E. Knight commented of *The Mysterious Case of the Allbright Academy* that the "suspenseful story features an all-too-plausible conflict between authoritarian control and personal freedom."

In her "Time-Traveling Twins" series for young readers, Stanley introduces look-alike siblings Liz and Lenny. With the help of their grandmother's magic hat, the twins are transported back to the pioneer days of 1843 in *Roughing It on the Oregon Trail.* Liz, Lenny, and Grandma return in *Joining the Boston Tea Party,* "a humorous and painlessly informative introduction to an important chapter in American history," observed Carey Ayres in *School Library Journal.* In this second story, a trip back to 1773 finds the trio enmeshed in the politics of the day, dressing as Mohawks and helping throw tea into Boston Harbor. *Booklist* reviewer Helen Rosenberg stated that "the dialogue bubbles, blending historical tidbits with modern-day humor." In *Thanksgiving on Plymouth Plantation* the three time-travelers celebrate harvest time with the first Pilgrims and their Wampanoag neighbors. "Stanley's facts are informative and instructive," noted a critic in *Kirkus Reviews.*

Stanley's self-illustrated books include "fractured" fairy tales such as *Rumpelstiltskin's Daughter, Goldie and the Three Bears,* and *The Giant and the Beanstalk.* In *Rumpelstiltskin's Daughter,* "a witty mix of fable and farce," in the words of *Booklist* critic Hazel Rochman, the title character outwits a greedy, foolish king. Friendship is the subject of *Goldie and the Three Bears,* as the independent-minded Goldie wanders into a strange home to seek help after becoming lost. There she discovers that one of the inhabitants enjoys many of the same things she does, and when Baby Bear arrives home, they share the joy of bouncing on his bed. "The pictures alone are delectable, at once saucy and tender,"

wrote *Horn Book* reviewer Barbara Bader. In *The Giant and the Beanstalk,* Stanley focuses on the gentle giant who must overcome his fear of heights to search for his kidnapped pet hen. A *Publishers Weekly* contributor remarked of this work that "the story leads up to a felicitous finale, but the twists and turns readers takes along the way make this tale as original as Stanley fans have come to expect."

Stanley offers her take on the Pygmalion myth in *The Trouble with Wishes,* a story set in ancient Greece. The work centers on Pyg, a talented artist who falls in love with his masterpiece, a sculpture of a beautiful goddess. When his creation comes to life, however, Pyg finds nothing but disappointment; the goddess is coldhearted, humorless, and arrogant and wants nothing to do with him. Fortunately for Pyg, his loyal apprentice, Jane, uses her skills to carve a special gift that helps lift his spirits. According to a *Publishers Weekly* contributor, "readers will find Stanley's highly humorous tale, enhanced by her trademark meticulously detailed art, a great deal of fun." A critic in *Kirkus Reviews* described *The Trouble with Wishes* as "a classy retelling of a classic myth highlighting the meaning of real companionship."

Bella at Midnight incorporates elements of William Shakespeare's *The Tempest* and *The Merchant of Venice* with Stanley's own childhood memories. Told by multiple narrators, the story follows Bella, a knight's daughter who is given up for adoption after her mother dies in childbirth. At the age of sixteen, Bella is recalled by her father, an embittered man who has since remarried, and joins his unhappy household. When she learns that a childhood friend faces danger in an enemy land, she embarks on a journey to rescue him and help restore peace in the region. "What raises this above other re-created fairy tales is the quality of the writing," Cooper asserted in her *Booklist* review of the novel. Susan Dove Lempke, writing in *Horn Book,* called *Bella at Midnight* a "nuanced reworking of the Cinderella story," while Kathleen Isaacs noted in *School Library Journal* that "Stanley has brewed a magical elixir that will warm the hearts of readers who like their adventures set in medieval worlds."

Stanley uses a fairy-tale styled setting for *The Silver Bowl,* the first part of a planned trilogy. Molly, a servant who is responsible for cleaning the silver bowl in the castle of her masters, can see visions of the future in the surface of the polished metal. The royal family is cursed, she discovers, and Molly is the one who must free them. In *The Silver Bowl,* "Stanley blends historical fiction and fantasy seamlessly, and her clear, rich language envelops and transports readers," Mandy Lawrence commended in *School Library Journal.* A contributor to *Kirkus Reviews* also praised the novel, writing that "Stanley concocts a delicious blend of familiar fairy-tale motifs and intriguing, well-rounded characters to create an engaging fantasy."

In *Saving Sky* Stanley imagined what might have happened after the September 11, 2001 attacks if the U.S. government had set up internment camps—like those for Japanese-Americans during World War II—to control and contain Americans of Middle Eastern descent. In the face of an escalating war, seventh-grader Sky stands up for Kareem, a classmate, and with her family keeps the Muslim boy hidden from government officials. "The main characters are well rendered and likable, and . . . Stanley succeeds in delivering the message that hope trumps fear," wrote Susan W. Hunter in *School Library Journal*. Frances Bradburn concluded in her *Booklist* review of *Saving Sky* that "readers will have much to discuss after finishing this beautifully written, disturbing book."

Biographical and Critical Sources

BOOKS

Children's Literature Review, Volume 46, Gale (Detroit, MI), 1998.
Cummins, Julie, editor, *Children's Book Illustration and Design,* PBC International, 1992.
St. James Guide to Children's Writers, 5th edition, St. James Press (Detroit, MI), 1999, pp. 1000-1001.
Silvey, Anita, editor, *Children's Books and Their Creators,* Houghton Mifflin (Boston, MA), 1995.

PERIODICALS

Booklist, May 15, 1978, Denise M. Wilms, review of *The Farmer in the Dell,* p. 1492; December 1, 1979, Marilyn Kaye, review of *Fiddle-I-Fee: A Traditional American Chant,* p. 556; September 15, 1983, Ilene Cooper, review of *The Conversation Club,* p. 173; October 1, 1986, Ilene Cooper, review of *Peter the Great,* p. 275; September 1, 1993, Bill Ott, "Should We Tell the Kids?," p. 56; June 1 & 15, 1999, Sally Estes, review of *A Time Apart,* p. 1826; March 1, 2000, Stephanie Zvirin, review of *Joan of Arc,* p. 1249; April 1, 2000, Stephanie Zvirin, review of *Roughing It on the Oregon Trail,* p. 1479; August, 2000, Ilene Cooper, review of *Michelangelo,* p. 2135; July, 2001, Ilene Cooper, review of *The Mysterious Matter of I.M. Fine,* p. 2007; September 15, 2001, Helen Rosenberg, review of *Joining the Boston Tea Party,* p. 224; December 15, 2001, Gillian Engberg, review of *Michelangelo,* p. 811; September 1, 2002, Ilene Cooper, review of *Saladin, Noble Prince of Islam,* p. 121; November 1, 2003, Ilene Cooper, review of *Goldie and the Three Bears,* p. 498; September 1, 2004, Carolyn Phelan, review of *Thanksgiving on Plymouth Plantation,* p. 137; June 1, 2004, Jennifer Mattson, review of *The Giant and the Beanstalk,* p. 1749; February 1, 2006, Ilene Cooper, review of *Bella at Midnight,* p. 49; December 15, 2008, Ian Chipman, review of *Mozart: The Wonder Child: A Puppet Play in Three Acts,* p. 42; June 1, 2010, Frances Bradburn, review of *Saving Sky,* p. 69; April 15, 2011, Michael Cart, review of *The Silver Bowl,* p. 53.

Bulletin of the Center for Children's Books, October, 1986, Betsy Hearne, review of *Peter the Great,* pp. 37-38; September, 1998, review of *Joan of Arc,* p. 32; February, 1999, review of *Raising Sweetness,* p. 218; October, 1999, review of *A Time Apart,* p. 70; October, 2001, review of *The Mysterious Matter of I.M. Fine,* p. 77.

Horn Book, November-December, 1995, Elizabeth S. Watson, review of *The True Adventure of Daniel Hall,* p. 758; March 1999, Roger Sutton, review of *Raising Sweetness,* p. 202; November 2000, Mary M. Burns, review of *Michelangelo,* p. 773; November, 2001, review of *Joining the Boston Tea Party,* p. 769; September-October, 2003, Barbara Bader, review of *Goldie and the Three Bears,* pp. 601-603; March-April, 2006, Susan Dove Lempke, review of *Bella at Midnight,* p. 194.

Kirkus Reviews, April, 1, 1978, review of *The Farmer in the Dell,* p. 370; February 1, 1990, review of *Fortune,* p. 185; August 15, 1990, review of *Good Queen Bess: The Story of Elizabeth I of England*; November 15, 1992, review of *Moe the Dog in Tropical Paradise,* p. 1449; July 1, 1993, review of *Charles Dickens: The Man Who Had Great Expectations,* p. 866; July 15, 1995, review of *The True Adventure of Daniel Hall,* p. 1030; August 1, 2001, review of *Joining the Boston Tea Party,* p. 1132; July 15, 2002, review of *Saladin, Noble Prince of Islam,* p. 1044; August 1, 2003, review of *Goldie and the Three Bears,* p. 1024; August 1, 2004, review of *Thanksgiving on Plymouth Plantation,* p. 749; September 15, 2004, review of *The Giant and the Beanstalk,* p. 921; November 15, 2006, review of *The Trouble with Wishes,* p. 1178; December 15, 2008, review of *Mozart*; August 1, 2010, review of *Saving Sky*; May 15, 2011, review of *The Silver Bowl*.

Kliatt, March, 2006, Michele Winship, review of *Bella at Midnight,* p. 17.

New York Times Book Review, November 9, 1986, Jean Fritz, "The Wedding Gift Had Tusks," p. 58; November 13, 1988, Peter F. Neumeyer, review of *Shaka: King of the Zulus,* p. 56; October 28, 1990, Sam Swope, review of *Fortune,* pp. 32-33; March 17, 1991, Marianne Partridge, review of *Good Queen Bess,* p. 26; May 18, 1997, Margaret Moorman, review of *Rumpelstiltskin's Daughter,* p. 28; November 15, 1998, Marina Warner, review of *Joan of Arc,* p. 28; October 17, 1999, review of *Raising Sweetness,* p. 30; November 16, 2003, "Still Eating That Porridge," p. 43.

Publishers Weekly, April 3, 1978, review of *The Farmer in the Dell,* p. 80; April 29, 1996, review of *Elena,* p. 73; July 8, 1996, review of *Leonardo da Vinci,* p. 84; July 22, 1996, Elizabeth Devereaux, "Diane Stanley: Illustrating a Life," p. 216; February 17, 1997, review of *Rumpelstiltskin's Daughter,* p. 219; February 1, 1999, review of *Raising Sweetness,* p. 84; September 6, 1999, review of *A Time Apart,* p. 105; January 31, 2000, review of *The True Adventures of Daniel Hall,* p. 109; May 22, 2000, review of *Roughing It on the Oregon Trail,* p. 93; August 28, 2000, review of *Michelangelo,* p. 83; July 30, 2001, review of *The Mysterious Matter of I.M. Fine,* p. 85; November 12, 2001, review of *Saving Sweetness,* p. 63; August 5, 2002, review of *Saladin, Noble Prince of Islam,* p. 73; August 19, 2002, review of *The Mysterious Matter of I.M. Fine,* p. 92; August 18, 2003, review of *Goldie and the Three Bears,* p. 79; September 13, 2004, review of *The Giant and the Beanstalk,* p. 78; September 27, 2004, review of *Thanksgiving on Plymouth Plantation,* p. 59; November 20, 2006, review of *The Trouble with Wishes,* p. 57; January 7, 2008, review of *The Mysterious Case of the Allbright Academy,* p. 54.

School Library Journal, January, 1980, Marjorie Lewis, review of *Fiddle-I-Fee,* p. 55; December, 1983, Pamela Warren Stubbins, review of *The Conversation Club,* pp. 60-61; September, 1998, Shirley Wilton, review of *Joan of Arc,* pp. 226-227; September 1999, John Peters, review of *A Time Apart,* p. 228; June 2000, John Sigwald, review of *Roughing It on the Oregon Trail,* p. 126; August 2000, Wendy Lukehart, review of *Michelangelo,* p. 208; August 2001, Carey Ayres, review of *Joining the Boston Tea Party,* p. 162; August 2001, Terrie Dorio, review of *The Mysterious Matter of I.M. Fine,* p. 189; September, 2002, Patricia D. Lothrop, review of *Saladin, Noble Prince of Islam,* p. 251; November, 2003, Lauralyn Person, review of *Goldie and the Three Bears,* p. 116; February, 2004, Nancy Menaldi-Scanlon, reviews of *Bard of Avon: The Story of William Shakespeare* and *Good Queen Bess,* both p. 82; August, 2004, Lynn K. Vanca, review of *Leonardo da Vinci,* p. 140; September, 2004, Julie Roach, review of *Thanksgiving on Plymouth Plantation,* p. 181; October, 2004, Grace Oliff, review of *The Giant and the Beanstalk,* p. 135; January, 2005, Ann W. Moore, review of *Saladin, Noble Prince of Islam,* p. 56; March, 2005, Kathleen T. Isaacs, review of *Saladin, Noble Prince of Islam,* p. 68; March, 2006, Kathleen T. Isaacs, review of *Bella at Midnight,* p. 230; March, 2008, Elaine E. Knight, review of *The Mysterious Case of the Allbright Academy,* p. 212; February, 2009, Wendy Lukehart, review of *Mozart,* p. 95; September, 2010, Susan W. Hunter, review of *Saving Sky,* p. 165; July, 2011, Mandy Lawrence, review of *The Silver Bowl,* p. 108.

Washington Post Book World, December 6, 1992, Phyllis Sidorsky, review of *Bard of Avon,* p. 18.

ONLINE

Diane Stanley Home Page, http://www.dianestanley.com (November 5, 2011).

HarperCollins Web site, http://www.harpercollins.com/ (November 5, 2011), "Diane Stanley."

National Center for Children's Illustrated Literature Web site, http://www.nccil.org/ (November 5, 2011), "Diane Stanley."

Autobiography Feature

Diane Stanley

Diane Stanley contributed the following autobiographical essay to *SATA:*

Because I was an only child, I grew up in a world of adults. Since my parents divorced in my infancy, I grew up among my mother's people, the Grissoms, and it was these extraordinary, eccentric, creative adults who formed my world. Most important to me were my mother, my aunt Nancy, and my grandmother Pearl. All three were, in their own individual ways, fascinating. I naturally wanted to be like them and, to some extent, I succeeded. But they were a very tough act to follow.

Though I am in many ways a continuation of that line of verbal, creative, book-loving, far-flung-traveling Grissoms, I am also a Stanley, the daughter of a father who is neat, precise, conservative, and single-minded. Some of these traits were passed on to me, making me feel, at times, like a pigeon in an aviary of exotic birds.

My father, Burt Stanley, was a young naval officer when he met my mother. He went on to be one of the flying aces in World War II and to make a career in the U.S. Navy, retiring with the rank of captain. He and my mother did not have a happy marriage. Their temperaments and backgrounds were too different from one another's. After the divorce, my father remarried and disappeared from my life. I only remember seeing him once while I was growing up, though we met again when I was sixteen and now see one another every year or so. I have two half-sisters and two step-brothers whom I also see occasionally, though I didn't know them when I was a child. At that time, divorce was not as common as it is today, and I often felt strange that I lived only with my mother. Although I have felt hurt that my father never wanted to see me when I was growing up, I realize now how torn apart children sometimes feel, going back and forth between their mothers and fathers. Since their lives and attitudes and rules were so very different, it might have been quite confusing for me to have gone on frequent visits. Perhaps it was for the best.

I was born in Abilene, Texas, on December 27, 1943. Apparently, the doctor predicted that I would arrive for Christmas, but I disappointed everyone by waiting two more days. Furthermore, the timing still wasn't right, because my mother was playing poker when she began to go into labor, and was reluctant to go to the hospital because she was winning.

Parents, Burt and Fay Stanley, 1940 (Photograph courtesy of Diane Stanley.)

Even though we left Abilene while I was still a baby, we returned there often—every summer and every Christmas at the very least—and the extended family was very close.

My grandfather, Ernest Grissom, had founded a department store in Abilene which featured high-fashion clothing. He had a wonderful eye for beautiful things, and his store made him a wealthy man, at least by the standards of west Texas. He and my grandmother, Pearl, traveled all over the world—China, India, Thailand, South America—and brought back stone Fu dogs, tiny shoes of embroidered silk from China, a monkey, the side off a painted Sicilian cart, Greek icons, and an endless list of rare and beautiful things. As a young mother in the 1920s, Pearl thought nothing of putting her children in the car and driving down to Mexico, though there were few decent roads then and bandits were still common. She was a pilot as well, which was certainly unusual for a woman and which took courage, since these were the early days of aviation.

My grandmother was artistic in many ways. Even the ordinary womanly tasks of keeping a home and choosing clothes were opportunities for expressing her originality. Amazing houses filled with folk art from all over the world arranged in original ways became a family tradition. She also took up weaving in middle age and had a large loom and a closet filled with hundreds of skeins of yarn. She was always making something, and it was never the sort of thing anyone else would think to make.

My warmest memory of my grandmother is of listening to her "little girl stories." She was a natural storyteller, for she had not only the gift of narrative, but also a beautiful voice. People were always telling her she should be a writer, but she told me once that she didn't believe she had anything important to say. She wrote some verses in her old age about losing her sight, which were published. They do not begin to reflect the warm, bright, unusual, complex woman I knew. That woman comes out in the sixty pages of childhood memories she dictated when in her eighties, and which are among my greatest treasures. I adored my grandmother, as did everyone who knew her.

Pearl and Ernie had three children. The oldest was Nancy, who also became a very important person in my life. The middle child was my mother, Fay. The youngest was a boy, Jack, who lived a tragic life and died in middle age.

As close as my mother was to her family, she was a city girl at heart, and once she had obtained her divorce, she took me to New York. The life I live today, as a mother of three children, is filled with car pools, soccer practice, birthday parties, Boy Scouts, and all the concerns and events of children. But when I was growing up, the one child of a glamorous divorcée living in the artsy West Village of New York in the 1940s, everything was quite different. I learned to order Shirley Temples in the lounges of elegant restaurants—places with live musicians who were often asked to play my favorite song, "Good Night, Irene." I developed a taste for lobster. I skated at Rockefeller Center in a black velvet coat with ermine trim and matching ermine muff. I went to the opera and saw Broadway plays. I read Hilaire Belloc and Oscar Wilde.

We lived in a charming ground-floor apartment on Perry Street, which we shared with Frances Herrick, a friend of Mother's. Frances had a regular job and lived a fairly ordinary life. My mother, on the other hand, being fortunate enough to have enough money from her family, did not have a job. She did work at writing, though,

and during that period—the first seven years of my life—she was successful in publishing some of her work. Her murder mystery, *Murder Leaves a Ring,* won a first-novel contest and was published by Holt, Rinehart. It was set in our apartment and even included a floor plan. The murder victim is discovered dead in the bathtub (wearing an evening dress). The "ring" in the title was, of course, the bathtub ring. In the Dell paperback edition of the book, the artist who did the cover illustration was obviously given a picture of my mother, because the lady slumped charmingly in the bathtub is a portrait of the author. Besides her mystery, Mother wrote short stories and produced a radio play which starred Tallulah Bankhead.

Mother's New York friends included many artists, actors, and writers, some of them famous. The poet Ruthven Todd was a close friend, and through him she met the artist Joan Miro and the poet Dylan Thomas. She fell in love with a German concert pianist, Helmut Behrwald, and I still have a medal given to him by Peter of Yugoslavia after a command performance. He was a warm and charming man, and the sound of beautiful music sometimes comforted my nap times. Helmut died suddenly of a heart attack while we were visiting in

Maternal grandmother, Pearl Bunkley Grissom, with (left) Fay, the author's mother, and Nancy, 1923 (Photograph courtesy of Diane Stanley.)

Abilene. Ironically, I was practicing the piano when I heard the news, and it made me very sad.

*

Of the early days in New York, I have a few random memories. I saw *Peter Pan* with Mary Martin numerous times. In fact, mother got so tired of seeing it that she used to get her friends to take me. I guess it never occurred to her to just tell me I had already seen it and didn't need to see it again—she was very indulgent with me in many ways.

I remember singing duets with her from Broadway musicals and acting out "operas" in the vein of Gian Carlo Menotti with my friends.

But what I remember most of all about New York was the garden. Most brownstone apartments in Manhattan have tiny, dark little yards in back. But our apartment backed onto a large garden which belonged to an Episcopal church the next block over. It was a magical place with high, ivy-clad walls, stone sculpture, fountains, flowers, and winding flagstone paths. There was a pond with goldfish in it and multicolored marbles embedded in the cement. How I loved that garden! Equally magical was the church itself—I had only to walk out my back door, across the garden, and into the back door of the church—where I sang in the junior choir. It seemed enormous to me (probably because I was small), and I remember the light coming through the stained glass, the high darkness or the place, and the smell of incense.

I loved being in plays, and one I particularly remember was *King Midas and the Golden Touch.* I had a Greek tunic sort of thing to wear, to which my mother had sewn stripes of shiny gold ribbon. I adored it! The afternoon of the play, we were to get there early to get our costumes and makeup on. I begged my mother to let me walk to school by myself. Unfortunately, she agreed, On crossing Hudson Street, I looked both ways but forgot about the cross street, and a taxi which was turning a corner hit me. I spent the evening at the hospital, though all I had were terrible bruises. My greatest sorrow was that I didn't get to be in the play.

Probably the most dramatic occurrence in those early days was the devastating fire which destroyed our apartment. I was awakened in the middle of the night with my room already full of smoke. We got out safely and spent the night with neighbors three doors down. Since the buildings were attached, I remember feeling terrified that the fire would spread. I thought and worried about fire for some time after that. It took many months to rebuild the apartment, during which time we lived with friends.

The summer after second grade, Mother and I went to Mexico City to spend the summer. On the way, we stopped in Abilene to visit, and while we were there, Mother had a physical checkup, because she was very thin and my grandparents were worried about her health. We proceeded to Mexico before all the results were in. We had only been there a few days when my grandparents arrived to take us back to Texas. Mother had tuberculosis.

There was no effective treatment for TB in those days. People were sent to special hospitals called sanitoriums, where they were quarentined to avoid spreading the disease to healthy people, kept comfortable, and waited for the body to heal itself, or not, as the case might be. For me, this meant the only parent I had ever known was taken away from me.

For several years, I lived with my aunt and uncle, Nancy and Hal Sayles. Nancy became my second mother, and Martha and Jim, my cousins, were like my brother and sister. Jim was one year older than me and Martha one year younger.

The Sayles household was as orderly and well run as it was exotic. They had live-in servants and a beautiful house full of Nancy's unusual touches. One I particularly remember was a long hallway with lighted display cases built into them. Each case was a dollhouse room, furnished with fine, hand-made miniature furniture, pictures, candlesticks, rugs, family photos—gathered from all over the world. She used to change it several times a year, and always decorated it for Christmas.

Nancy was a world traveler, but her interest was in remote places where ancient cultures still thrived, She particularly loved Asia, Mexico, and Central America. In her sixties, she became a serious collector of pre-Columbian art and an authority on Guatemalan textiles, selling her photographs from remote villages to the costume collection of the Metropolitan Museum in New York. Until her seventies she was leading tours to Guatemala.

Her house was one where people liked to come. There was a small refrigerator filled with sodas, and we had no rules about how many we could have. Our friends felt free and comfortable there.

We spent a lot of time outside, even in the blazing west Texas summers, digging in the dry creek bed looking for Indian artifacts, soaring across the creek on our rope swing, playing cowboys and North Americans, catching crayfish when the creek was full, and many other small-town pastimes.

Jim used to tell me stories. One was of an adventurous cat named Kitty-pair-a-kitty (I believe this was because he was one of a pair of kittens, though I never was quite sure). At any rate, he got into all kinds of trouble, and cars and motorcycles came into his adventures a lot, those things being much on Jim's mind at the time. There was also a series on the king of the fairies and all his court who supposedly lived in our backyard and performed circus acts one night, using the clothesline as

Diane at age two (Photograph courtesy of Diane Stanley.)

a high wire. I kept saying that if there really were fairies, why couldn't I see them? He promised to take me to their hideout, and when he finally did, it seems they had all gone on vacation. But he had gone to some trouble to make a little cave with a door in it. He said some magic words and the door slowly opened by itself. In fact, he had rigged up a string which ran underground and which he unobtrusively opened with his thumb while I gazed openmouthed at this undeniable wonder. Inside, there was a tiny note of apology from the vacationing king, which I kept.

*

I was an active, gangly, rumpled, accident-prone sort of child, and I'm very glad I had those years, though I missed my mother very much. When people today say that children are too busy with activities and have so many pressures on them that they don't have time to "be a child," I think those sweaty, dirty, carefree afternoons down by the creek are just the kind of playful goofing-off they mean that children are missing. I had lots of it. If I had art lessons or ballet lessons or played any sport (at which I would have been a klutzy disaster), then I have forgotten it. I remember dressing up in Nancy's fine lingerie and playing princess and acting out stories with our dolls. For at least those few years, I was a child among children, and it was fun.

When I was about eleven, my mother recovered from her tuberculosis, and we moved again, this time to La Jolla, California. We had a house a few blocks from the beach, and my play now featured kite-making and-flying, bike-riding, lots of roller-skating, and endless exploring of the rocky sections of the beach with its tide pools and caves.

I had a little white poodle named Poochie. Poodles were all the rage in the 1950s and were clipped in little pom-poms and sometimes even dyed pink or purple, but Poochie wore his fur "natural" and his white tended towards brownish, as he spent a lot of time on the beach with me. His actual name was Puccini Barculous Ferocious Atrocious Gregarious Stanley the First. I felt this was a very witty name. I might as well say at this point that I was something of a show-off, being once again a child among adults, and anxious to be every bit as intellectual and clever as they were. I doubt if this went down very well with the other children.

Anyway, Poochie and my best friend Lynn and I spent our days together, usually outdoors, summer and winter (this was, after all, southern California). Or we made things, such as the papier-mâché horse's head which Lynn and I needed in order to dress up as a horse for Halloween.

We made up plays which we recorded on my new tape recorder, a big, old-fashioned machine with loose tape reels threaded in by hand. This was long before audio-cassettes; personal tape recorders were a new thing then, and they were only for recording, not for playing music. My favorite play we did was *izor,* a parody of *Zorro,* a popular television show. Zorro was a sort of Spanish colonial Robin Hood, a nobleman who put on a black outfit and mask and went around foiling the evil plans of cruel overlords. He was noted for his fancy sword work, and his trademark was a "Z" which he sliced into whatever was nearby, in three neat strokes (swish, swish, swish), to show that he had been there. He could even do this on people's chests, neatly cutting the clothes but not the skin. Now "izor" had a similar habit, but since *his* name began with an "i," he always ended up killing people when he went to dot it. This allowed us to make all sorts of death-agony sounds. Though "izor" was always contrite, he was just too stupid to stop dotting his *i*'s.

I was now growing into an active, gangly, rumpled sort of teenager, advanced intellectually but socially still a child. To make it worse, I skipped the eighth grade and was thus in class with boys and girls a year or two older than I was. I read a lot and was not stylish about my dress. I certainly wasn't popular.

But I was on the school newspaper, I sang in several choral groups, and I was president of the drama club. This was my big interest, and I took private acting lessons. My thirteenth summer I played Puck in *A Midsummer Night's Dream* at an outdoor theater in Balboa

Park. In high school I earned enough points to be a National Thespian. I planned to act on Broadway when I grew up. It is strange that once I got to college, I put all thoughts of the theater behind me, so interested did I become in other things. But perhaps it isn't surprising that my oldest daughter plans to be an actress, and my son is interested in acting, too.

Another thing that seems odd to me is that my natural interest and talent in art did not come to the foreground earlier. I certainly shone whenever we had to draw something in school, or carve something out of a bar of soap. I remember taking watercolors down to the beach and attempting to paint the sea. And I was forever making things.

Writing, however, was something I did well and often as a young person. I wrote short stories, made a family newspaper, composed poems, and made A's in English. Because my mother was a writer, I often thought that I, too, could be a writer.

Certainly, I was an avid reader. I read everything from comics to classics. We had a lot of books in the house, and I read them all. As a small child, I had loved *Babar* and *Madeline* and the poems and stories of A.A. Milne.

Later, I devoured *Anne of Green Gables* and *The Secret Garden*. By junior high, I was reading adult books, Hawthorne and Hugo as well as *Gone with the Wind, Auntie Mame,* and *Lost Horizon.* I loved the dark, melodramatic novels of Thomas Hardy, and romantic books like *Jane Eyre* and *Green Mansions*. I regret that I didn't discover Dickens until later—but better late than never. I cannot stress enough what a big part reading has always played in my life. It comforted me when I was sad or lonely, broadened my understanding of the world, enriched my vocabulary, entertained me, made me think, made me laugh, made me cry, helped me grow. I could never have become a writer if I weren't first a reader.

When I was sixteen, my mother, who for some time had been ill, had to be hospitalized. I moved back to Abilene and finished high school there. Once again, I moved in with my aunt and uncle and my cousins.

It would be hard to imagine two cultures more different than urban southern California and a small town in west Texas. California teenage social life in the late fifties was centered around coffeehouses, folk music, poetry, and trying to act like beatniks. In Texas, everything was hunting, football, and cheerleaders and all the girls wanted to look like First Lady Jackie Kennedy. We

Diane with her mother, who was recuperating from tuberculosis, about 1952 (Photograph courtesy of Diane Stanley.)

wore matching cashmere sweater sets, circle skirts with lots of petticoats, and penny loafers. For church we wore pillbox hats over our huge, teased hairdos and little white gloves. People talked differently, and thought differently, and in order to fit in, I had to become a whole new person. It seems like I've been doing this all my life, since I have lived in so many places. The good side of it is that I have not solidified into a rigid personality who can only view things one way. Perhaps being challenged over and over again also helped me to become a writer.

I graduated from Abilene High School in 1961 and entered Trinity University in San Antonio the following fall. It was a small, Presbyterian, liberal arts college, and I was happy there. I made a lot of friends, enjoyed my classes, made good grades, and loved the independence of being on my own.

Women in the early 1960s were not expected to have careers, and I assumed that my education was for the improvement of my mind rather than preparation for a job. My major was in the social sciences: history, political science, sociology. This was not very practical, but I assumed that I would become a wife and mother, and that it really didn't matter.

My senior year I took a drawing class first semester, which I enjoyed, and a figure-drawing class second semester, which I adored. Though I had had no other art training. I seemed instinctively to know what to do. It felt as if I had been doing it all my life.

At the end of the year, my art teacher called me into his office for a conference. He told me that I was the only person in the class who was not an art major, and that he had given me the only *A*. He told me I had talent. This changed my life: I believed him.

Having graduated in 1965, with no white knight on the horizon, I moved to Houston where I shared an apartment with several girlfriends from Trinity. I got a job as a lab technician in a hospital and took more life drawing at night. I also fell in love with a young man fresh out of the Harvard Business School, working at his first job. His name was Peter Vennema, and although we later went our separate ways, we met up again and, fourteen years after we first met, we got married. But I'm getting ahead of the story.

Working in a hospital, I learned about medical illustration, a field in which artists are trained in medicine and then do illustrations for medical and scientific books. Being the kind of artist who loves detail and works small, this seemed just right for me. So for the next four years, I worked towards becoming a medical illustrator.

I spent a year at the University of Texas studying art and finishing the pre-med requirements for graduate school. Then I spent another year studying art at the Edinburgh College of Art in Scotland.

Diane (left, standing) with cousin Martha and second mother, Nancy Sayles (seated left), and cousin Jim (Photograph courtesy of Diane Stanley.)

I had never been to Europe. Now I was going for the first time, alone, and planning to stay there a year. I was thrilled and I was frightened. It turned out to be a wonderful year. I rented a spare room in a family's apartment. In Britain, such lodgings are called "digs". My digs were rather bleak and very cold. I was only allowed to take a bath twice a week, and for this the water heater was turned on especially. At other times, I could heat up water in a teakettle for washing my hair or taking a "canary bath." I also remember that they did not have a refrigerator and so the wife did her shopping each day for that day's meals. I did not eat with them, however, and spent all my time in my little room, bundled up in a quilted robe, with my space heater sending out its few feeble rays of warmth.

But the city was beautiful, with its grey stone buildings, the grand "royal mile" with its castle at one end and a palace at the other, and its twisting cobblestone streets running up and down steep inclines. I ate a lot of omelettes to save money and, whenever I could, I would take a trip. Over Christmas break, I went to Moscow and Leningrad, via Warsaw and East Berlin. This was the first really exotic place I had ever been, and I was fascinated. This was the beginning of my "Russian phase" in which I read all the great Russian novels, beginning with *War and Peace,* studied Russian art and history, and unknowingly planted the seeds of the first biography I would write years later, *Peter the Great.*

In the spring (thanks to a gift from my aunt Nancy), I went to Italy and the Greek islands. The following summer, another American girl and I covered the great cities of Europe, including several behind the Iron Curtain, and ended up picking apples in a kibbutz in Israel.

Returning to the United States, I began my two years of graduate work at Johns Hopkins University College of Medicine. We studied histology, neuroanatomy, and gross anatomy, in which we dissected a cadaver. I did not enjoy this, especially because it smelled of chemical preservatives. I also sketched in the operating room.

I received my master's degree in 1970, and that summer I married Peter Zuromskis, who had received his M.D. in the same class. During the next seven years, we lived in various places as he did his internship and residency training. We spent a year in Boston, three years in Virginia Beach, where my daughters Catherine (1971) and Tamara (1973) were born. We spent three more years in Annapolis, Maryland, then moved back to Massachusetts. Shortly after this, the marriage ended in divorce.

During all these moves, I worked as a freelance medical illustrator and full-time mother. My two daughters, bright and beautiful, became the center of my life. We progressed through lullabies and diapers and first steps and ear infections to the point where they were old enough not to tear books or smear them with peanut butter. Reading to them was one of the delights of my day. I began visiting the library every week. It was a comfortable branch library in Annapolis with enough playthings to keep the girls occupied while I searched the shelves for the ten or twelve best books. This generally took about an hour. My interest was so keen that the librarian began to set aside books she thought I would like. Without exactly realizing it, I was doing a self-taught course in children's literature.

*

I'm not sure exactly when I knew that I wanted to become an illustrator of children's books, but this ambition became clear and firm. I began to research technical details which would be necessary in doing this kind of art work. I began experimenting with water color and pen and ink. After about a year I had completed a number of pictures suitable for children's books. This constituted my artist's portfolio.

At that time, we were planning to move to the Boston area and made a trip there from Maryland to look for a house. I made an appointment with John Keller, the editor in chief at Little, Brown & Company, publishers. I brought my portfolio to show to him, since this is how illustrators get work. Apparently, he liked what he saw because he asked me to illustrate a book for his company. This was, without a doubt, one of the happiest days of my life.

Daughters Tamara (above) and Catherine on top of a pyramid in Mexico, 1982 (Photograph courtesy of Diane Stanley.)

The project John suggested was an illustrated version of the nursery rhyme "The Farmer in the Dell." Back in Annapolis, during my children's nap times, I worked away on the art. In 1978 it was published: my first book!

At that time, big changes were taking place in my life. I was getting divorced and had moved to New York City. I lived with my two daughters in an apartment in the West Village, not far from where we had lived when I was a child. Katie and Tamara went to St. Luke's School, where I had gone. Even the beautiful garden was still there, as magical as ever. I visited it with my children.

Part of the reason for choosing that part of the city was that my mother was living nearby, on Bethune Street. She was working as the chief copywriter for the cosmetics firm, Fabergé, and had written another book, *Portrait in Jigsaw*. She had remarried in 1970 to Dr. Carl Shulman, a professor of engineering at City College of New York. Carl was a scientist with the soul of an artist. Though physics and mathematics were an essential part of who he was, his curiosity about the world, his humor, his sophistication, and his complete unpretentiousness made him a true delight. He and Mother seemed like the most unlikely couple imaginable: she was tall, outgoing, and flamboyant; he was short, unconcerned with his appearance, reserved, and intellectual. What people didn't always know was that

Mother had a great mind under all that flash and dazzle, and Carl was funny and playful. They had a wonderfully happy marriage for fifteen years, ending when he died in 1985 following bypass surgery.

My favorite Carl story is the one when he went to Abilene with Mother for Christmas. Pearl said she had always wanted to figure out a way to "snow" on her friends when they came caroling. Carl tucked that thought away in his mind and set to work. The following Christmas, they arrived with a machine which would make snow. It didn't work perfectly—it sort of sleeted on the carolers. Nevertheless, it made a sensation.

Carl, who was an amateur pilot, had once flown Mother to Nantucket to watch an eclipse. They fell in love with this beautiful island off the coast of Massachusetts, with its grey-shingled houses and cobblestoned Main Street. She and Carl built a house there, right on the beach, overlooking the dunes. It was the place where we gathered as a family. We still go there every summer, and it is my favorite place on earth.

Mother was a tremendous help to me the two years I lived in New York City. It was difficult juggling small children and a job. This was the first time I had had a full-time job since my girls were born. Sadly, she would die of cancer at the end of November 1990. The previous spring, although she was already weakened by the disease, she traveled with us to Indonesia. The month before her death, she and my aunt Nancy spent a week together in Mexico. Six months after Mother's death, Nancy, too, died of cancer. Both of them lived their lives fully to the end.

In New York City, I worked briefly at Dell Publishers as a designer in the publicity department. Then I worked at G.P. Putnam's Sons as art director in their children's book division. Book design had been a particular interest of mine in art school, and working at Putnam's was a joy. I firmly believe that the people who work in children's books are a particularly delightful breed. I made a lot of close friends in those days, and I loved my work.

In the evenings, after taking care of my housekeeping tasks and my "mommy" responsibilities, I began the second part of my day, for I was continuing to illustrate books. In these midnight hours I completed the art for *Half-a-Ball-of-Kenki,* by Verna Aardema; *Little Mouse Nibbling,* by Tony Johnston; and *Fiddle-I-Fee,* an American folk chant. These books are all out-of-print, and the style of illustration varied wildly from one book to another. Partly, this was because I was trying to find a style which suited me. But it was also an intentional attempt on my part to find a way of working which suited the story. I did not want to become an art machine, continuously churning out identical pictures.

By a bizarre coincidence, my job at Dell was in an office building directly next door to the apartment owned by the parents of Peter Vennema, whom I had dated so many years before. By further coincidence, my boss at Dell happened to mention the name to me, for otherwise I would never have known. I dropped by to say hello, and was lucky to find them in, since Mr. Vennema had retired and now spent little time in the city. Peter, who was living in Houston, soon heard I was in New York, and when he had an opportunity to come north on business he took me to the theater. After that we saw one another as often as we could, which wasn't easy, living thousands of miles apart.

Peter is a quiet and self-assured man. Though he studied engineering and business, his interests are varied and he is a serious reader. He has lived in England, France, and South Africa and shares my love of travel and curiosity about other cultures and about history. We feel easy and comfortable together and share the same goals and ideals.

And so, on September 8, 1979, we got married. I gave up my job and moved to Texas. We bought a house in a pleasant neighborhood with a nice yard, where the girls could play, and a playground two blocks away. I settled in to illustrate fulltime. I did nine more books either by other authors—such as *Sleeping Ugly* by Jane Yolen—or folk and fairy tales like *Petrosinella* and *The Month Brothers.* I could do about three of these books in a year. Now I find I have to work hard to do one, since my current books are longer and more complicated.

In 1981, my third child was born, a boy this time. We named him John Leslie. I now had children of both sexes and three "flavors": a redhead (Catherine), a brunette (Tamara), and a blond (John). Starting all over again with babyhood at thirty-eight was wrenching, but I soon got used to it. The next eight years passed by in a whirl of car pools and homework and slumber parties mixed with teething, bottles, and endless trips around the block with the stroller.

*

It was during this time that I began making a real effort to write a story I could illustrate. After several false starts, including one story about a Russian peasant and a dancing bear (which later became *Fortune*) and another about a cat that gets into a territorial dispute with a cuckoo clock (which was rewritten years later as *Siegfried*), I finally wrote *The Conversation Club.* This club of anthropomorphic mice was inspired somewhat by the natural exuberance of my large family. In the story, the mice all talk at the same time, the result being complete gibberish. This has been known to happen at our dinner table.

I was working principally with an editor, Meredith Charpentier, whom I had followed when she moved from one publisher to another, and she published *The Conversation Club,* my first book as an author. It was followed by *A Country Tale,* with more anthropomorphic animals, cats this time. My girlhood was spent

Tamara, John, Peter, Diane, and Catherine at home, 1989 (Photograph courtesy of Diane Stanley.)

with any number of beloved cats, and I always had at least one until my daughter, Tamara, developed an allergy to cats. Since John is allergic to dogs, we are petless. But this didn't keep me from writing books about animals, as I did in *Captain Whiz-Bang, Siegfried,* and *Moe the Dog in Tropical Paradise.*

While I work on my illustrations, I frequently listen to books on tape. One book I particularly enjoyed was the biography of Peter the Great of Russia by historian Robert K. Massie. Suddenly it popped into my head that Peter, who was an extremely colorful and eccentric character, would make a nice subject of a book for children. One phone call to Meredith in New York was enough to begin the project, my first biography.

Peter the Great would be a standard thirty-two-page picture book, so I did not have room for a great amount of text. The first challenge was to choose what to tell and what to leave out. I was fairly ruthless this first time out, ignoring his military adventures and his marriages. There was much about Peter the Great that

was cruel or shocking, and I left these parts out as inappropriate for young readers. Several years later, in writing *Shaka,* I would be more thorough and more honest.

The second challenge was to make the story as interesting as possible to a young reader, and for this I searched for colorful anecdotes which brought out Peter's personality. In all my biographies, I now search for the telling anecdote, in hopes that it will capture the child's imagination.

Finally, I wanted the pictures to be as accurate as I could possibly make them, yet I wanted them to be fun to look at. I chose a somewhat naive style and worked in gouache, an opaque watercolor that gives brilliant, flat color. Every element in the pictures was based upon a documented source—either a portrait (so I'd know what the particular people in the story looked like), a costume book, a photograph of a particular room or building where an event took place, or prints and paintings of the period to document anything from furniture to how a horse would be bridled. The two pieces of information that were hardest to find were the sailboat in which Peter first learned to sail (I finally found several prints showing what it looked like) and the room in which he died, which I had to reconstruct from written descriptions. I have continued to take this kind of care with the details in the pictures in all my biographies.

When *Peter the Great* was published, we were all surprised by how successful it was and how many awards it won, including being chosen an ALA notable book. And when I went to speak at schools and at conferences for teachers and librarians, I was urged to do more such books. Many people felt I had created a unique and much-needed kind of book. It was the beginning of a new direction in my work.

From my husband's time in South Africa came the idea to do a book about Shaka, who founded the Zulu nation in the early part of the nineteenth century. It was difficult dealing with a figure who remains controversial and whose culture left no written records. I would have to reconstruct a great deal from the oral tradition and two books written by Englishmen who knew Stanley only in his later years. To this massive task of research, my husband lent an eager and competent hand, spending hours in the library and getting books from distant sources through interlibrary loan. In the end, it became clear that, though he did not write the final text, Peter should be acknowledged as coauthor. Since that time, he has been an integral part of the research phase on all my biographies.

Shaka: King of the Zulus was named a *New York Times* Best Illustrated Book and received many other awards and honors. It was the hardest book I had ever undertaken, and I felt grateful and proud.

I took time out to illustrate a fairy tale I had written some years before. It had once been set in Russia and featured a dancing bear. I now moved it to Persia and made the bear a tiger. *Fortune,* as the book was called, was a sheer delight from start to finish and felt like a vacation after the pressure of a forty-page, heavily researched biography. I did the gouache paintings in the ancient Persian style, with collage borders.

The next historical subject was Queen Elizabeth I of England. One of my editors, Cindy Kane, then at Four Winds Press, asked a group of librarians what book they would like to see from Diane Stanley. One of them suggested Elizabeth. Cindy suggested it to me and *Good Queen Bess* was born. The hardest part about writing Queen Elizabeth's story was simply that there is so much to tell: so many wonderful characters crossed her path, so many fascinating events were going on in her time. I find with each book I do, I spend more time writing and rewriting. I hope that means that each is better than before. *Good Queen Bess* was also an ALA notable book and was a *Boston Globe/Horn Book* nonfiction honor book. It won *Parenting* magazine's Reading Magic award and was named one of *Parents* magazine's Best Kids' Books of 1990.

My mother was the author of my next biography, *The Last Princess,* the story of Kaiulani of Hawai'i. It grew from her interest in Hawaiian history begun when she and my father were stationed there in 1941. In fact, she was at Pearl Harbor when it was bombed (my father was out on an aircraft carrier). She had suggested several times that I write about Kaiulani, the tragic princess who never got to be queen and who died young after watching her country be annexed by the United States. In the end, Mother wrote it and I illustrated it. I could not have known when we planned this mother-daughter project that she would not live to see it published. She had the color proofs of the book in her hospital room and showed them to all the nurses. I am very grateful that I didn't wait another year to do the book. I only wish she could have lived to see the awards come in, for *The Last Princess,* too, was an ALA notable book and a *Parents* magazine best book.

As my books have become more complicated and take a full year to do, I have felt less able to do more whimsical books. Thus, I have begun writing stories to be illustrated by other artists. It has been a delight to see what these talented illustrators have done with my stories: Bruce Degen illustrated *The Good-Luck Pencil* with the wonderful hidden extras he would later go hog-wild with in the "Magic Schoolbus" books; John Sandford illustrated *Siegfried* in rich and glowing colors and gave the book a look which was both sophisticated and cozy; and Elise Primavera took *Moe the Dog in Tropical Paradise* into her heart so perfectly that Moe and his friend Arlene seem very real to me. To My delight, Elise also illustrated another of my stories, *Saving Sweetness. The Gentleman and the Kitchen Maid* was illustrated by Dennis Nolan.

Looking at the life I have made for myself, I feel terribly grateful to have found work that is satisfying and useful. Sitting down each morning, either to my word processor or my drawing board, is something I do gladly. I often find that as the day progresses towards car-pool time or dinner time, I am reluctant to stop. If I didn't have obligations to my family, I would probably work myself to a state of exhaustion. The fact is that I love my work.

To balance my work is my family life, for which I am also grateful. I have three bright, attractive children—Catherine, my thespian; Tamara, deeply creative and a possible future writer; and John, who wants to do everything from soccer to musical comedy. I have a wonderful husband who is a perfect partner in everything I do. For what more could a person ask? Free time, maybe. But that's about all.

*

Stanley contributed the following update to her autobiography in 2011:

Reading over my entry from 1991 was like opening a time capsule. The past as I wrote it then (on my "word processor"!) is much as I remember it now; but reading the last few paragraphs, in which I described the world I was living in and how the future looked from there, was like looking at an old picture of myself in a beehive hairdo. Was that really me? Wow, how things have changed!

Since I ended with my family, I might as well start there. Catherine is no longer a thespian. She went off to Harvard, majored in art history, and ended up with a doctorate in visual culture from the University of Rochester. She is now an assistant professor at the University of New Mexico, specializing in the history of photography. She is married to the wonderful Daniel, a professor of English, and they just became the proud parents of Clementine Fay Worden, the most beautiful baby in the world. Fay, of course, was my mother's name, so in yet another way she continues in our memories and our lives.

Tamara stayed true to her creative potential, getting her B.A. from Johns Hopkins in the Writing Seminars program—then she stunned us all by going to law school.

But we shouldn't have been so surprised, because in addition to being creative, Tamara has always been an idealist—the kind of idealist who follows through by taking action. And so, unlike most of her fellow students at U. Penn Law School, she didn't join a big law firm, but became a public defender. She lives in Grass Valley, California, with Biscuit the Wonder Dog, who shares her interests in running, hiking, camping, and swimming in the river.

John went off to Princeton and majored in English, then settled in Manhattan. He worked for a while at 101 Productions, a theater management company that managed such Broadway hits as *The History Boys* and *Spamalot*. But he was really more interested in film and television, so he moved on to work in production accounting, currently for the CBS drama *Blue Bloods*. He's still playing soccer, in a Manhattan soccer league.

And I'm still lucky to have "a wonderful husband who is a perfect partner in everything I do," except that now, instead of helping me with research for picture-book biographies, Peter listens with apparent interest as I wrestle with my many plot dilemmas, and makes help-

Diane Stanley, 1991 (Photograph courtesy of Diane Stanley.)

ful suggestions like, "They could escape out the water gate," or "What if you had a rat-catcher?" He's a keeper, no doubt about it.

So my family has evolved, as families do—but so has my work. In fact, that's the part about my twenty-year-old entry that feels the most dated. Back then, I saw myself as a picture-book person, and the biographies were still in their infancy. I hadn't even thought of writing a novel.

So I'll pick up where I left off (and set the record straight), with *Saving Sweetness.* I did publish such a book, and a sequel to it called *Raising Sweetness* (two of my all-time favorites, by the way), but Elise Primavera didn't do the illustrations; G. Brian Karas did, and the art is truly brilliant. (Instead, Elise illustrated another one of my books, *Woe Is Moe,* which she did quite beautifully.) My interest was already shifting to nonfiction—but I didn't yet know how far it would take me, how long I would follow that path, and how it would come to define me as an author and an artist.

Bard of Avon: The Story of William Shakespeare was a breakthrough book for me. I also think it's one of my best. Though I've never viewed my biographies as a series, since each one is different in any number of ways, I was starting to settle in on certain elements of format that I would use in all the books that followed. Like *Good Queen Bess, Bard* was forty-eight pages long, and I was beginning to play with front and back matter. More and more, my books would include these "extras"—a map, an introduction, a pronunciation guide, a glossary, a list of important dates, and/or a "what happened next" kind of postscript. They all have bibliographies, often with suggested books for young readers.

Bard begins with an author's note explaining how little we actually know about Shakespeare's daily life. So the story I was about to tell was woven from many strands—the world in which he lived, the history and nature of the theater in Shakespeare's time (the first in Europe since antiquity), the plays he wrote, and the famous people whose lives he touched. But it was the two-page "Note on Language" in the back of the book that was the real departure—and the most fun. I talked about the proper spelling of names. Was it Kemp or Kempe? Apparently it didn't matter. There were no dictionaries back then, no rules of spelling, and even basic words for common things (like eggs) varied from village to village. I finished by giving a long list of familiar words and phrases that Shakespeare brought into our language—from "tongue-tied" to "dead as a doornail." *Bard* was named a *Booklist* Top of the list, an ALA notable book, and a *Horn Book* Fanfare selection, among many other awards.

Charles Dickens: The Man Who Had Great Expectations was the first book for which we traveled to the location to do research. We visited everything Dickens-related in all of England, shooting roll after roll of film.

But the crowning moment was our serendipitous arrival at Gad's Hill Place, just in time for a fundraising "cream tea and tour of the house." It's a private girl's school now and isn't open to the public, so we were lucky indeed. I was able to visit Dickens' book-lined study, where he wrote *A Tale of Two Cities* and *Great Expectations;* and I stood in the room where he died. Having read so much about the man—unlike Shakespeare, there was a lot of information—I felt a very personal connection with Charles Dickens. I truly felt his spirit in that house, which he first saw as a boy and bought many years later. It was the sort of place where a great man would live, the great man he hoped one day to be, and the symbol of all he'd accomplished.

There followed other trips for other books. I have been in the rooms where Michelangelo, Leonardo da Vinci, and Joan of Arc were born, and it was thrilling every time, but perhaps never so much as with Dickens, because I knew him so well.

Cleopatra was an altogether different matter. Though we did go to Egypt, and in particular to Alexandria, we couldn't walk through the halls of her palace or take pictures of the room where she had herself unrolled from a carpet to the astonishment of Julius Caesar—because her palace, her tomb, and the famous Pharos lighthouse (one of the seven wonders of the ancient world) lie deep beneath the waters of Alexandria Harbor, along with the rest of Greco-Roman Alexandria. Not a single building from that period is still standing. But fragments of them can be seen in a few museums, and they suggest that the architecture of Alexandria in Cleopatra's time was a combination of classical Greek and Roman details and traditional Egyptian elements. Using these clues, I reconstructed her palace in my illustrations.

Each book brings its own particular challenges, and *Cleopatra* brought several. Besides the absence of physical evidence, there is little reliable biographical material. As a defeated (and dangerous) enemy of Rome, her portrait busts were destroyed, and so were all written accounts of her life. The oldest record we have—and the best description of her as a person—comes from Plutarch, a Greek historian who was also a Roman citizen. What he wrote, a hundred years after Cleopatra's death, was filtered through a strong Roman bias. I did the best I could with what has come down to us (as has everyone else who's tackled Cleopatra's life), but I told my readers in an author's note that much of her story is suspect because it was written by her enemies.

In my illustrations for biographies I always tried to reflect the culture of my subject through the style of art, and in the decorative elements. In *Shaka* I used Zulu beadwork as a theme, and for *Cleopatra* I used mosaic, an art form common in Greece and Rome. Since she was of Greek heritage (descended from Ptolemy, a general of Alexander the Great) and lived in Roman times, mosaic seemed appropriate—if exceedingly time-consuming, painting all those endless little squares. *Cleopatra* was named an ALA notable book and selected a *Booklist* Editor's Choice and *Publishers Weekly* Best Book.

Joan of Arc met all my requirements for a biographical subject: she was an important person who lived in interesting times, her life story was dramatic, and her world would be fun to illustrate. But nothing is perfect. I had to explain the Hundred Years' War before we even got started, I had to find a way to write straight history about someone who conversed with saints and angels, and my heroine was burned at the stake at the tender age of nineteen. Try illustrating that!

Joan of Arc followed in the footsteps of the previous biographies, winning the same top awards, and I was beginning to have a greater sense of my purpose in doing that particular kind of book. I was introducing young readers to important historical figures they would not encounter in school until they were much older. By learning about them now, while still in elementary school, they would open a mental file on these famous people, a place and a context for the random references that would inevitably come their way. I'd rather they didn't meet them first in the form of parody, thinking Leonardo and Michelangelo were animated Ninja turtles.

From Leonardo da Vinci, **Morrow Junior Books, 1996, "showing my cut and paste technique."** (Illustration courtesy of Diane Stanley.)

Writing about Leonardo da Vinci brought a new challenge. I wanted to show my readers his actual art, but I didn't want it to look like an art history book. So I had photographs of his paintings printed to size, according to my dummy sketches, then pasted them onto the paper and painted the rest of the scene around them. To make it look more natural, I occasionally had something overlapping a small part of one of the pictures, meaning I would have to carefully cut that shape away (Leonardo's profile, for example) with an X-Acto blade. Did I mention that nothing's easy?

Since Leonardo was one of the greatest draughtsmen to ever wield a pen, I wanted my readers to see his drawings too. I found some antique-looking paper online and Xeroxed Leonardo's drawings onto it. (This is legal, by the way; I checked with the lawyers at William Morrow. The art itself has long been in the public domain, and if it isn't clear that you copied it out of any particular book, you are perfectly safe.) Step two was to tear the edges, as if these were fragments torn from one of Leonardo's notebooks. These heavenly drawings went the top of every text page. *Leonardo da Vinci* won the NCTE Orbis Pictus Award, was a *Boston Globe/Horn Book* Award honor book, an ALA notable book, and a Best Book selection of both *Publishers Weekly* and *Booklist.*

Michelangelo was much harder to like than Leonardo, though I certainly felt I knew him. The primary materials I had to work with were wonderful, especially his letters and poems, which reveal Michelangelo to have been a sour, cranky, depressive sort of man. While at work on the Sistine Chapel ceiling, his letters did not mention the astonishing work he was doing. They were all about money and full of complaints—some quite legitimate, since he had to go all the way to Bologna to get his payment from the pope. He said he had no friends of any kind, and didn't want any. Raphael called him "lonely as a hangman." These are the kind of details a writer revels in, and Michelangelo offered more than his share.

Once again I brought Michelangelo's actual art directly into my illustrations, but this time I did it on the computer. I did my sketches digitally, using a Wacom tablet and stylus, then scanned the art and combined the two. The final step was to print the sketch on good watercolor paper, complete with full-color Michelangelo art already in place, and paint in the rest. In all honesty, I don't think it worked very well for some of the sculptures. Though I tried to "take down the shine" of the marble, they didn't seem to live in the same world as the rest of the picture.

Michelangelo was an Orbis Pictus honor book, a *School Library Journal* best book, and a *Booklist* editor's choice. That same year I was awarded a *Washington Post*/Children's Book Guild award for the body of my work in nonfiction. It was a tremendous honor and a nod to all the biographies that had come before.

On September 11, 2001, I was just finishing the elaborate, Persian miniature-inspired illustrations for *Saladin, Noble Prince of Islam*. I remember thinking—along with countless other, more important things—that I might as well throw the art away. No one would buy the book. Later, I decided that maybe I'd been too pessimistic. Perhaps people would want to learn more about Islam and the history of the conflict between east and west, going back to the time of the Crusades. Perhaps it would lay the groundwork, in a small way, for tolerance and understanding.

That was my reasoning, anyway, and I was right on both counts. The reviewers and award committees responded warmly, and saw the book as important. *Saladin* was an ALA notable book, an IRA Notable Book for a Global Society selection, and a *Publishers Weekly* and *Booklist* Best Book choice. But it didn't sell, and despite being one of my newest books, it's now out of print. That makes me very sad.

My last biography, *Mozart: The Wonder Child,* was a labor of love and a voyage of discovery. I'd long admired the paintings of the early Renaissance, most of which were done in egg tempera, the precursor to oil paints. But I didn't think anyone did that anymore. I thought it was impossibly hard—ageing the wooden panels for years, making your own gesso coating, and grinding your own colors. And even if I was willing to go to all that trouble, where would I get the supplies, and who would teach me how to use them?

Before I go any further, let me step away for books for a moment and return to my personal life (there's a connection here, trust me). In 2003, with our last child in college and no further obligations to keep us in Houston, Peter and I decamped for Santa Fe, New Mexico. We were both able to take our work with us (Peter owns a manufacturing company in Michigan, which he's always run from a distance), and moving had long been part of the plan, but we envisioned an orderly search, over a period of time, for the perfect place to live. Peter is the least-impulsive person on the planet, and while I am less cautious, I do like to plan and think things out. Yet we made this important decision on the basis of two trips to Santa Fe, first for my cousin Martha's wedding, then six months later for her daughter's. One was in summer, one in winter—two seasons! After almost twenty-five years of living in Houston, this (along with the mountains, clear air, low humidity, and little traffic) was exciting! On our third trip, we bought a building lot. On the fourth, we hired an architect.

Looking back on that impetuous decision, the most amazing thing is that we underestimated how much we would like Santa Fe, and how living there would change us. Before I moved here I had never built a house, rarely hiked, never skied (all right, I did ski once when I was sixteen, but it was not a happy experience), didn't care for gardening, and was only mildly interested in opera. I have now built two houses, am an avid and fairly ac-

"My first egg tempera painting, largely copied from Botticelli." (Illustration courtesy of Diane Stanley.)

complished skier, and I belong to a weekly women's hiking group (the Hiking Honeys or the Walkie Talkies, we can't decide which). I love working in my garden, and I madly look forward to the Santa Fe Opera's short but wonderful season (the rest of the year I go to the Met Live Broadcasts at the local Lensic Theater). Change is good. We are very happy here. (So are a lot of other people, so I can count on my Houston friends to come and visit.)

Santa Fe is full of galleries. Every third local you meet is probably an artist. So wouldn't you know it was the perfect place to find someone to teach me how to paint in egg tempera? Of course it was! It was even the sort of place where someone would run a business called True Gesso Panels, making panels for artists like "Andy" (realist painter Andrew Wyeth) and others who were much less famous. No need to age wood or make my own gesso. I could order my panels made to size with a perfect, smooth finish—ready for me to paint on.

The teacher I found, Koo Schadler, is by far the best teacher of any subject I've ever had in my life. I became, I blush to admit, something of a Koo groupie. And I was not alone in this. She is an amazing artist, a generous teacher, and a beautiful human being. I took four workshops from her, including one in Italy, after which I figured it was time to stop taking classes and start painting.

I would buy fresh eggs from the farmers' market (something else to love abut Santa Fe) and make my own paints by mixing and grinding powdered colors with diluted yolk of egg. Then I would painstakingly apply layer after whisper-thin layer of glazes, one over the other—warm, then cool, then warm again—giving the beautiful, luminous quality for which egg tempera is justly famous. When I decided it was a nifty idea to illustrate a forty-eight page picture book in this technique, it also resulted in the repetitive-stress rotator cuff injury from which I've only just recovered.

The finished art for *Mozart: The Wonder Child,* on large, heavy panels, completely filled a suitcase (with a little bubble wrap for protection) and weighed a ton. I hand-carried the art to the offices of HarperCollins in New York City and there I abandoned the suitcase, which had seen better days. Then I came back to Santa Fe and packed my art materials away. I was finished with picture books. It's been three years since then, and I still haven't picked up a paintbrush. I keep waiting for that longing to come back, waiting to feel like something vital is missing from my life. But so far that hasn't happened. I'm as busy as ever, still loving my work, but I'm writing long fiction instead.

Once again I need to jump back in time. In 1998 I decided to find out if I could write a novel. My picture books had always been longer and more complicated than the form really called for. Maybe I was better suited to longer fiction. So I took one of my mother's ideas, one I'd always liked but which she'd never gotten around to writing. She'd read about a British filmmaker who wanted to make a documentary on the Iron Age. So he rounded up a bunch of volunteers, including families with children, and had them live for a year on a reconstructed Iron Age farm, keeping everything as accurate as possible. This struck me as a wonderful setting, a realistic time-travel story with many possibilities for drama. So I set to work, and when I had a hundred polished pages, I sent them to my long-time and much-beloved editor, Meredith Charpentier. Her response, in a nutshell, was that a setting is not a plot.

Not to be dissuaded, I ditched the hundred pages and started again (with a plot this time), and Meredith was pleased with the results. I was struck by how much I loved the whole experience, despite my initial failure. I was far more emotionally involved than I'd ever been with my writing before, and I loved having the room to spread out and develop a story that was complex, subtle, and multi-layered. *A Time Apart* was named an ALA best book for young adults and one of *Booklist*'s top-ten first novels. I knew I could write a novel now, and I knew it would not be my last.

As the nineties passed into the naughts (or whatever we're calling the decade), I started alternating novels with picture books. I wrote two mysteries, *The Mysterious Matter of I.M. Fine* (in which the villain is a chil-

dren's book author) and a sequel, *The Mysterious Case of the Allbright Academy.* These books were fun to do, and were quite successful. But mysteries aren't really my genre.

Among my more-recent picture books was an updated version of the Rumpelstiltskin story in which the miller's daughter does not marry the greedy king who locked her up in a room full of straw and ordered her to spin it into gold by morning or die. (And really, who would?) *Rumpelstiltskin's Daughter* is one of my personal favorites and was a very successful book. It was nominated for nine state award lists and won four of them, and was an ALA notable book, a *School Library Journal* best book, and a *Booklist* editor's choice.

Not surprisingly, I decided to try doing more re-imagined fairy tales. There followed *Goldie and the Three Bears, The Giant and the Beanstalk,* and *The Trouble with Wishes,* the last based on the Greek myth Pygmalion.

One night I was lying in bed, trying to come up with another picture-book idea, taking Cinderella for my model and looking for a fresh approach. I started thinking about the stepsisters and stepmother and wondering why they were so famously wicked. The Muse was on duty that night, and in a flash I saw their whole story: The father/husband would be a merchant and would be lost at sea. Since they'd borrowed heavily to pay for the goods he was carrying on the voyage, a loan they couldn't possibly repay, the mother and her young daughters would be turned out of their comfortable house, with nothing but the clothes on their backs. They'd be shunned by their neighbors, swindled by a servant, and forced to throw themselves on the mercy of the mother's sister, who would enjoy their downfall enormously.

This was clearly not a picture book, it was a novel; and I was all on fire to write it. So for the first time in my career I put a book aside (*The Trouble with Wishes*) and plunged into something new. I decided to tell the story in multiple-point-of-view first person, allowing me to further develop my characters and to attack the story from a number of different angles. It would be set in a fairly realistic late Middle Ages, a period I knew quite well, having researched so many biographies set in roughly that period. I wanted to get as many details right as possible, but I wouldn't be constrained by historical accuracy, since these were fictional countries and kings. And magical things could happen. I have never—I repeat never—had so much fun as I did writing that book! *Bella at Midnight* was named a *School Library Journal* best book and a *Booklist* editors' choice.

It was around this time that my editor, Meredith Charpentier, passed away. She had been my friend and mentor for over twenty years, since she edited my second book, *Half-a-Ball-of Kenki* by Verna Aardema. An author who is lucky enough to fall into the hands of such a gifted editor will do whatever it takes to keep her. So I had followed Meredith from Frederick Warne to Macmillan, then Four Winds, and finally to William Morrow & Co. where we'd settled in for the long haul.

The relationship between an editor and an author is not just about business. There has to be trust and understanding on both sides. You have to speak the same language. And for me, at least, there has to be friendship, too. And so I was enormously lucky, having lost Meredith, to find another incredible editor in Rosemary Brosnan. Like Meredith, Rosemary can say The Hard Thing with delicacy and kindness, pull me out of holes

I've dug for myself, give wise advice, and cheer when cheering is called for. Editors don't get the attention they deserve, and I've been blessed with two of the best.

In 2008 I was awarded the Mazza Medallion for Artistic Diversity, an award given every other year by the Mazza Museum of Children's Art in Findlay, Ohio. The winner is selected by other illustrators, so it was especially flattering to be chosen. And it's undeniably true that I've been diverse in my work, having done illustration in virtually every medium imaginable, except for oils: pencil, colored pencil, ink-resist with overlays, pen-and-ink, stipple, collage, watercolor dry-brush, pas-

Thanksgiving in Berkeley, 2006 from left, clockwise, Peter, Diane, John, Tamara, and Catherine (Photograph courtesy of Diane Stanley.)

tels, gouache, acrylics, egg tempera, and many combinations of the above. Yet as I went up on that stage to accept the medallion, I was keenly aware of the irony that I was being given an award for something I was about to abandon, because my heart had moved on. I'd come into children's books through the art door and ended up in the writing room.

For my next novel I chose a controversial topic, a subject I felt deeply about, but which might be (and probably was) considered too political. *Saving Sky* is a quasi-dystopian Anne Frank story set in a post-9/11 America as it might have been had the terrorists possessed the power, money, and organizational skill to continue attacking on a regular basis. War can change a nation, as it did in the United States during World War II, when the government rounded up innocent Japanese Americans and confined them in internment camps. In much the same way, in *Saving Sky* I have the government rounding up and incarcerating "persons of suspicious origins and associations." If that sounds extremely broad, a license to arrest pretty much anyone you want—it is. It also comes, word for word, from a law passed (though quickly rescinded) in England during World War II.

When my main character, Sky Brightman, realizes that her classmate, Kareem, is about to be arrested, she helps him escape, and Sky's family gives him refuge on their ranch in rural New Mexico. While the premise is politically charged, *Saving Sky* is really about human courage, the best kind of family love, the nature of friendship, and what it means to sacrifice your own safety in order to do the right thing. *Saving Sky* was chosen one of the top-ten books by the New England Children's Booksellers advisory council and was named a Bank Street College of Education best book. It also won the Arab-American Award for literature for or by Arab Americans.

With my book *The Silver Bowl*—the first in a trilogy—I have happily returned to medieval fantasy. My heroine, Molly, is a scruffy child with no education, a troubling gift for seeing the future, and a father who considers her to be a burden. Sent away at the tender age of seven to work in the castle kitchens, Molly is eventually put to work polishing the king's great silver hand basin, which speaks to her and shows her visions of the past. Molly learns that there is a curse on the royal family (a hundred curses, actually, all of them in the silver bowl) and she has been called to stop them.

What Molly discovers about herself and her mysterious family history while rescuing the prince and battling demons led me quite naturally to Book II, *The Cup and the Crown*. The manuscript is finished and in Rosemary's capable hands. It takes place in a mysterious walled city, hidden behind a range of impenetrable mountains, where Molly's grandfather was born, and from which he later escaped. It features a raven as a point-of-view character, an engaging rat catcher named

Richard Strange, and a dour magus named Sigrid who can read Molly's mind. I am now well into to Book III, tentatively titled *The Princess of Cortova*. Though it's still early, *The Silver Bowl* is one of *Booklist*'s Top Ten Books in the SciFi/Fantasy category, and was named one of the best books of the year by *Kirkus*.

I've noticed in the last few years that my writing has deepened and my thought process has intensified. I am constantly thinking about my characters, or scenes, or plot points. Sometimes I wonder if it's healthy to have such a rich inner life, filled with people who don't actually exist, to which impossible things keep happening. Is it a sign of my growth as a writer, or of getting older, or simply the fruit of long experience? Whatever it means, it's a part of who I am now—a person very different from the one I was twenty years ago.

And yet my summary, written way back then, remains true. I'm grateful to have three wonderful children (and a wonderful new granddaughter). I'm lucky to have a husband who is a partner in all I do. And I still feel "terribly grateful to have found work that is satisfying and useful."

* * *

STEIN, Tammar 1979(?)-

Personal

Born c. 1979; married; has children. *Education:* University of Virginia, B.A. (English literature and astronomy), 1998. *Religion:* Jewish.

Addresses

Home—Clearwater, FL. *E-mail*—tammarstein@hotmail.com.

Career

Novelist.

Member

Society of Children's Book Writers and Illustrators.

Awards, Honors

Sydney Taylor Award Notable Children's Book of Jewish Content selection, Association of Jewish Libraries, American Library Association Best Book for Young Adults selection, and New York Public Library Pick for Teens selection, all 2006, all for *Light Years*.

Writings

Light Years, Alfred A. Knopf (New York, NY), 2005.
High Dive, Alfred A. Knopf (New York, NY), 2008.
Kindred, Alfred A. Knopf (New York, NY), 2011.

Sidelights

Raised in both the United States and Israel, Tammar Stein draws on her knowledge of diverse cultures, as well as her experiences living in Europe, in her novels for young adults. Committing to a career as a writer in high school, Stein studied English literature while attending the University of Virginia. It was there that she wrote the short story that she would eventually expand into her first novel, *Light Years.* The process of revision took Stein over five years, but resulted in what *School Library Journal* contributor Kathleen Isaacs described as a "well-paced first novel" that will appeal to young adults "interested in other ways of seeing the world." In the years since, Stein has expanded her literary output to additional critical acclaim, producing the novels *High Dive* and *Kindred.*

When readers first meet Maya Laor in *Light Years,* the college freshman is having a difficult time adjusting to life at the University of Virginia, where she intends to study astronomy. Unlike most of her fellow students, Maya is an Israeli whose military service has bestowed both maturity and insight. The twenty year old is also

Cover of Tammar Stein's young-adult novel Kindred, *which finds a college freshman drawn into an epic battle between good and evil.*
(Jacket cover copyright © 2011 by Alfred A. Knopf. Reproduced by permission of Alfred A. Knopf, an imprint of Random House Children's Books, a division of Random House, Inc.)

reeling from the recent death of her boyfriend, Dov, a casualty of a Palestinian suicide bomber targeting a small café in Tel Aviv. Because Dov was at the café waiting for her, Maya feels responsible for his death, and such feelings are incongruous within a college culture focused on partying and intercollegiate sports rivalries. As Stein draws readers into Maya's world, she alternates her first-person narrative between the young woman's present and past, and it is only with the help of a sincere and caring older student named Justin that the young woman is able to reconcile her two worlds and understand what was and was not her fault.

Reviewing *Light Years* in *Kirkus Reviews,* a contributor noted that Stein's description of "the everyday fears of people living in Israel, as well as the beauty of the region, ring true," while Hazel Rochman praised Maya in *Booklist* as a multifaceted character who is "needy and angry, sarcastic and warm." In helping to illuminate a world view that accepts violence as a part of daily life, *Light Years* "provides insight that builds compassion and leaves readers with a sense of hope and healing," concluded *Kliatt* contributor Michele Winship. For a *Publishers Weekly* reviewer, Stein is to be congratulated for producing "a moving and insightful" debut.

Arden, the nineteen-year-old narrator of Stein's novel *High Dive,* is also well traveled, but her current trip is not of her choosing. Neither was the death of Arden's father in an automobile accident, or her mother's deployment to Iraq as a nurse with the U.S. Army. Although Arden has been charged with closing up the family's vacation home in Sardinia, she does not believe she is up to the task and when an opportunity comes to join a group of carefree Texas college girls on a tour of Europe she takes it. While jumping from Paris to Switzerland to Italy, where good food and parties await them, Arden avoids her sadness, but she knows that this impulsive, carefree trip stands in stark contrast to the danger her mother faces each and every day. Ultimately the young woman realizes that she can no longer avoid the responsibilities life has put in her path, and by confronting her reality she learns that support often comes to one facing a new challenge. Praising *High Dive* as "hopeful and real," a *Kirkus Reviews* writer added that Arden's mature perspective "is realistic when placed within the context of her life." "Stein deftly portrays anguish, uncertainty, and unexpected joys," asserted *School Library Journal* contributor Roxanne Myers Spencer, and in *High Dive* "not a moment drags as Arden's bittersweet journey unfolds."

Stein draws on questions of religious faith and free will in *Kindred,* which is enriched by the author's study of the true nature of angels as revealed through biblical scholarship. Moses and Miriam are eighteen-year-old twins who have been steeped in dual theologies: while their father is a rabbi, their mother once took holy orders as a nun and both parents now teach religion on the college level. As *Kindred* opens, Miriam is at college when she is visited by the archangel Raphael. Because the teen understands angels to be threatening creatures, she takes seriously Raphael's message that God wishes her to protect a fellow student from imminent disaster. The disaster turns out to be an explosion in Tabitha's dorm, but Miriam is unable to get the girl out of the building in time to prevent serious injury. Soon her brother Moses arrives on campus and announces that he is doing the bidding of the devil by trying to convince a teenage boy named Jason to commit a destructive act. Realizing that she and Mo have been positioned like pawns on opposing sides of the good vs. evil spectrum, Miriam drops out of school and gets a job writing for a small-town newspaper. A newly diagnosed chronic digestive disease adds to her stress level, along with a new romance with fellow journalist Emmitt; meanwhile, worries over her brother are overshadowed by her belief that keeping Jason from committing violence is also part of God's command, and she dare not fail Him a second time.

Kindred "demands thought and reflection" as it weaves questions of faith, morality, and man's true nature into its story, according to *Booklist* contributor Francisca Goldsmith. Such demands are "made easier," the critic added, "by [Stein's] smooth writing and an engaging cast of rounded characters." A "riveting tale" in the opinion of a *Publishers Weekly* contributor, *Kindred* meshes "family, medical, and supernatural dramas with a sweet romantic subplot." For Elissa Gershowitz, reviewing Stein's novel in *Horn Book,* the work engages readers on multiple levels: The "lofty theological" underpinnings of Miriam's challenges will provoke reflection while "the compelling characters . . . keep the story down to earth," Gershowitz maintained.

Biographical and Critical Sources

PERIODICALS

Booklist, December 1, 2004, Hazel Rochman, review of *Light Years,* p. 647; January 1, 2011, Francisca Goldsmith, review of *Kindred,* p. 96.
Bulletin of the Center for Children's Books, March, 2005, Elizabeth Bush, review of *Light Years,* p. 309; February, 2011, April Spisak, review of *Kindred,* p. 299.
Horn Book, March-April, 2011, Elissa Gershowitz, review of *Kindred,* p. 125.
Kirkus Reviews, December 15, 2004, review of *Light Years*; May 15, 2008, review of *High Dive.*
Kliatt, January, 2005, Michele Winship, review of *Light Years,* p. 11; May, 2008, Myrna Marler, review of *High Dive,* p. 17.
Publishers Weekly, January 17, 2005, review of *Light Years,* p. 57; December 20, 2010, review of *Kindred,* p. 54.
St. Petersburg Times, February 13, 2011, Colette Bancroft, "Imagining the Real Angels" (profile), p. L8.
School Library Journal, January, 2005, Kathleen Isaacs, review of *Light Years,* p. 137; June, 2008, Roxanne Myers Spencer, review of *High Dive,* p. 151; March, 2011, Eric Norton, review of *Kindred,* p. 171.

Voice of Youth Advocates, June, 2005, Abbe Goldberg, review of *Light Years,* p. 139; April, 2011, Leah Sparks, review of *Kindred,* p. 70.

ONLINE

Tammar Stein Home Page, http://www.tammarstein.com (March 2, 2012).

*   *   *

STUVE-BODEEN, Stephanie 1965-
(S.A. Bodeen)

Personal

Born 1965, in WI; married Tim Bodeen; children: Bailey, Tanzie. *Education:* University of Wisconsin, River Falls, B.S. (secondary education), 1988; Spalding University, M.F.A. (writing), 2003.

Addresses

Home—OR. *E-mail*—ssbodeen@yahoo.com.

Career

Teacher and children's book author. Peace Corps volunteer in Tanzania, East Africa, c. 1990; has taught junior- and senior-high school.

Awards, Honors

Ezra Jack Keats New Writer Award, Minnesota Book Award, Charlotte Zolotow Award Highly Commended designation, Bank Street College Children's Book of the Year selection, and American Library Association (ALA) Notable Book designation, all 1999, all for *Elizabeti's Doll;* Patterson Prize, Society of School Librarians International Honor Book designation, Bank Street College Outstanding Merit designation, and Parent's Choice Fiction Award, all 2001, all for *Mama Elizabeti;* Bank Street College Book of the Year designation, 2002, and Outstanding Achievement in Children's Literature selection, Wisconsin State Library Association, 2004, both for *Elizabeti's School;* Parent's Choice Recommended designation, 2003, and African Studies Association Children's Africana Book Award, Pennsylvania Young Reader's Choice Award finalist, and *Storyteller's World* Award, all 2004, all for *Babu's Song;* ALA Quick Picks for Reluctant Readers selection, and Bank Street College Children's Book of the Year designation, both 2009, both for *The Compound;* ALA Quick Picks for Reluctant Readers selection, and Bank Street College Children's Book of the Year designation, both 2011, both for *The Gardener;* Oregon Book Award finalist, and Peace Corps Writers' Award for Best Children's Writing, both 2011, both for *A Small Brown Dog with a Wet Pink Nose.*

Writings

PICTURE BOOKS

Elizabeti's Doll, illustrated by Christy Hale, Lee & Low (New York, NY), 1998.

We'll Paint the Octopus Red, illustrated by Pam De Vito, Woodbine House (Bethesda, MD), 1998.

Mama Elizabeti, illustrated by Christy Hale, Lee & Low (New York, NY), 2000.

Elizabeti's School, illustrated by Christy Hale, Lee & Low (New York, NY), 2002.

Babu's Song, illustrated by Aaron Boyd, Lee & Low (New York, NY), 2003.

The Best Worst Brother, illustrated by Charlotte Fremaux, Woodbine House (Bethesda, MD), 2005.

A Small Brown Dog with a Wet Pink Nose, illustrated by Linzie Hunter, Little, Brown (Boston, MA), 2006.

Also author of *A Home for Salty,* written for the Friends of San Pablo Bay National Wildlife Refuge. Contributor to anthologies, including *Memories of Sun: Stories of Africa and America,* HarperCollins (New York, NY), 2004.

Author's works have been translated into Spanish.

YOUNG-ADULT NOVELS

(As S.A. Bodeen) *The Compound,* Feiwel & Friends (New York, NY), 2008.

(As S.A. Bodeen) *The Gardener,* Feiwel & Friends (New York, NY), 2010.

Adaptations

The Compound was adapted for audiobook, Brilliance Audio, 2008.

Sidelights

Although Stephanie Stuve-Bodeen has always enjoyed writing, she did not concider making it a career until after her children were born. Raised on a dairy farm in Wisconsin, Stuve-Bodeen went to Tanzania as a Peace Corps volunteer after graduating from the University of Wisconsin—River Falls. Her experiences in Africa inspired the setting and characters for her first picture book, *Elizabeti's Doll,* as well as for other books that follow Stuve-Bodeen's likeable young protagonist: *Mama Elizabeti* and *Elizabeti's School.* In more-recent years she has also focused on older readers, producing the well-received young-adult novels *The Compound* and *The Gardener,* both published under her pen name S.A. Bodeen.

The idea for *Elizabeti's Doll* came from Stuve-Bodeen's experiences staying with a Tanzanian village family for a week during her Peace Corps stint. "I was in a mud hut with rats under my bed at night . . . ," she recalled to John Coyne for *PeaceCorpsWriters.org.* "I spent my days with the family's six kids and their entourage, who were extremely imaginative when it came to creating toys." Several years later, while at dinner with other former Peace Corps volunteers, a dining companion "mentioned a girl in her village with a rock for a doll. I remembered the same, and wrote the story at 3 a.m. the next day."

In *Elizabeti's Doll* Stuve-Bodeen describes a little girl's adjustment to the birth of a new baby brother, Obedi. Wanting a baby of her own to care for, Elizabeti finds a smooth, oblong rock that becomes her doll. Naming the "doll" Eva, Elizabeti bathes and feeds it, and ends up saving Eva from the cooking fire where her older sister inadvertently places it. *Elizabeti's Doll* drew warm praise for its unpretentiousness and its sensitivity to Tanzanian culture. A reviewer for *Publishers Weekly* hailed it as an "impressive debut" that is enhanced by "well-balanced prose" and a fittingly gentle tone. In *School Library Journal,* Martha Topol described Stuve-Bodeen's story as "a splendid celebration of life and the power of a child's imagination."

Elizabeti returns In *Mama Elizabeti* as the girl finds herself put in charge of younger brother Obedi after her mother gives birth to a new baby sister. Because of her experience caring for the rock doll Eva, Elizabeti hopes to fulfill her new role with ease, but squirmy, curious, and playful Obedi is a lot more difficult than Eva. Calling *Mama Elizabeti* "funny and tender," *Black Issues*

Christy Hale collaborates with author Stephanie Stuve-Bodeen on the picture book **Mama Elizabeti,** *part of a series about a young Tanzanian girl.* (Illustration copyright © 2000 by Christy Hale. Reproduced by permission of Lee & Low Books, Inc.)

Stuve-Bodeen introduces readers to a young girl living in an African village in her award-winning picture book Elizabeti's Doll, *featuring artwork by Christy Hale.* (Lee & Low Books, 1998. Illustration copyright © 1998 by Christy Hale. Reproduced by permission.)

Book Review contributor Khafre Abif added that Stuve-Bodeen's story is a good choice "for mothers hoping to spend some quality reading time with their daughters."

Elizabeti's School finds the young girl leaving her brother behind for her first day at school. With neatly braided hair, new shoes, and a new uniform, she is excited to follow her older sister, Pendo, to school, until she reaches the schoolyard and anxiety sets in. Noting that the book "distills the essence of the school experience" and "first-day jitter," a *Kirkus Reviews* contributor praised Stuve-Bodeen for allowing North American readers a "winning peek at a life that's different but the same." As with the other "Elizabeti" books, *Elizabeti's School* depicts a "family life . . . rich in love and warmth," according to Lynda Ritterman, the *School Library Journal* critic recommending Stuve-Bodeen's picture book as "the perfect story for sharing with young children."

In *Babu's Song* Stuve-Bodeen introduces readers to an elderly mute Tanzanian toymaker who makes a music box for his grandson, Bernardi. When the boy sells his grandfather's gift at market in the hopes of buying a soccer ball with the proceeds, confessing his action to Babu results in a wise outcome that allows Bernardi to follow his dreams. Praising *Babu's Song* in *School Library Journal,* Luann Toth added that Stuve-Bodeen tells her story "with economy of language but with heaps of feeling," while a *Publishers Weekly* reviewer wrote that "the rapport between grandfather and grandson emerges as genuinely heartwarming."

Stuve-Bodeen also explores sensitive topics in *We'll Paint the Octopus Red* and *The Best Worst Brother,* both which focus on a child with Down syndrome. She

tells *We'll Paint the Octopus Red* through the eyes of Emma, who is nervous about having a younger sibling until her father helps her imagine all the fun she will have with the new baby. When Isaac is born with Down syndrome, Emma learns that, although her new brother will be able to play with her as she had hoped, he will do things more slowly. Illustrated by Charlotte Fremaux, *The Best Worst Brother* finds both children older: Isaac is now a toddler and Emma is in elementary school. Although Emma is frustrated by her brother's inability to learn words and clumsiness, her persistent efforts to teach the little boy eventually yield a heartening success.

In *School Library Journal* Lisa Gangemi Kropp described *We'll Paint the Octopus Red* as a thoughtful and appropriate choice for young readers. "The fine text gets right to a child's level of understanding," wrote Ilene Cooper in her *Booklist* review, the critic adding that Stuve-Bodeen sidesteps complex issues that children will not understand. Appraising *The Best Worst Brother,* Robyn Walker noted in *School Library Journal* that this picture-book sequel features "softly colorful" illustrations by Freemaux that allow the "simple" text "with a fairly wide audience."

Stuve-Bodeen addresses the universal childhood crusade of being allowed to have a pet in *A Small Brown Dog with a Wet Pink Nose.* Featuring colorful digital artwork by Linzie Hunter, the story follows Amelia as she overdramatizes her need for a puppy. Rather than the usual strategy of begging, pleading, and nagging, however, Amelia develops an unique way to win over her parents: create an endearing—and well-behaved—pretend pup named Bones and make him a part of the family. When the imaginary Bones runs away, the girl's parents join her in the search, and readers are not surprised when their search leads to a real-life puppy. "Amelia is an endearing character," wrote *School Library Journal* contributor Donna Cardon, and the "cheery" retro-styled illustrations by Hunter "perfectly match Stuve-Bodeen's text." "Rarely have children been offered such a devious strategy for landing a mutt," observed *Booklist* contributor Daniel Kraus, and a *Publishers Weekly* contributor predicted that "young readers will enjoy participating in [Amelia's] . . . success" in achieving her goal.

Stuve-Bodeen's first novel for older readers, *The Compound,* also marks her move into science fiction. In the story, nine-year-old Eli was only three when his family moved into an underground bunker in response to news of an imminent nuclear attack. The underground dwelling is almost a duplicate of the wealthy family's above-ground mansion, and life has been fairly comfortable. However, the compound has resources to sustain the family for only so long, and time is running out. Worried about returning above ground, Eli also wonders about his parents' choices, especially as the stresses of living together in a confined space begin to take their toll on the family's sanity.

Characterizing *The Compound* as "a true edge-of-the-seat thriller," Dylan Thomarie added in *School Library Journal* that Stuve-Bodeen's story touches on "social issues . . . that could lead to great classroom discussions," while *Horn Book* contributor Claire E. Gross wrote that the "unique premise" of the novel produces a "tense portrait of a family in crisis [that] probes the psychological and moral costs of survival."

Another child faces his worries about survival in *The Gardener,* which introduces a boy named Mason. Mason has been raised by his single mom and spends much of his time at the nursing home where she works. Because his face was disfigured by a dog bite years before, he is an outsider at school, but at the nursing home he is drawn into a friendship with Laila, a pretty young patient who has recently awakened from a coma. Although Laila is confused, she is clearly afraid of someone at the home, and the strange scars on her back signal to Mason that something is indeed wrong. As he investigates, the boy discovers a connection to Trodyn Industries, where his mother once worked and now reviles. He soon discovers that Laila is part of an experiment by Trodyn to transform children into autotrophs—beings that can live without food or drink—and she is not the only person at the nursing home who is afraid of someon known only as The Gardener.

"Bodeen leads her characters through intricate mazes of conflict created when good intentions and scientific knowledge run amok," wrote *Journal of Adolescent & Adult Literacy* contributor Theo Massey in reviewing *The Gardener,* and she leaves readers "with endless questions about the choices" they will "face as science and technology continue to open doors that, once opened, can never be closed again." Hayden Mass predicted in *School Library Journal* that *The Gardener* will have appeal to reluctant readers as well as sci-fi fans due to its "likeable protagonist and . . . juicy premise."

Biographical and Critical Sources

PERIODICALS

Black Issues Book Review, July, 2000, Khafre Abif, review of *Mama Elizabeti,* p. 74.

Booklist, September 15, 1998, Ilene Cooper, review of *We'll Paint the Octopus Red;* August, 2000, Connie Fletcher, review of *Mama Elizabeti,* p. 2150; February 15, 2001, Henrietta M. Smith, review of *Elizabeti's Doll,* p. 1161; June 1, 2003, Gillian Engberg, review of *Babu's Song,* p. 1788; December 1, 2009, Daniel Kraus, review of *A Small Brown Dog with a Wet Pink Nose,* p. 53.

Horn Book, July, 2000, Martha V. Parravano, review of *Mama Elizabeti,* p. 448; November-December, 2002,

Aaron Boyd creates the artwork for Stephanie Stuve-Bodeen's warm-hearted picture book **Babu's Song.** (Lee & Low Books, 2003. Illustration copyright © 2003 by Aaron Boyd. Reproduced by permission.)

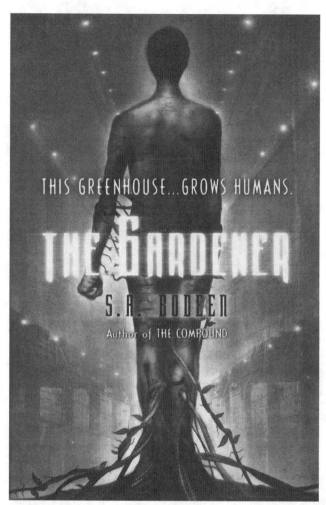

Cover of Stuve-Bodeen's young-adult science-fiction novel **The Gardener.** (Jacket cover art © 2010 by Matt Mahurin. Reproduced by permission of Feiwel & Friends, an imprint of St. Martin's Press.)

Martha V. Parravano, review of *Elizabeti's School*, p. 741; May-June, 2008, Claire E. Gross, review of *The Compound*, p. 307.

Journal of Adolescent & Adult Literacy, February, 2011, Theo Massey, review of *The Gardener,* p. 384.

Kirkus Reviews, August 15, 2002, review of *Elizabeti's School,* p. 1237; April 15, 2003, review of *Babu's Song,* p. 612; December 1, 2009, review of *A Small Brown Dog with a Wet Pink Nose.*

Publishers Weekly, March 17, 2003, review of *Babu's Song,* p. 75; December 7, 2009, review of *A Small Brown Dog with a Wet Pink Nose,* p. 46.

School Library Journal, September 1998, Martha Topol, review of *Elizabeti's Doll,* pp. 183-184; December 1998, Lisa Gangemi Kropp, review of *We'll Paint the Octopus Red,* p. 92; July, 2000, Martha Topol, review of *Mama Elizabeti,* p. 88; September, 2002, Lynda Ritterman, review of *Elizabeti's School,* p. 206; December, 2003, Luann Toth, review of *Babu's Song,* p. 128; July, 2004, Lisa G. Kropp, review of *Elizabeti's School,* p. 45; September, 2005, Robyn Walker, review of *The Best Worst Brother,* p. 187; July, 2008, Dylan Thomarie, review of *The Compound,* p. 94; January, 2010, Donna Cardon, review of *A Small*

Brown Dog with a Wet Pink Nose, p. 82; June, 2010, Hayden Bass, review of *The Gardener,* p. 94.

ONLINE

PeaceCorpsWriters.org, http://www.peacecorpswriters.org/ (January 9, 2001), John Coyne, interview with Stuve-Bodeen.

Stephanie Stuve-Bodeen Home Page, http://www.rockfora doll.com (March 1, 2012).

Stephanie Stuve-Bodeen Web log, http://latteya.livejournal. com (March 1, 2012).*

*   *   *

SYLVESTER, Kevin

Personal

Born in Youngstown, NY; married; wife's name Laura; children: Erin, Emily. *Education:* University of Toronto, B.A. (philosophy and English; Latin minor); graduate work at Ontario College of Art and Design.

Addresses

Home—Toronto, Ontario, Canada. *E-mail*—sylvester artwork@gmail.com.

Career

Author-illustrator and broadcaster. Canadian Broadcasting Corporation Radio, host of "Morning Sports," 1999-2006; guest on radio programs, including *Inside Track, Q, Sounds like Canada, Sunday Edition,* and *The Current.* Producer of radio documentaries.

Awards, Honors

Stephen Leacock Award for Humor nomination, 2002, for *Shadrin Has Scored for Russia;* Silver Birch Award Honor selection, Ontario Library Association, 2006, and Rocky Mountain Award Honor selection, 2007, both for *Sports Hall of Weird;* Silver Birch Award, 2009, for *Gold Medal for Weird;* Silver Birch Award for Fiction, 2011, for *Neil Flambé and the Marco Polo Murders,* and nomination, 2012, for *Neil Flambé and the Aztec Abduction;* Silver Birch Award for Nonfiction nomination, 2012, for *Game Day;* Hackmatack Children's Choice Award shortlist, 2011, and Silver Birch Award shortlist, 2012, both for *Don't Touch That Toad, and Other Strange Things Adults Tell You* by Catherine Rodina.

Writings

(Self-illustrated) *Shadrin Has Scored for Russia: The Day Canadian Hockey Died: A Mockumentary,* Stoddart (Toronto, Ontario, Canada), 2001.

(Self-illustrated) *Sports Hall of Weird,* Kids Can Press (Toronto, Ontario, Canada), 2005.

(Self-illustrated) *Gold Medal for Weird,* Kids Can Press (Toronto, Ontario, Canada), 2007.

Game Day: Meet the People Who Make It Happen, Annick Press (Toronto, Ontario, Canada), 2010.

(Self-illustrated) *Splinters,* Tundra Books of Northern New York (Plattsburgh, NY), 2010.

"NEIL FLAMBÉ" MIDDLE-GRADE NOVEL SERIES; SELF-ILLUSTRATED

Neil Flambé and the Marco Polo Murders, Key Porter Books (Toronto, Ontario, Canada), 2010.

Neil Flambé and the Aztec Abduction, Key Porter Books (Toronto, Ontario, Canada), 2010.

Neil Flambé and the Crusader's Curse, Key Porter Books (Toronto, Ontario, Canada), 2012.

Neil Flambé and the Tokyo Treasure, Key Porter Books (Toronto, Ontario, Canada), 2012.

ILLUSTRATOR

Catherine Rodina, *Don't Touch That Toad, and Other Strange Things Adults Tell You,* Kids Can Press (Toronto, Ontario, Canada), 2010.

Carol-Ann Hoyte and Heidi Bee Roemer, editors, *And the Crowd Goes Wild! A Global Gathering of Sports Poems,* 2012.

Contributor to periodicals, including *Literary Review of Canada.*

Sidelights

With his bachelor's degree in philosophy and English, Kevin Sylvester may seem like an unlikely candidate for a career as a sportscaster. However, the Canadian writer was a popular broadcaster on Canada's CBC Radio for almost a decade, covering national competitions as well as many Olympic games. Sylvester's first published book, the self-illustrated *Shadrin Has Scored for Russia: The Day Canadian Hockey Died: A Mockumen-*

Sportscaster Kevin Sylvester turns his creative talent to picture-book creation in stories such as **Splinters.** (Copyright © 2010 by Kevin Sylvester. Reproduced by permission of Tundra Books.)

tary, had its start as a radio play in which he made fun of Canada's 1972 Summit Series win against the USSR. In the years since, Sylvester has developed a new creative niche, writing for younger readers and also illustrating his own stories. He entertains middle-grade readers in his "Neil Flambé" mystery series, which is based on a character he created for radio, and his self-illustrated picture book *Splinters,* which tells a sports-related story with roots in a popular fairy tale.

Sylvester's "Neil Flambé" novels begin with *Neil Flambé and the Marco Polo Murders,* which introduces an overly self-confident fourteen-year-old amateur sleuth with a highly honed sense of smell. Neil's off-putting air of self-importance comes from the fact that he also a top chef who keeps the staff at his Vancouver restaurant busy turning away diners without reservations. When several local chefs begin turning up dead it seems prudent for the teen to start investigating. Along with each murdered chef, a strange smell lingers, and the killer leaves a note, written in Italian, that references fourteenth-century explorer Marco Polo. The longer the killing spree continues, the more those chefs still standing are suspected of murder. "As pressure mounts for Neil, readers will hope this insufferable young chef is innocent," predicted a *Publishers Weekly* contributor," and in *School Library Journal* Julie Shatterly praised *Neil Flambé and the Marco Polo Murders* as "an engaging and lively read" featuring "an interesting teen" as its central character. Sylvester's young hero "is cocky without being completely obnoxious," maintained *Resource Links* contributor Roseanne Gauthier, the reviewer adding that the book's "writing and line drawings are clever and full of life."

Readers find Neil in Mexico City in *Neil Flambé and the Aztec Abduction,* as his efforts to win a two-week-long cooking competition take a back seat to the kidnapping of girlfriend Isabella Tortellini leads to threats of worse unless he throws the contest. Neil seems to have lost his culinary golden thumb in *Neil Flambé and the Crusader's Curse,* as customers begin to grumble and critics start to dish out complaints rather than serving up praise in their reviews of his formerly popular restaurant. Noting that Sylvester's "sketches . . . add spice, interest and enjoyment to each page" of *Neil Flambé and the Aztec Abduction,* Mary Thomas added in her *Canadian Review of Materials* appraisal that the second "Neil Flambé" novel keeps the series on an even keel by providing a "goofy, mystery plot, . . . fad-food tie-ins, . . . [and] feuding chefs."

In *Splinters* Sylvester turns to younger readers in his story of a little girl who dreams of only one thing. For Cindy Winters, the goal of life is to play ice hockey, but her family is too poor to afford her entry into a local hockey league. The determined girl takes a series of odd jobs to save up the money needed, but once a member she is kept from the playing field by the coach's jealous daughters, the Blister sisters. From her spot on the bench, Cindy watches each practice, earning her

titular nickname in the process. Finally, a visit from Charmaine Prince, who is hosting try-outs for the regional All-Star Hockey Team, inspires Cindy to track down her fairy goaltender, sharpen her blades, and achieve her stick-wielding destiny.

Predicting that *Splinters* "may become a Canadian classic" due to its engaging story about the nation's most-popular sport, Suzanne Pierson added in her *Canadian Review of Materials* review that Sylvester's self-illustrated story features "playful watercolour and pencil" art that adds "just the right amount of detail to support the story line for young readers." The author's "puckish . . . take on the Cinderella story is reflected in [the] squiggly, exaggerated" lines of his art, quipped a *Kirkus Reviews* writer, and Daniel Kraus noted in *Booklist* that the "expressive faces" of Cindy and her fellow characters "are nimble enough to keep up with the" fast-moving story in *Splinters.* Also praising the illustrations as "spot-on," Catherine Callegari concluded in *School Library Journal* that Sylvester's story "meets its goal in being clever," and in *Quill & Quire* Megan McChesney deemed the art in *Splinters* to be as "charming, vibrant, and full of emotion."

Sylvester draws on his knowledge of professional sports in his nonfiction books *Sports Hall of Weird* and *Gold Medal for Weird,* both which collect unheralded but fascinating moments that have been edited out of the résumés of golfers, hockey players, soccer players, and other professional athletes as well as fans and others in the sporting game. From mid-game fêtes of heroism and off-kilter competitions to haunted sports stadiums and a team roster listing the recently deceased to the over-the-top antics of rabid fans: all this and more are chronicled in Sylvester's humorous prose. Reviewing *Gold Medal for Weird,* Gail Lennon noted in *Resource Links* that the book presents "a fountain of facts" which are "humorously illustrated with Sylvester's cartoons," and *Quill & Quire* critic Paul Challen dubbed *Sports Hall of Weird* "a delightful . . . package that will tweak that love of the strange that many young readers develop along with their fondness for sports."

Another sports-related book, *Game Day,* allows readers to go behind the scenes and learn about twenty unusual jobs that are based around the world of professional athletic competition. Writing that Sylvester's goal in this book is to show that "people off the field are just as much superstars as those playing on it," Matthew Weaver dubbed *Game Day* a "nifty collection" of stories in his *Voice of Youth Advocates* review. Praising the same work in *Booklist,* John Peters wrote that Sylvester shows that "the choice of occupations are diverse and quirky enough to intrigue career-minded teens," while *School Library Journal* critic Kim Dare noted of *Game Day* that the author "imparts some solid tidbits of advice in his chatty, conversational narrative."

Biographical and Critical Sources

PERIODICALS

Booklist, September 1, 2010, Daniel Kraus, review of *Splinters,* p. 120; February 1, 2011, John Peters, review of *Game Day: Meet the People Who Make It Happen,* p. 64.

Canadian Review of Materials, June 18, 2010, Suzanne Pierson, review of *Splinters;* November 18, 2010, Dave Jenkinson, review of *Game Day;* November 26, 2010, review of *Neil Flambé and the Aztec Abduction.*

Kirkus Reviews, August 1, 2010, review of *Splinters.*

Publishers Weekly, March 15, 2010, review of *Neil Flambé and the Marco Polo Murders,* p. 55.

Quill & Quire, February, 2005, Paul Challen, review of *Sports Hall of Weird;* September, 2010, Megan Mc-Chesney, review of *Splinters.*

Resource Links, June, 2005, Eva Wilson, review of *Sports Hall of Weird,* p. 28; October, 2007, Gail Lennon, review of *Gold Medal for Weird,* p. 25; February, 2010, Roseanne Gauthier, review of *Neil Flambé and the Marco Polo Murders,* p. 13.

School Library Journal, April, 2010, Julie Shatterly, review of *Neil Flambé and the Marco Polo Murders,* p. 169; September, 2010, Catherine Callegari, review of *Splinters,* p. 134; January, 2011, Kim Dare, review of *Game Day,* p. 130.

Voice of Youth Advocates, December, 2010, Matthew Weaver, review of *Game Day,* p. 483.

ONLINE

Canadian Broadcasting Corporation Web site, http://www.cba.ca/ (March 3, 2012), "Kevin Sylvester."

Kevin Sylvester Web log, http://kevinarts.blogspot.com (March 3, 2012).*

T-V

TOBIA, Lauren

Personal

Born in Bristol, England; married; children: two daughters. *Education:* University of the West of England, B.A. (illustration; with honours), 2006.

Addresses

Home—Southville, Bristol, England. *Agent*—Mandy Suhr, Miles Stott Children's Literary Agency, Pembrokeshire, England. *E-mail*—look@laurentobia.com.

Career

Illustrator and graphic designer. Formerly worked as an intensive-care nurse.

Member

Illustrator's Guild, Society of Children's Book Writers and Illustrators.

Awards, Honors

Branford Boase Award, 2008, for *Good Luck, Anna Hibiscus!* by Atinuke; CYBILS Literary Award in Early Chapter-Book category, 2011, for *Have Fun, Anna Hibiscus!* by Atinuke; Sheffield Children's Book Award shortlist, 2012, for *Anna Hibiscus' Song* by Atinuke.

Illustrator

Atinuke, *Anna Hibiscus,* Walker Books (London, England), 2007.

Jull Atkinsand, *Yasmin's Parcels,* Evans (London, England), 2008.

Atinuka, *Hooray for Anna Hibiscus!,* Walker Books (London, England), 2008.

Franzeska G. Ewart, *A Heart for Ruby,* Walker Books (London, England), 2009.

Pippa Goodhart, *Happy Butterfly,* Franklin Watts (London, England), 2009.

Lauren Tobia (Reproduced by permission.)

Anituke, *Good Luck, Anna Hibiscus!,* Walker Books (London, England), 2009, Kane/Miller (La Jolla, CA), 2011.

Anituke, *Anna Hibiscus' Song,* Kane Miller (La Jolla, CA), 2011.

Anituke, *Have Fun, Anna Hibiscus!,* Walker Books (London, England), 2010, Kane/Miller (La Jolla, CA), 2011.

Michelle Robertson, *How to Find a Fruit Bat,* Orchard Books (London, England), 2012.

Anituke, *Welcome Home, Anna Hibiscus!,* Walker Books (London, England), 2012.

Sidelights

A former nurse, Lauren Tobia decided to pursue her lifelong dream of becoming an illustrator after raising her two daughters. In 2006 Tobia graduated from the University of the West of England with an honors degree in illustration. Quickly attracting the interest of Walker Books, she began her multi-book collaboration with Nigeria-born author Atinuke on the "Anna Hibiscus" books, which include *Anna Hibiscus, Good Luck, Anna Hibiscus!, Hooray for Anna Hibiscus!, Have Fun, Anna Hibiscus!,* and *Welcome Home, Anna Hibiscus!* Anna's exploits can also be enjoyed by younger readers in the picture book *Anna Hibiscus' Song.*

In *Anna Hibiscus* beginning readers meet a little girl who lives in amazing West Africa with her twin baby brothers, her father, and her Canadian-born mother. Supported by friends and her father's extended family, Anna is allowed to follow where whimsy and curiosity take her. In each of Atinuke's books the author shares several vignettes from the little girl's fun-filled life, from visiting the seaside and enjoying a family party to starting her first entrepreneurial venture as an orange seller. *Good Luck, Anna Hibiscus!* and *Have Fun, Anna Hibiscus!* both follow Anna's preparation for traveling away from home as well as her long trip to North America, where she spends the Christmas holiday with Granny Canada and her dog Qimmac, while *Hooray for Anna Hibiscus!* collects four stories about the girl's day-to-day adventures with her loving African family. "A lovely, rare bird of a series," according to *School Library Journal* contributor Nicole Waskie-Laura, the "Anna Hibiscus" books "provid[e] . . . a modern view of another culture in warm, approachable language."

"Tobia . . . knows how to really bring these stories to life," wrote Elizabeth Bird in her *School Library Journal* Web log review of Atinuke's first two "Anna Hibiscus" stories. "Every character in these books looks exactly right," and "Anna herself is charming." "With just a few swipes of the pen," added Bird, the illustrator "can conjure up a situation fraught with stress or the nicest, homiest family scene. If kids start yearning to belong to a gigantic fun family like the one Anna Hibiscus belongs to, at least some of the credit is going to have to go to Lauren Tobia for capturing this idyllic community." Also praising the illustrator, a *Publishers Weekly* contributor wrote that the books' art "accentuates Anna Hibiscus's outsized personality and loving report with her family," and *Horn Book* contributor Robin L. Smith asserted that the books' "detailed illustrations add depth and energy to the stories" and appeal to Atinuke's intended audience of beginning readers.

Biographical and Critical Sources

PERIODICALS

Guardian (London, England), March 1, 2008, Julia Eccleshare, review of *Anna Hibiscus,* p. 20.
Horn Book, May-June, 2011, Robin L. Smith, reviews of *Good Luck, Anna Hibiscus!* and *Have Fun, Anna Hibiscus!,* both p. 80.

Publishers Weekly, August 8, 2011, review of *Anna Hibiscus' Song,* p. 44.
School Library Journal, August, 2011, Nicole Waskie-Laura, reviews of *Good Luck, Anna Hibiscus!* and *Have Fun, Anna Hibiscus!,* both p. 67.

ONLINE

Lauren Tobia Home Page, http://laurentobia.com (March 8, 2012).
Miles Stott Children's Literary Agency Web site, http://http://www.milestottagency.co.uk/ (March 1, 2012), "Lauren Tobia."
School Library Journal Web log, http://blog.schoollibrary journal.com/afuse8production/ (August 11, 2010), Elizabeth Bird, reviews of both *Anna Hibiscus* and *Horray for Anna Hibiscus!*
Walker Books Web site, http://www.walker.co.uk/ (March 1, 2012), "Lauren Tobia."

*   *   *

TOWNSEND, Kari Lee 1968-
(Kari Lee Harmon)

Personal

Born 1968, on a U.S. military base in Portugal; father in the U.S. Air Force; married Brian Townsend (a pharmaceutical specialty sales rep); children: Brandon, Joshua, Matthew, Emily. *Education:* Attended Jefferson Community College (NY), Champlain Community College, and State University of New York (SUNY) Plattsburgh; SUNY Albany, B.A. (English education); SUNY Oswego, M.A. (English education). *Hobbies and other interests:* Reading, travel, photography.

Addresses

Home—New York. *Agent*—Christine Witthohn, Book Cents Literary Agency; cw@bookcentsliteraryagency.com. *E-mail*—karileetownsend@gmail.com.

Career

Author and editor. Former substitute teacher; freelance editor, beginning 2008.

Awards, Honors

Golden Duck Award nomination for Excellence in Children's Literature, 2010, for *Talk to the Hand;* Best Amateur Sleuth award nomination, *Romantic Times,* and Agatha Award nomination for Best First Mystery, both 2011, both for *Tempest in the Tea Leaves.*

Writings

"DIGITAL DIVA/SAMANTHA GRANGER EXPERIMENT" NOVEL SERIES; FOR YOUNG ADULTS

Fused, Sourcebooks Jabberwocky (Naperville, IL), 2010 published in e-book edition as *Talk to the Hand,* The Story Vault, 2012.

Rise of the Phenoteens (e-novel), The Story Vault, 2011.
Let Freedom Ring (e-novel), The Story Vault, 2011.

"FORTUNE TELLER MYSTERY" NOVEL SERIES

Tempest in the Tea Leaves, Berkley (New York, NY), 2011.
Corpse in the Crystal Ball, Berkley (New York, NY), 2012.
Trouble in the Tarot, Berkley (New York, NY), 2013.

OTHER

(Under name Kari Lee Harmon) *Destiny Wears Spurs* (e-book; for adults), The Story Vault, 2012.
Project Produce (e-book; for adults), The Story Vault, 2012.

Author of *Sleeping in the Middle*.

Sidelights

"Writing is hard!," Kari Lee Townsend told *SATA*, in sharing her experiences as a published writer. "Breaking into this business is even harder. 'Blah, blah, blah,' you say. 'What does she know? She's already published. She's already living her dream.'

"I'm here to tell you I do know what it feels like to be rejected, but I also know what it takes to succeed. A lot of hard work, perseverance, and determination. I truly believe the only people who will never achieve their dreams are those who give up. You can succeed but only if you want it badly enough.

"It took me fourteen years to sell my first manuscript, three of which were with an agent. I felt like giving up plenty of times, but I never did, thankfully. My agent landed me two three-book deals in two different genres at two different houses just five months apart. Sounds like Cinderella, I know, and in a way it is. Cinderella had to work her butt off until she finally got everything she ever dreamed of. You can, too.

"Many people assume if an editor likes your work, they can simply say yes and buy your book. Often times that editor has to get at least one yes from some other person, but many times, they have to get a yes from an entire committee. Buying a book is not that simple, and the average person doesn't realize all an editor has to go through to get the go-ahead to make an offer. That editor can love your voice and writing style, but if the publisher doesn't have a need for a book of that nature in their lineup, or already has something similar, or hasn't had good luck in the past with that subject matter then chances are, the answer is going to be no even if they adore the author.

"I can't tell you how many times over the years editors have loved my voice, writing style, etc, but couldn't buy my book. I used to be so upset and wallow in self-pity, thinking I must not be any good. They kept asking, 'what else do you have?,' but I wasn't listening. I just kept saying, 'Well, nothing, really.' My light-bulb moment came when I finally realized they did like me, they just couldn't use what I had. So I thought why not come up with something they actually could use instead of simply writing whatever I wanted. This is a business, after all, and you have to be aware of what's going on in it if you're ever going to make it.

"First, look at all aspects of the dream you're interested in. Think about trying something new. You never know what you might like until you give it a try. I write funny and I love a bit of romance and I always have some form of mystery anyway, so writing action adventure 'tween stories and adult cozy mysteries turned out to be perfect for me. I still write funny, I still have romance, and I still have plenty of mystery. The point is don't be afraid to put yourself out there and play around. See what fits.

"Next, make sure you do your homework. I'm not saying follow a trend. I'm just saying be aware of them. For example, with my cozy mysteries, I looked to see what was selling. I noticed some really fun, light paranormal themes, cooking themes, and craft themes that did really well. I chose the paranormal because that interested me. So then I took a close look at what the publisher already had on their list and what they didn't. Then I made a list of paranormal themes I might like to try. Finally, I came up with three blurbs and asked my agent which one she thought was the strongest. She actually ran them by the editor who loved my work but had asked what else does she have, and the editor chose the one she wanted to see the most. So I wrote a proposal specifically for her, and low and behold, she bought the first three books!

"If I had done what I normally did and stopped at 'Well, I don't have anything, really,' then I never would have sold. Instead, I put myself out there and came up with something. Editors are human, too. They want to say yes. They just sometimes need a little help on our end. So tell me, are you willing to go after your dreams? Are you willing to put yourself out there and try something new? I say go for it. Anything is possible if you're willing to put in the work. Good luck to you!"

Biographical and Critical Sources

PERIODICALS

Kirkus Reviews, October 15, 2010, review of *Fused.*
New York Journal of Books, November 1, 2010, review of *Fused.*
Romantic Times, August, 2011, review of *Tempest in the Tea Leaves..*

ONLINE

Kari Lee Townsend Group Mystery Web log, http://www.mysteriesand margtaritas.blogspot.com (January 28, 2012).

Kari Lee Townsend Home Page, http://www.karilee
townsend.com (January 28, 2012).

*   *   *

VERNON, Ursula

Personal
Daughter of an artist. *Education:* Macalester College,
degree (anthropology). *Hobbies and other interests:*
Birdwatching, iaido.

Addresses
Home—Cary, NC.

Career
Author and illustrator. Creator of art for card game
Reiner Knizia's Black Sheep.

Awards, Honors
Webcomics Choice Award for Outstanding Black-and-
White Art, 2005, 2006, and for Outstanding Anthropo-
morphic Comic, 2006; Will Eisner Comics Industry
Award nomination for Talent Deserving of Wider Rec-
ognition, 2006, for *Digger.*

Writings

Black Dogs: The House of Diamond (middle-grade novel),
   illustrated by Chris Goodwin, Sofawolf Press (St.
   Paul, MN), 2007.

SELF-ILLUSTRATED

It Made Sense at the Time . . . : Selected Sketches, Sofawolf Press (St. Paul, MN), 2004.
Digger (anthology; originally published at *Diggercomic.
   com*), ongoing volumes, Sofawolf Press (St. Paul,
   MN), beginning 2005.
*Nurk: The Strange, Surprising Adventures of a (Some-
   what) Brave Shrew,* Harcourt (Orlando, FL), 2008.

*SELF-ILLUSTRATED; "DRAGONBREATH" CHAPTER-BOOK
SERIES*

Dragonbreath, Ahoy!, Dial Books (New York, NY), 2009.
Attack of the Ninja Frogs, Dial Books for Young Readers
   (New York, NY), 2010.
Curse of the Were-Wiener, Dial Books (New York, NY),
   2010.
Lair of the Bat Monster, Dial Books for Young Readers
   (New York, NY), 2011.
No Such Thing as Ghosts, Dial Books for Young Readers
   (New York, NY), 2011.

Revenge of the Horned Bunnies, Dial Books for Young
   Readers (New York, NY), 2012.

Creator of comics, including "Irrational Fears" and
"Little Creatures."

Adaptations
*Nurk: The Strange, Surprising Adventures of a (Some-
what) Brave Shrew* was adapted for audiobook, ready
by Bill Knowlton, Full Cast Audio, 2009.

Sidelights
Award-winning comics artist Ursula Vernon is the author of the Web comic "Digger," the story of a wombat
trapped in a strange land. In addition to continuing to
expand the story in "Digger," Vernon has produced several other Web comics and has also gained fans through
her middle-grade fantasy *Black Dogs: The House of
Diamond.* Her characteristic mix of a whimsical story
and humorous cartoon characters also entrances young
readers in her "Dragonbreath" series of chapter books,

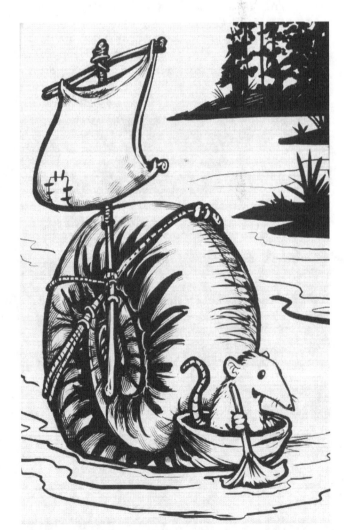

*Cartoonist Ursula Vernon entertains picture-book readers with her
whimsical* **Nurk,** *the story of an adventurous shrew.* (Copyright © 2008 by
Ursula Vernon. Reproduced by permission of Houghton Mifflin Harcourt Publishing
Company. All rights reserved.)

and she shares a quirky tale about a young rodent whose life changes after a daring rescue in *Nurk: The Strange, Surprising Adventures of a (Somewhat) Brave Shrew.*

In "Digger" Vernon's furry hero assembles an unusual selection of friends that includes a talking statue, a prophetic slug, a lonely hyena, and a mysterious shadow creature, all which help the young wombat find her way back to her home. Originally published twice weekly on the *Graphic Smash* Webcomic site and now available on *DiggerComic.com,* "Digger" has earned Vernon the loyal fan base that led to publication of a multi-volume print anthology collecting the wombat's adventures.

Dragonbreath, Ahoy! starts off Vernon's popular "Dragonbreath" chapter-book saga, which mixes comic-book panels and a straightforward narrative text. Danny Dragonbreath is the only dragon attending classes at the Herpitax-Phibbias School for Reptiles and Amphibians. He worries that, because of his differences, he may not live up to the expectations of his classmates, especially when they ask him to act like a traditional dragon and breathe fire. A visit to an ocean-dwelling relative and an attack by a giant squid inspire Danny to use his dragon abilities, although fire-breathing does not prove to be the best defense under water. Reviewing *Dragonbreath, Ahoy!,* Tina Martin noted in *School Library Journal* that "the exchanges between the . . . nervous Wendell

Vernon creates a saga of multi-species friendship and adventure in her self-illustrated "Dragonbreath" saga, which includes **Curse of the Were-Weiner.** (Copyright © 2010 by Ursula Vernon. Reproduced by permission of Dial Books for Young Readers, a division of Penguin Group (USA), Inc.)

and nonchalant Danny make this a laugh-out-loud read." "Young readers will sympathize with Danny," wrote Kat Kan in her *Booklist* review of the "Dragonbreath" series opener, and a *Kirkus Reviews* writer predicted that "Danny D's first outing will leave readers in stitches—and on tenderhooks—waiting for the next one."

Vernon continues her "Dragonbreath" series in *Attack of the Ninja Frogs,* as Danny and nerdy iguana friend Wendell team up with a foreign-exchange student named Suki the salamander to save her from an attack of sword-wielding amphibians and ultimately end up in the bamboo forests of Japan. A *Kirkus Reviews* critic described *Attack of the Ninja Frogs* as a "hilarious weave of smart-alecky prose and two-toned" comic-book-style cartoon art.

Curse of the Were-Wiener finds Danny and Wendell faced with a particularly awful lunch in the school cafeteria, while *Lair of the Bat Monster* follows their trip south to the Mexican home of Danny's feathered-lizard relative, a trip that turns dramatic and requires Wendell to be a hero. In *No Such Thing as Ghosts* readers can follow along as the two friends experience some surprising Halloween adventures, while *Revenge of the Horned Bunnies* finds Danny and Wendell at summer camp where they join Christiana and Danny's cousin Spencer in a battle against some quite un-cuddly flop-eared creatures.

"School lunch bites—literally—in the third impossibly droll escapade" in the "Dragonbreath" series, wrote a *Kirkus Reviews* writer in a review of *Curse of the Were-Weiner,* while in *Booklist* Kan reassured parents that Vernon's *No Such Things as Ghosts* "is just spooky enough for young readers." "More charged up than daunted by encounters in previous episodes," Danny Dragonbreath faces off against another entertaining adventure in *Revenge of the Horned Bunnies,* surviving his latest foe with the help of "nerdy sidekick Wendell," according to a *Kirkus Reviews* writer.

In *Black Dogs* Vernon introduces a young woman named Lyra, who resolves to revenge the massacre of her parents. Along the way, Lyra falls in with Sadrao, a soldier from Khamir, as well as with two elves and a half-blood wizard. Together with her band, she joins the defenders of the elven nation of Anu'tintavel in their battle against a powerful wizard. Reviewing *Black Dogs* in *Library Journal,* Jackie Cassada recommended the book for its mix of "political and social intrigue as well as [for] the adventurous swordplay."

Biographical and Critical Sources

PERIODICALS

Booklist, May 15, 2009, Kat Kan, review of *Dragonbreath, Ahoy!,* p. 55; October 15, 2010, Kat Kan, review of *Curse of the Were-Wiener,* p. 52.

Bulletin of the Center for Children's Books, September, 2009, Hope Morrison, review of *Dragonbreath, Ahoy!,* p. 43.

Kirkus Reviews, May 1, 2008, review of *Nurk: The Strange, Surprising Adventures of a (Somewhat) Brave Shrew;* December 15, 2009, review of *Attack of the Ninja Frogs;* July 15, 2010, review of *Curse of the Were-Weiner;* January 15, 2011, review of *Lair of the Bat Monster;* July 15, 2011, review of *No Such Things as Ghosts.*

Library Journal, December 1, 2006, Jackie Cassada, review of *Black Dogs: The House of Diamond,* p. 115.

School Library Journal, August, 2008, Tim Wadham, review of *Nurk,* p. 104; January, 2010, Tina Martin, review of *Dragonbreath, Ahoy!,* p. 82; July, 2010, Nancy D. Tolson, review of *Attack of the Ninja Frogs,* p. 71.

ONLINE

Digger Web site, http://www.diggercomic.com (March 12, 2012).

Ursula Vernon Home Page, http://ursulavernon.com (March 12, 2012).*

*   *   *

VIGILANTE, Danette

Personal

Born in Brooklyn, NY; married; children: two daughters.

Addresses

Home—New York, NY. *E-mail*—danette@danette vigilante.com.

Career

Author.

Writings

The Trouble with Half a Moon, G.P. Putnam's Sons (New York, NY), 2011.

Contributor of column to *Red Hook Star Review,* beginning 2010.

Sidelights

A born-and-raised New Yorker, Danette Vigilante sets her middle-grade novel *The Trouble with Half a Moon* in the same Brooklyn neighborhood where she grew up. In the story, thirteen-year-old Dellie is distraught when her younger brother Louis is killed during a car accident, and his death makes living in her high-crime urban neighborhood that much harder. Although her working-class Puerto Rican parents attempt to make the

Danette Vigilante (Reproduced by permission.)

best of things, her mom becomes overprotective and now curtails Dellie's activities when she is not in school. Although she understands her mother's grief, the teen begins to feel overwhelmed by the unfairness of life when a single mom moves into the downstairs apartment in their public-housing complex and makes no effort to hide her abusive relationship with her boyfriend. When the woman's son, five-year-old Corey, turns to Dellie for affection, guilt over Louis's death inspires the teen to become the boy's protector. Meanwhile, her relationship with Kayla, Dellie's best friend, starts to unravel and a cute boy named Michael seems intent on spending time with her.

Praising Vigilante for imbuing her fiction debut with a "realistic sense of the diverse neighborhood community" in which she sets her story, Hazel Rochman added in her *Booklist* review of *The Trouble with Half a Moon* that Dellie's "grief, anger, and heartbreaking coming-to-terms are realistic." The author's use of a "first-person, present-tense narration allows readers to feel Dellie's pain and confusion," asserted a *Kirkus Reviews* writer, and in *School Library Journal* Cheryl Ashton predicted of Vigilante's novel that "Dellie's story will speak to young people who've needed a little faith to get them through tough times."

"I grew up in a housing project where every few days, a little boy would knock on some of the neighbor's doors asking for food," Vigilante explained to *SATA.* "Sometimes he would ask for a slice of bread or an egg. Even though I was just a kid myself, my heart broke every time he'd come to our door, his small hands cupped waiting for something to be placed in them and a tiny, shy smile on his lips. If we had it, I happily gave him what he needed and wondered just what such a small boy could do with those things. Would he make toast? What about the raw egg? And most importantly, why didn't he have any food in his apartment?

"This boy stayed in my heart for years until I had the courage to write his story and give him what every child should have: safety, love, happiness, and a full belly. This little boy desperately needed to be rescued, not just by anyone but by someone very brave. From this, my first novel, *The Trouble with Half Moon,* was born.

"My hope is for my readers to take away with them this thought: Even the smallest good deed holds the power to lead to something great. Maybe even life changing."

Cover of Danette Vigilante's young-adult novel The Trouble with Half a Moon, *which is set in her Brooklyn home town.* (Jacket cover photograph © 2011 by Manjari Sharma. Reproduced by permission of G.P. Putnam's Sons, a division of Penguin Young Readers Group, a member of Penguin Group (USA), 345 Hudson Street, New York, NY 10014.)

Biographical and Critical Sources

PERIODICALS

Booklist, January 1, 2011, Hazel Rochman, review of *The Trouble with Half a Moon,* p. 111.
Bulletin of the Center for Children's Books, January, 2011, Deborah Stevenson, review of *The Trouble with Half a Moon,* p. 255.
Kirkus Reviews, December 1, 2010, review of *The Trouble with Half a Moon.*
School Library Journal, March, 2011, Cheryl Ashton, review of *The Trouble with Half a Moon,* p. 173.

ONLINE

Danette Vigilante Home Page, http://www.danettevigilante. com (March 2, 2012).
Danette Vigilante Web log, http://danettevigilante.blogspot. com (March 2, 2012).

*   *   *

VOELKEL, J&P
See VOELKEL, Pamela

*   *   *

VOELKEL, Pamela
(J&P Voelkel, a joint pseudonym)

Personal
Born in England; immigrated to United States, 2001; married Jon Voelkel (an advertising executive and author). *Hobbies and other interests:* Traveling, studying Maya history.

Addresses
Home—Norwich, VT. *E-mail*—voelkel@jaguarstones. com.

Career
Author. Former copywriter and creative director in advertising.

Writings

"JAGUAR STONES" MIDDLE-GRADE NOVEL TRILOGY

(With husband, Jon Voelkel, as J&P Voelkel) *Middleworld,* Egmont USA (New York, NY), 2010.
(With Jon Voelkel as J&P Voelkel) *The End of the World Club,* Egmont USA (New York, NY), 2011.

Adaptations
The "Jaguar Stones" novels were adapted for audiobook by Listening Library.

Sidelights

Pamela Voelkel was working as a copywriter and creative director at an advertising agency in England when she met her future husband, advertising colleague Jon Voelkel. Raised in Peru and Colombia, where he became steeped in the mix of mystery and danger in South America's mountains and deserts, rivers, jungles, and coastline, Jon inspired his new wife with the same enthusiasm. Now living in Vermont, the couple share this passion with middle-grade readers in their "Jaguar Stones" novels, published as J&P Voelkel.

The "Jaguar Stones" series begins in *Middleworld,* as fourteen-year-old video-game expert Max Murphy is less tha enthusiastic about a summer vacation spent digging up artifacts in Central America with his archaeologist parents. Arriving in San Xavier, Max finds that his parents have disappeared, but Lola, a Mayan girl, helps the American visitor with his search and reveals to Max that he is actually an emissary of her ancient people. The two teens' quest takes them into the rain forest where ancient secrets and modern-day criminals await them.

In her *Booklist* review of *Middleworld,* Jennifer Mattson remarked on the Voelkels' obvious "knowledge of the ancient Maya" and wrote that the "unusual Mesoamerican backdrop" of the couple's "Indiana Jones-influenced adventure . . . will keep readers interested and looking forward to future entries." According to a *Publishers Weekly* critic, the novel is propelled by its "exotic settings and . . . breakneck pace," and *School Library Journal* critic Ellen Fader noted the mix of "suspense and intrigue, human sacrifice, smuggling, and secret doors and escape routes through pyramids." Lesley Farmer asserted in *Kliatt* that in *Middleworld* "the Voelkels have created an adventurous Mayan world" and their story "will leave readers eager for the second book in the series."

Max and Maya return in *The End of the World Club,* as they confront concerns over the end of the earth as predicted by the Mayan calendar. The teens' quest for a precious gem prophesied to save the world leads them from Central America to Spain, where they are pursued by a powerful god who also hopes to acquire the stone. The fate of Max's parents ultimately hangs in the balance as the two teens make their return to the ancient underworld city of Xibalba, where an attempted rescue and a daring gamble await. Recommending the novel to fans of Rick Riordan's "Percy Jackson and the Olympians" novels, Connie Fletcher added in *Booklist* that *The End of the World Club* serves up "a fact-packed, thrilling ride" that is rich with Mayan elements.

In their writing collaboration, Jon Voelkel crafts the high-action storyline while Pamela develops the stories' characters and actions as the teens navigate a maze of challenges during the course of each adventure. In addition to writing, the Voelkels travel widely to expand their knowledge of Mayan history and culture, all which they share on their interactive Web site, Jaguarstones. com.

Cover of Jon and Pamela Voelkel's Mayan adventure Middleworld, *the first novel in their "Jaguar Stones" series.* (Cover illustration copyright © 2011 by Cliff Nielsen. Copyright © J&P Voelkel, 2011. Reproduced with permission of Egmont USA.)

Biographical and Critical Sources

PERIODICALS

Booklist, November 15, 2007, Jennifer Mattson, review of *Middleworld,* p. 61; February 1, 2011, Connie Fletcher, review of *The End of the World Club,* p. 78.

Kirkus Reviews, November 15, 2010, review of *The End of the World Club.*

Kliatt, November, 2007, Lesley Farmer, review of *Middleworld,* p. 14.

Publishers Weekly, September 17, 2007, review of *Middleworld,* p. 55.

School Library Journal, October, 2007, Ellen Fader, review of *Middleworld,* p. 164.

ONLINE

Jaguar Stones Web site, http://www.jaguarstones.com/ (February 12, 2012), "Pamela Voelkel."*

W

WATTS, Frances
[A pseudonym]
(Alexandra Lavau)

Personal
Born Alexandra Lavau, in Lausanne, Switzerland; immigrated to Australia at age three; partner of David Francis. *Education:* Macquarie University, Ph.D. (English literature), 1995.

Addresses
Home—Sydney, New South Wales, Australia. *E-mail*—franceswatts@ymail.com.

Career
Writer and editor. ABC Books, Sydney, New South Wales, Australia, children's book editor; Little Hare Books, Sydney, commissioning editor for five years; freelance editor of adult books; author of children's books.

Awards, Honors
Honour Book designation, Children's Book Council of Australia (CBCA), 2006, for *Kisses for Daddy;* Eve Pownall Award, CBCA, 2008, for *Parsley Rabbit's Book about Books;* Notable Book designation, CBCA, 2009, for *Extraordinary Ernie and Marvelous Maud,* and 2011, for both *A Rat in a Stripy Sock* and *The Song of the Winns.*

Writings

This Dog Bruce, illustrated by Bridget Strevens-Marzo, Little Hare Books (Surry Hills, New South Wales, Australia), 2004.

Kisses for Daddy, illustrated by David Legge, Little Hare Books (Surry Hills, New South Wales, Australia), 2005.

Frances Watts (Photograph courtesy of ABC Books. Reproduced by permission.)

Parsley Rabbit's Book about Books, illustrated by David Legge, ABC Books (Sydney, New South Wales, Australia), 2007.

Captain Crabclaw's Crew, illustrated by David Legge, ABC Books (Sydney, New South Wales, Australia), 2009.

A Rat in a Stripy Sock, illustrated by David Francis, ABC Books (Pymble, New South Wales, Australia), 2010.

Goodnight, Mice!, illustrated by Judy Watson, ABC Books (Pymble, New South Wales, Australia), 2010.

"ERNIE AND MAUD" SERIES; ILLUSTRATED BY JUDY WATSON

Extraordinary Ernie and Marvelous Maud, ABC Books (Sydney, New South Wales, Australia), 2008, Eerdmans Books for Young Readers (Grand Rapids, MI), 2010.

The Middle Sheep, ABC Books (Sydney, New South Wales, Australia), 2008, Eerdmans Books for Young Readers (Grand Rapids, MI), 2010.

The Greatest Sheep in History, ABC Books (Sydney, New South Wales, Australia), 2009, Eerdmans Books for Young Readers (Grand Rapids, MI), 2011.

Heroes of the Year, ABC Books (Pymble, New South Wales, Australia), 2011, Eerdmans Books for Young Readers (Grand Rapids, MI), 2012.

"GERANDER"/"SONG OF THE WINNS" CHAPTER-BOOK TRILOGY

The Song of the Winns, illustrated by David Francis, ABC Books (Pymble, New South Wales, Australia), 2010, published as *The Secret of the Ginger Mice,* Running Press Kids (Philadelphia, PA), 2012.

The Spies of Gerander, illustrated by David Francis, ABC Books (Pymble, New South Wales, Australia), 2011.

"SWORD GIRL" SERIES

The Secret of the Swords, illustrated by Gregory Rogers, Allen & Unwin (Sydney, New South Wales, Australia), 2012.

The Poison Plot, illustrated by Gregory Rogers, Allen & Unwin (Sydney, New South Wales, Australia), 2012.

Sidelights

Frances Watts is a pseudonymous Swiss-born Australian writer who is perhaps best known in the United States for her "Ernie and Maud" series. Illustrated by Judy Watson, these books chronicle the adventures of a young superhero and his unusual sidekick, a feisty sheep. Watts, who also edits books under her real name, Alexandra Lavau, noted in a *Kids Book Review* online interview with Megan Blandford that "kids' books are the natural outlet for my humour, my voice. I can give life to the quirky characters that pop into my head, consider questions I have about the world, push my imagination in unexpected directions. It's very liberating."

In *Extraordinary Ernie and Marvelous Maud* a quartet of aging superheroes decides that the group needs new blood, but the only person to enter their competition is a decidedly ordinary lad named Ernie Eggers. After being paired with a talking sheep named Maud, however, Ernie develops a knack for handling trouble, taking down a trio of bullies as well a bothersome dog that nips at his partner's heels. A reviewer in *Children's Bookwatch* noted that the work "contains just the right combination of humor and action," and a *Publishers*

Weekly critic applauded "the slapstick premise" in *Extraordinary Ernie and Marvelous Maud* as well as the partners' growing relationship.

The Middle Sheep, the second installment in the "Ernie and Maud" series, concerns Maud's decision to adopt a sidekick of her own. When Ernie becomes upset with his woolly partner's apparent disinterest in fighting crime, Valiant Vera, a member of the Superheroes Society, issues an ultimatum to the feuding duo: cooperate with each other or leave the group. According to a *Kirkus Reviews* writer, *The Middle Sheep* "is just right for readers ready for the challenge of a chapter book."

In *The Greatest Sheep in History* Ernie and Maud come to the rescue when Chicken George, a terrifying and terribly misunderstood villain, steals the notes of a speaker at the National Superheroes Convention. "Children will respond most to the story's action," observed Hazel Rochman in her *Booklist* review of *The Greatest Sheep in History,* and Aleesah Darlison stated in Sydney, Australia's *Sun Herald* that Watts' story offers "plenty of giggles."

Discussing why she writes, Watts explained to *SATA:* "I was lucky to be born into a book-loving family; books have always been a part of my life. (Well, really, they are more like an obsession!) But I wouldn't be a reader today if I hadn't been introduced to many wonderful books as a child, and it's this positive experience of books and reading that I hope to inspire with my own books.

"So I write books to share (like *Kisses for Daddy* and *Goodnight, Mice!*) and books about the power of dreams (*A Rat in a Stripy Sock*); books that educate while entertaining (*Parsley Rabbit's Book about Books*) and funny books that show readers it's okay to be yourself (like the 'Ernie and Maud' series). And most recently I have been working on the 'Gerander' trilogy (published in the United States as the 'Song of the Winns' trilogy), which is full of action and adventure and courage and friendship to make kids want to read and read and keep on reading. I want to get kids of all ages hooked on books!"

Biographical and Critical Sources

PERIODICALS

Booklist, June 1, 2008, Connie Fletcher, review of *Kisses for Daddy,* p. 89; July 1, 2011, Hazel Rochman, review of *The Greatest Sheep in History,* p. 58.

Children's Bookwatch, June, 2010, review of *Extraordinary Ernie and Marvelous Maud.*

Kirkus Reviews, July 1, 2010, review of *The Middle Sheep.*

Publishers Weekly, February 15, 2010, review of *Extraordinary Ernie and Marvelous Maud,* p. 130.

School Library Journal, July, 2011, Nancy Mackenzie, review of *The Greatest Sheep in History,* p. 81.

Sunday Age (Melbourne, Victoria, Australia), June 22, 2008, Frances Atkinson, review of *Extraordinary Ernie and Marvelous Maud,* p. 27; October 16, 2011, Michelle Hamer, review of *The Spies of Gerander,* p. 17.

Sun Herald (Sydney, New South Wales, Australia), September 30, 2007, Amanda Holohan, review of *Parsley Rabbit's Book about Books,* p. 73; July 6, 2009, Aleesah Darlison, review of *The Greatest Sheep in History,* p. 13.

ONLINE

Frances Watts Home Page, http://www.franceswatts.com (March 1, 2012).

Kids Book Review Web site, http://www.kids-bookreview.com/ (September 8, 2010), Megan Blandford, "Author Interview: Frances Watts."

Lateral Learning Web site, http://www.laterallearning.com/ (March 1, 2012), "Frances Watts."

*   *   *

WERTZ, Michael

Personal

Married Andrew Cowitt (a musician and programmer). *Education:* University of California, Santa Cruz, B.A. (French language), 1990; California College of the Arts, B.F.A. (illustration; with distinction), 1998.

Addresses

Home—Oakland, CA. *Agent*—Abigail Samoun, Red Fox Literary; info@redfoxliterary.com. *E-mail*—michael@wertzateria.com.

Career

Commercial graphic artist and illustrator. California College of the Arts, instructor in Photoshop illustration, 1999-2002. *Exhibitions:* Work included in exhibitions at various galleries, and at San Francisco Society of Illustrators Show, 1997.

Member

Graphic Artists Guild.

Awards, Honors

Awards from Los Angeles Society of Illustrators, 1998, 1999, 2001, 2003; Graphic Artists Guild National Recognition Award, 2000, 2001; Lee Bennett Hopkins Honor Book selection, Notable Book selection, National Council of Teachers of English, and ABC Best Books for Children selection, all 2009, all for *A Curious Collection of Cats* by Betsy Franco.

Writings

SELF-ILLUSTRATED

Dog Dreams, Ginko Press (San Francisco, CA), 2011.

ILLUSTRATOR

Mary M. Cerullo, *The Truth about Great White Sharks,* photographs by Jeffrey L. Rotman, Chronicle Books (San Francisco, CA), 2000.

Mary M. Cerullo, *The Truth about Dangerous Sea Creatures,* photographs by Jeffrey L. Rotman, Chronicle Books (San Francisco, CA), 2003.

Arne Johnson and Karen Macklin, *Indie Girl: From Starting a Band to Launching a Fashion Company, Nine Ways to Turn Your Creative Talent into Reality,* Zest Books (San Francisco, CA), 2008.

Betsy Franco, *A Curious Collection of Cats,* Tricycle Press (Berkeley, CA), 2009.

Betsy Franco, *A Dazzling Display of Dogs,* Tricycle Press (Berkeley, CA), 2010.

Contributor to periodicals, including *American Illustration, Communication Arts Illustration Annual, Frontiers, Los Angeles Times, Macworld, New Yorker, New York Times, Oakland Magazine, San Francisco Chronicle, Step-by-Step, Utne Reader,* and *Washington Post.* Contributor to anthologies, including *Bliss Live It!: Bliss Give It!,* Girl Scouts of the USA (New York, NY), 2010.

Sidelights

Specializing in retro-inspired screen-print graphics, San Francisco-area artist Michael Wertz has worked on de-

Michael Wertz teams up with poet Betsy Franco to create the picture book **A Dazzling Display of Dogs.** (Illustration copyright © 2011 by Michael Wertz. Reproduced by permission of Tricycle Press, an imprint of Random House Children's Books, a division of Random House, Inc.)

signs for advertising in addition to creating posters, product designs, and movie trailers. Beginning with pencil sketches, Wertz creates dynamic images in which stylized shapes and typography interplay against simple backgrounds to produce eye-catching color contrasts. The graphic appeal of his images have made them a perfect fit for children's picture books, making his illustrations a central feature of stories by Betsy Franco and Mary M. Cerullo. The "childlike drawings" Wertz creates for Cerullo's *The Truth about Dangerous Sea Creatures* "add a lot of visual appeal" to the study of underwater predators, according to *School Library Journal* contributor Arwen Marshall, while Nora Jane Natke asserted in the same publication that Cerullo's *The Truth about Great White Sharks* benefits from the artist's design experience through its "attractive" mix of "line drawings . . . varied typefaces, and eye-catching graphics."

Franco's companion volumes *A Curious Collection of Cats* and *A Dazzling Display of Dogs* pair pet-centered concrete poems with Wertz's unique and colorful images. In *A Curious Collection of Cats* the poet shares playful poems in short forms such as haiku and limerick, and her words are wound "up and down or in curving jumps" throughout the artist's "playful images," according to *Booklist* contributor Hazel Rochman. Praising the same book as "an ideal match of subject and form," Susan Dove Lempke added in her *Horn Book* review that Wertz adds "visual interest" to a book that "convey[s] the silliness of cats and their humans without every being silly" itself. Author and illustrator go to the dogs in their second collaboration, as "Franco celebrates animals complete with loveable quirks and downright silliness," according to Lempke. Dubbing *A Dazzling Display of Dogs* "exuberant," a *Publishers Weekly* contributor added that "the whimsy of Franco's poems is matched by [Wertz's] . . . modern-meets-retro collages."

Biographical and Critical Sources

PERIODICALS

Booklist, March 15, 2009, Hazel Rochman, review of *A Curious Collection of Cats*, p. 62; December 15, 2010, Hazel Rochman, review of *A Dazzling Display of Dogs*, p. 44.

Horn Book, May-June, 2009, Susan Dove Lempke, review of *A Curious Collection of Cats*, p. 314; January-February, 2011, Susan Dove Lempke, review of *A Dazzling Display of Dogs*, p. 104.

Kirkus Reviews, October 15, 2003, review of *The Truth about Dangerous Sea Creatures*; December 1, 2010, review of *A Dazzling Display of Dogs*.

Publishers Weekly, November 29, 2010, review of *A Dazzling Display of Dogs*, p. 48.

School Library Journal, July, 2000, Nora Jane Natke, review of *The Truth about Great White Sharks*, p. 92; December, 2003, Arwen Marshall, review of *The Truth about Dangerous Sea Creatures*, p. 132; August, 2008, Elaine Baran Black, review of *Indie Girl: From Starting a Band to Launching a Fashion Company, Nine Ways to Turn Your Creative Talent into Reality*, p. 146; April, 2009, Teresa Pfeifer, review of *A Curious Collection of Cats*, p. 147; January, 2011, Lauralyn Persson, review of *A Dazzling Display of Dogs*, p. 88.

ONLINE

Michael Wertz Home Page, http://www.wertzateria.com (March 2, 2012).

Red Fox Literary Web site, http://www.redfoxliterary.com/ (March 2, 2012), "Michael Wertz."*

* * *

WILKINSON, Lili 1981-

Personal

Born April 7, 1981, in Melbourne, Victoria, Australia; daughter of John (a sound recorder) and Carole (a children's author) Wilkinson. *Education:* Melbourne University, B.A. (creative arts; with honours); work toward Ph.D. *Hobbies and other interests:* Bicycling, Japanese food, quilting.

Addresses

Home—Melbourne, Victoria, Australia. *Agent*—K.T. Literary; contact@ktliterary.com. *E-mail*—lili@lili wilkinson.com.au.

Career

Author. Teacher of English in Japan; State Library of Victoria, Melbourne, Victoria, Australia, Web site manager at Centre for Youth Literature until 2011.

Awards, Honors

Barbara Jefferis Award Highly Commended selection, 2010, and Ameila Bloomer listee, Rainbow Room listee, and Stonewall Honor Book selection, all American Library Association, all 2012, all for *Pink;* White Raven Award, International Youth Library, 2008, and Ena Noel Award, International Board on Books for Youth, 2011, both for *Scatterheart.*

Writings

Joan of Arc: The Story of Jehanne Darc, Black Dog Books (Fitzroy, Victoria, Australia), 2007.

Scatterheart, Black Dog Books (Fitzroy, Victoria, Australia), 2007.

The (Not Quite) Perfect Boyfriend ("Girlfriend Fiction" series), Allen & Unwin (Crows Nest, New South Wales, Australia), 2008.

(Editor) *Short: A Collection of Interesting Short Stories and Other Stuff from Some Surprising and Intelligent People,* Black Dog Books (Fitzroy, Victoria, Australia), 2008.

Angel Fish, Black Dog Books (Fitzroy, Victoria, Australia), 2009.

Pink, Allen & Unwin (Crows Nest, New South Wales, Australia), 2009, Allen & Unwin (London, England), 2010. HarperTeen (New York, NY), 2011.

Company of Angels, Catnip, 2010.

A Pocketful of Eyes, Allen & Unwin (Crows Nest, New South Wales, Australia), 2011.

Love-Shy, Allen & Unwin (Crows Nest, New South Wales, Australia), 2012.

Contributor to periodicals, including *Age, Meanjin, Voiceworks,* and *Write4Children.* Contributor to anthologies, including *Right Book Right Time,* 2007; *Trust Me,* edited by Paul Collins, 2008; and *Read to Succeed: Strategies to Engage Children and Young People in Reading for Pleasure.*

Sidelights

Following in the tradition of her mother, Australian children's fantasy author Carole Wilkinson, Lili Wilkinson earned her first byline at age thirteen when one of her stories was published in a magazine. A degree in creative arts led to a job at Melbourne's State Library of Victoria, where Wilkinson created teen-friendly resources for the Centre for Youth Literature. Her focus on adolescents has also extended to writing: since 2007 Wilkinson has produced one young-adult novel a year, on average, in addition to editing the anthology *Short: A Collection of Interesting Short Stories and Other Stuff from Some Surprising and Intelligent People.* While her books have been popular in her native Australia, where they range from teen series romance to historical novels such as *Scatterheart,* Wilkinson is best known to U.S. readers for her novel *Pink.*

When readers first meet her in *Pink,* Ava Simpson has achieved the ambitions of her liberal-minded academic parents: she has died her hair inky black, has perfected her trendy Goth image, and now spends her time with perpetually disillusioned, overbearing, and pompously intellectual best friend Chloe, who is also her lesbian partner. However, like any adolescent, Ava wants to break with her parents and test her own wings. To do so she throws over her old life in favor of a new start as a scholarship student at the Billy Hughes School for Academic Excellence. With her hair back to its normal color, and a fashionable outfit in an appealing shade of pink, Ava is befriended by Alexis and her clique of popular friends, who romantically link the new student with good-looking classmate Ethan. As a friend of Alexis, it is de rigeur for Ava to audition for the school musical, and when she is passed over for a part she decides to help out behind the scenes. While Ava behaves in one way when with her popular friends, she acts very differently among the stage crew, all who despise Alex-

is's clique and cultivate their bohemian eccentricities. While Ava realizes that she has several roles to juggle in real life, it feels to her that she is miscast in all of them.

"Wilkinson takes a witty, refreshing look at high school and adolescence" in *Pink,* according to *Voice of Youth Advocates* contributor Sara Martin, and in *Booklist* Karen Cruze wrote that the author's "snarky wit" makes her novel "a refreshing addition to the LGBT oeuvre." Wilkinson's mastery of "sharp dialogue and perceptive insights" results in "a wise and often hilarious novel," asserted Sandra Bennett in her appraisal of the coming-of-age story for *School Librarian,* and Jennifer Schultz noted in *School Library Journal* that *Pink* "authentically captures the social awkwardness of high school life and love."

Biographical and Critical Sources

PERIODICALS

Booklist, January 1, 2011, Karen Cruze, review of *Pink,* p. 97.

Bulletin of the Center for Children's Books, January, 2011, Karen Coats, review of *Pink,* p. 256.

School Librarian, winter, 2010, Rachel Ayers Nelson, review of *Company of Angels,* p. 249; spring, 2011, Sandra Bennett, review of *Pink,* p. 58.

School Library Journal, March, 2011, Jennifer Schultz, review of *Pink,* p. 176.

Voice of Youth Advocates, April, 2011, Sara Martin, review of *Pink,* p. 71.

ONLINE

Lili Wilkinson Home Page, http://liliwilkinson.com.au (February 28, 2012).

Scottish Book Trust Web site, http://www.scottishbooktrust.com/ (March 15, 2012), interview with Wilkinson.

* * *

WILLEN, Janet

Personal

Born in NJ; married. *Education:* New York University, B.A.; New School for Social Research (now The New School), M.A. (political philosophy). *Religion:* Jewish.

Addresses

Home—Silver Spring, MD. *E-mail*—janet@janetwillen.com.

Career

Writer and editor for publishers, including Harcourt, Brace, Funk & Wagnalls, and *Nation's Business* magazine.

Janet Willen (Reproduced by permission.)

Member

Society of Children's Book Writers and Illustrators.

Awards, Honors

(With Marjorie Gann) Notable Books for a Global Society selection, International Reading Association, 2012, for *Five Thousand Years of Slavery.*

Writings

(With sister, Marjorie Gann) *Five Thousand Years of Slavery,* Tundra Books of Northern New York (Plattsburgh, NY), 2010.

Author of educational materials.

Sidelights

As a schoolchild in New Jersey, Janet Willen learned about slavery in the United States and grappled with the question of how people could think they had the right to own other people. In their book *Five Thousand Years of Slavery,* Willen and coauthor/sister Marjorie Gann explore slavery throughout the world, sharing stories of slaves and slave owners from antiquity to the present day. "Some experts believe there are more people enslaved today than every before," Willen informed *Washington Jewish Week* contributor Aaron Leibel in discussing her reasons for writing the book. "The abolition movement says something positive about human nature to me," she added, referencing the movement to abolish slavery that started in the eighteenth century. "It shows that we can make a difference in the world, that there is good in all of us to help us fight evil when we see it."

Willen worked for over three decades as a writer and editor specializing in educational materials before she began her extensive research for *Five Thousand Years of Slavery.* She also volunteered as a tutor to middle-school and younger children for more than twenty years, sharing her love for reading and writing. During the six years it took to complete their manuscript, the sisters researched their subject thoroughly and also gained the feedback of experts in the field. With Willen in Maryland and Gann in Canada, this was a long-distance collaboration. Dividing the task of writing between them, they critiqued each others' work in order to give their text a unified voice. "We read each chapter aloud, revising when needed, so that by the end, we often couldn't tell who'd written which section," Willen explained to *SATA.* "We think this indicates that we achieved a uniform style." *Five Thousand Years of Slavery* is also enhanced with visual elements such as paintings, engravings, and photographs.

Willen and Gann's history takes readers back to the ancient world, where victorious Sumerian armies enslaved their captives, and wealthy Romans depended on female slaves to perform the many laborious tasks required to maintain an upscale household. From there the story moves forward in time, as European colonization spread slavery throughout the Western world and Africans were imported to work the plantations of the Americas. The importance of slavery in the Southern United States prior to the outbreak of the Civil War is also covered, as is slavery in the vast Pacific region. The book leads up to the present day and to those desperately pool parents in developing countries who feel compelled to gain much-needed money by selling their children's labor.

Cover of Willen and Marjorie Gann's collaborative history **Five Thousand Years of Slavery.** (Jacket photo: AP Photo/Apichart Weerawong. Reproduced by permission of Tundra Books.)

In his *School Library Journal* review of *Five Thousand Years of Slavery,* Gerry Larson recommended Willen and Gann's book as a "groundbreaking study [that] brings the disturbing subject into historical and contemporary focus," and in *Booklist* Hazel Rochman described the text as "encyclopedic in scope and minutely detailed." Noting that it "reads like a storybook," Judith Hayn added in *Voice of Youth Advocates* that the inclusion of "poignant and inspirational stories of enslaved individuals, whether many years ago or in contemporary societies," also merits praise. "Gann and Willen are engaging storytellers," asserted Val Ken Lem in a review of the resource for *Canadian Review of Materials,* and their care in "[de]emphasizing the true nature of much of the human trafficking of both children and adults" shows them to be "cognizant of the innocence of their youngest readers." Citing the "timeliness, international focus and . . . accuracy" of *Five Thousand Years of Slavery,* a *Kirkus Reviews* writer recommended the work as a "first look at a terrible topic."

Biographical and Critical Sources

PERIODICALS

Booklist, May 1, 2011, Hazel Rochman, review of *Five Thousand Years of Slavery,* p. 73.

Canadian Review of Materials, January 14, 2011, Val Ken Lem, review of *Five Thousand Years of Slavery.*

Kirkus Reviews, December 15, 2010, review of *Five Thousand Years of Slavery.*

Quill & Quire, January, 2011, Jill Bryant, review of *Five Thousand Years of Slavery.*

School Library Journal, March, 2011, Gerry Larson, review of *Five Thousand Years of Slavery,* p. 179.

Toronto Star, February 24, 2011, Deirdre Baker, review of *Five Thousand Years of Slavery.*

Voice of Youth Advocates, February, 2011, Judith Hayn, review of *Five Thousand Years of Slavery,* p. 582.

ONLINE

Open Book Toronto Web site, http://www.openbooktoronto.com/ (February 1, 2011), interview with Willen and Marjorie Gann.

Washington Jewish Week Online, http://washingtonjewishweek.com/ (May 18, 2011), Aaron Leibel, "Haunted by Slavery."

*   *   *

WOLFERMANN, Iris 1972-

Personal

Born 1972, in Germany; married; children: daughters. *Education:* Hochschool der Künste (Berlin, Germany), degree; attended Central St. Martin's College of Art & Design (London, England).

Addresses

Home—Berlin, Germany. *E-mail*—i.wolfermann@gmx.de.

Career

Illustrator and fine artist.

Illustrator

Barbara Zoschke, *Flanke ins Weltall,* Patmos Verlag/Sauerländer, 2005.

Hans Christian Andersen, *Die Schneekönigin,* Carlsen, 2006.

Herbert Rosendorfer and Julia Andreae, *Amadeus and Pauline,* ArsEdition, 2006.

Astrid Lindgren, *Pippi Longstocking,* Cornelsen Verlag (Berlin, Germany), 2006.

Jutta Treiber, *Der König tanzt,* Annette Betz Verlag/Carl Ueberreuter, 2007.

Nina Wilkening, *Rund um Zeit erfahren,* Cornelsen Verlag (Berlin, Germany), 2007.

Guak Young-ijk, *Around and Around and Around, Woongjin,* ThinkBig (South Korea), 2008.

Caroline Lahusen and Jens Schröder, *Bob und die Jagd auf den weißen Löwen,* Thienemann Verlag, 2009.

Caroline Lahusen and Jens Schröder, *Bob und die Rache des Pharao,* Thienemann Verlag, 2009.

Werner Färber, *Das Krokodil im Silbersee,* Jacoby & Stuart, 2009.

Bruno Hächler, *I Am Who I Am,* NordSüd (New York, NY), 2010.

Paivi Stalder, *My Wish Tonight: What Children Wish,* translated from the German, NorthSouth (New York, NY), 2010.

Contributor to periodicals, including *Berliner Zeitung, incognito, Das Magazine, Der Tagenspeigel,* and *Die Zeit.* Contributor of illustrations to educational publications.

Biographical and Critical Sources

PERIODICALS

Booklist, May 1, 2010, Ian Chipman, review of *I Am Who I Am,* p. 90.

Publishers Weekly, May 24, 2010, review of *I Am Who I Am,* p. 52.

School Library Journal, July, 2010, Laura Butler, review of *I Am Who I Am,* p. 60; February, 2011, Lauralyn Persson, review of *My Wish Tonight: What Children Wish,* p. 90.

ONLINE

Iris Wolfermann Home Page, http://www.iriswolfermann.de (March 2, 2012).*

WOON, Yvonne 1984-

Personal

Born 1984, in MA. *Education:* Columbia University, M.F.A., 2010. *Hobbies and other interests:* Etymology, supernatural phenomenon, New England history.

Addresses

Home—New York, NY. *Agent*—Ted Malawer, Upstart Crow, P.O. Box 25404, Brooklyn, NY 11202. *E-mail*—yvonnewoonbooks@gmail.com.

Career

Novelist.

Writings

"DEAD BEAUTIFUL" NOVEL SERIES

Dead Beautiful, Disney/Hyperion (New York, NY), 2010.
Life Eternal, Hyperion (New York, NY), 2012.

Adaptations

Dead Beautiful was adapted for audiobook, Brilliance Audio, 2010.

Sidelights

Yvonne Woon was still completing graduate school when the first installment of her "Dead Beautiful" novel series was published. Although *Dead Beautiful* and its sequel, *Life Eternal,* tap into the current teen vogue for paranormal romance, Yoon "takes a new and unconventional look at the undead," according to a *Kirkus Reviews* writer, "focusing on story and characters" rather than "gore and mayhem."

In contrast to its dark subject, *Dead Beautiful* takes readers to sunny California, where Renée Winters is celebrating her sixteenth birthday. When her parents die mysteriously, she becomes the ward of her grandfather. From the West Coast, the grief-stricken teen flies to northern Maine and the boarding school that will become her new home. School does not seem to offer much: Gottfried Academy has a classics-based curriculum that seems academically archaic to the forward-thinking teen. Things look up when she meets and falls in love with Dante Berlin, despite the fact that he is hiding a strange and dramatic secret. As their relationship deepens the couple shares secrets, and soon they are joined in the search to uncover a series of strange murders that leads to the truth about their strange school.

"Detailed world building and setting contribute as much to the story as character and plot," noted Cindy Welch in her *Booklist* review of *Dead Beautiful,* and in *Pub-* *lishers Weekly* a critic described Renée as "an unusually analytical and composed narrator." The first-time novelist "pulls off some interesting twists and captures readers with the romantic connection between René and Dante," observed Emily Chornomaz in her *School Library Journal* review of the novel. "Well-written, intriguing and . . . different," according to a *Kirkus Reviews* writer, *Dead Beautiful* "ends with much to explore" in Yoon's promised sequels.

René returns in *Life Eternal,* but the lighthearted California teen seems much older than her chronological age might suggest. Since thwarting death due to Dante's fateful kiss, she now studies in Montreal, at Saint Clément. In addition to coping with her own transformation, she must also deal with Dante's absence and the fact that she might lose him altogether due to the inevitable death of non-life-taking vampires. As she researches the science of vampirism that is taught at Gottfried Academy, René learns about a group of scholars who have found a way to thwart their destiny and achieve permanent life. "Romantic, suspenseful, and far from over," according to a *Kirkus Reviews* writer, *Life Eternal* "will leave readers wanting more," according to the critic.

Cover of Yvonne Woon's highly praised debut novel Dead Beautiful, *in which a sixteen year old receives a tragic inheritance.* (Jacket cover by Jonathan Barket and Paul Aniszewski. Reprinted by permission of Disney-Hyperion, an imprint of Disney Book Group, LLC. All rights reserved.)

Biographical and Critical Sources

PERIODICALS

Booklist, September 15, 2010, Cindy Welch, review of *Dead Beautiful,* p. 72.

Kirkus Reviews, August 1, 2010, review of *Dead Beautiful;* December 1, 2011, review of *Life Eternal.*

Publishers Weekly, August 23, 2010, review of *Dead Beautiful,* p. 50.

School Library Journal, October, 2010, Emily Chornomaz, review of *Dead Beautiful,* p. 129.

Voice of Youth Advocates, October, 2010, Stacey Hayman, review of *Dead Beautiful,* p. 360.

ONLINE

Yvonne Woon Home Page, http://yvonnewoon.com (February 25, 2012).*